The Haynes Automotive
Heating & Air Conditioning Systems Manual

by Mike Stubblefield
and John H Haynes Member of the Guild of Motoring Writers

The Haynes Repair Manual for automotive heating and air conditioning systems

(8F8 - 10425)
(1480)

ABC

2

Haynes Publishing Group
Sparkford Nr Yeovil
Somerset BA22 7JJ England

Haynes Publications, Inc.
861 Lawrence Drive
Newbury Park
California 91320 USA

Acknowledgments

We are grateful for the help and cooperation of Chrysler Corporation, Ford Motor Company, General Motors Corporation, Mac Tools, Inc., Snap-On Tool Corporation, Robinair Division of Sealed Power Corporation and Everco Industries, Inc. for their assistance with technical information, certain illustrations and photos.

© **Haynes North America, Inc. 1989, 1993, 2000**

With permission from J.H. Haynes & Co. Ltd.

A book in the Haynes Automotive Repair Manual Series

Printed in the U.S.A.

ISBN 1 56392 381 5

Library of Congress Catalog Card Number 88-83195

While every attempt is made to ensure that the information in this manual is correct, no liability can be accepted by the authors or publishers for loss, damage or injury caused by any errors in, or omissions from, the information given.

00-256

Contents

Preface.. 0-5

Chapter One
Basic theory of air conditioning system operation................... 1-1

Chapter Two
Basic air conditioning and heating system components........ 2-1

Chapter Three
Typical automotive air conditioning systems............................ 3-1

Chapter Four
Service and diagnostic tools.. 4-1

Chapter Five
Heating and air conditioning system service and repair......... 5-1

Chapter Six
Troubleshooting.. 6-1

Glossary.. GL-1

Index.. IND-1

Notes

Preface

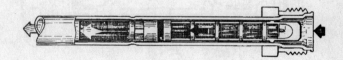

There was a time when every good mechanic understood the basic systems of the automobile pretty well. But that time has passed. The days of the renaissance repairman are over. As systems have become more complicated, the investment in training and tools necessary to service the entire range of automotive technology found on a typical modern vehicle has widened to the point that no one actually "fixes cars" anymore. Instead, most modern mechanics specialize. Today, we have engine builders, front end specialists, tune-up specialists, transmission specialists, etc. Unfortunately, this approach has created an aura of "black magic" around the more esoteric of these topics.

Automotive air conditioning is certainly one subject that is poorly understood by nearly all do-it-yourselfers and a lot of professionals as well. The reasons for this situation come down to motivation, money and knowledge.

Unlike performance-related topics such as degreeing a cam, rejetting a carburetor, etc., air conditioning theory, service and troubleshooting is, frankly, pretty dry stuff. A well maintained air conditioning system won't make a vehicle faster. But it will make it more comfortable. Unfortunately, performance - not comfort - is what gets young mechanics going. Consequently, they don't usually grow up saying "I want to be an air conditioning technician."

Then there are the special tools. Even if you are the kind of person who is attracted to air conditioning work, the tools needed to diagnose, repair and maintain a typical system are highly specialized and expensive. They're so specialized, in fact, that they can't be used for much else. Only a professional who chooses the field as a career can justify the kind of investment it takes to become an air conditioning specialist.

Another reason air conditioning seems so mysterious is that little useful knowledge of the basics is readily available. Lots of books explain how to service specific systems, but few bother with the underlying principles of operation. This is unfortunate, because a good grasp of basic theory can enable a mechanic to understand any air conditioning system.

Heating and air conditioning

If carefully read and understood, this book should help any mechanic understand the fundamentals of air conditioning systems. It begins with a discussion of basic air conditioning theory, followed by a description of each of the components found in typical heating and air conditioning systems. Any real comprehension of what follows after that is only possible if the first two chapters are read and understood. The rest of the book is devoted to routine maintenance, service procedures, repairs and troubleshooting.

Only two things are not included in this volume:

1) removal and installation procedures and
2) compressor overhauls.

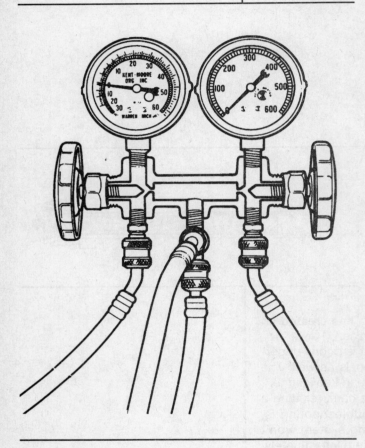

For specific air conditioning and heating system component removal and installation procedures, refer to the *Haynes Automotive Repair Manual* for the vehicle in question. If - after using this book to troubleshoot an air conditioning system - you conclude that the compressor is malfunctioning, we recommend that you remove it and install a rebuilt unit. There are several reasons for this. First, time is money.

The money you will save by rebuilding the compressor yourself is more than offset by the money you will have to invest in specialized tools that may not work on other compressors. In this day of rebuilt components, it doesn't make much sense to rebuild a critical component like the compressor when you can obtain a rebuilt one for a few dollars more. Second, there simply is not enough space in this volume to include the overhaul procedure for every air conditioning compressor available.

Other than these two items, however, you will find most everything you need to know about how air conditioning systems work, how to maintain them, service them, troubleshoot them and repair them in this manual.

One final note: The astute reader will notice that little mention has been made so far of heating systems. That's because- aside from heater core replacement (covered in *Haynes Automotive Repair Manuals* when possible) - heating systems are pretty easy to maintain and fix. Because heating and air conditioning systems are so interrelated, it's impossible to discuss one without the other.

Basic theory of air conditioning system operation

Automotive air conditioning is generally regarded as one of the two most significant contributions by American automotive engineering to the evolution of the automobile (the automatic transmission is the other). At first, air conditioning was an expensive option found only on the most luxurious automobiles. As time went on, it became more available, and affordable, to the general motoring public. Today, air conditioning systems are such a widely used option that we seldom give them much thought, until they break and we have to fix them. And that's what this book is all about - how to keep A/C systems operating and how to fix them when they break. The heating system has also been included in this volume because it is an integral part of most modern automotive "climate control" systems. In many instances, it's impossible to work on the air conditioning system without working on the heating system as well.

But before we get into maintaining or servicing either system, it's essential that you know the principles of air conditioning and heating system operation. This chapter provides a clear description of these principles. Make sure you understand them clearly before you try to maintain, diagnose or repair the air conditioning or heating system in your vehicle. Neglecting the material in this first chapter could get you into trouble later.

The comfort zone?

Studies have shown that most people feel comfortable in a relatively narrow temperature zone of about 70 to 80° F **(see illustration)**. When the effect of humidity is taken into consideration, this range becomes a little wider. Humidity is simply the amount of moisture in the air. When the air has absorbed as much moisture as it can, the relative humidity is said to be 100%. If the humidity is relatively high, say 70%, we may still feel comfortable down in the mid-60's; if the humidity is low enough, say 30%, we can even tolerate the low 90's without much discomfort. The actual amount of humidity varies in accordance with the temperature, because warm air holds more moisture than cold air.

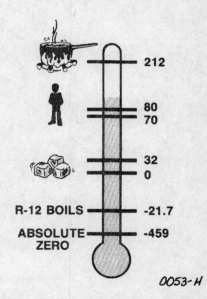

0053-H

Most people feel comfortable in a relatively narrow temperature zone between 70 and 80°F

What this means in practical terms is that you can feel just as cool when the temperature is 80°F and the relative humidity is 30% as when the temperature is 70°F and the relative humidity is 90%.

The key to whether you feel hot or cold is the ability of your body perspiration to evaporate quickly and easily. If the air is dry, perspiration evaporates quickly and the heat leaving the body makes it feel cool. But when the moisture content of the air is high, perspiration cannot evaporate as rapidly, so less body heat is removed and you feel warmer.

Most automotive air conditioning and heating systems are integrated into a "climate control" system that controls the temperature, humidity and air circulation by cooling the air inside the passenger compartment when it's hot outside and heating it when the outside air is cold. We'll look at typical air conditioning and heating system components and controls in Chapter Two. In this chapter, we examine the underlying physical phenomena which enable all air conditioning and heating systems to accomplish these tasks.

Heat

Without heat, a heating system would be impossible, and air conditioning would be unnecessary. What, exactly, is heat? Here's what the American Heritage Dictionary has to say about heat:

A form of energy associated with the motion of atoms or molecules in solids and capable of being transmitted through solid and fluid media by conduction, through fluid media by convection, and through empty space by radiation."

The dictionary goes on to define other meanings for heat, but the one above best characterizes heat for the purposes of this discussion. Fancy terms like "conduction," "convection" and "radiation" notwithstanding, the gist of the above definition is that *heat is basically energy*.

When viewed in its broadest sense, energy takes many forms, manifests itself in many ways and can be transformed from one form to another in many complex ways. But heat is always there in some way. Let's take a few examples. The sun, obviously, gives off vast quantities of energy, heat being one of the more obvious ones. On a smaller scale, any fire also gives off heat. The connecting rods, crankshaft and drivetrain of an internal combustion engine convert the chemical energy released in the explosion of gasoline vapors into the kinetic energy of the moving automobile, in the process creating a lot of heat because of the friction created by all those moving parts rubbing against one another. And every time the driver applies the brakes to stop the vehicle, the friction generated between the brake pads and rotors, and between the tires and the road, transforms the kinetic energy of the moving vehicle into heat.

But when you hear the word "heat," do you think of kinetic energy, friction, internal combustion, fires or the sun? Probably not. The first thought that crosses your mind is the palpable effect of heat on your body when you are in close proximity to a heat source. In other words, the word "heat" makes you think of the *physiological sensation of being hot*. That's because we humans are pretty sensitive to heat, or the absence of it.

Remember, there is a relatively narrow temperature range within which we feel truly comfortable. Put another way, we must have the right amount of heat to feel comfortable. Sure, some people have learned to survive at the extreme edges of this range, but the majority of us like to be in that comfort zone of about 70 to 80° F. In this zone, we feel good. That's why air conditioning and heating systems are so popular in our vehicles, homes and offices. Without them, we would sometimes be uncomfortable.

Before we examine the principles of operation of modern air conditioning systems, let's take a quick look at the basics of the typical heating system, which is considerably simpler than an air conditioning system.

The heating system

The internal combustion engine is nothing more than a big heat pump that converts chemical energy into mechanical energy. The temperature in the combustion chamber ranges from 1200° to 1800°F.

About a third of this heat is actually used for pushing the piston down on its power stroke. Another third escapes out the exhaust system. The remainder is conducted through the cylinder walls and cylinder head into the engine cooling system. The heater harnesses this waste heat generated by the engine to heat the passenger compartment.

Heat moves from warmer to cooler substances

A basic characteristic of heat is that it always moves from a warmer to a cooler substance **(see illustration)**. For example, place an ice cube in your hand and hold it for a minute. Your hands feel cold and the ice cube starts melting. The heat is transferring from your hands to the ice cube. We will talk more about the movement of heat in the following discussion about air conditioning. Now let's look at the three means by which heat is transferred.

If you place an ice cube in your hand, it quickly starts to feel cold because the heat is transferring from your hand to the ice cube - heat always moves from a warmer to a cooler substance

Convection, conduction and radiation

Convection **(see illustration)** is the movement of heat that occurs in liquids and gases when the heated portion rises and is displaced by the cooler portion, creating a circular movement known as a "convection current." Turn on the faucet for the hot water in the shower. Note that it's hot, even though the heater is some distance away. The moving water carries the heat to the shower nozzle. Similarly, when air warmer than the surrounding air is forced into the passenger compartment, it moves up, forcing the cooler air down. This constant displacement of cooler air by warmer air eventually distributes the heated air evenly throughout the passenger compartment.

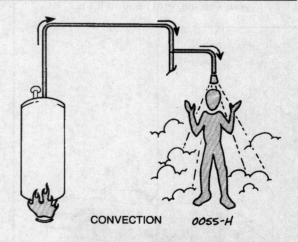

CONVECTION

What happens when you turn on the hot water faucet in the shower? Hot water comes out the shower nozzle, even though the hot water heater is some distance away, because the water - or any liquid or gas, for that matter - has the ability to carry heat from one place to another - this phenomenon is known as convection

Heating and air conditioning

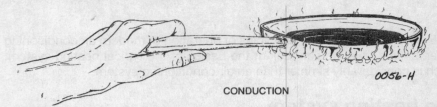

CONDUCTION

When you pick up a cast iron pan from the stove, the handle feels warm, even though it's not directly exposed to the flame, because the heat "conducts" through the metal pan to the handle - do the same thing with an aluminum pan, however, and you could burn your hand, because aluminum is a better conductor of heat than cast iron (in other words, the rate of heat transfer depends on the thermal conductivity of the substance)

When you feel the heat on a sunny day, it's because infra-red (invisible) waves from the sun are radiating through space, falling on your vehicle, and heating it up

The sun, of course, isn't the only heat source - everything with heat radiates (because it's moving from warmer to cooler substances, remember?). Add up the heat radiating off your vehicle, its engine, the road, etc. and you can see why it gets hot inside the passenger compartment

Conduction **(see illustration)** is the transfer of heat through a solid material. Pick up a cast iron pan from the stove. Note that the handle is warm. The heat has conducted through the hot metal pan to the cooler handle. Do the same thing with an aluminum pan and you may burn your hand. That's because the rate of transfer depends on the thermal conductivity of the material. And aluminum is a better conductor than cast iron. All "heat exchangers" (devices that transfer heat from a heated liquid to the air, or vice versa) are constructed from metals like aluminum and copper, which are considered the best thermal conductors.

Radiation **(see illustration)** is the transfer of heat by those waves located in the "infra-red" portion of the "electromagnetic spectrum." Because infrared waves have wavelengths longer than those of visible light rays, they are invisible. But when you see "heat waves" rolling off a hot asphalt road or the hood of a hot car, that's radiation. The important thing to remember about radiation is that anything that is heated up will give off radiating heat.

Using these three methods of heat transfer, we can describe any heating system. At the heart of the system is a small heat exchanger, commonly known as a heater core. The core is nothing more than a convoluted section of metal tubing through which hot engine coolant is pumped. The heat in the coolant moves through the walls of the tubes and into hundreds of tiny, wafer thin cooling fins attached to the tubing (conduction). An electric fan blows air through the core and heat is transferred from the fins to the cooler air as it passes over them (radiation). This heated air is then forced through a series of ducts and outlets into the passenger compartment, where it warms the air (convection).

Air conditioners

Chances are that every vehicle you've ever owned has a heater, but you have probably owned one without an air conditioner. If so, you know what it's like to spend an hour, or a day, confined to the passenger compartment of such a vehicle on a hot day **(see illustration)** When exposed to direct sunlight while parked or driven on a hot day with the windows rolled up, inside temperatures can exceed 140°F. Heat radiated by the sun falls on the metal and glass skin of the roof, body panels and windows, is conducted through the skin and radiated into the passenger compartment. Even heat radiating up off the hot pavement enters the vehicle in a similar fashion. The engine, exhaust system and transmission all shed a huge amount of heat, which also finds its way into the passenger compartment. Even the occupants themselves give off heat. Many modern vehicles have only two roll-down windows, no vent windows and poor ventilation systems. For these vehicles, air conditioning systems aren't just a convenience, they're a necessity. Spending time in one of these vehicles on a hot day with a broken air conditioner is extremely uncomfortable. That's why it's essential that you keep it in top condition. Before you can do that though, you need to know a few things about the principles of air conditioning.

Though you might be able to service an air conditioning system without really understanding how it works, you will have a tough time trying to troubleshoot it when something goes wrong. So take the time to fully understand the following principles before attempting to work on an air conditioning system.

What is automotive air conditioning?

Automotive air conditioning is the process by which air is cooled, cleaned and dehumidified before entering, or re-entering, the passenger compartment. Basically, an air conditioning system removes heat from the passenger compartment by absorbing it and carrying it outside, where it is released into the atmosphere.

This process is possible because we have learned how to manipulate three simple natural phenomena:

1 *Heat transfer*
2 *The "latent heat of vaporization"*
3 *The effect of pressure on boiling or condensation*

No true comprehension of air conditioning is possible until you understand these three underlying principles because they form the basis of all air conditioning systems.

Heat transfer

If two materials of different temperatures are placed near each other, the heat in the warmer material will always travel to the colder material until both are the same temperature.

Take, for example, a bottle of warm beer sitting next to a tray of ice cubes on the kitchen counter **(see illustration)**. The colder tray of ice cubes does not transfer its colder temperature to the bottle of beer next to it. Instead, the heat in the beer automatically flows to the ice cube tray.

How much heat? In order to express the amount of heat that transfers from one substance to another, a standard of measurement known as the British Thermal Unit (BTU) has been created. One BTU is equal to the amount of heat required to raise the temperature of one pound of water 0.55°C (1°F) **(see illustration)**. For example, to raise the temperature of one pound of water from 0°C (32°F) to 100°C (212°F), one BTU of heat must be added for each 0.55°C (1°F) rise in temperature, or a total of 180 BTUs of heat. Conversely, in order to lower

Heat transfer

What happens if you place a bottle of room temperature beer next to a tray of ice cubes? The bottle of beer cools off because its heat travels from the beer to the ice cubes (not because the cold of the ice cubes is transferred to the beer!)

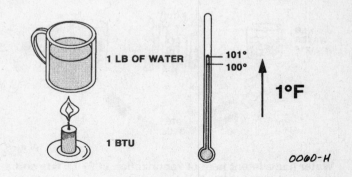

One British Thermal Unit (BTU) is equal to the amount of heat required to raise the temperature of one pound of water one degree Fahrenheit

the temperature of one pound of water from 100°C (212°F) to 0°C (32°F), 180 BTUs of heat must be removed from the water.

Latent heat of vaporization

When a liquid boils (changes to a gas), it absorbs heat without raising the temperature of the resulting gas. When the gas condenses (changes back to a liquid), it gives off heat without lowering the temperature of the resulting liquid.

For example, place one pound of water at 0°C (32°F) in a container over a flame. With each BTU of heat that the water absorbs from the flame, its temperature rises 0.55°C (1°F). Thus, after it has absorbed 180 BTUs of heat, the water reaches a temperature of 100°C (212°F). But then a funny thing happens. Even though the flame continues to transfer heat to the water, the temperature of the water remains at 100°C (212°F). It also starts to boil, or change from a liquid to a gaseous state. And it continues to boil until the entire pound of water has passed into the atmosphere as vapor. If, instead of escaping into the atmosphere, the vapor from the whole pound of water were somehow trapped in a container and checked with a thermometer, it too would indicate a temperature of 100°C (212°F). In other words, even though the flame undoubtedly transferred more than 180 BTUs of heat to the water, there could not have been more than an 82°C (180°F) rise in the water's temperature (it went from 32 to 212°F, right?). Where did the rest of the heat go? It was absorbed by the water as it boiled off and disappeared with the vapor. If the vapor contacted cool air, however, the hidden heat would reappear and flow into the cooler air as the vapor condensed back to water. In scientific terms, this phenomenon is known as the "latent," or hidden, heat of vaporization.

Water has a latent heat of vaporization of 970 BTUs and a boiling point of 100°C (212°F). What this means is that as a pound of water reaches a temperature of 100°C (212°F), it will absorb 970 BTUs of heat as it changes to vapor. Conversely, the vapor will give off 970 BTUs of heat in condensing back to water **(see illustration)**.

This remarkable transfer of heat that occurs when a liquid boils or a vapor condenses, is the basic principle of operation for all air conditioning systems.

The amount of heat that a liquid can absorb as it vaporizes is not the only critical characteristic to consider. It must also have a low boiling point. In other words, the temperature at which it boils must be lower than the substance to be cooled.

Place our bottle of beer, for example, at a room temperature of, say, 21.6°C (70°F) next to boiling water. The heat will flow from the (higher temperature) water to the (cooler temperature) beer. Thus, we get one warm beer, because the boiling point of water is too high.

In order to make practical use of the heat transfer that occurs when a liquid boils, we have to find some liquid with a low boiling point. A commercial refrigerant boils at extremely low temperatures of approximately -29.85°C (-21.7°F) in an open container. In other words, here's a liquid that will boil, and vaporize, way below the temperature of any passenger compartment this side of Bemidji, Minnesota, and will absorb tremendous

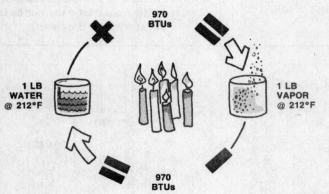

0061-H

Water has a latent heat of vaporization of 970 BTUs and a boiling point of 212°F - in other words, as a pound of water reaches a temperature of 212°F, it will absorb 970 BTUs of heat as it changes to vapor; conversely, the vapor will shed 970 BTUs of heat as it condenses back to water

amounts of heat without getting any warmer itself. We'll get back to refrigerant in a moment. First, we need to discuss the third principle of air conditioning operation.

Effect of pressure on boiling or condensation

The saturation temperature (the temperature at which boiling or condensation occurs) of a liquid or a vapor increases or decreases in accordance with the pressure to which it is subjected.

In the typical "fixed orifice tube" (we'll discuss that term in the next chapter) air conditioning system, liquid refrigerant is stored in the condenser under high pressure. When the liquid refrigerant is released into the evaporator by the fixed orifice tube, the resulting decrease in pressure and partial boiling lowers its temperature to the new boiling point. As the refrigerant flows through the evaporator, the passenger compartment air passes over the outside surface of the evaporator coils. As it boils, the refrigerant absorbs heat from the air and cools the passenger compartment **(see illustration)**. The heat from the passenger compartment is absorbed by the boiling refrigerant and hidden in the vapor. The refrigeration cycle is now under way. To complete the cycle, three things need to happen:

1 *The heat in the vapor must be disposed of*
2 *The vapor must be converted back to liquid for reuse*
3 *The liquid must be returned to the starting point in the refrigeration cycle*

The compressor and condenser perform these functions. The compressor pumps the refrigerant vapor - which contains the "latent," or hidden, heat- out of the evaporator and suction accumulator drier, then forces it, under high pressure, into the condenser which is located in the outside air stream at the front of the vehicle. The increased pressure in the condenser raises the refrigerant condensation or saturation temperature to a point higher than that of the outside air. As the heat transfers from the hot vapor to the cooler air, the refrigerant condenses back to a liquid. The liquid, under high pressure now, returns through the liquid line back to the fixed orifice tube for reuse.

But how can heat be transferred from a comparatively cooler vehicle passenger compartment to the hot outside air? The answer lies in the difference between the refrigerant pressure that exists in the evaporator, and the pressure that exists in the condenser. In the evaporator, the suction of the compressor reduces the pressure, and the boiling point, below the temperature of the passenger compartment. Thus, heat transfers from the passenger compartment to the boiling refrigerant. In the condenser, which is pressur-

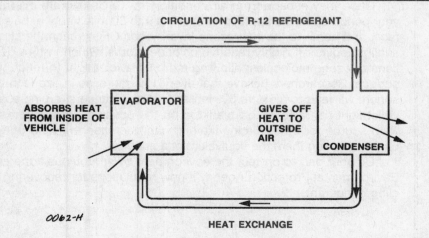

CIRCULATION OF R-12 REFRIGERANT

EVAPORATOR

ABSORBS HEAT FROM INSIDE OF VEHICLE

GIVES OFF HEAT TO OUTSIDE AIR

CONDENSER

HEAT EXCHANGE

0062-H

In its simplest terms, refrigerant absorbs heat from the passenger compartment at the evaporator, transfers it through a tube and sheds it to the outside air at the condenser

ized by the compressor, the condensation point is raised above the temperature of the outside air. Thus, the heat transfers from the condensing refrigerant to the outside air. The fixed orifice tube and the compressor simply create pressure conditions that allow the third law of nature to work.

Refrigerant-12

The movement of heat and the change of state of a substance leads us now to Refrigerant-12 (R-12 or Freon), which is the chemical substance dichlorodifluoromethane (CCl_2F_2) used as a "heat carrier" in earlier air conditioning systems.

Why R-12? Because it can change states and carry heat away as required by the air conditioning system and it can do so while remaining within the normal operating temperature range of an air conditioning system. Although water can also change states, R-12 can do it more rapidly and at a much lower temperature.

R-12 is used in earlier automotive air conditioners because of its low boiling point (the point at which evaporation occurs). At any temperature above-21.6°F, R-12 will change state, vaporize and absorb great quantities of heat from inside the vehicle. This creates the "cooling effect" of the air conditioning system.

R-12 was the preferred chemical for many years because it has some very desirable characteristics. It is non-toxic (as long as it isn't exposed to an open flame), non-corrosive, odorless, soluble in oil, harmless to natural rubber components and easy to handle when used properly. In large quantities, however, R-12 can discolor chrome and stainless steel components.

When exposed to an open flame, drawn into the engine or detected with a Halide (propane) leak tester, R-12 can turn into phosgene gas, which is poisonous. **You should NEVER inhale phosgene gas!**
SERVICE TIP: When servicing an air conditioning system, remember to keep the work area well ventilated. When discharging an air conditioning system, keep vehicles with running engines away from the work area.

But the real drawback of R-12 is that, despite its numerous desirable characteristics, it is a member of the chemical family known as chlorofluorocarbons (CFCs), which consist of one or two carbon atoms surrounded by chlorine and fluorine atoms. Recent scientific studies indicate that the ozone layer of the earth's atmosphere, which absorbs more than 99% of the damaging ultraviolet light emitted by the sun, is being seriously depleted as a result of CFC leakage from air conditioning and refrigeration systems.

Once they escape from air conditioners, CFCs migrate over a 15 to 30 year period up to the stratosphere, some 9 to 30 miles above the earth's surface, and home to the vital ozone layer. When CFCs reach the stratosphere, sunlight splits off highly reactive chlorine atoms, which in turn destroy millions of ozone molecules, allowing more ultraviolet light to reach the earth's surface. Researchers believe that every 1% decrease in ozone in the stratosphere will lead to a 5% to 6% increase in skin cancers. An increase in ultraviolet light can also kill off plankton on the ocean's surface that serve as a food source for other marine life and can decrease the yield of agricultural crops by giving them the equivalent of a sunburn.

Do your part to protect the environment by scrupulous adherence to the Environmental Protection Agency's new regulations for recovering and recycling refrigerant.

The pressure-temperature relationship of R-12

The most important characteristic of R-12 is the relationship between pressure and temperature. If the pressure of R-12 is low, the temperature will also be low. If the pressure is high, the temperature will also be high **(see illustration)**.

Within the 20 to 80 psi range, the temperature and pressure of R-12 vary directly. A one psi increase in pressure yields a one degree Fahrenheit change in temperature. So an increase or decrease in R-12 temperature can be obtained by varying the R-12 pressure.

For an air conditioning system to operate at peak efficiency, the R-12 must reach the coldest state (the lowest pressure), at which it can operate without icing, in the evaporator and its warmest (highest pressure) in the condenser. Recall that, in our discussion about latent heat of vaporization, we mentioned that R-12 vaporizes at a low temperature and absorbs great quantities of heat. In the evaporator, the R-12 is under very low pressure. Thus a low temperature is also obtained. This temperature is much lower than the temperature of the air inside the vehicle. Thus, the heat will travel to the colder R-12. As the heat is absorbed, the R-12 vaporizes and carries the heat from the evaporator to the condenser.

At the condenser, the R-12 is at a high temperature and pressure. The temperature of the R-12 is higher than the outside air at the condenser. The heat flows from the condenser to the atmosphere; thus the heat is released outside the vehicle. By giving off heat, the R-12 condenses back to a liquid and the cycle starts over again **(see illustration)**.

These two changes of state - evaporation and condensation - occur during every air conditioning cycle. Heat is absorbed from inside the vehicle by the cold, liquid R-12 flowing through the evaporator. Evaporation takes place and the heat-laden R-12 vapors move out of the evaporator to the compressor.

The compressor increases the pressure and the temperature of the R-12 vapors. The vapors are then pumped to the condenser where the heat is transferred to the outside air and condensation takes place (the R-12, while giving off its heat, returns to a liquid form).

At sea level, under atmospheric pressure, R-12 vaporizes at -21.6°F. By pressurizing R-12, it vaporizes at higher temperatures. This is the same process that occurs in radiators. When a pressure cap rated at 15 psi is installed on a radiator, water - which normally boils at 212°F - will boil at about 265°F. Thus, by pressurizing R-12 to between 15 and 30 psi, the point of vaporization can be increased to between 11 and 32°F, which is the desirable level in most evaporators. At even higher pressures (180 to 230 psi), R-12 will condense back into a liquid at temperatures between 130 and 150°F, which is desirable in most condenser units.

There are two major advantages in using R-12. First, it's able to cycle through changes of state within a wide range of temperatures and pressures that exist within the air conditioning system. Second, with R-12, it's possible to use economical air conditioning control devices (which will be discussed in Chapter Two).

If you have read and understood everything in this chapter, you now know how a heater heats and how an air conditioner cools. A heating system simply transfers

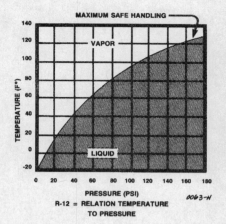

The most important characteristic of R-12, or refrigerant, is the relationship it maintains between pressure and temperature: If the pressure of R-12 is low, the temperature will also be low; if the pressure is high, the temperature will also be high - and, as the graph shows, within the 20 to 80 psi range, temperature and pressure vary directly

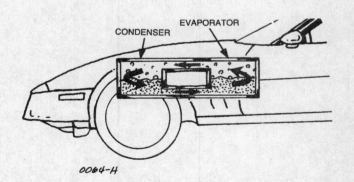

At the condenser, the R-12 is at a high temperature and pressure - higher, in fact, than the outside air around the condenser, so the heat in the R-12 flows away, through the condenser tubing and fins and into the outside air - by giving off heat, the R-12 condenses back to a liquid again and the cycle starts all over

heat from the hot engine coolant to the passenger compartment through convection, conduction and radiation. An air conditioning system is nothing more than a combination of various mechanical components utilizing a chemical medium, R-12, to absorb heat from inside the vehicle and transfer it to the outside air. The remaining cooler air contains less moisture, adding to the cooling sensation. In effect, one might say that an air conditioning system does not really cool a vehicle, but actually "unheats" it. Now we are ready to discuss the components of heating and air conditioning systems, and how they work together, in more detail.

R-134a

As part of a worldwide effort to protect the ozone layer, the United States joined 75 other countries as a Party to the international treaty known as the Montreal Protocol in 1990. The USA committed to phasing out R-12 and other ozone-depleting substances by the year 2000. The 1990 Clear Air Act Amendments incorporated this production of CFCs by the end of 1995. Automobile manufacturers have now phased out R-12 and switched to a new refrigerant - known as HFC-134A, or R-134a - which is a hydrofluorocarbon (HFC)-based substance. Because of the absence of chlorine in its molecule structure, R-134, R-134a is 95 percent less harmful to stratospheric ozone than R-12.

But R-134a isn't perfect: It's slightly less efficient at transferring heat than R-12; The latent heat of vaporization (the amount of energy required to change from vapor to a liquid) for R-12 is 36.2 Kcal/Kg @ 0° C: R-134a's latent heat of vaporization is 47.9 Kcal/Kg @ 0° C. In other words, R-134a consumes a little more energy in shedding the heat it has absorbed and transferred from the passenger compartment than does R-12. Practically speaking, this means that an R-134a system must operate at slightly higher pressures, and some of the system components - the compressor, the condenser and the evaporator - must be a little more robust and a little larger. It also means that more airflow across the condenser will be necessary, which may result in reduced air conditioning system performance in heavy traffic

Basic air conditioning and heating system components

Heating system components

Strictly speaking, there are very few components in the heating system-the heater core, the hoses that connect it to the engine's cooling system and an electric blower (fan) that draws air into the heater case and blows it through the heater core.

Other components - such as the water pump and thermostat - are really part of the engine cooling system and their functions are well documented elsewhere. The rest of the heating system - the heater case (or heater box), the blend doors, the dash control assembly, the control valve (if equipped), any temperature sensors, etc. - are really heater controls. Typical control components are covered later in this chapter.

The heater core is located under the dash, inside a large (usually plastic) assembly known as the heater case (or heater box). On vehicles with an integrated air conditioning and heating system, this assembly is usually referred to as a heater/evaporator case because the evaporator and the heater are both housed in it. Hoses deliver engine coolant to the heater core and transport it back to the engine. If the heater is equipped with a control valve, it's located in-line in the heater hose. Think of the heater core **(see illustration)** as a small radiator. Like the radiator, the heater core is also a heat exchanger which sheds the engine heat carried by the coolant. It accomplishes this task by conducting the heat through the tubing walls and into thousands of tiny cooling fins. So, like the radiator, the heater core actually helps to cool the engine. But instead of radiating the heat into the outside air, the heater core radiates it into the air inside the heater box, which is blown by an electric fan into the passenger compartment. That's all there is to it. We will look at the heating system in more detail in Chapter Three.

Like a radiator, the heater core carries engine coolant through its tubing and transfers the heat from the coolant through the tubing walls into cooling fins which shed the heat into the air being blown through the heater case by the blower assembly

Basic types of air conditioning systems

There are two basic types of vehicle air conditioning systems. As we discussed in Chapter 1, in a typical vehicle air conditioning system, high-pressure liquid refrigerant in the condenser is released into the evaporator, via a device, which decreases the refrigerant pressure. The type of device used to decrease the refrigerant pressure gives us the basic difference between the type of air conditioning system; the device used may be either an *expansion valve*, or an *orifice tube*. Let's take a quick look at the two types of systems in more detail.

Air conditioning system using an expansion valve

The five basic components used in this type of system are:

1) *Compressor (driven by the engine)*
2) *Condenser (located at the front of the vehicle, in front of the radiator)*
3) *Receiver/drier (located in the engine compartment)*
4) *Expansion valve (usually attached to the evaporator)*
5) *Evaporator (located inside a housing in the dash, with the heater core)*

Let's follow the refrigerant as it flows through this type of system **(see illustration)**. The **compressor** compresses the refrigerant from a low-pressure vapor to a high-pressure vapor. The high-pressure vapor is pumped into the **condenser**, where it is condensed by the cooling airflow to a high-pressure liquid. The high-pressure liquid is pumped to the **receiver/drier** (sometimes referred to as a filter/drier), where it is cleaned and all moisture is removed. The clean, dry high-pressure liquid is pumped to the **expansion valve**, where it is changed to a low-pressure mixture of liquid and vapor. The low-pressure refrigerant mixture is then pumped to the **evaporator**, where the remaining liquid is turned back to a low-pressure vapor, cooling the air passing over the evaporator as it does so. From the evaporator, the low-pressure vapor passes back to the compressor, which pumps it through the system again.

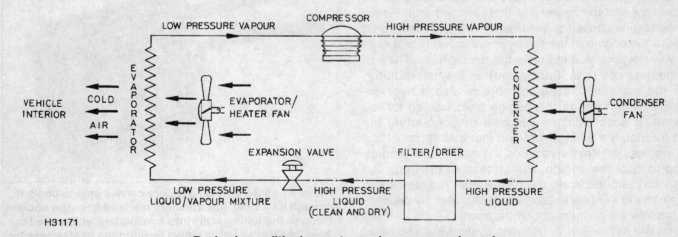

Basic air conditioning system using an expansion valve

H31171

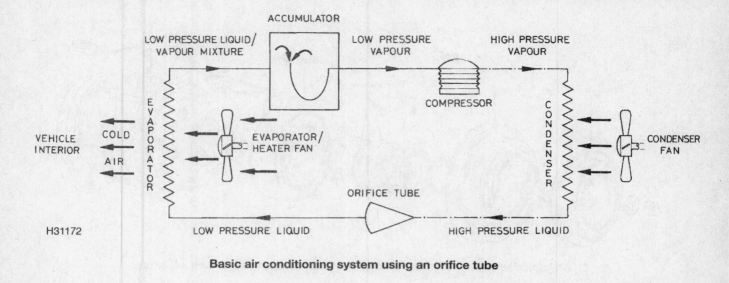

Basic air conditioning system using an orifice tube

Air conditioning system using an orifice tube

The five basic components used in this type of system are:

1) *Compressor (driven by the engine)*
2) *Condenser (located at the front of the vehicle, in front of the radiator)*
3) *Orifice tube (located in the refrigerant line, or in the evaporator)*
4) *Evaporator (located inside a housing in the dash, with the heater core)*
5) *Accumulator (located in the engine compartment)*

Let's trace the flow of the refrigerant through this type of system **(see illustration)**. The **compressor** compresses the refrigerant from a low-pressure vapor to a high-pressure vapor. The high-pressure vapor is pumped into the **condenser**, where it is condensed by the cooling airflow to a high-pressure liquid. The high-pressure liquid is pumped to the **orifice tube**, where the flow is restricted, changing the refrigerant to a low-pressure liquid. The low-pressure liquid is then pumped to the **evaporator**, where the liquid is partly converted to a vapor, cooling the air passing over the evaporator as it does so. From the evaporator, the low-pressure mixture of liquid and vapor is pumped to the **accumulator**, where the remaining liquid is boiled back to vapor. The pure low-pressure vapor passes back to the compressor, which pumps it through the system again.

Air conditioning components

There are five basic components in every automotive air conditioning system:

1) *Compressor*
2) *Condenser*
3) *Accumulator or receiver-dryer*
4) *Expansion valve or orifice tube*
5) *Evaporator*

No air conditioning system can operate without all five components. A number of additional components, whose function is to control and maximize the efficiency of specific systems, are also employed in all systems. We will examine those components in the second half of this chapter. First, let's look at the five primary components in detail.

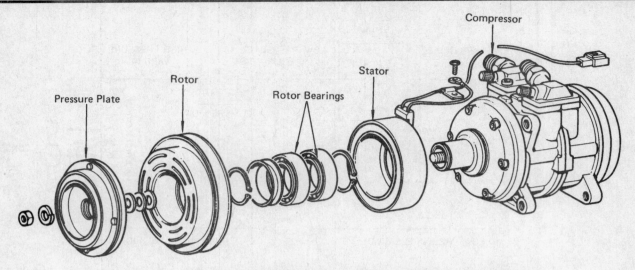

Pressure Plate   Rotor   Rotor Bearings   Stator   Compressor

An exploded view of a typical electro-magnetic compressor clutch assembly

Compressor

Compressors vary considerably in design but they all perform the same two functions: pumping refrigerant through the system and increasing its pressure and temperature so it will condense and release heat. The following paragraphs will give you a brief idea of how the two basic types of compressors work. Since we aren't going to cover compressor rebuilding, this rudimentary knowledge should suffice.

Compressor clutch

All automotive air conditioning compressors are belt-driven from the engine's crankshaft. An electro-magnetic clutch **(see illustration)** disengages the compressor from the belt when compressor operation is unnecessary, or unwanted.

The clutch is engaged or disengaged both by the control panel on the dash and by the actual demands of the system. In some systems, the clutch constantly "cycles" compressor operation on and off. In others, the compressor runs continuously as long as the system is turned "on."

Older compressors had a "rotating coil" clutch design. The magnetic coil that engages or disengages the compressor is mounted within the pulley and rotates with it. Electrical connections for the clutch operation are made through a stationary brush assembly and rotating slip rings, which are part of the field coil assembly.

A stationary coil design is employed in all contemporary air conditioning compressors. In this type, the magnetic coil is mounted on the end of the compressor and the electrical connections are made directly to the coil leads.

Function

The compressor is the pump that circulates refrigerant through the system. The suction side of the compressor pulls in refrigerant in a low pressure, low temperature form. The refrigerant is then pumped through the compressor to the discharge or outlet side where it's compressed, raising its temperature. It's now ready once more to condense and release heat. The pressurized, heated refrigerant vapor is forced out of the compressor, through the high pressure line, to the condenser.

Operation

Basically, all compressors fall into one of two categories: piston type and rotary vane type. As the name implies, piston type compressors have one or more (up to ten) pistons arranged in either an inline, axial, radial or vee configuration. Rotary vane compressors have no pistons.

Piston-type compressors

Piston type compressors **(see illustration)** go through an intake stroke and a compression stroke for each cylinder. On the intake stroke, the refrigerant from the low side (evaporator side) of the system is drawn into the compressor. The intake of refrigerant occurs through reed valves. These one-way valves control the flow of refrigerant vapors into the cylinder.

During the compression stroke, the gaseous refrigerant is compressed. This increases both the pressure and the temperature of the heat-carrying refrigerant. The outlet (discharge) side reed valves then open to allow the refrigerant to move into the condenser. The outlet reed valves may be considered the beginning of the high side of the system.

The most common piston-type compressors have multiple pistons **(see illustration)**, operated by a "squish plate" attached to the compressor shaft. As the shaft turns, the squish plate moves the pistons to compress the refrigerant. Many compressors use several sets of twin, horizontally-opposed pistons.

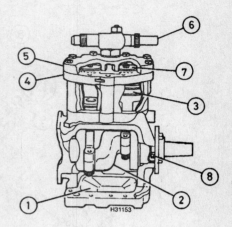

Cutaway view of a typical two-cylinder piston-type compressor

1   Oil sump
2   Crankshaft
3   Piston and ring assembly
4   Valve plate
5   Cylinder head
6   Service valve fitting
7   Reed valve assembly
8   Crankshaft seal assembly

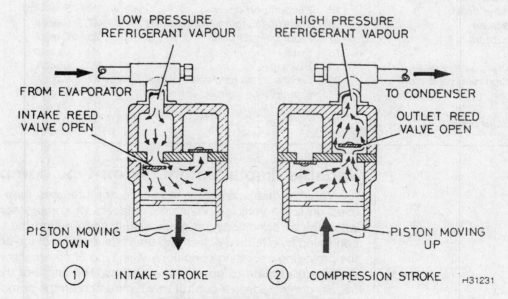

Diagram of compressor operation

1   **Intake stroke** - *gaseous refrigerant from low (evaporator) side of system is drawn into compressor through one-way reed valve.*
2   **Compression stroke** - *gaseous R-12 is compressed into high pressure, high temperature, heat-carrying refrigerant and pushed out one-way reed valve to condenser*

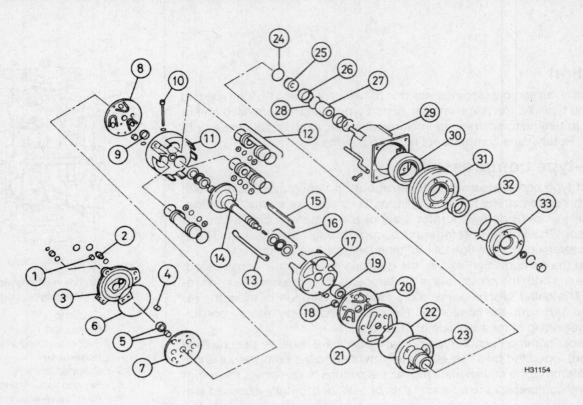

Exploded view of a typical six-cylinder compressor

1	Low-pressure cut-out (superheat) switch	12	Piston assembly	23	Front cylinder head
2	Pressure relief valve	13	Discharge tube	24	O-ring
3	Rear cylinder head	14	Shaft and squish plate	25	Seal
4	Suction screen	15	Suction port cover	26	Seal seat
5	Oil pump rotors	16	Thrust bearing and races	27	Sleeve
6	O-ring	17	Front cylinder body	28	Circlip
7	Rear discharge valve plate	18	Bush	29	Casing
8	Rear suction reed valve plate	19	Bearing	30	Clutch coil
9	Bearing	20	Front suction reed valve plate	31	Pulley
10	Oil tube	21	Front discharge reed valve plate	32	Bearing
11	Rear cylinder body	22	O-ring	33	Clutch plate and hub assembly

Variable displacement piston-type compressors

Variable displacement piston-type compressors **(see illustration)** are used on some vehicles. Variable displacement compressors run constantly when the air conditioning system is switched on, and the refrigerant flow is controlled by effectively changing the displacement of the compressor to suit the prevailing operating conditions. This type of compressor uses a variable-angle squish plate to operate the pistons. The angle of the squish plate is usually controlled via a control valve, mounted on the compressor, which allows varying amounts of high-pressure refrigerant to enter the compressor crankcase. The control valve senses the suction pressure on the low side of the compressor, which varies in accordance with the evaporator temperature and the compressor speed.

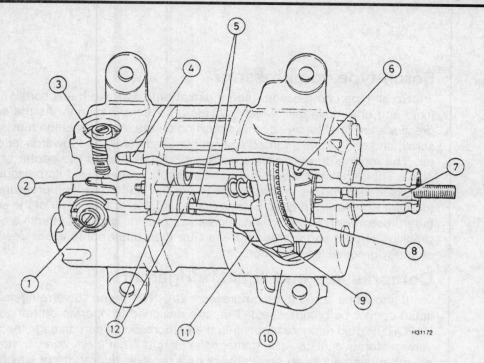

Cutaway view of a typical variable displacement piston-type compressor

1   Main control valve
2   Discharge port
3   Auxiliary control valve
4   Suction port
5   Connecting rods
6   Squish plate drive linkage
7   Input shaft
8   Thrust bearing squish plate
9   Anti-rotation swivel
10 Crankcase
11 Anti-rotation shaft
12 Pistons

Rotary vane type compressors

Rotary vane type compressors consist of a rotor with several vanes and a precisely shaped housing **(see illustration)**. As the compressor shaft rotates, the vanes and housing form chambers. The refrigerant is drawn through the suction port into the chambers, which become smaller as the rotor turns. The discharge port is located at the point where the gas is completely compressed.

The vane type compressor employs no sealing rings. The vanes are sealed against the housing by centrifugal force and lubricating oil. The oil sump is located on the discharge side, so the high pressure tends to force it around the vanes into the low pressure side. This action insures continuous lubrication. Because it depends upon a constant supply of oil, the vane type compressor is susceptible to damage if the system charge is lost. Usually, some sort of protection device is employed to disengage the clutch if system pressure drops too low.

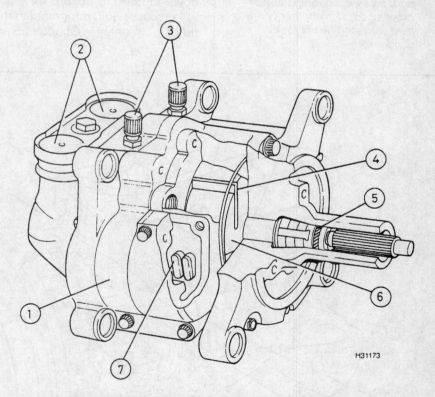

Cutaway view of a typical rotary vane-type compressor

1   Discharge valve cover
2   Suction and discharge ports
3   Service fittings
4   Vane
5   Shaft seal
6   Rotor
7   Reed valve

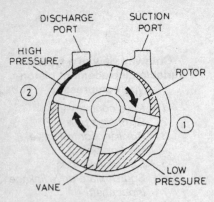

Diagram of compressor operation

1. **Intake** - *As a low pressure chamber sweeps by the suction port, gaseous refrigerant from low (evaporator) side of system is drawn through one-way reed valve.*

2. **Exhaust** - *As rotor rotates, chamber decreases in size, compressing refrigerant. As chamber sweeps by discharge port, pressurized refrigerant is expelled through another one-way reed valve and heads for the condenser.*

Scroll-type compressors

Scroll-type compressors **(see illustration)** have two metal scrolls, one fixed and one moveable, which provide an eccentric motion. As the compressor shaft rotates, an eccentric bushing on the shaft drives the moveable scroll, and refrigerant is forced against the fixed scroll, and towards its center. The motion creates an increase in pressure toward the center of the scroll. The refrigerant vapor moves in a circular pattern, and its pressure is increased as it moves toward the center of the scroll. The high pressure refrigerant is released through a delivery port located at the center of the scroll **(see illustration)**. Scroll-type compressors provide a longer effective compression stroke, and a smoother start-up than other compressor designs, and they produce less vibration.

Compressors and liquid refrigerant

It should be noted that compressors CANNOT pump liquid refrigerant (a liquid cannot be compressed). They are designed to operate on refrigerant VAPOR. If liquid refrigerant gets into the compressor, it can damage the reed valves. Moreover, it can also damage the pistons. That's why every system is equipped with either an accumulator or a receiver-drier (both of which are covered later) to absorb excess moisture and protect the compressor. We will discuss liquid refrigerant in the system - how it gets there and how to get rid of it - in detail in Chapters 5 and 6.

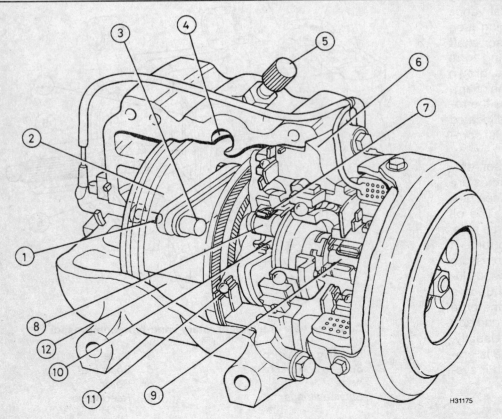

Cutaway view of a typical scroll-type compressor

1. Refrigerant temperature sensor
2. Moveable scroll
3. Delivery port
4. Intake port
5. Low pressure service valve
6. Front plate
7. Needle bearing
8. Stud pin
9. Crankshaft
10. Eccentric bushing
11. Ball coupling
12. Fixed scroll

H31175

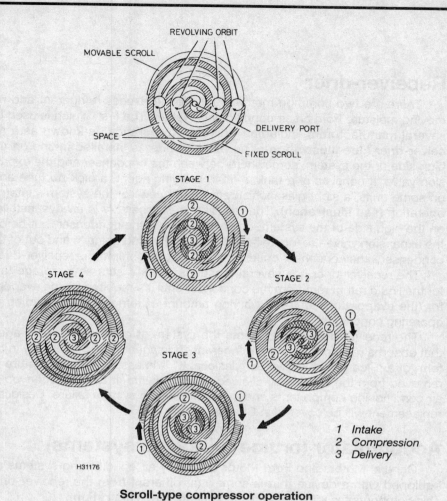

MOVABLE SCROLL
REVOLVING ORBIT
SPACE
DELIVERY PORT
FIXED SCROLL

STAGE 1

STAGE 2

STAGE 3

STAGE 4

1 Intake
2 Compression
3 Delivery

H31176

Scroll-type compressor operation

Condenser

The condenser (see illustration), sometimes referred to as the refrigerant coil, is nothing more than a heat exchanger. It's similar in design to the evaporator, the heater core and the radiator. The condenser is mounted directly in front of the radiator where it can receive the full air flow created by vehicle forward motion and by the engine fan. This configuration affords the maximum surface area for heat transfer within a minimum amount of engine compartment space.

The condenser receives the heated, pressurized refrigerant vapor from the compressor's discharge hose. The refrigerant vapor enters at the top of the condenser and flows through the coils, conducting heat through the walls of the tubing and into the cooling fins, then radiating off the fins into the cooler atmosphere.

As the refrigerant vapors are cooled and flow down through the condenser, they gradually condense back into liquid form. At that point where the refrigerant vapors turn to liquid, they shed the greatest amount of heat.

In an air conditioning system that's operating under an average heat load, the condenser will have a combination of hot refrigerant vapor in the upper two-thirds and warm liquid refrigerant which has condensed in the lower third of the coils. This high pressure liquid refrigerant flows out of the condenser and moves to the evaporator.

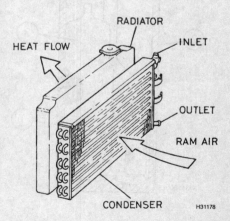

RADIATOR
HEAT FLOW
INLET
OUTLET
RAM AIR
CONDENSER
H31178

The condenser looks and works just like a heater core, evaporator or radiator and is always installed right in front of the radiator to receive the full airflow from the vehicle's forward motion

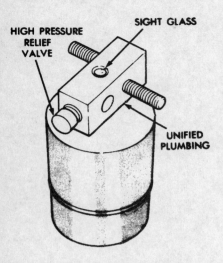

The receiver-drier performs two functions: it acts as a storage tank for the liquid refrigerant until it's required by the evaporator and it protects the system by absorbing moisture from the R-12 into a "desiccant bag" of silica gel

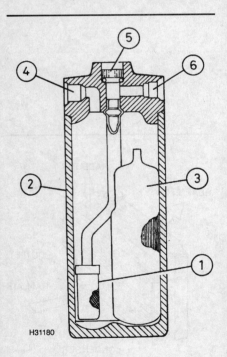

Cutaway view of a typical receiver/drier assembly

1 Filter screen
2 Receiver/drier housing
3 Dessicant bag
4 Inlet
5 Sight glass
6 Outlet

Receiver-drier

There are two common methods for storing excess refrigerant and removing moisture from an air conditioning system. The first, which is used by several manufacturers, including Chrysler Corporation, is known as a receiver-drier (see illustration). The receiver-drier is installed in-line on the high side of the system, somewhere between the condenser and the expansion valve. It consists of a tank, a filter, a drying agent, a pick-up tube and, on some units, a sight glass which affords a "view" of the system's internal operation (see illustration). The receiver-drier assembly is always installed on the high side of the system, downstream from the condenser, but before the expansion valve - to locate it, find the metal tubing going in and out of the condenser - the condenser outlet pipe will go straight into the receiver-drier.

The receiver-drier has several functions. First, it acts as a storage tank for the liquid refrigerant from the condenser until it's required by the evaporator (the evaporator requires a varying amount of refrigerant, depending on operating conditions).

The receiver-drier also protects the system. It contains a drying agent that absorbs moisture from the refrigerant. This agent, which is usually in the form of a silica gel, is known as "desiccant." It is essential that moisture be removed from the system - if allowed to accumulate, it can wreak havoc on air conditioning components and eventually cause system failure. Desiccant replacement will be covered in Chapter 5.

Accumulator (orifice tube type systems)

General Motors and Ford Motor Company air conditioning systems are equipped with a device that is somewhat different from the receiver-drier. This component is known as an accumulator (see illustration).

Unlike the receiver-drier, which is mounted on the high side of the system, the accumulator is located on the low side of the system, usually right at the evaporator outlet. However, its two-fold function - to store excess refrigerant and remove moisture from the system - is the same as that of the receiver-drier. If any liquid refrigerant is passed out of the evaporator, it's stored by the accumulator. Because liquids cannot be compressed, liquid re-

A typical accumulator assembly is not always this easy to see - this one's on a Pontiac Fiero, so it's not obscured by the engine - but, like all accumulators, it's mounted on the firewall right at the evaporator outlet pipe

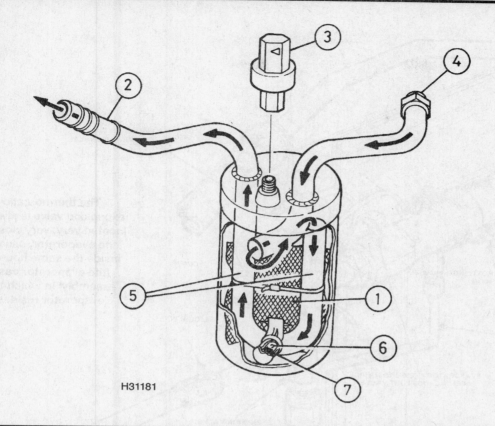

Cutaway view of a typical accumulator assembly

1. Dessicant bag
2. Outlet pipe
3. Pressure-sensitive compressor clutch cycling switch
4. Inlet pipe
5. Vapor return tube
6. Liquid bleed hole
7. Filter screen

H31181

frigerant can damage the compressor. And, like the receiver-drier, the accumulator also utilizes desiccant to remove moisture from the system (**see illustration**).

Moisture in the system

If a component malfunctions or a hose leaks, allowing moisture to contaminate the system, the desiccant must be replaced. In many systems, this can require replacing the accumulator or the receiver-drier, because the desiccant is often non-removable. Some designs, however, permit desiccant removal without junking the entire accumulator or receiver-drier.

But if moisture in the system is suspected, the accumulator or receiver drier is normally replaced, because moisture combines with refrigerant to form hydrochloric acid, which is highly corrosive to components. And if moisture gathers on the expansion valve or orifice tube (see below), it can freeze, blocking the flow of refrigerant and preventing the cooling action at the evaporator.

Controlling refrigerant flow to the evaporator

To obtain optimal cooling performance from any system, the flow of refrigerant to the evaporator must be controlled and complete evaporation of the liquid refrigerant within the evaporator must be assured. These two tasks are accomplished by a thermostatic expansion valve or a fixed orifice tube.

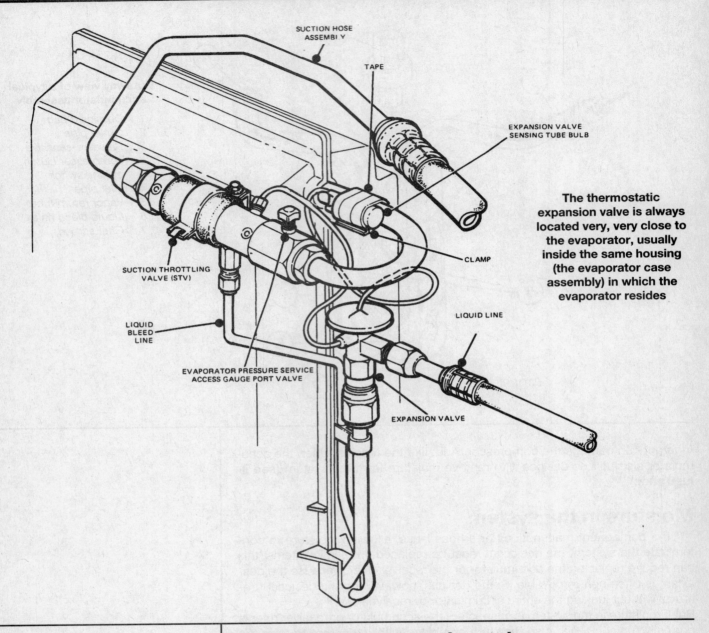

SUCTION HOSE ASSEMBLY

TAPE

EXPANSION VALVE SENSING TUBE BULB

The thermostatic expansion valve is always located very, very close to the evaporator, usually inside the same housing (the evaporator case assembly) in which the evaporator resides

CLAMP

SUCTION THROTTLING VALVE (STV)

LIQUID LINE

LIQUID BLEED LINE

EVAPORATOR PRESSURE SERVICE ACCESS GAUGE PORT VALVE

EXPANSION VALVE

Thermostatic expansion valve

The thermostatic expansion valve **(see illustration)**, which is located in the line between the receiver-drier and the evaporator (usually right at the evaporator), meters, modulates and controls the flow of refrigerant:

1   **Metering** - A metered orifice within the valve changes the pressure of the incoming liquid refrigerant from high pressure to low pressure.

2   **Modulating** - A thermostatically-controlled valve located inside the expansion valve body fluctuates toward an open or closed position as required to control the liquid refrigerant passing through the orifice. This ensures that the evaporator receives the proper amount of refrigerant. The low pressure created at the expansion valve makes it possible for the liquid refrigerant to vaporize as it passes through the evaporator coils, absorbing heat from the vehicle's interior.

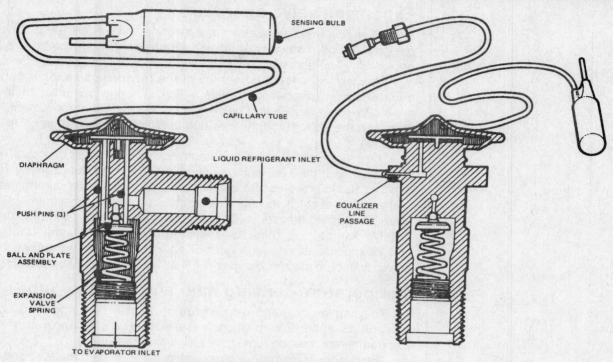

SENSING BULB

CAPILLARY TUBE

DIAPHRAGM

LIQUID REFRIGERANT INLET

PUSH PINS (3)

EQUALIZER LINE PASSAGE

BALL AND PLATE ASSEMBLY

EXPANSION VALVE SPRING

TO EVAPORATOR INLET

Cutaway of a typical (Ford) thermostatic expansion valve:

1) *Regulated by a spring-loaded valve, refrigerant flows through the valve*
2) *The valve is regulated by a pressure-controlled diaphragm through push pins linking the diaphragm and valve*
3) *The pressure in the diaphragm chamber varies in accordance with the pressure inside a temperature sensing bulb located close to the evaporator and the capillary tube which links it to the diaphragm chamber*
4) *An increase in refrigerant temperature at the evaporator outlet increases the pressure in the temperature bulb and tube system, which exerts downward pressure on the expansion valve diaphragm, opening the valve*
5) *A decrease in refrigerant temperature decreases the pressure in the bulb and tube, lessening the pressure on the diaphragm and allowing the valve to close*

3   Controlling - The valve must quickly respond to changes in heat load conditions. As increased heat is sensed, the valve will move toward an open position to increase the flow of refrigerant. Decreased heat loads or increased compressor output volume due to increased engine speed will cause the valve to move toward a closed position, restricting the amount of refrigerant entering the evaporator.

Atomization of low pressure liquid refrigerant

Refrigerant from the receiver-drier enters the expansion valve as a liquid under high pressure. As it passes through the metering orifice in the valve, the refrigerant is forced through the small orifice and sprayed out the other side. The result is a pressure differential, i.e. lower pressure and temperature, which allows the atomized refrigerant to flow through the evaporator and easily vaporize. Because it's at a lower temperature than the interior air of the vehicle, the refrigerant will absorb heat and carry it away from the passenger compartment.

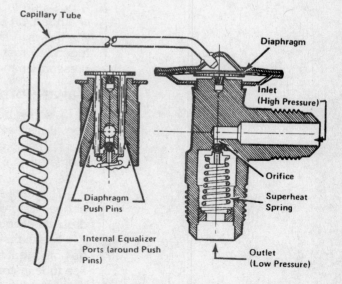

Capillary Tube

Diaphragm

Inlet (High Pressure)

Diaphragm Push Pins

Orifice

Superheat Spring

Internal Equalizer Ports (around Push Pins)

Outlet (Low Pressure)

Cutaways of another typical expansion valve (Volkswagen); note the similarity between this design and the Ford unit

Expansion valve operation

Note: *The following explanation of expansion valve operation is for a typical design used on many air conditioning systems. Though some detail differences may exist between this and other types, the principles are the same.*

Typically, refrigerant flow through the thermostatic expansion valve is controlled by a spring-loaded valve, which, in turn, is controlled by the difference in pressure above and below the valve. Diaphragm movement is transmitted to the valve through operating pins linking the diaphragm plate and the valve.

The pressure above the diaphragm (upper diaphragm chamber) varies in accordance with the pressure supplied by the temperature sensing bulb and capillary tube. The pressure below the diaphragm (lower diaphragm chamber) varies in accordance with the temperature of the refrigerant entering the valve. The spring adjusts valve operation and controls a temperature differential known as "superheat" (see Valve spring below). It's important that you understand how this device works. The expansion valve is the "brain" of a receiver drier type system. So even if it's still not clear yet, keep reading.

Temperature sensing bulb and capillary tube

The capillary tube, tube end (bulb, coil or plain end) and upper diaphragm chamber form a closed system filled with a temperature-sensitive gas (refrigerant, carbon dioxide or a similar substance).

The capillary tube, coil or plain end is clamped onto the evaporator outlet pipe (or installed in a well in the pipe). It's insulated from the outside air with special tape, so it measures only the temperature of the refrigerant as it leaves the evaporator.

Any increase in refrigerant temperature at the evaporator outlet increases the pressure in the temperature bulb and tube system. This in turn exerts a downward pressure on the diaphragm, opening the valve. Similarly, a decrease in refrigerant temperature decreases the pressure in the temperature bulb system. This lessens the pressure on the diaphragm, allowing the valve to close.

The lower diaphragm chamber reflects the evaporator inlet temperature. A passage in the expansion valve from the outlet passage leads to this chamber. On some valves, an external tube is connected to the refrigerant line between the evaporator and the compressor. These passages allow refrigerant pressure to reach the underside of the diaphragm, balancing the pressure on the upper side of the diaphragm.

Valve spring

A spring below the valve tends to move the valve toward the closed position. It also acts in conjunction with the diaphragm to control valve movement. The spring is preset to provide proper valve action and also allows for a differential of 4 to 16°F between the evaporator inlet and outlet temperatures.

This temperature differential is called "superheat." The few extra degrees of heat ensures that the vapor at the evaporator outlet doesn't contain any droplets of liquid refrigerant when it is returned to the compressor.

The expansion valve spring is preset and cannot be adjusted. It should be noted that late model GM and Ford systems use an expansion tube or orifice tube instead of an expansion valve and do not have the spring and temperature differential feature. That's why the accumulator is located on the outlet side of the evaporator, where it can collect any residual liquid refrigerant that might pass through the evaporator.

Servicing the expansion valve

Expansion valves are preset at the factory, so a defective valve must be replaced with a new one. Expansion valves with a filter screen should have the screen replaced whenever the system is open.

The internally equalized expansion valve (like the units already shown) has a drilled equalizing passage between the outlet chamber and the lower side of the diaphragm. A variation of the internally equalized expansion valve is known as the Suction Throttling Valve, Pilot Operated Absolute, or, simply, STV POA. On systems equipped with this design, the equalizer line is attached to a special fitting on the STV unit. The line allows refrigerant pressure to be applied to the lower diaphragm in the same manner as the internally equalized type.

The externally equalized valve has a line and fitting which are connected from the lower side of the diaphragm to a point on the low side hose between the evaporator and the compressor.

Typical configurations

Like other air conditioning system components, expansion valves undergo constant evolution. Manufacturers have introduced a number of different expansion valve designs in recent years. Functionally, the valve described above is typical of many units, including the following variations. Also, operation changes little from one design to another.

Chrysler Corporation "H" valve **(see illustration)** - First used in 1974, this type gets its name from its distinctive "H" configuration. There are two refrigerant passages which form the legs of the "H." One passage is in the refrigerant line from the condenser to the evaporator and contains a ball and spring

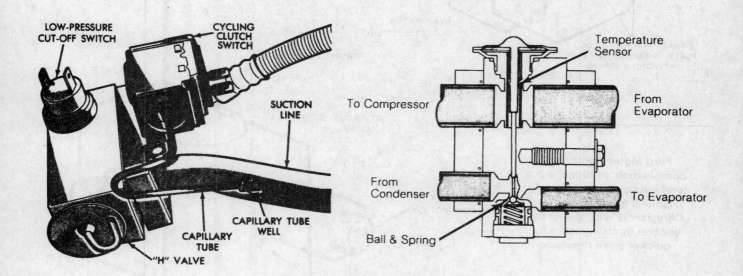

A typical Chrysler "H" valve (left); a cutaway of the same valve (right), which gets its name from the refrigerant passages which form the legs of the "H":

1   *One passage, which contains a ball and spring valve, is in the refrigerant line from the condenser to the evaporator.*
2   *The other passage, which contains the valve's sensing element, is in the refrigerant line from the evaporator to the compressor.*

Heating and air conditioning

valve. The other passage is in the refrigerant line from the evaporator to the compressor and contains the valve's temperature sensing element.

In 1976, Ford Motor Company introduced the combination (or block) type valve, which combines an expansion valve (similar to Chrysler's "H" valve) and the STV into one housing **(see illustration)**. This design puts the operation of these two valves in close proximity for quicker valve response.

In 1980, Ford introduced the minicombination valve. Its configuration is basically similar to that of the earlier valve, but the "H" expansion valve is smaller and the STV has been redesigned to eliminate the internal piston and separate housing manifold.

The manifold assembly has a manifold block which attaches to the evaporator. The expansion valve and STV are attached to the manifold by short sections of tubing **(see illustration)**.

After 1978, Ford expansion valves have used a ball-and-slotted seat arrangement **(see illustrations)**. The slotted seat keeps the valve from closing completely. A slight amount of refrigerant is always allowed to flow into the evaporator with this arrangement. This provides additional refrigerant and refrigerant oil to the compressor to lubricate and cool it during minimum system cooling requirements (expansion valve closed). This type of valve is known as the By-pass Orifice (BPO) Expansion Valve.

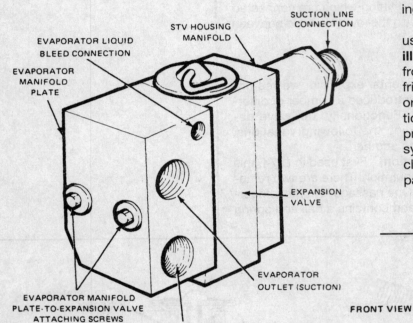

EVAPORATOR LIQUID BLEED CONNECTION

EVAPORATOR MANIFOLD PLATE

STV HOUSING MANIFOLD

SUCTION LINE CONNECTION

EXPANSION VALVE

EVAPORATOR OUTLET (SUCTION)

EVAPORATOR MANIFOLD PLATE-TO-EXPANSION VALVE ATTACHING SCREWS

EVAPORATOR INLET

Ford Motor Company's combination, or block, valve combines an expansion valve (similar in design to the Chrysler "H" valve) with the suction throttling valve for quicker valve response

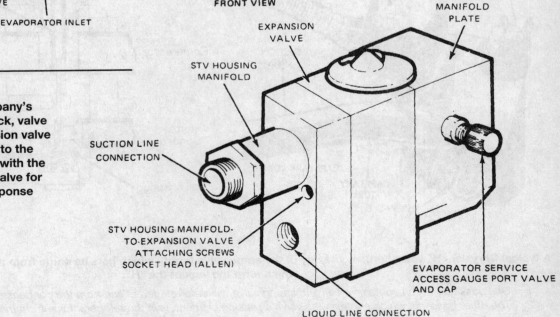

FRONT VIEW

EXPANSION VALVE

STV HOUSING MANIFOLD

EVAPORATOR MANIFOLD PLATE

SUCTION LINE CONNECTION

STV HOUSING MANIFOLD-TO-EXPANSION VALVE ATTACHING SCREWS SOCKET HEAD (ALLEN)

EVAPORATOR SERVICE ACCESS GAUGE PORT VALVE AND CAP

LIQUID LINE CONNECTION

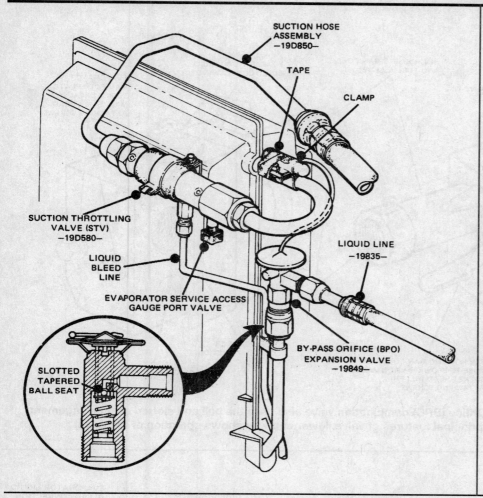

SUCTION HOSE
ASSEMBLY
—19D850—

TAPE

CLAMP

SUCTION THROTTLING
VALVE (STV)
—19D580—

LIQUID
BLEED
LINE

EVAPORATOR SERVICE ACCESS
GAUGE PORT VALVE

LIQUID LINE
—19835—

SLOTTED
TAPERED
BALL SEAT

BY-PASS ORIFICE (BPO)
EXPANSION VALVE
—19849—

Ford Motor Company's By-pass Orifice (BPO) expansion valve uses a ball and slotted seat arrangement - the slotted seat keeps the valve from closing completely, allowing a small amount of refrigerant to flow into the evaporator, thus providing additional refrigerant and oil to the compressor for lubrication and cooling when the system is not operating at capacity - upper illustration shows location of principal components of assembly at evaporator, lower cutaway shows operation of the valve

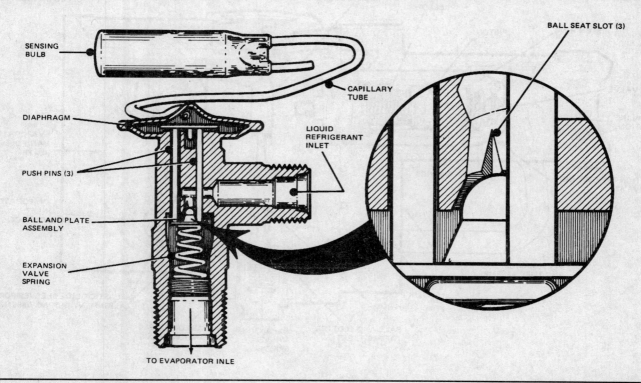

SENSING
BULB

CAPILLARY
TUBE

BALL SEAT SLOT (3)

DIAPHRAGM

LIQUID
REFRIGERANT
INLET

PUSH PINS (3)

BALL AND PLATE
ASSEMBLY

EXPANSION
VALVE
SPRING

TO EVAPORATOR INLE

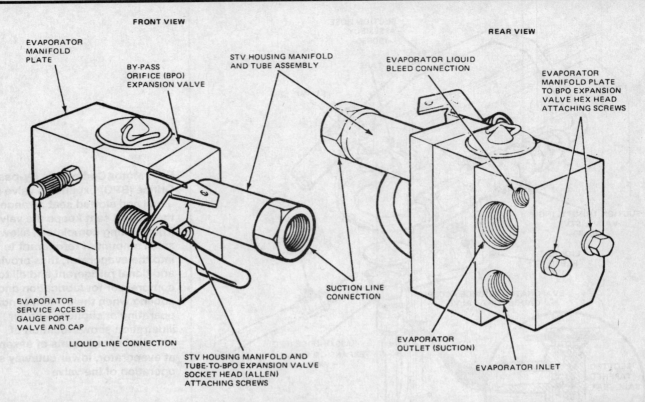

FRONT VIEW

REAR VIEW

EVAPORATOR
MANIFOLD
PLATE

BY-PASS
ORIFICE (BPO)
EXPANSION VALVE

STV HOUSING MANIFOLD
AND TUBE ASSEMBLY

EVAPORATOR LIQUID
BLEED CONNECTION

EVAPORATOR
MANIFOLD PLATE
TO BPO EXPANSION
VALVE HEX HEAD
ATTACHING SCREWS

EVAPORATOR
SERVICE ACCESS
GAUGE PORT
VALVE AND CAP

LIQUID LINE CONNECTION

STV HOUSING MANIFOLD AND
TUBE-TO-BPO EXPANSION VALVE
SOCKET HEAD (ALLEN)
ATTACHING SCREWS

SUCTION LINE
CONNECTION

EVAPORATOR
OUTLET (SUCTION)

EVAPORATOR INLET

**Ford Motor Company's By-pass Orifice (BPO) combination valve also uses the ball and slotted seat arrangement
(upper illustration shows principal features of valve, lower cutaway shows operation of the valve)**

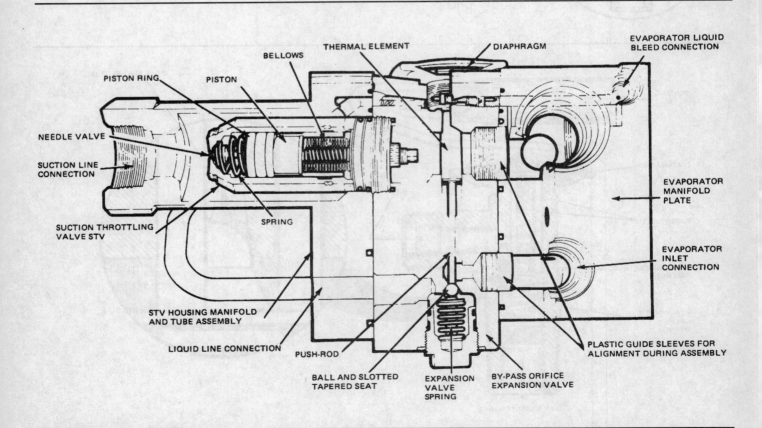

PISTON RING

PISTON

BELLOWS

THERMAL ELEMENT

DIAPHRAGM

EVAPORATOR LIQUID
BLEED CONNECTION

NEEDLE VALVE

SUCTION LINE
CONNECTION

SUCTION THROTTLING
VALVE STV

SPRING

EVAPORATOR
MANIFOLD
PLATE

EVAPORATOR
INLET
CONNECTION

STV HOUSING MANIFOLD
AND TUBE ASSEMBLY

LIQUID LINE CONNECTION

PUSH-ROD

BALL AND SLOTTED
TAPERED SEAT

EXPANSION
VALVE
SPRING

BY-PASS ORIFICE
EXPANSION VALVE

PLASTIC GUIDE SLEEVES FOR
ALIGNMENT DURING ASSEMBLY

Orifice tubes

The orifice tubes **(see illustrations)** used on all current Ford and General Motors vehicles, and some foreign makes, perform the same function as the expansion valve but have a different configuration.

General Motors' 1975 design was a straight tube of sintered metal and was referred to as an expansion tube. The plastic orifice tubes used on current Ford FFOT systems and on 1976 and later GM CCOT systems have filter screens to remove contaminants and a calibrated orifice tube to meter refrigerant flow.

Both designs create the necessary pressure drop by metering a steady flow of refrigerant while the compressor is operating. A cycling clutch switch, either a thermostatic type or a pressure sensing type, turns the compressor on and off. The intermittent operation of the compressor controls the refrigerant flow and pressure. Like the expansion valve, the expansion and orifice tube are mounted on the inlet side of the evaporator.

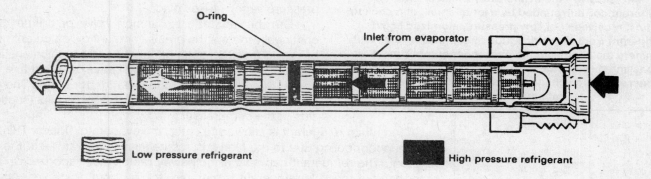

O-ring

Inlet from evaporator

Low pressure refrigerant

High pressure refrigerant

Cutaway of a typical modern orifice tube (this one's from a Volvo)

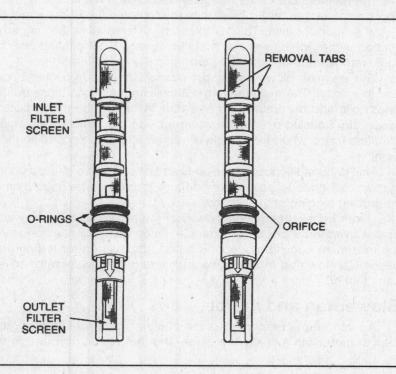

REMOVAL TABS

INLET FILTER SCREEN

O-RINGS

ORIFICE

OUTLET FILTER SCREEN

Cutaway of Ford Motor Company "fixed orifice" tube assembly - no matter what they're called or who uses them, all orifice tubes work the same way: they have filter screens to remove contaminants and a calibrated orifice tube to meter refrigerant flow

Heating and air conditioning

A typical evaporator (and blower motor) assembly (Pontiac Fiero shown) - the evaporator, which is simply a refrigerant coil surrounded by a lot of small, thin cooling fins, receives cool, low pressure, atomized liquid refrigerant from the orifice tube or expansion valve and transfers the heat from the passenger compartment air passing through the coils and cooling fins into the refrigerant, which changes to a low pressure vapor as it absorbs the heat

Evaporator

Like the heater core and condenser, the evaporator **(see illustration)** consists of a refrigerant coil packed in a dense arrangement of thin cooling fins. Because it must be located under the dash, it provides a maximum amount of heat transfer in a minimum amount of space. The evaporator is usually installed in a housing under the dash panel or cowl. When the air conditioning system is turned on, warm air from the passenger compartment is blown through the coils and fins of the evaporator.

The evaporator receives refrigerant from the thermostatic expansion valve or orifice tube as a low pressure, cold atomized liquid. As the cold refrigerant passes through the evaporator coils, heat moves from the warm air into the cooler refrigerant.

When the liquid refrigerant receives enough heat, a change of state - from a low pressure liquid into a low pressure vapor - takes place.

The thermostatic expansion valve or orifice tube continually meters the precise amount of refrigerant necessary to maintain optimum heat transfer, which ensures that all of the liquid refrigerant will have changed to a vapor by the time it reaches the evaporator outlet. The vaporous refrigerant then continues on to the inlet (suction) side of the compressor.

If too much refrigerant is allowed to enter, the evaporator floods. This results in poor cooling due to the higher pressure (and temperature) of the refrigerant. The refrigerant can neither boil away rapidly nor vaporize. On the other hand, if too little refrigerant is metered, the evaporator starves. Again, poor cooling is the result because the refrigerant boils away or vaporizes too quickly before passing through the evaporator.

The temperature of the refrigerant vapor at the evaporator outlet will be approximately 4 to 16°F higher than the temperature of the liquid refrigerant at the evaporator inlet. This temperature differential is the "superheat," described earlier, which ensures that the vapor will not contain any droplets of liquid refrigerant that would be harmful to the compressor.

The warm air blown across the evaporator usually contains some moisture (humidity). The moisture in the air will normally condense on the evaporator coils and be drained off as water. A drain tube in the bottom of the evaporator housing directs the water outside the vehicle. That's why a puddle often forms when the vehicle is parked after the air conditioner has been running.

This dehumidification of the air is an added feature of the air conditioning system that adds to passenger comfort. It can also be used as a means of controlling fogging of the windows.

Under certain conditions, however, too much moisture may accumulate on the evaporator coils. For example, when humidity is extremely high and the maximum cooling mode is selected, the evaporator temperature might become so low that moisture would freeze on the evaporator coils before it can drain off.

Blower fan and motor

An important component in the cooling action of the evaporator is the blower motor/fan (usually the same one that blows air through the heater

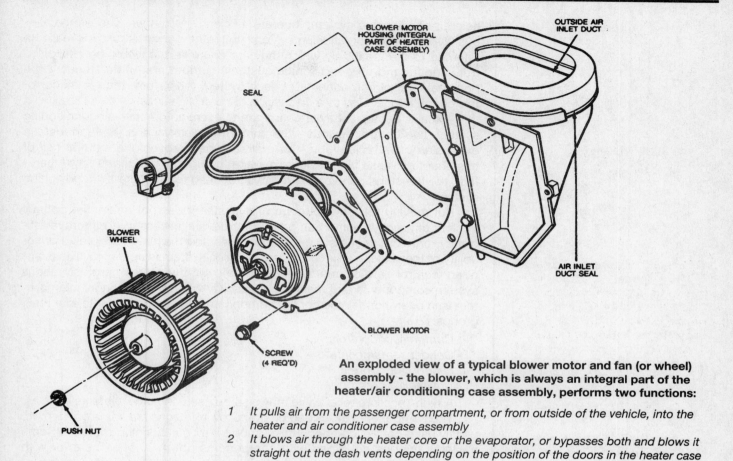

BLOWER MOTOR HOUSING (INTEGRAL PART OF HEATER CASE ASSEMBLY)

OUTSIDE AIR INLET DUCT

SEAL

AIR INLET DUCT SEAL

BLOWER WHEEL

SCREW (4 REQ'D)

BLOWER MOTOR

PUSH NUT

An exploded view of a typical blower motor and fan (or wheel) assembly - the blower, which is always an integral part of the heater/air conditioning case assembly, performs two functions:

1   *It pulls air from the passenger compartment, or from outside of the vehicle, into the heater and air conditioner case assembly*
2   *It blows air through the heater core or the evaporator, or bypasses both and blows it straight out the dash vents depending on the position of the doors in the heater case*

core), also located in the evaporator housing. The blower **(see illustration)** draws warm air from the passenger compartment over the evaporator and blows the "cooled" air out into the passenger area. The blower motor is controlled by a fan switch with settings from Low to High.

High blower speed will provide the greatest volume of circulated air. A reduction in speed will decrease the air volume. But the slower speed of the circulated air will allow the air to remain in contact with the fins and coils of the evaporator for a longer period of time. The result is more heat transfer to the cooler refrigerant. Therefore, the coldest air temperature from the evaporator is obtained when the blower is operated at its slowest speed. The next section examines various typical controls and describes how they make air conditioning more efficient.

Air conditioning system control components

The components discussed in the first half of this chapter are the basic hardware found in every automotive air conditioning system. But although they are necessary to make it work, they're not sufficient to make it work efficiently. That's why every air conditioning system used in an automobile must also have certain control devices which constantly monitor its operation and ensure optimum efficiency. A number of different means are employed to help air conditioning systems operate efficiently. When we discuss the various "types" of air conditioning systems in the next chapter, we will really be referring to the means by which they are controlled. It would be difficult to truly understand air conditioning systems without first understanding the principal control components of each system. Therefore, the remainder of this chapter is devoted to a discussion of control devices.

Actually, because they are common to every automotive air conditioning system, two control devices - the compressor clutch and the thermostatic expansion valve/orifice tube - have already been covered in the first half of this chapter. These two devices regulate the flow of refrigerant (and, therefore, the transfer, and eventual removal, of heat) through the air conditioning system.

But moving refrigerant through the system does not guarantee optimal cooling efficiency. Numerous other controls are necessary to improve efficiency, protect various system components and maintain acceptable driveability of the vehicle while the air conditioning system is operating. These ancillary control devices improve the efficiency of the system, protect various system components and maintain driveability when the air conditioning system is in operation. These control components can be divided into four main groups:

Compressor controls
Condenser fan controls
Evaporator controls
Driveability controls

A high-pressure relief valve may also be used on some systems.

The components described on the following pages are some of the more widely used control components on modern air conditioning systems. Some systems may be equipped with components not mentioned here, or with components that are variations on the ones described here. The following information is intended to be a general introduction. If you need specific details of a particular system, consult the manufacturer.

Compressor controls

Compressors used in modern vehicle air conditioning systems are designed to either run constantly, whenever the system is switched on, or to cycle on and off as necessary to maintain the desired temperature inside the vehicle. Most modern constantly-running systems use a variable displacement compressor because the refrigerant flow can be controlled without switching the compressor on and off (see *Variable displacement piston-type compressors*). Note that constantly-running compressors still use a compressor clutch to allow the compressor to be disengaged when the air conditioning system is turned off, and when necessary for safety reasons (low or excessive system pressure, for example).

The compressor can be switched on and off by controlling the power supply to the compressor clutch coil. Switching the compressor off and on can be used to prevent excessively high or low system operating pressures, respectively, to prevent the system from overcooling the vehicle interior, and to protect the compressor itself from damage caused by extreme operating conditions. And on systems with a cycling compressor, the compressor can be switched on and off to control the refrigerant flow.

The most commonly used compressor controls are the:

Low-pressure cut-out switch

High pressure cut-out switch
Trinary switch
Ambient temperature switch
Pressure-sensing (cycling) switch (orifice tube type systems)
Thermal fuse/superheat switch
Thermostatic switch
Compressor crankcase pressure control valve (variable
    displacement compressors)

Various other compressor controls may be used, particularly on modern vehicles with engine management systems, on which the compressor clutch is often controlled by the engine management system electronic control unit (ECU) or powertrain control module (PCM). For example, the compressor may have a maximum recommended rotating speed beyond which the internal components might be damaged. On these systems, the compressor clutch is disengaged if the engine speed reaches a level that is dangerous to the compressor. On some models, if the driver decides to floor the accelerator pedal when the engine speed is low, the compressor clutch can be disengaged to increase the engine power available for acceleration.

Low pressure cut-out switch

The switch is usually wired in series with the compressor clutch, and is used to stop the compressor if the system pressure falls below a predetermined level, which will usually be caused by a refrigerant leak, an obstruction in the refrigerant circuit, or very low temperature. If the refrigerant pressure is low because of a leak, or if there is no pressure, compressor oil may have been lost along with the refrigerant, and the compressor may be damaged by a loss of lubrication if it continues operating.

If the refrigerant pressure drops below a predetermined level, the switch contacts open, stopping the compressor. If the pressure rises above the predetermined level, the switch contacts close, and the compressor is switched on again.

Besides stopping the compressor when there's a refrigerant leak, the low pressure cut-out switch also stops the compressor when the ambient temperature falls to a very low level (causing low pressure), because there's a risk of damage to the compressor seals, gaskets and reed valves due to poor oil circulation.

On expansion valve-type systems, the low pressure cut-out switch is usually installed on the high pressure side of the system, typically in the receiver/drier or the expansion valve assembly **(see illustration)**. On orifice tube-type systems, the switch is fitted to the low side of the system, usually in the accumulator.

High pressure cut-out switch

This switch is usually wired in series with the compressor clutch, and is used to stop the compressor if the system pressure rises beyond a predetermined level, usually because of an obstruction somewhere in the refrigerant circuit or an overheated condenser.

If the refrigerant pressure reaches a predetermined level, the switch contacts open, stopping the compressor. If the pressure drops back below the predetermined level, the switch contacts close, and the compressor is reactivated.

The switch is installed on the high pressure side of the system, in the compressor or in the refrigerant line **(see illustration)**.

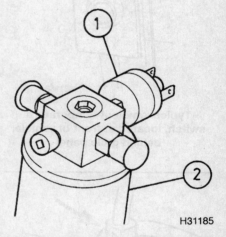

H31185

Typical low pressure cut-out switch location (expansion valve system with receiver/drier)

1   Low pressure cut-out switch
2   Receiver/drier

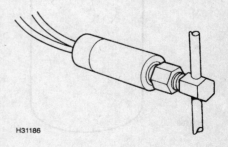

H31186

Typical high pressure cut-out switch, located in refrigerant line

Heating and air conditioning

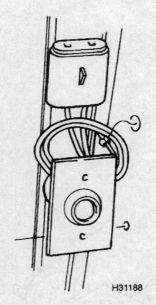

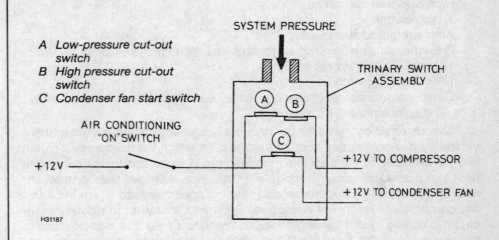

A Low-pressure cut-out switch
B High pressure cut-out switch
C Condenser fan start switch

AIR CONDITIONING "ON" SWITCH

+12V

SYSTEM PRESSURE

TRINARY SWITCH ASSEMBLY

+12V TO COMPRESSOR

+12V TO CONDENSER FAN

H31187

Schematic view of a typical trinary switch

Typical ambient temperature switch, located at front of vehicle, behind grille panel

H31188

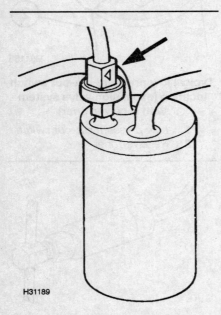

Typical pressure-sensitive (cycling) switch (arrow), located on accumulator

H31189

Trinary switch

This switch **(see illustration)** is basically a high pressure cut-out switch, low pressure cut-out switch and condenser fan switch combined into one assembly. If the system pressure falls, the low pressure switch opens and stops the compressor. If the system pressure is too high, the high pressure switch opens and stops the compressor. If the condenser temperature rises beyond a preset threshold, the fan switch closes, activating the condenser cooling fan. Trinary switches are common on expansion valve-type systems, and are usually installed on the receiver/drier.

Ambient temperature switch

The ambient temperature switch **(see illustration)** measures the outside air temperature, and is used in some systems to prevent compressor operation when the outside air temperature is low. If the compressor is operated in extremely cold conditions, it can cause poor oil circulation, damaging the compressor seals, gaskets and/or valves.

If the ambient temperature drops below the range suitable for compressor operation, the switch opens, preventing current flow to the compressor, which stops the compressor. When the ambient temperature reaches the preset minimum operating temperature, the switch contacts close, and the compressor is started again.

The switch is usually located at the front of the engine compartment, behind the front grille panel, where it can quickly and accurately sense outside air temperature.

Pressure-sensitive (cycling) switch (orifice tube type systems)

The pressure-sensitive (cycling) switch **(see illustration)** senses the pressure on the low side of the system, and uses the pressure as an indicator to evaporator temperature **(see illustration)**. The compressor is then cycled on and off by the switch to control the evaporator temperature. The switch also provides protection against freezing, and stops the compressor when the ambient temperature (and thus the system pressure) is low. The switch usually acts as a low pressure cut-out switch too.

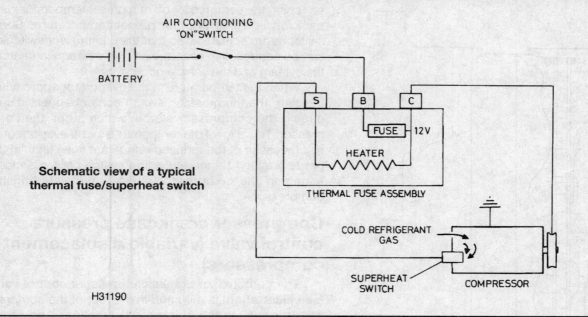

Schematic view of a typical thermal fuse/superheat switch

H31190

Thermal fuse/superheat switch

A thermal fuse and superheat switch **(see illustration)** are used to stop the compressor in the event of low system pressure. The two components are used on some vehicles instead of a low pressure cut-out switch. The superheat switch is located in the rear of the compressor and is exposed to the flow of cold refrigerant. The switch contacts are normally open, but if a predetermined temperature threshold is reached (caused by a reduction in refrigerant flow), the contacts close, grounding the heater circuit in the thermal fuse through the body of the compressor. When the air conditioning circuit is switched on, the thermal fuse and its heater coil receive a 12-volt supply from the battery; when the superheat switch contacts close, closing the circuit and allowing the heater coil to heat the fuse. The heater coil will eventually melt the fuse, which cuts the voltage to the compressor coil, stopping the compressor.

The thermal fuse is usually mounted on a compressor bracket. If the thermal fuse blows, it must be replaced. A blown fuse is easy to identify: its casing is melted.

Thermostatic switch

The thermostatic switch **(see illustration)** used on some systems controls the compressor in accordance with the evaporator temperature. The switch uses a temperature-sensing capillary tube to sense evaporator temperature. The capillary action causes the switch contacts to open or close in accordance with the evaporator temperature. The switch operates within a predetermined temperature range,

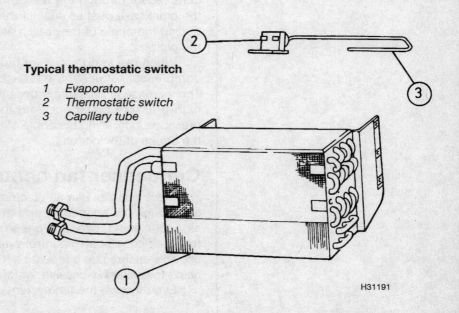

Typical thermostatic switch

1 Evaporator
2 Thermostatic switch
3 Capillary tube

H31191

Heating and air conditioning

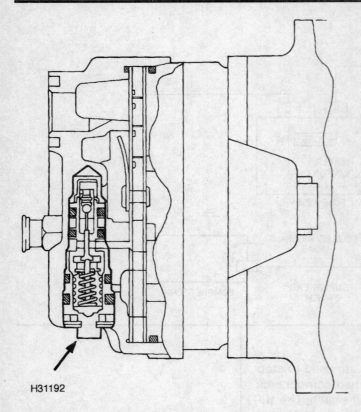

H31192

Cutaway view of rear of typical variable displacement compressor, showing crankcase pressure control valve location (arrow)

switching the compressor off at a preset temperature and back on again at another preset temperature. Some switches are adjustable so that the compressor switching can be controlled in accordance with the requirements of the system and the vehicle occupants.

When the temperature in the evaporator approaches freezing, the thermostatic switch contacts open, disengaging the compressor clutch, which stops the compressor. This allows the temperature in the evaporator to rise (because of the reduced refrigerant flow) until, at the predetermined temperature, the switch contacts close, engaging the compressor clutch, and restarting the compressor.

Compressor crankcase pressure control valve (variable displacement compressors)

The compressor crankcase pressure control valve **(see illustration)** is mounted in the rear of the compressor. It regulates the compressor crankcase pressure. The crankcase pressure controls the angle of the variable-angle squish plate, which in turn controls the compressor displacement (see *Variable displacement piston-type compressors*).

The control valve contains a pressure-sensitive diaphragm, which is exposed to pressure on the suction side of the compressor. The diaphragm acts on a valve exposed to the compressor high-side pressure. The diaphragm also controls the opening and closing of a bleed port which is exposed to suction side pressure.

When the temperature of the evaporator decreases, or the speed of the compressor increases (because of higher engine speed), the low-side pressure (suction) at the compressor decreases. This reduction in pressure is sensed by the control valve, which allows pressure from the high side of the compressor through the bleed port into the crankcase. The high pressure in the crankcase pushes against the undersides of the compressor pistons, reducing the angle of the squish plate, and effectively shortening the stroke of the pistons.

When the temperature of the evaporator increases, or the speed of the compressor reduces, the low-side pressure at the compressor increases. The increase in pressure moves the control valve diaphragm to close off the high-pressure bleed port into the crankcase. This reduces the crankcase pressure, increasing the angle of the squish plate, and effectively lengthening the stroke of the pistons.

Condenser fan controls

Most vehicles use an electric cooling fan to ensure an adequate flow of air through the condenser and the cooling system radiator. On vehicles with air conditioning, two fans are often installed, and they're usually connected to the air conditioning control system and operate when the system is turned on. This ensures an adequate airflow through the condenser at all times, and helps to prevent excessive system pressure.

Even though the fan system does not have a direct effect on the operation of the air conditioning system, a fan that doesn't operate when required can quickly lead to excessive system pressure and temperature.

The most commonly used condenser fan controls include the:

Cooling fan switch
Air conditioning system high-pressure fan switch
Air conditioning system trinary switch
Air conditioning system "On" switch
Pressure-sensitive air conditioning system fan switch

Cooling system fan temperature switch

This switch is really part of the engine cooling system. It switches on the cooling fan(s) when the engine coolant reaches a predetermined temperature. When the coolant temperature drops below a second predetermined temperature (which is usually lower than the "switch-on" temperature), the switch opens again, interrupting power to the fan(s). On many vehicles, the cooling fan(s) will run even when the ignition is switched off.

Air conditioning system high-pressure fan switch

On some vehicles, a high-pressure switch in the air conditioning system refrigerant circuit activates the cooling fan(s) when the refrigerant pressure rises above a predetermined level, usually right after the compressor starts to operate. When the air conditioning system is switched off, the cooling fan system is controlled solely by the cooling system fan temperature switch. On some vehicles, the air conditioning system high pressure fan switch may provide an input signal to the engine management system.

Air conditioning system trinary switch

On some vehicles, an air conditioning system high pressure fan switch is incorporated into the trinary switch (see *Compressor controls*).

Air conditioning system ON switch

Many vehicles have an air conditioning system ON fan switch, which activates the fan(s) when the air conditioning system is turned on. This ensures that there is always an adequate airflow through the condenser.

Pressure-sensitive air conditioning system fan switch

This type of switch is sometimes used on vehicles with a variable-displacement compressor (which runs constantly). This switch controls the cooling fan(s) in accordance with the compressor high-side pressure, and is located in the compressor refrigerant discharge line. The switch operates in conjunction with the cooling system fan temperature switch.

Evaporator controls

Evaporator controls are used to control the temperature of the evaporator by regulating the flow of refrigerant through the evaporator. (Of course, the evaporator temperature is also controlled by the cycling of the compressor, which indirectly controls the flow of refrigerant through the evaporator.) Evaporator controls are used mainly on older U.S.-built vehicles with compressor which run constantly. Evaporator controls are seldom found on modern U.S. vehicles, or on any European or Japanese vehicles.

Evaporator controls help prevent freezing and help keep the air conditioning system operating efficiently. As already noted, the flow of refrigerant through the evaporator is the key to the efficient operation of an air conditioning system. Sometimes, under certain operating conditions, the condensation which forms on the outside of the evaporator may freeze, which can block the evaporator fins, and reduce the airflow through the evaporator. This reduces the evaporator's cooling ability, and thus the cooling efficiency of the system.

The most commonly used evaporator controls include the:

Suction throttling valve (STV)
Pilot Operated Absolute Suction Throttling Valve (POA STV)
Valves-In-Receiver (VIR)
Evaporator-Equalized Valves-In-Receiver (EEVIR)
Evaporator Pressure Regulator (EPR) valve

Suction Throttling Valve (STV)

The suction throttling valve (STV) was used on some early expansion valve type air conditioning systems to control the refrigerant flow leaving the evaporator. In an air conditioning system that uses an STV, the compressor is running constantly as long as the system is switched on. A typical STV opens or closes in response to refrigerant pressure to keep the pressure in the evaporator within a predetermined range. This maintains the evaporator temperature at a level that ensures efficient operation of the air conditioning system without allowing the evaporator to freeze up.

Pilot Operated Absolute Suction Throttling Valve (POA STV)

Most modern STVs are of the pilot operated absolute (POA) type. A POA STV **(see illustration)** is really nothing more than a spring-loaded valve, controlled by an evacuated bellows and needle valve assembly inside a housing. The valve operates independently of atmospheric pressure, and is unaffected by changes in altitude. By providing an opposing force to evaporator pressure, the valve can maintain the evaporator pressure with a high degree of accuracy (within a 1 psi range).

As long as the evaporator pressure remains above a predetermined level, the POA STV remains open to allow refrigerant to flow freely out of the evaporator. When the pressure drops below the predetermined level, the valve closes, and the refrigerant flow from the evaporator is restricted. The pres-

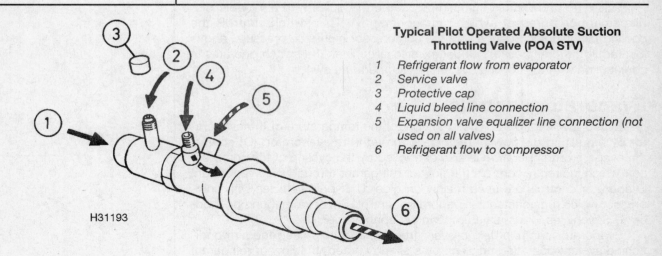

H31193

Typical Pilot Operated Absolute Suction Throttling Valve (POA STV)

1   Refrigerant flow from evaporator
2   Service valve
3   Protective cap
4   Liquid bleed line connection
5   Expansion valve equalizer line connection (not used on all valves)
6   Refrigerant flow to compressor

sure in the evaporator then increases, which raises the temperature and prevents icing on the outside of the evaporator. The opening and closing cycle of the valve continues as long as the compressor is running.

Valves-In-Receiver (VIR)

The valves-in-receiver (VIR) unit **(see illustration)** combines the functions of an expansion valve, a POA STV and a receiver/drier into one assembly. The VIR is usually installed near the evaporator. In a VIR unit, the temperature-sensing bulb and capillary tube for the expansion valve are eliminated because the diaphragm end of the expansion valve is directly exposed to the refrigerant vapor entering the VIR assembly from the evaporator outlet.

Evaporator-Equalized Valves-In-Receiver (EEVIR)

The evaporator-equalized valves-in-receiver (EEVIR) unit is a modified version of the VIR. It has a redesigned expansion valve in order to eliminate temperature fluctuations in the system which occur under certain operating conditions. The expansion valve is also modified so that it is always partly open instead of completely closed. This helps to prevent freezing at the expansion valve (which will block the flow of refrigerant and prevent the system from operating).

Evaporator Pressure Regulator (EPR) valve

The evaporator pressure regulator (EPR) valve **(see illustration)** is usually installed at the inlet port of the compressor. The valve maintains the evaporator outlet pressure within predetermined limits. An EPR valve performs the same function as the STV.

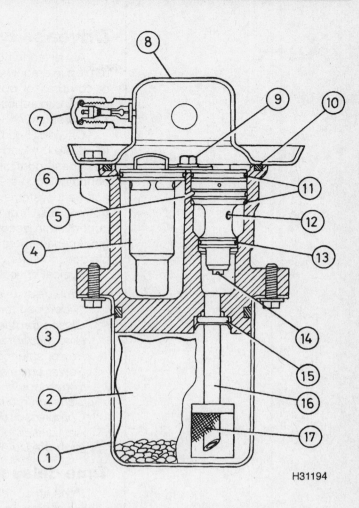

H31194

Cutaway view of typical Valve-In-Receiver (VIR) assembly

1	Receiver/drier housing	11	Expansion valve upper O-rings
2	Dessicant bag	12	Expansion valve capsule
3	Valve housing-to-receiver O-ring	13	Expansion valve lower O-ring
4	POA valve capsule	14	Expansion valve inlet
5	Equalizer port	15	Liquid pick-up tube O-ring
6	POA valve O-ring	16	Liquid pick-up tube
7	Service valve	17	Pick-up tube filter screen
8	Inlet connector housing		
9	Valve capsule retaining screw and washer		
10	Inlet connector housing-to-valve housing O-ring		

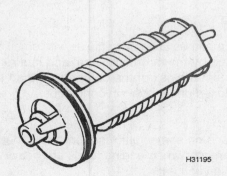

H31195

Typical Evaporator Pressure Regulator (EPR) valve

Driveability controls

An air conditioning compressor takes a significant amount of power to run (on average, somewhere between 10 and 15 horsepower), and the effect of compressor operation, in conjunction with other demands placed on the engine, can impose loads which reduce vehicle performance. This is a significant problem on vehicles with small capacity engines.

Driveability controls are used to control the operation of the compressor to relieve the load on the engine under conditions when driveability may suffer. These controls don't usually affect the cooling performance of the air conditioning system. On most modern vehicles equipped with engine management systems, the compressor clutch is controlled by the electronic control unit (ECU) or the powertrain control module (PCM). The compressor is controlled in accordance with the information received from the various engine management system sensors, to ensure that the driveability of the vehicle doesn't suffer. This reduces the need for separate driveability controls.

Typical driveability controls include the:

Time delay relay
Wide-open throttle switch
Closed throttle switch
Low vacuum switch
Power steering pressure switch
Power brake switch
Engine coolant high temperature switch
Constant run relay
Compressor delay timer
Anti-dieseling relay
High-pressure relief valve

Time delay relay

If the air conditioning system is already switched on prior to starting the vehicle, a time delay relay is sometimes used to delay the engagement of the compressor for a few seconds after engine start-up.

Wide-open throttle switch

A wide-open throttle switch is sometimes used on vehicles with small capacity engines. The switch is operated by the throttle linkage. When the throttle pedal is fully depressed, the switch activates a relay that interrupts the compressor clutch circuit. This reduces the load on the engine, and improves acceleration.

Closed throttle switch

A closed throttle switch is sometimes used on vehicles with small capacity engines. The switch is operated by the throttle linkage, and interrupts the compressor clutch circuit to prevent the risk of the compressor load stalling the engine when the throttle is closed under overrun conditions.

Low vacuum switch

Low vacuum switches are used on some vehicles to interrupt the operation of the air conditioning compressor when engine loads are heavy (which is indicated by low intake manifold vacuum).

Power steering pressure switch

On vehicles with small capacity engines and power steering, the power steering system has little effect on the performance of the engine under normal driving conditions. But during parking maneuvers, the power steering system imposes its heaviest loads on the engine. When parking, the engine speed and power output are usually low, so an air conditioning compressor is likely to impose even further demands on the engine, and can even cause rough idling and stalling.

To prevent these problems, some vehicles are equipped with a power steering pressure switch, which disengages the compressor whenever the power steering hydraulic pressure exceeds a predetermined level.

Some vehicles are equipped with a more sophisticated version of this system in which the switch sends a signal to the ECU or PCM, which adjusts the engine idle speed to compensate for the higher steering load without disengaging the compressor.

Power brake switch

On some vehicles with a small capacity engine, the engine can even stall if the air conditioning compressor is running when the brakes are applied. These vehicles use a power brake switch to disengage the compressor under certain braking conditions to prevent the engine from stalling.

Engine coolant high temperature switch

The air conditioning condenser is usually positioned in front of the engine cooling system radiator. The air conditioning system transfers heat to the air passing through the condenser, which then has to pass through the radiator. When the ambient temperature is high, the already heated air passing over the radiator is unable to carry away sufficient heat from the engine coolant, and engine overheating can occur.

To prevent the possibility of overheating, some vehicles are equipped with a coolant temperature switch that disengages the compressor clutch when the coolant temperature exceeds a predetermined level.

Constant run relay

Some vehicles are equipped with a constant run relay that is controlled by the engine management system, and is used to maintain idle quality. The relay prevents compressor cycling when the engine is idling, for a predetermined period after normal driving. If the engine is allowed to idle for an extended period, the relay returns the compressor to its normal cycling mode for a short time, to prevent the evaporator from freezing up.

Compressor delay timer

This device is sometimes used on vehicles equipped with an engine management system. When the engine is idling (or running below a predetermined speed), and the air conditioning system is switched on, the timer delays the engagement of the compressor clutch for a few seconds while the engine idle speed is raised, to compensate for the additional load. The compressor clutch is engaged as soon as the engine idle speed has stabilized.

Anti-dieseling relay

Some engines have a tendency to keep running, or "diesel," after the ignition has been switched off. The compressor is used to prevent dieseling on some carbureted vehicles. As soon as the ignition is switched off, the compressor clutch is engaged for a few seconds. This additional load stalls the engine immediately.

Heating and air conditioning

High-pressure relief valve

Many systems incorporate a high-pressure relief valve as a safety device in the event that pressure inside the system exceeds safe levels. (Some systems use a disc instead of a valve; when a predetermined pressure is reached, the disc will burst.) Most pressure relief valves will close when the system pressure has returned to a safe level. Excessive pressure can be caused by an overheated condenser or an overcharge of refrigerant.

The high-pressure relief valve is usually located on the receiver/drier (expansion valve type systems) or on the compressor. It's usually mounted in a safe place so that there's no risk of refrigerant being discharged toward anyone working on the vehicle.

If the high-pressure relief valve opens for any reason, the system will require recharging with refrigerant and compressor oil.

R-134a system components

The compressor, condenser and evaporator on R-143a systems - though similar in appearance and function - are larger and more robust than their counterparts on R-12 systems. Otherwise, there's little physical difference between the components used on R-12 systems and those used on R-134q systems. However, components designed for use in one kind of system cannot be interchanged with those designed for another system. Mixing parts from two different systems could result in component failure and damage to the system.

3 Typical automotive air conditioning systems

Now that you're familiar with the basic components and controls of automotive air conditioning systems, let's look at how they work together in typical modern systems. We will also look at some older systems too. Though it's doubtful many of them are still in use nowadays, a brief description of their operation should provide you with a better perspective on the operation of contemporary systems.

High and low sides of the air conditioning system?

Before we look at the individual components of an automotive air conditioning system, it's important to keep in mind that all air conditioning systems have a "high" and a "low" side **(see illustration)**. The dividing line for the two sides always occurs at the same point in the system.

The high side is the portion of the system in which high pressure, and high temperature, exists. The high side stretches from the outlet or discharge side of the compressor, through the condenser and, if equipped, the receiver drier, to the expansion valve or orifice tube.

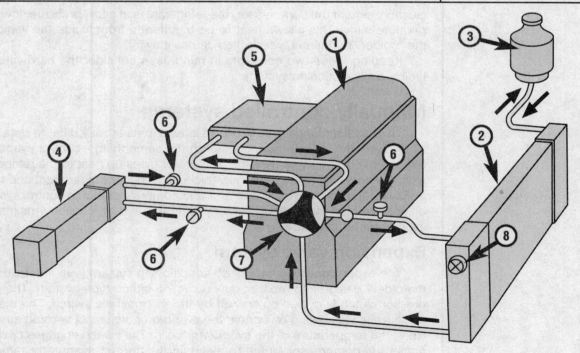

A typical heating system:

1 Engine cylinder block	3 Expansion tank	5 Intake manifold	7 Coolant pump
2 Radiator	4 Heater core	6 Bleeder screws	8 Cooling fan switch

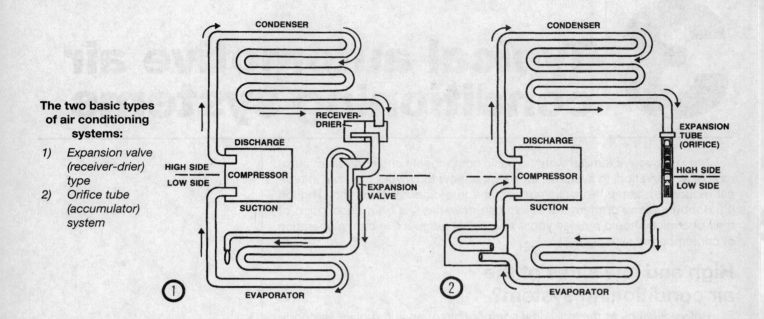

The two basic types of air conditioning systems:

1) *Expansion valve (receiver-drier) type*
2) *Orifice tube (accumulator) system*

The compressor raises the pressure (and the temperature) so the refrigerant can condense and release heat as it moves through the condenser. A "pressure differential" is created at the expansion valve or orifice tube - the dividing point on the front side of the system. We will explain the expansion valve and orifice tube in detail later in this chapter.

The low side is the other half of the system. On this side, from the expansion valve, through the evaporator and accumulator (if equipped) to the inlet (suction) side of the compressor, the refrigerant is in a low pressure, low temperature state. This allows heat to be transferred from inside the vehicle to the "colder" refrigerant, which then carries it away.

Keeping these two concepts in mind, let's consider the hardware in a typical air conditioning system.

Manually controlled systems

The various manually controlled systems in use today differ in detail, but all of them are designed to accomplish the same thing - control evaporator temperature. Air flowing over the evaporator gives up heat to the refrigerant, which removes this heat from the vehicle passenger compartment and transports it to the condenser. Evaporator and compressor clutch control systems differ somewhat in operation but they perform a similar function - maintaining evaporator temperature.

Expansion valve system

The expansion valve type of air conditioning system **(see illustration)** is the oldest design and most common cycling clutch type system. The compressor clutch is cycled on and off by the thermostatic switch. The thermostatic switch is located on or near the evaporator, where its sensing tube can "feel" the temperature of the evaporator coils. The switch engages or disengages the compressor clutch to maintain the correct evaporator temperature. This process keeps the cooled air entering the vehicle at a constant temperature. This type of system was once typical of OEM air conditioning systems.

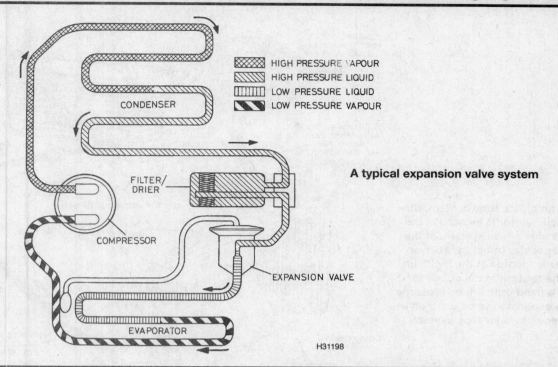

HIGH PRESSURE VAPOUR
HIGH PRESSURE LIQUID
LOW PRESSURE LIQUID
LOW PRESSURE VAPOUR

CONDENSER

FILTER/DRIER

COMPRESSOR

EXPANSION VALVE

EVAPORATOR

A typical expansion valve system

H31198

Orifice tube system

There are three principal differences between an orifice tube type system and the expansion valve type described above. First, the receiver-drier is replaced by an accumulator. Second, unlike the receiver-drier, which is located in the high side of the system at the condenser, the accumulator is located in the low side at the evaporator outlet. Third, a fixed orifice tube replaces the conventional expansion valve.

The orifice tube system **(see illustrations)** is employed on many General Motors and Ford vehicles. The GM system is known as a Cycling Clutch Ori-

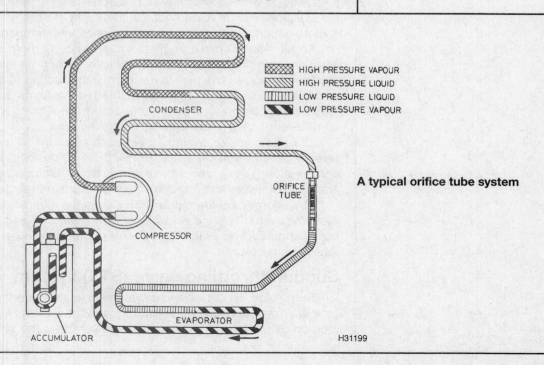

HIGH PRESSURE VAPOUR
HIGH PRESSURE LIQUID
LOW PRESSURE LIQUID
LOW PRESSURE VAPOUR

CONDENSER

ORIFICE TUBE

COMPRESSOR

EVAPORATOR

ACCUMULATOR

A typical orifice tube system

H31199

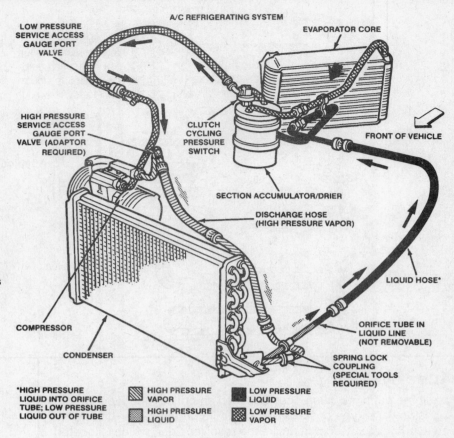

A/C REFRIGERATING SYSTEM

LOW PRESSURE SERVICE ACCESS GAUGE PORT VALVE

EVAPORATOR CORE

HIGH PRESSURE SERVICE ACCESS GAUGE PORT VALVE (ADAPTOR REQUIRED)

CLUTCH CYCLING PRESSURE SWITCH

FRONT OF VEHICLE

SECTION ACCUMULATOR/DRIER

DISCHARGE HOSE (HIGH PRESSURE VAPOR)

COMPRESSOR

CONDENSER

LIQUID HOSE*

ORIFICE TUBE IN LIQUID LINE (NOT REMOVABLE)

SPRING LOCK COUPLING (SPECIAL TOOLS REQUIRED)

*HIGH PRESSURE LIQUID INTO ORIFICE TUBE; LOW PRESSURE LIQUID OUT OF TUBE

HIGH PRESSURE VAPOR

HIGH PRESSURE LIQUID

LOW PRESSURE LIQUID

LOW PRESSURE VAPOR

In an orifice tube system, the accumulator is located in the low side of the system, at the evaporator outlet (a receiver-drier is located in the high side of the system at the condenser) and a fixed orifice tube replaces the expansion valve used on a receiver-drier type system

fice Tube (CCOT). Ford calls its system Ford Fixed Orifice Tube (FFOT).

Earlier orifice tube systems used a standard thermostatic switch which turned the compressor off and on in accordance with evaporator temperature. Most newer systems have a pressure-sensing switch that controls compressor operation in accordance with system pressure. Measuring pressure is more accurate and responsive than measuring temperature.

Small displacement engines have difficulty maintaining a stable idle when the compressor clutch is continually cycling on and off. In 1985, General Motors solved this problem with the introduction of the DA-V5 compressor, which does not cycle at all. Instead, it varies its output in accordance with system demand. Other manufacturers followed suit, and now many compressors have a non-cycling, variable output.

The accumulator, which serves as a reservoir for any liquid refrigerant flowing out of the evaporator, prevents liquid refrigerant from reaching the compressor. Like the receiver-drier, the accumulator stores excessive refrigerant. It also filters and removes moisture from the refrigerant.

The **accompanying illustration** shows the different locations of the thermostatic switch and the pressure sensing switch. Keep in mind that they're both clutch cycling switches, but one measures temperature and the other measures pressure.

Suction throttling valve (STV) system

Some older air conditioning systems use a suction throttling valve or STV **(see illustration)** as the main evaporator control. This type of system is common on older General Motors and Ford vehicles. The valves themselves dif-

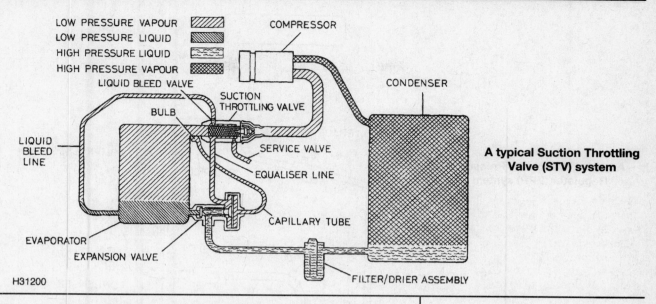

LOW PRESSURE VAPOUR
LOW PRESSURE LIQUID
HIGH PRESSURE LIQUID
HIGH PRESSURE VAPOUR
LIQUID BLEED VALVE
COMPRESSOR
CONDENSER
BULB
SUCTION THROTTLING VALVE
LIQUID BLEED LINE
SERVICE VALVE
EQUALISER LINE
CAPILLARY TUBE
EVAPORATOR
EXPANSION VALVE
FILTER/DRIER ASSEMBLY
H31200

A typical Suction Throttling Valve (STV) system

fer in configuration but, functionally, they're all pretty similar. Basically, all of them maintain proper evaporator temperatures by modulating evaporator pressure. The compressor in an STV system runs continuously instead of being cycled on and off. This type of system is no longer in favor with the manufacturers because it requires too much energy (fuel) for operation.

The suction throttling valve, also known as a pilot operated absolute (POA) valve on some systems, is mounted on the outlet side of the evaporator. Because refrigerant flow from the evaporator is being regulated by the valve to maintain evaporator temperatures, this device allows the compressor to run all the time.

Valves-in-receiver system

The valves-in-receiver type system **(see illustration)** is another older General Motors design. The controls - expansion valve and pilot operated absolute suction throttling valve - are located in the same housing as the receiver-drier. This unit is mounted in the high pressure side between the condenser and the evaporator inlet.

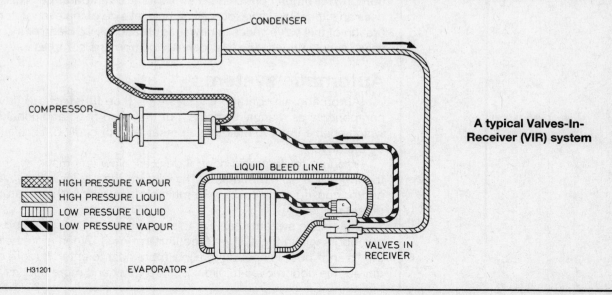

CONDENSER
COMPRESSOR
HIGH PRESSURE VAPOUR
HIGH PRESSURE LIQUID
LOW PRESSURE LIQUID
LOW PRESSURE VAPOUR
LIQUID BLEED LINE
VALVES IN RECEIVER
EVAPORATOR
H31201

A typical Valves-In-Receiver (VIR) system

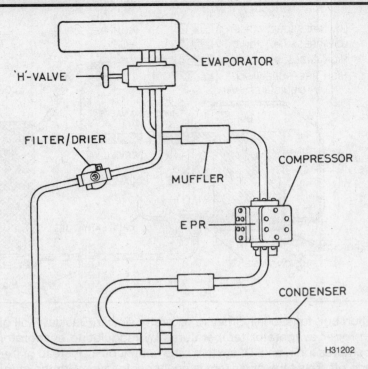

A typical Evaporator Pressure Regulator (EPR) system

Like the standard suction throttling valve type system, the valves-in-receiver (VIR) system requires continuous compressor operation whenever cooling is required. The VIR unit controls refrigerant flow to the evaporator and to the compressor.

Evaporator pressure regulator (EPR) system

The evaporator pressure regulator type system **(see illustration)** is used only on Chrysler Corporation vehicles with a twin-cylinder compressor. Unlike the suction throttling valve (STV) and valves-in-receiver (VIR) units, which are mounted in-line, but outside the compressor, the evaporator control valve is located within the low pressure side of the compressor. The EPR or evaporator temperature regulator (ETR) valve senses the pressure of the incoming refrigerant and opens or closes to regulate the flow of refrigerant through the compressor, thus controlling the evaporator temperature. This system also uses an expansion valve located at the inlet side of the evaporator (the configuration of this valve varies in newer applications). To clean or inspect the EPR valve, simply remove the inlet connection from the compressor.

Automatic systems

Automatic air conditioning systems **(see illustration)** have the same components as manual systems, but they also have additional components which enable them to maintain a preset level of cooling, or heating, selected by the driver.

Vacuum or electronic control devices allow automatic systems to sense the in-vehicle air temperature. The system then adjusts the level of heating and/or cooling as necessary to maintain the vehicle temperature within the preset range.

Automatic systems achieve this equilibrium by opening and closing various doors within the system **(see illustrations)**. When more heat is needed, the "blend" door is opened to allow more heat to enter. If more cooling is required, the door moves to allow less warm air and more cool air to enter.

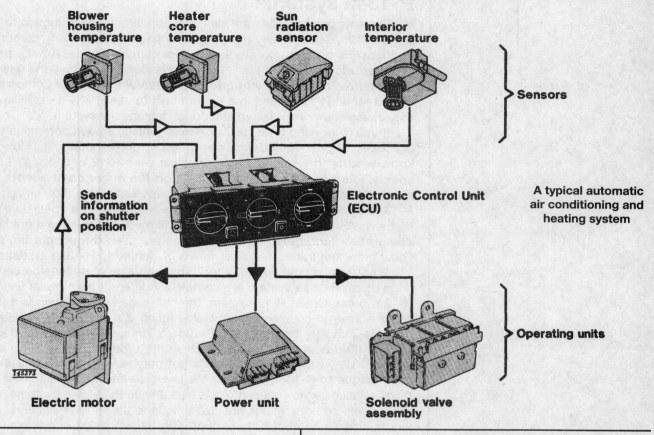

Blower housing temperature

Heater core temperature

Sun radiation sensor

Interior temperature

Sensors

Sends information on shutter position

Electronic Control Unit (ECU)

A typical automatic air conditioning and heating system

Operating units

Electric motor

Power unit

Solenoid valve assembly

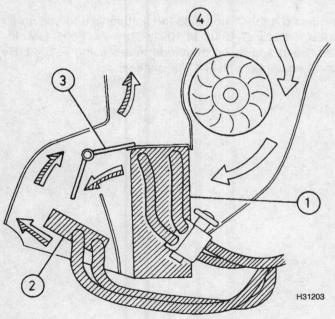

Airflow through heater/evaporator housing, with temperature control set to maximum heating

1 Evaporator
2 Heater core
3 Air blend flap
4 Heater/blower motor/evaporator fan

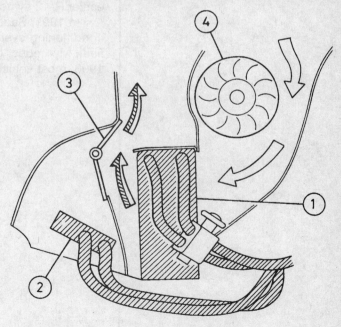

Airflow through heater/evaporator housing, with temperature control set to maximum cooling

1 Evaporator
2 Heater core
3 Air blend flap
4 Heater/blower motor/evaporator fan

H31203

R-134a systems

Systems using R-134a are similar in appearance and function to system using R-12. Although they use physically larger, heavier-duty compressors, condensers and evaporators, cycling clutch, orifice tubes, pressure switches, receiver-driers, etc. - are virtually identical to the parts used on R-12 systems. *But they're not interchangeable!* Installing a component designed for an R-12 system in a system built to use R-134 a - or vice-versa - may cause component failure and could damage the system.

If you're working on a 1992 or newer vehicle, always determine whether is uses R-12 or R-134a before servicing or troubleshooting it. How so you know whether the system in your vehicle uses R-12 or R-134a? *Look for special identification decals or labels on the major components*. For instance, some 1992 and later Ford Taurus models with a 3.0L engine use an R-134a system. Ford distinguishes these models with a special yellow tag that says "R-134a NON-CFC" on it. These models also have a gold colored compressor, and green colored O-rings are used throughout the system. Other manufacturers use similar means of identifying R-134a systems.

What else should you look for? The high-side and low-side service fittings on an R-134a system are completely different from those used on an R-12 system. On an R-12 system, the high-side service fitting is a 3/8-inch 24 for screw-on couplers; the low-side fitting is a 7/16-inch 20 (also known as a 1/4-inch flare fitting). On an R-134a system, the high-side and low-side service fittings are special 1/2-inch Acme-type fittings with no external threads. They have internal threads but they're for the specially-designed caps unique to R-134a systems; the low-side service valve uses a special quick-release service coupler that's also unique to R-134a systems. And the valve cores on both fittings are also unique to the R-134a systems. In other words, there's no possibility of confusing these fittings with those used on earlier R-12 systems.

In 1991, Saab introduced a 1992 model as the first vehicle to use an air conditioning system designed for R-134a. In 1992, Chrysler, Ford, GM, Infiniti, Mercedes, Nissan, Saab and Volvo debuted models using R-134a. By 1993, most vehicles were equipped with R-134a systems.

4 Service and diagnostic tools

Manifold gauge set (test gauges)

The manifold gauge set **(see illustrations)** is unquestionably the most important tool used in air conditioning system servicing. Nearly all service work performed on automotive air conditioning systems requires the use of test gauges. Test gauges enable a technician to determine the system's high (head) pressure side and low (suction) side vacuum, determine the correct refrigerant charge, perform diagnosis procedures and help determine whether the system is operating efficiently.

Because pressures must be compared in order to determine how the system is operating, the gauge set is designed to allow both the high and low sides to be read at the same time. **Note:** *Some vehicles (older model Chryslers with EPR valves or Fords with POA valves, for instance) also require the use of a third (auxiliary) gauge (see below).*

A typical manifold gauge set has . . .

1 A hand valve for the low side of the system
2 A gauge for the low side of the system
3 A gauge for the high side of the system
4 A hand valve for the high side of the system
5 A valve for attaching the high side service hose
6 A service valve for attaching devices such cans of refrigerant and vacuum pumps
7 A valve for attaching the low side service hose

Also note that the gauges on this unit are glycerine-filled to keep the needles steady, a nice feature to have for accurate work

This gauge set has a few features the previous one didn't have

1 *A Schrader valve allows you to purge the hoses or evacuate the system without interfering with the regular center service hose and also provides a place to hook up the low side hose- when it's not in use - to keep it clean (the valve on the other end protects the high side hose)*
2 *A "sight glass" in the front of the manifold allows you to visually monitor the condition of the refrigerant as it passes through the manifold (a nice feature, since a lot of newer systems don't have a sight glass anymore)*
3 *To reduce the likelihood of turning a valve the wrong way, the hand valves are mounted on the front of the manifold*
4 *A T-type center service valve allows you to access both vacuum and refrigerant at the same time*

A top-of-the-line instrument like this can handle four hoses at one time, allowing you to evacuate or charge the system, or both, without unhooking the other hoses

The "low side" gauge

The low side gauge, which is most easily identified by the BLUE housing and hand valve, is used to measure the low side pressure at the service ports provided on the low side of the system by the manufacturer. The low side gauge pressure scale reads from 0 to between 130 and 150 pounds per square inch (psi) in a clockwise direction. The vacuum scale reads from 0 to 30 inches of mercury in a counterclockwise direction. The low side gauge is sometimes called a compound gauge because it has a dual purpose - to indicate either pressure or vacuum.

The "high side" gauge

The high side gauge, which usually has a RED housing and hand valve, is strictly a pressure gauge. It reads from 0 to 500 psi in a clockwise direction.

Auxiliary gauge

An auxiliary gauge may be required for testing older Chrysler vehicles with Evaporator Pressure Regulator (EPR) valves or Fords with Pilot Operated Absolute (POA) valves. It can be either a separate gauge used in conjunction with a two-gauge set or an integral gauge in a three-gauge set. The 0 to 150 psi reading provided by the gauge will be within the same range as shown on a low side gauge. Therefore, the auxiliary gauge should be the same type as used for low side testing. On older model Chryslers, the gauge is attached to the additional cylinder head inlet fitting on the compressor. On Fords, it's attached to the suction fitting.

Manifold hand valves

The purpose of the manifold is to control refrigerant flow. When the manifold gauges are attached to the system, pressure is indicated on both gauges at all times during normal conditions. During testing, both the low and high side hand valves are in the closed position (turned clockwise all the way until the valve is seated). You will note that even with the hand valves closed, the high and low side pressures are still indicated on the respective gauges. That's because the valve stems do not prevent refrigerant from reaching the gauges. They simply isolate the low and high sides from the central service hose port on the manifold.

When both hand valves are closed or when one or the other is open, the low and high side gauges will give good readings. However, when both valves are open, gauge readings are not accurate because high side pressure escapes into the low side of the manifold and influences the low side gauge reading.

Warning: *NEVER OPEN THE HIGH SIDE HAND VALVE WHILE THE AIR CONDITIONING SYSTEM IS IN OPERATION! High pressure refrigerant will force its way through the high side of the manifold test gauge and into the refrigerant can(s), if attached. The pressure can be high enough to rupture the can or even burst the fitting at the safety can valve, resulting in damage and physical injury.*

Manifold gauges for R-134a systems

Manifold gauges for 134-a systems work exactly the same was as R-12 gauges. But you can't use the same set of gauges for both systems. They use completely different couplers and hoses. The gauge face on manifold gauges for R-134a systems have an identification plate that says "for R-134q use only" or something similar. And that's exactly what is meant ! DO NOT try to use a set of R-134a gauges on a R-12 system. And don't try to use a set of R-12 gauges on an R-134a system, either. The fittings are totally different, so each type of gauge is totally incompatible with the fittings and hoses used on the other system.

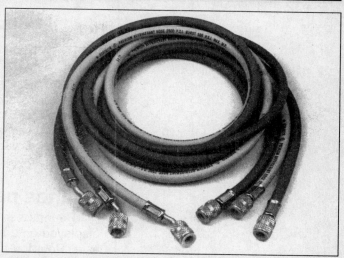

The hoses you select are just as important as the gauges you use them with - a cheaply constructed hose can burst, causing serious injury, so make sure you buy high quality hoses from a reputable manufacturer (also, try to purchase hoses that are long enough and have the correct fittings for the system you intend to service). Hoses for R-134a systems have different, larger fittings, and a black stripe down each hose

Hoses

R-12 hoses are always solid blue (low-side), solid red (high-side) and solid yellow (utility hose); R-134a hoses are also blue, red and yellow but have a black stripe running the length of each hose. R-134a hoses also have different, larger service fittings than those on R-12 hoses. Don't try to adapt old R-12 hoses by installing the newer R-134a fittings – R-134a hoses look the same as the reinforced rubber or thermoplastic R-12 hoses, but they're lined with a special nylon barrier that prevents the newer refrigerant from leaking through the walls of the hose. (For more information on R-134a hoses, refer to *R-134a hoses* in Chapter 5).

Measuring pressure

Pressure, which is measured when checking and diagnosing the air conditioning system, is usually expressed in pounds per square inch (psi). The reading on the manifold gauges is known as "pounds per square inch gauge," or simply "psig," because it's affected by atmospheric pressure changes, such as changes in altitude. A pressure reading which is not affected by atmospheric pressure is known as "pounds per square inch absolute," or "psia."

Atmospheric pressure

Atmospheric pressure, which is expressed and measured in pounds per square inch, is the pressure exerted on the earth's surface at any given point. Atmospheric pressure is 14.7 psia at sea level, but this figure varies with altitude. It's approximately 1/2-pound less for each 1000 feet of elevation. Pressure, and gauge readings, also vary slightly due to the weather, because changes in the weather mean changes in the barometric (atmospheric) pressure.

Pounds per square inch absolute (psia)

Pounds per square inch absolute, or psia, is sort of an "ideal" measure of pressure which is unaffected by barometric (atmospheric) conditions or by altitude. It begins with a zero psi reading in a perfect vacuum. Aside from providing a handy reference point when referring to changes in atmospheric pressures at various altitudes, absolute pressures are seldom used in air conditioning work.

Pounds per square inch gauge (psig)

Pounds per square inch gauge, or psig, are the units of measurement displayed on a typical manifold gauge set. This type of gauge is referred to as a "Bourdon-tube" gauge. A Bourdon-tube gauge consists of a semicircular, or coiled, flexible metal tube attached to a gauge that records the degree to which the tube is straightened by the pressure of the gas or liquid inside.

A Bourdon-tube gauge is calibrated to read zero at sea level on a "typical" day (with atmospheric pressure at 14.7 psi). At higher elevations, of course, where the atmospheric pressure is lower, the gauge reading will be lower.

Correcting the gauge pressure reading for altitude

Atmospheric pressure is low at high elevations. The corrected gauge pressure within a closed system can be computed by subtracting the gauge altitude correction factor from the reading. Don't forget to do this when checking the system's low side pressures.

Altitude pressure variations

Altitude (feet above sea level)	Absolute pressure of atmosphere (psi)	Gauge altitude correction (psi)*
0	14.7	0
1000	14.2	0.5
2000	13.7	1.0
3000	13.2	1.5
4000	12.7	2.0
5000	12.2	2.5
6000	11.7	3.0
7000	11.3	3.4
8000	10.9	3.8
9000	10.5	4.2
10000	10.1	4.6
Etc.		

Subtract the indicated correction from the gauge readings.

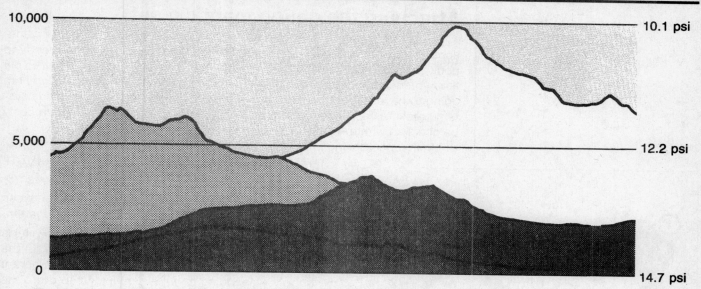

The higher the elevation, the lower the atmospheric pressure and the greater the necessary gauge correction)

Measuring vacuum

When checking and diagnosing air conditioning systems, vacuum is customarily measured in inches of mercury, or "in-Hg." "Perfect" vacuum is defined as 29.92 in-Hg at sea level with the atmospheric pressure at 14.7 psia.

Besides its pressure readings, the compound (low pressure) gauge on the manifold set also has a vacuum section which reads in inches of mercury. The compound gauge measures vacuum accurately only at the elevation for which it is calibrated. At high altitudes, the gauge reads low. Air conditioning specifications are normally expressed in sea level terms, so at higher altitudes the gauge reading should be corrected to sea level.

Altitude vacuum variations

Altitude (feet above sea level)	Complete vacuum (in-Hg)	Gauge altitude correction (in-Hg)*
0	29.92	0
1000	28.92	1.0
2000	27.82	2.1
3000	26.82	3.1
4000	25.82	4.1
5000	24.9	5.0
6000	23.92	6.0
7000	23.02	6.9
8000	22.22	7.7
9000	21.32	8.6
10000	20.52	9.4
Etc.		

* Add the indicated correction to the gauge reading.

Attaching the gauge manifold set

Now that you know how to read the gauges and how to correct for variations in vacuum and pressure caused by different altitudes, you're ready to hook them up. Pay close attention and you'll learn how to do it right. Every time you need to diagnose a problem in the air conditioning system, you are going to have to examine the system's overall performance, particularly system pressures and refrigerant flow. These performance parameters can only be checked with the manifold gauge set.

In theory, hooking up a set of gauges is simplicity itself:

1 The low side hose (usually blue) is attached between the low side gauge and the low side of the system.

2 The high side hose (usually red) is attached between the high side gauge and the high side of the system.

3 The service hose (usually yellow, sometimes white) is attached between the service (center) fitting on the manifold and either a vacuum device or refrigerant supply, depending on what you intend to do to the system.

In reality, hooking up the test gauges isn't always this simple, because the high and low side service valves differ somewhat - in size, configuration and ease of access - from system to system. So don't be surprised if you buy or borrow a gauge set only to find that it doesn't hook up as easily as you had hoped. Fortunately, there are service adapter fittings available for every conceivable purpose. Let's look at the common ones.

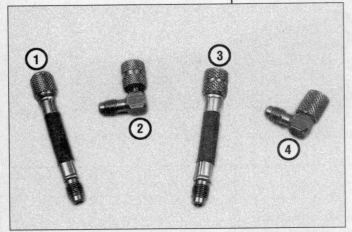

To prevent wasting money on fittings you'll never use, try to purchase service adapter fittings individually, as you need them - some common adapters are shown here

1 *Flexible GM high side adapter with 1/4-inch male fitting on one end and 3/16-inch female on the other*

2 *90-degree adapter with 1/4-inch male and 1/4-inch female ends*

3 *Flexible high side adapter with 1/4-inch male and 1/8-inch female fittings*

4 *Ford 90-degree high side adapter with 1/4-inch male and 1/8-inch female fittings*

Service adapter for R-12 systems

Like screwdrivers or wrenches or other common tools, service adapter fittings are available individually, or in sets **(see illustrations)**. Unless you know that you will be servicing all types of systems, adapter fitting sets are not the way to go. Buy adapters individually as the need arises. That way you won't end up with a bunch of useless fittings.

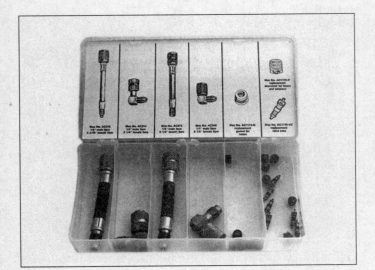

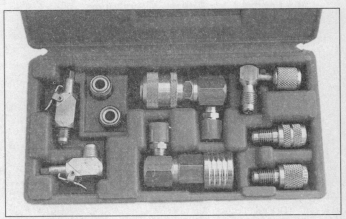

Adapter kits such as the two shown here usually include all the individual adapters shown in the previous illustration and, sometimes, lots more - but you'll pay for adapters you may not need

There are so many clever adapters that space doesn't permit an exhaustive compilation in this book. However, there are several that no mechanic should be without when servicing an air conditioning system.

First, you will probably need a high side fitting adapter, either because the service valve on the system is inaccessible, or because its outside diameter (OD) and/or thread pitch doesn't match the OD and/or thread pitch of the high side hose fitting, or because the service valve is pointing in a direction that makes a convenient hook-up difficult. While any one of these problems might seem intimidating enough in itself, you may even be looking at a combination of two or even all three of the above. Amazingly, there is a solution for every one of them!

For instance, there are high side adapter fittings available in straight and 90° configurations, as short flexible hose models and even as quick disconnect couplers. There are even anti blow-back refrigerant check valves which prevent refrigerant discharge when disconnecting high side service hoses.

Companies such as Mac Tools, Inc. and Snap-On Tools Corporation offer a variety of adapters in various configurations. The first step, obviously, is to obtain a Mac or Snap-On catalog, or both of them, and start studying the fittings. If you're a professional mechanic, you probably see a Mac or Snap-On dealer once a week when he stops by your shop. If you're a home mechanic, call the local dealer and ask him when he will be stopping by a shop in your neighborhood. Take the vehicle you will be servicing to make sure the fitting adapters mate properly with the service valves on the system and with the service hoses on the manifold gauges.

Service fitting for R-134a systems

The service fittings for R-134a systems are completely different in design, size and appearance from those used on R-12 systems. Instead of a _-inch flare or 7/16-inch 20) fitting they use a 1/2-inch Acme fitting. So the threaded fittings on R-134a manifold gauges, bulk refrigerant drums, hoses, etc. look completely different from the fittings on their counterparts intended for use with R-12 systems. Practically speaking, this mean that if you wish to service an R-134a system, you'll have to obtain new everything – gauges, hoses, refrigerant drum, etc.

Thermometers

Thermometers **(see illustration)** are essential for air conditioning and heating system diagnosis. Get a thermometer that reads between 25° and 125°F (a 0° to 220°F range is even better). Conventional thermometers are available in standard and dial configurations. Dial types are easier to read, tougher and more versatile than standard types.

The digital thermometer is also becoming popular, despite its high cost, because it's faster, more accurate and easier to read. Because some digital thermometers can be equipped with air, surface or immersion probes, they are much more versatile than conventional thermometers.

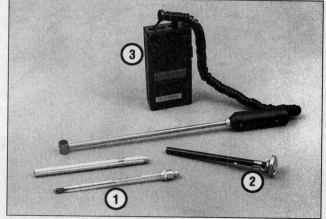

A variety of thermometers are currently available . . .

1   *A conventional mercury column thermometer - delicate, hard-to-read and expensive*
2   *A dial type thermometer - rugged, easy-to-read and cheap*
3   *A digital thermometer - acceptably rugged, easy-to read, expensive, but quick responding and most accurate*

System evacuation tools

Vacuum pumps

If an air conditioning system has had 1) refrigerant removed to service or repair the system, 2) refrigerant loss caused by component failure or 3) shows evidence of refrigerant contamination, it must be evacuated to get rid of all moisture and air before it can be recharged with refrigerant.

Air and moisture are extracted from the system with a vacuum pump. Pumping draws air from within the closed system to create negative pressure, or vacuum. By lowering the pressure inside the system into a vacuum condition, the boiling point of water, or moisture, is also lowered to a point at which evaporation easily occurs. This vaporized moisture is then easily drawn out by the vacuum pump.

The vacuum necessary to vaporize moisture in the system for evacuation varies with the altitude. At sea level, where the air pressure is 14.7 psi, water boils at 212°F. To evacuate a system, it is necessary to lower the boiling point of water in the system to a point that is lower than the "ambient" air temperature (the temperature of the air surrounding the vehicle). At an ambient temperature of, say, 75°F, you must draw at least 29.5 inches of vacuum (in-Hg) to bring the boiling point of water down to 72°F.

As altitude increases, the vacuum gauge reading is affected significantly. For instance, it isn't possible to obtain a vacuum reading of 29.5 inches once you're above sea level. That's because for each 1000 feet of altitude, the vacuum requirement decreases by 1 in-Hg. So the vacuum gauge must be corrected by 1 in-Hg for every 1000 feet of altitude to compensate for the change in atmospheric pressure. Thus, at 1000 feet, a gauge reading of 28.5 in-Hg will be the same as 29.5 in-Hg at sea level. The good news is that this will still accomplish the same job of lowering the boiling point enough to evacuate the moisture from the system. **Note:** *For other vacuum corrections, refer to the altitude vacuum variation chart in the manifold test gauge section of this chapter.*

Once the desired vacuum reading is obtained, regardless of the altitude, continue pumping for about 30 minutes to completely rid the system of moisture. **Note:** *A completely saturated system may require many hours of pumping to remove all the moisture, as the process of vaporizing the moisture and moving the vapor out of the coils and hoses is much slower than simply removing air alone.*

Air power (venturi type) vacuum pumps

There are two kinds of vacuum pumps generally available. The cheaper of the two is the air power, or venturi type, pump **(see illustration)**. The venturi type pump is easy to use and maintenance free. It has no moving parts and requires no lubricating oil. What's the catch? Well, it requires a compressor that can pump at least 80 or 90 psi. And a compressor that pumps 80 to 90 psi for half an hour is using a lot of electricity. How do you use this type of vacuum pump? Follow these steps:

1 Before using a venturi type pump, always discharge the refrigerant first.

2 Connect the manifold gauge set center service hose to the vacuum pump inlet labeled VACUUM.

3 Open the high and low side manifold gauge hand valves as far as possible.

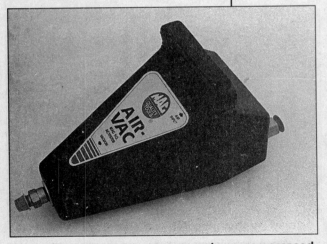

Venturi type vacuum pumps operate on compressed air (about 80 to 90 psi air power from a compressor) to pull down a vacuum in the system in about 1/2-hour - this type of pump is inexpensive to buy, but uses a lot of electricity (to run the compressor for 1/2-hour)

4 Connect an air hose to the vacuum pump inlet labeled AIR INPUT or AIR INLET.

5 Note the reading indicated by the low side gauge and begin timing the evacuation when the gauge indicates a vacuum reading. **Note:** *If, after a couple of minutes, no vacuum is indicated on the low side gauge, inspect the system for leaks and repair it before proceeding. Check the gauge set hose connections first.*

6 After about five minutes of pumping, the required vacuum reading (which, remember, varies with altitude) should be indicated on the low side gauge. When this reading is obtained, close both the gauge valves and then disconnect the air hose. **Note:** *If the required vacuum reading is not obtained within 10 minutes, inspect the gauge set hose connections, the hand valves and the system fittings for leaks. After correcting the problem, repeat Steps 1 through 5 and continue the evacuation process.*

7 Allow several minutes for the system to stabilize and check the low side gauge to determine whether the system is maintaining vacuum.

   a) If the system is holding vacuum, reconnect the air hose, open both hand valves and continue pumping for at least 30 minutes to complete the evacuation process.

   b) If the system is losing vacuum, check to make sure the leak is not at the gauge set connections. If the leak is not at the connections, charge the system, use a leak detector to locate the source of the leak, discharge the system, repair the leak and repeat the evacuation process.

8 When the evacuation process is complete, close the gauge valves and disconnect the air hose.

9 Check the low side gauge to make sure the system maintains vacuum.

10 Disconnect the air pump at the center hose.

11 Recharge the system.

Rotary vane type vacuum pumps

The rotary vane type pump **(see illustration)**, which has a small electric motor driving the pump, is considerably more expensive than a venturi type pump. It also requires some maintenance - the pump must be routinely lubricated. But it doesn't require the use of a compressor to evacuate the system, so it uses a lot less electricity than a venturi type.

To operate a rotary vane type pump:

1 Make sure the pump is free by rotating the shaft.

2 Remove the exhaust dome and fill the pump with oil to at least the mid-point of the oil level sight glass.

3 Make sure that the vacuum breaker O-ring valve is closed tight.

4 Make sure that the electrical power matches the motor wiring (normally 115 volts, but some pumps are 220 volt models).

The rotary vane type pump is powered by an electric motor, is much more expensive to buy than venturi type pumps but is much more economical to operate

5   Check all hoses and connectors for leaks. Use the shortest plumbing that will work.

6   Install a shut-off valve on the end of the service hose that will connect the pump to the test gauge manifold.

7   Connect the shut-off valve to the center service port of the manifold.

8   Start the pump. You will note a gurgling sound as the refrigerant passes through the pump. This should be followed by a short period of almost no sound coming from within the pump. The pump will then develop a rapping sound which only occurs when it's under a deep vacuum (normally 250 microns or less).

9   After the system is pumped down to the desired vacuum level, close the shut-off valve and open the vacuum breaker valve until the pump makes a gurgling sound. Failure to break the vacuum within the pump at this time can result in damage to the pump when it restarts.

10   Turn off the motor.

Servicing a rotary vane type vacuum pump

1   Change the oil whenever there is a change in the performance of the pump. The oil should always be changed after pumping down a very dirty or burned out system. Always drain the pump while it's still warm. Recharge the pump with the oil specified by the manufacturer.

2   Purging the pump periodically is helpful because it often cures many ills that develop as a result of poor maintenance:

   a)   Rotate the pump shaft by hand to make sure it's free so the motor can operate the unit.

   b)   Run the pump with the intake closed until the pump is warm.

   c)   Shut it off, open the intake and drain the pump oil. With the drain open, the exhaust dome removed and the pump operating, slowly pour 2 ounces of the specified oil into the open intake fitting. As you hear the oil pass through the pump, cover the exhaust opening. This will cause the purging oil and any residual oil and sludge to flow rapidly out of the drain fitting. Repeat this step until all signs of contamination disappear.

   d)   When the purging is completed, close the drain fitting and, pouring through the exhaust dome hole, fill the pump with new, clean vacuum oil to the mid-point of the oil level gauge. **Note:** *It's normal for the oil level to rise somewhat as the pump warms up, but if the rise is excessive, the oil is contaminated*.

   e)   If the pump is going to be out of service for some time after shutdown, drain the oil, purge the pump and fill it with new, clean oil. This will prevent corrosion by any contaminants that may be present in the old pump oil. Cover the intake and exhaust openings.

R-12 system charging tools and equipment

Until about 1996, a do-it-yourselfer could save a bundle by charging his or her air conditioning system at home with small, inexpensive 14-ounce cans, which were available at any auto parts store. Two or three cans usually did the job.

But times change. As a result of recent Federal legislation designed to protect stratospheric ozone from further depletion, 14-ounce cans of R-12 are no longer sold to do-it-yourselfers; they're now available only to EPA-certified professional automotive air conditioning technicians. The thinking behind this decision is that do-it-yourselfers without proper tools and training

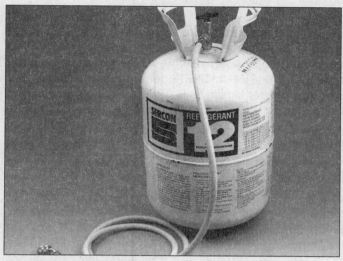

To use a bulk refrigerant drum, simply attach a service hose between the bulk can valve and the service valve on the manifold gauge set

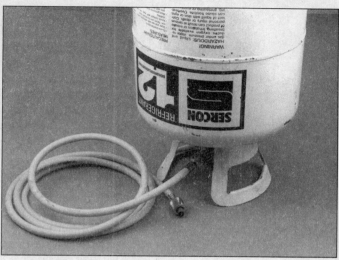

When adding refrigerant to the system from a bulk drum, invert the drum to ensure that liquid, rather than vapor, is released from the container when the valve is open

will simply keep adding small can of refrigerant to a leaking system instead of first fixing the leak. As of January 1, 1993, all professional shops are required to recover and recycle all refrigerant discharged from automotive air conditioning systems. It's highly unlikely that any home mechanic will ever purchase refrigerant recovery/recycling equipment. So the government feels that the best way to discourage do-it-yourselfers from discharging their systems into the atmosphere is to make it difficult for them to obtain small cans to recharge the system.

There may be a way around this dilemma in your area, but it isn't cheap: Uncertified do-it-yourselfers can still (when this was written) legally to purchase 20-pound or larger bulk refrigerant drums. However, most automotive parts stores carry only two sizes: Either the small cans (for professionals only), or 30-pound drums, which are very expensive. Basically, recharging with a 30-pound drum means you'd have to buy 10 time as much refrigerant as you'd need to charge a typical system at home. Obviously, it doesn't make much economic sense to take this route unless you own a lot of vehicles requiring air conditioning service. However, if you choose to so this, refer to the recharging information in Chapter 5 and any changing information the refrigerant manufacturer provides.

What about R-134a systems?

Finally, what about new systems using R-134a? After all, R-134a is 95 percent less destructive to the ozone layer that R-12. Can you charge an R-134a system at home? Yes, you can. At least for now. But first you'll have to invest in some new tools. Besides the R-134a itself, you will have to purchase a new service adapter hose with the new R-134a fittings. Your old can tappers, four-way dispensing valves, service hoses, etc. cannot be attached to a can of R-134a, nor can they be connected to the service valve on the low side of an R-134a system. And, to add R-134a with a set of manifold gauges, you'll have to purchase a new set of gauges and hoses designed to fit the unique service fittings on an R-134a system.

Don't even think about using your old R-12 charging tools on an R-134a system! Or vice versa! No adapters allowing you to use the same tools with both R-12 and R-134a systems will available because mixing these two refrigerants is a recipe for disaster. They're absolutely incompatible.

There is one other issue: Under Federal law, R-134a must soon be captured, recycled or reused, just like R-12. The Federal government has decided to control R-134a in a manner similar to R-12 because, even though it is relatively benign with respect to ozone destruction, it's considered a "greenhouse gas," i.e., its release into the atmosphere may contribute to raising global mean temperatures.

Don't mix refrigerants!

As mentioned earlier, R-12 and R-134a are completely incompatible. DO NOT, under any circumstances, ever mix them together in one system. Do not put even the smallest amount of R-134a in an R-12 system. If you do, you will damage the components and maybe the whole system. Ditto for their respective lubricants. R-134a systems use a special polyalkylene glycol (PAG)-based lubricant which is incompatible with the lubricants used in R-12 systems. Nor can R-12 lubricants be used in R-134a systems. Lubricant cross-contamination can result in damage to seals and bearings in the compressor.

Leak testers

Any time more than 1/2 pound of refrigerant is required to charge the system over a period of one year, a leak is indicated. Leakage - either through loose fittings, deteriorated hoses or seals or damaged metal lines - is the usual cause for low refrigerant charge. Most leaks are caused by normal engine vibration, which loosens threaded fittings and even causes metal lines to fatigue and crack over a period of time. Snugging the fittings will usually eliminate the former; repair or replacement is necessary for the latter. But checking for, locating and repairing more subtle leaks can be time consuming.

When refrigerant was a dollar a can and plentiful and R-12 was considered a harmless substance, finding a leak was more of an annoyance than anything. Now, of course, with the discovery of holes in the ozone layer over the Arctic and Antarctic – and the fears of scientists that we may be putting ourselves at greater risk of getting skin cancer as a result of ozone depletion – fixing leaks has become more of an annoyance. Not only is it environmentally responsible to be sure your air conditioner system doesn't leak – it's also a good idea from a dollars-and-cents point of view. With R-12 and R-134a very expensive, you can't AFFORD leaks in your air conditioning system.

Until recently, dye charged refrigerant cans were commercially available. These 14-ounce cans of refrigerant contained a red or fluorescent dye that made it easy to detect leaks in the system. However, dye-charged refrigerants are no longer available.

Bubble detector

This is an inexpensive way to find a leak, and a good one, especially if you've been unable to pinpoint the location of the leak using other methods. Simply apply a commercial bubble detector solution, or even a soap and water solution, to the suspected leak with a small brush. Apply the solution to all fittings and connections where leaks could occur. The leaking refrigerant will cause the detector or soapy solution to form bubbles. Tighten or repair the fittings as needed.

Halide (propane) torch leak detectors

Once a common tool in professional shops, the halide leak detector is seldom used any more, not because it isn't good at finding leaks but because of the manner in which it detects leaks. This type of detector uses a propane flame which draws the leaking refrigerant over a hot copper alloy reactor plate. A dramatic change in flame color occurs when there is refrigerant (indicating a leak) in close proximity to the flame. But, due to the fact that poisonous phosgene gas is formed when this type of leak detector comes into contact with refrigerant gas, we don't recommend the purchase or use of this type of detector. However, if you already have one, or have access to one, we have included the procedure for using it in Chapter 5. Be extremely careful and observe all the precautions included.

Halogen (electric) leak testers

The most sophisticated, most sensitive and easiest-to-use leak tester is the ion pump halogen leak tester **(see illustration)**. The most unique feature of this technological marvel is its pumping mechanism. The importance of a suction pump in instruments used for detecting refrigerant gas leaks has been recognized for quite some time. Up until recently, however, the use of bellows, valves and other mechanical moving parts has made suction pump equipped leak detectors bulky, inefficient and unreliable. These problems are eliminated by the ion pump, which is small, efficient and has no moving parts.

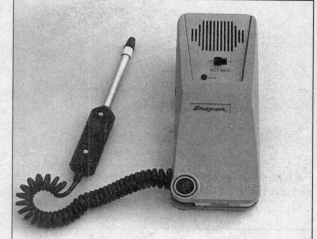

One of the most sensitive detectors of refrigerant gases is the negative corona discharge type of ionization detector. In such a sensor, an electrical discharge is set up between a pair of electrodes inside a chamber. The negative electrode is a very sharp wire; the positive electrode is a flat or cylindrical metal plate. When the electrical discharge is set up and current is flowing, a movement of air occurs. This "electrical wind," which is the result of friction between the moving charges (ions) in the corona and the molecules of the air surrounding it, always flows from the negative electrode toward the positive electrode. The halogen leak detector utilizes this air flow to draw air and refrigerant gas into the sensor, eliminating the need for mechanical suction.

The ion pump harnesses the electrical energy generated in the sensing element to produce a precise and reliable flow of air through the sensing element chamber. The air flow rate of the ion pump is self-regulating, enabling it to detect leaks as small as 1/10 ounce per year.

Although it's expensive, the halogen leak detector is worth the money if you want a safe, simple and sensitive means of finding leaks fast. It's also less harmful to the environment than the halide, or propane, type detector.

Though newer models have digital circuits that constantly adjust the level of sensitivity to the conditions, older units have to be adjusted for the proper level of sensitivity in accordance with the magnitude of a leak. The newer models are also ready to use as soon as they are turned on; older models take about five minutes to warm up.

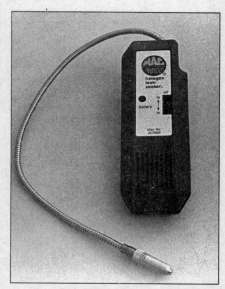

A pair of typical ion pump halogen leak testers - using them is simple, quick, convenient, accurate and safe, but they're expensive

Electronic sight glass (non-accumulator type systems)

In recent years, a small hand-held electronic sight glass **(see illustration)** has been marketed by a few automotive tool companies. This sophisticated device, which operates on the same principle as sonar, detects the presence of bubbles in the liquid line. Although it can be used on any receiver-drier type system, the electronic sight glass should not be used on an accumulator type system because, for reasons which are explained in Chapter 5, there are always some bubbles in the liquid line on an accumulator type system. But for non-accumulator type systems, the electronic sight glass is a handy tool.

Two sensors are used - one for transmitting and one for receiving. The sensors are in the form of C-clamps for easy attachment to the outside of any metal refrigeration line. No mechanical penetration of the line is necessary for the ultrasonic waves to pass through it.

Before the electronic sight glass, there was no accurate method to determine the level of refrigerant charge in a system. Nor was there any way to accurately introduce a partial charge into newer air conditioning systems. In fact, most manufacturers stipulate that when the charge is low, it should be completely dumped and the system should be refilled with the factory specified amount of refrigerant. This practice is not only time consuming and expensive, it also unnecessarily contaminates the environment.

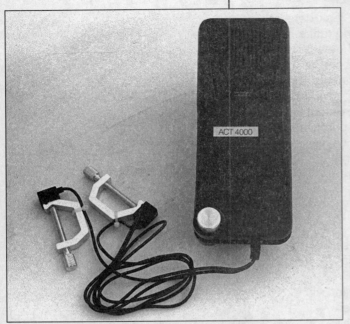

A typical electronic sight glass - this space age device detects the presence of bubbles in the refrigerant using a tiny sonar system

5 Heating and air conditioning system service and repair

Heating system

Service and repair

The heating system is so simple and (usually) trouble free that maintenance is often overlooked. However, there are two items which should be an essential part of every tune-up or inspection of the air conditioning and heating system:

1 Because the air which passes through the heater core is usually supplied from outside the vehicle through openings provided in the top or the sides of the cowl, these openings must be inspected periodically to ensure that they are kept free of leaves and other obstructions that might block the flow of air.

2 The heater hoses and the heater control valve (if equipped), must be in good working order. Some control valves are cable operated, others are vacuum operated. We will discuss how to check both kinds.

3 It is vital that the tubing of the heater core and the radiator be kept free from rust and scale accumulations. The hoses connecting the heater core to the cooling system must also be kept free of obstructions.

Inspecting the heating system

Note: *The following heating system checks should be a routine part of every cooling system inspection (outlined in detail in every Haynes Automotive Repair Manual). The following recommendations are directed primarily at the cooling system itself.*

1 An inspection of the heating system should always begin with the hoses. Carefully inspect each heater hose along its entire length. Replace a hose if it's cracked, swollen or deteriorated. Cracks will show up better if the hose is squeezed.

2 Pay close attention to the hose clamps that secure the hoses at either end. Hose clamps can pinch and puncture hoses, resulting in coolant leaks.

3 Make sure that all hose connections are tight. A leak will usually show up as white or rust colored deposits on the area adjacent to the leak. If wire type clamps are used on the hoses, it's a good idea to replace them with screw type clamps.

4   Clean the front of the radiator and air conditioning condenser with compressed air or a soft brush. Remove all bugs, leaves, mud, etc. embedded in the radiator fins. Be extremely careful not to damage the cooling fins or cut your fingers on them.

5   Check the coolant level. If it has been dropping - and no leaks are detectable - have the radiator cap and cooling system pressure tested at a service station.

6   Change the coolant at least once a year to ensure that the rust inhibitors are not depleted. Once these inhibitors are worn out, rust and scale begin forming in the cooling passages of the engine block, in the radiator and in the heater core.

Obviously, changing the engine coolant once a year will go a long way toward preventing the buildup of rust or scale deposits in the heating system, but there is no way to be sure that a preventive maintenance program has been carried out on a used vehicle.

If you have recently purchased a used vehicle, or if the heating system performance is unsatisfactory, chances are that the heater core, or the heater hoses, are blocked. It's time to flush the system.

Flushing the system

Some owners seem to think that "flushing" consists of nothing more than opening the petcock or drain valve on the bottom of the radiator and the one or two drain cocks on the engine block, sticking a garden hose into the radiator and turning on the water. Unfortunately, this kind of flush does little.

Normally, outside faucets are only connected to cold water, so sticking the hose into the radiator filler opening and running cold water through the system until the water coming out the drain cock turns clear flushes the radiator - but nothing else. Cold water won't open the thermostat, so the engine cooling passages remain closed off. Because the engine drains are open, some of the coolant in the block is drained off, but because there is no circulation, residue from old dirty coolant remains in the engine. And it is this stuff that we are primarily concerned with removing, because it eventually finds its way into the radiator, the heater hoses, the heater control valve and the heater core.

The following flushing procedure is designed to ensure that the entire cooling and heating systems are cleaned out.

1   Set the heater temperature controls to High.

2   If the vehicle is equipped with a vacuum-operated heater control valve (used on many vehicles with air conditioning), run the engine at idle during the following flushing procedure. The valve will only stay open with the engine running.

3   Open the radiator drain cock and drain the coolant. Do not open the engine drain cocks.

4   Remove the radiator cap.

5   Place a container under the heater supply fitting at the block (**see illustration**). Detach the hose from the fitting, point the hose downward and drain it into the container. Make sure that the container is big enough to catch the water that will drain from this hose when the water is turned on.

6   Connect the water supply hose to the heater hose fitting on the engine block. If you're using a piece of hose with the right diameter, simply push it onto the fitting and hose clamp it on. If you're using a garden hose, you'll have to hold the nozzle against the fitting.

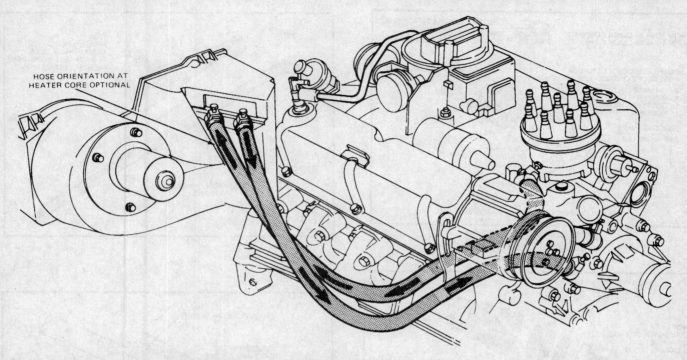

HOSE ORIENTATION AT
HEATER CORE OPTIONAL

The easiest way to find the heater hoses is to locate them where they come out of the firewall, then trace them forward and detach them from the water pump and intake manifold (or block) - as a rule of thumb, you should force clean water through the heater hoses and the heater core in the direction opposite normal flow (the hose attached to the water pump carries coolant back to the engine, so that's the one you want to use)

7   Turn on the water and flush for 3 to 5 minutes without the engine running (unless you have a vacuum-actuated heater control valve). Sometimes, it helps to squeeze the outlet or upper radiator hose during the last minute of flushing to remove any trapped liquid.

8   Turn off the water and close the radiator petcock. The radiator and the engine cooling passageways should be clean.

9   Now remove both heater hoses **(see illustration on next page)** and, if equipped, the heater control valve. Make sure that the hose between the valve and the engine, and the return hose, are both free of obstructions.

10 Carefully inspect the control valve for any signs of leakage or corrosion. On older vehicles which have not received annual coolant changes, severely corroded control valves are quite common. To check the control valve for proper function, attach a hand-held vacuum pump, apply vacuum and squirt water into one pipe with the garden hose. If the valve is functioning properly, the water will come out the other pipe. If the water squirts all over you instead of coming out the other pipe, replace the valve. Now, release the vacuum. The valve should not allow any water through. If it does, replace it.

11 Finally, with the heater control valve (if equipped) removed, squirt water through either heater hose and through the heater core. If the water coming out the other hose is discolored, continue flushing until it's clean.

12 Install the heater control valve and hook up the heater hoses.

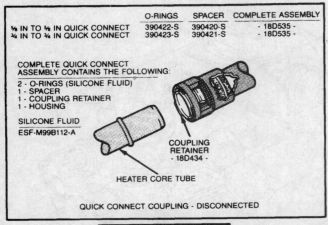

	O-RINGS	SPACER	COMPLETE ASSEMBLY
⅝ IN TO ⅝ IN QUICK CONNECT	390422-S	390420-S	- 18D535 -
¾ IN TO ¾ IN QUICK CONNECT	390423-S	390421-S	- 18D535 -

COMPLETE QUICK CONNECT
ASSEMBLY CONTAINS THE FOLLOWING:
2 - O-RINGS (SILICONE FLUID)
1 - SPACER
1 - COUPLING RETAINER
1 - HOUSING

SILICONE FLUID
ESF-M99B112-A

COUPLING
RETAINER
- 18D434 -

HEATER CORE TUBE

QUICK CONNECT COUPLING - DISCONNECTED

TO CONNECT COUPLING

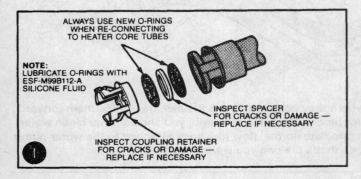

ALWAYS USE NEW O-RINGS
WHEN RE-CONNECTING
TO HEATER CORE TUBES

NOTE:
LUBRICATE O-RINGS WITH
ESF-M99B112-A
SILICONE FLUID

INSPECT SPACER
FOR CRACKS OR DAMAGE —
REPLACE IF NECESSARY

INSPECT COUPLING RETAINER
FOR CRACKS OR DAMAGE —
REPLACE IF NECESSARY

1

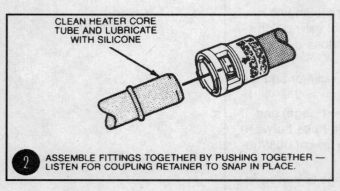

CLEAN HEATER CORE
TUBE AND LUBRICATE
WITH SILICONE

2 ASSEMBLE FITTINGS TOGETHER BY PUSHING TOGETHER —
LISTEN FOR COUPLING RETAINER TO SNAP IN PLACE.

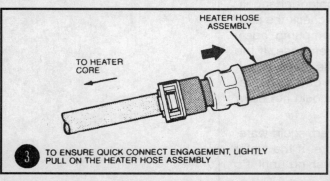

HEATER HOSE
ASSEMBLY

TO HEATER
CORE

3 TO ENSURE QUICK CONNECT ENGAGEMENT, LIGHTLY
PULL ON THE HEATER HOSE ASSEMBLY

HEATER HOSE
DISCONNECT TOOL
⅝ INCH T85T-18539-AH1
¾ INCH T85T-18539-AH2

EXTENSION HANDLE
T85T-18539-AH3

1

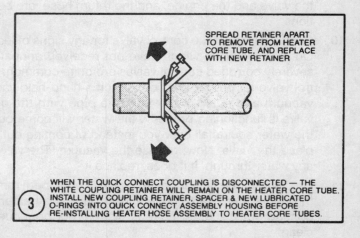

COUPLING RETAINER

HEATER HOSE
DISCONNECT TOOL

HEATER
CORE
TUBE

HEATER
HOSE
ASSEMBLY

PUSH HEATER HOSE ASSEMBLY TOWARDS HEATER CORE
TUBE TO ENSURE LOCKING TABS ARE FULLY EXPOSED, THEN
PUSH TOOL OVER COUPLING RETAINER WINDOWS TO
COMPRESS RETAINER LOCKING TABS — THEN PULL HOSE
ASSEMBLY AWAY FROM HEATER CORE TUBE.
REMOVE TOOL THEN CONTINUE PULLING HOSE ASSEMBLY
AWAY FROM HEATER CORE TUBE.

2 NOTE: WHEN COMPRESSING WHITE COUPLING RETAINER,
THE TOOL MUST BE PERPENDICULAR AND ON THE HIGHEST
POINT OF THE COUPLING RETAINER AS SHOWN ABOVE.

SPREAD RETAINER APART
TO REMOVE FROM HEATER
CORE TUBE, AND REPLACE
WITH NEW RETAINER

3 WHEN THE QUICK CONNECT COUPLING IS DISCONNECTED — THE
WHITE COUPLING RETAINER WILL REMAIN ON THE HEATER CORE TUBE.
INSTALL NEW COUPLING RETAINER, SPACER & NEW LUBRICATED
O-RINGS INTO QUICK CONNECT ASSEMBLY HOUSING BEFORE
RE-INSTALLING HEATER HOSE ASSEMBLY TO HEATER CORE TUBES.

Most heater hose couplings aren't this tricky - these special fittings are found on late model Ford vehicles

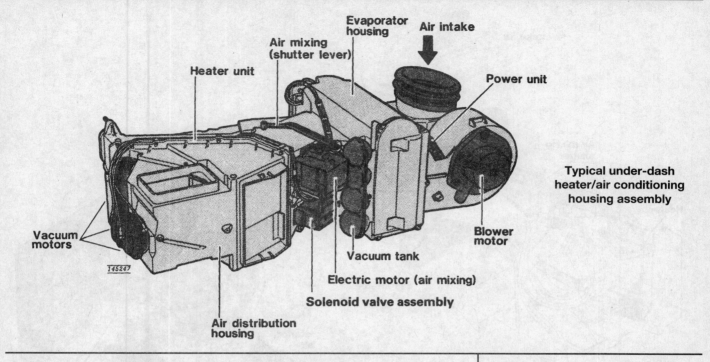

Heater unit

Air mixing (shutter lever)

Evaporator housing

Air intake

Power unit

Typical under-dash heater/air conditioning housing assembly

Vacuum motors

145247

Blower motor

Vacuum tank

Electric motor (air mixing)

Solenoid valve assembly

Air distribution housing

13   Add the specified amount of a 50/50 solution of water and antifreeze to the system. When the coolant level in the radiator reaches the filler neck, turn the engine heater controls to High, start the engine and allow it to warm up until the thermostat opens. When the thermostat opens, coolant will circulate into the engine cooling passages and into the heater system. Check the coolant level again and add more coolant as necessary.

Heater and air conditioning ducts

The elaborate system of ducting under the dashboard of your vehicle is designed to put heated or air conditioned air right where you want it. Most vehicles have ducts that allow the driver to direct the heated or cooled air toward the floor, the front seat occupants or the inside of the windshield for defrosting, or a combination of the above. Air is forced through various vents in the dash via a series of cable or vacuum operated doors. Usually, the more expensive the vehicle, the more elaborate the duct system.

The cable system is virtually foolproof. Cables rarely have to be replaced during the service life of the vehicle. The first tip-off that something is wrong with a cable usually occurs when it becomes difficult to move the control lever on the control head for the heater and air conditioner. If this happens, the door at the other end of the cable is probably jammed. Don't try to force the lever or you'll probably break the cable. Instead, refer to the *Haynes Automotive Repair Manual* which covers your vehicle, remove the dash or under dash trim plates and try to free up the door.

Some heating and air conditioning systems utilize vacuum lines instead of, or in addition to, cables for actuating the doors. And the latest designs employ electrically actuated doors, or a combination of electrical and vacuum operated doors **(see illustrations)**. These systems are highly complex and their diagnosis and repair is sometimes even beyond the scope of professional mechanics! Service on such systems is best left to an air conditioning technician.

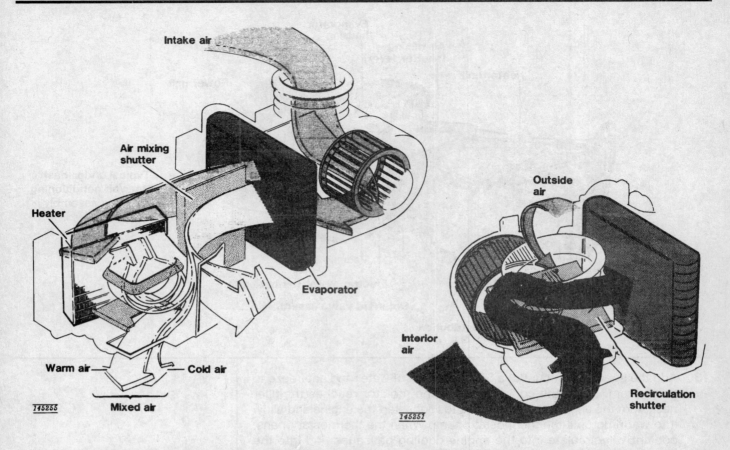

Intake air

Air mixing
shutter

Heater

Warm air — — Cold air

145255   Mixed air

Evaporator

Outside
air

Interior
air

145251

Recirculation
shutter

**Heated, air-conditioned and/or outside air are mixed inside the under-dash ducting by opening
and closing various doors**

Because this book is intended as a general guide, it would be virtually impossible to explain how to replace every heater control cable employed in every modern vehicle. This information would fill a book by itself. Most *Haynes Automotive Repair Manuals* include a detailed removal and installation procedure for replacing heater cables (unless the procedure is too complex for the home mechanic).

Air conditioning system
Safety precautions

1   Never strike a section of copper or aluminum tubing or a heat exchanger in a charged refrigeration system. A blow from a heavy tool could easily cause the relatively soft material to rupture.

2   If you have to apply force to a pressurized refrigerant threaded fitting, always use a back-up wrench to avoid the direct transfer of excessive torque to a section of refrigerant tubing. Whenever possible, use wrenches specially designed for "1/4inch flare nut" fittings (R-12 systems) or for 1/2-inch "Acme" fittings (R-134a systems).

3   Wear gloves when connecting or disconnecting service gauge hoses.

4   Always wear eye protection when working around refrigerant and air conditioning systems. Since the system's high side is under high pressure, severe injury to the eyes could result if a hose were to burst. Re-

frigerant also evaporates rapidly when exposed to the atmosphere, causing it to freeze anything it contact. That's why it's a good idea to protect skin and clothing with a shop coat. And a bad idea to wear loose clothing or things like ties or jewelry that could get caught in the drivebelts.

5 Because refrigerant is heavier than oxygen, high concentrate of refrigerant can displace oxygen in a confined area and act as an anesthesia. This is particularly important when leak-testing or soldering because toxic gas formed when refrigerant comes in contact with a flame.

6 Never operate an air conditioning system without first verifying that test gauges are backseated, if equipped, and that all fittings throughout the system are snug.

7 Never apply heat of any kind to a refrigerant line or storage vessel.

8 Always store refrigerant containers in a cool place. Never allow them to sit out in the sun or near a heat source. And never expose them to an open flame.

9 Never store refrigerant drums around corrosives like battery acid. Drums may corrode and then burst.

10 Always wear goggles when working on an air conditioning system. And keep a bottle of sterile mineral oil and a quantity of weak boric acid solution nearby for emergencies (refrigerant is readily absorbed by this oil). If refrigerant contacts your eyes, immediately use a few drops of mineral oil to wash them out, then wash them clean with the weak boric acid solution.

11 Frostbite from refrigerant should be treated by first gradually warming the area with cool water and then gently applying petroleum jelly. A physician should be consulted.

12 Always keep refrigerant drum fittings capped when not in use. Avoid sudden shock to the drum which might occur from dropping it or from banging a heavy tool against it. Never carry a drum in the passenger compartment of a vehicle.

13 Always have the system discharged before painting a vehicle, if the paint must be baked on, and before welding anywhere near refrigerant lines.

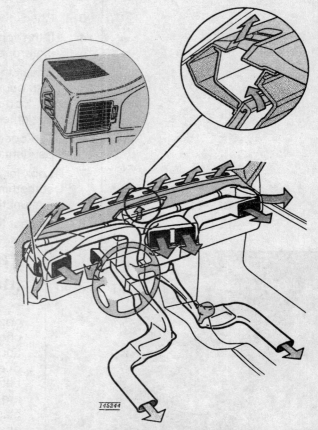

The heated, air-conditioned and/or outside air is routed through a series of ducts to heat or cool various parts of the vehicle interior

Preliminary system inspection

Before performing any of the service procedures outlines in this chapter, you must correct any conditions that might have an adverse effect on the operation of the system. First, be sure that you have read and understand the safety precautions outlined above. Then make sure that the following items have been checked before you proceed to service the system:

1 Check the cooling system. Inspect the water pump and all cooling hoses for leaks.

2 Check the compressor and engine drivebelts. They must be in good condition and properly adjusted.

3   Check the fan clutch. Make sue it's operating properly.

4   If the vehicle is equipped with a heavy-duty fan, make sure it's operating properly.

5   Check the condenser fins. They must not be bent, damaged or clogged with bugs, leaves or mud. If the fins are in need of some work, special fin "combs," available at auto part stores, can be used to clean and straighten them.

6   The operation of most modern air conditioning systems is heavily dependent on vacuum. Check all vacuum lines and connections for leaks.

7   Look for mechanical failures. Sometimes a malfunction can be traced to something as simple as a defective motor, heater air ducts or doors malfunctioning, or even a heater valve malfunction.

8   Inspect the compressor front seal and pressure relief valve for leaks.

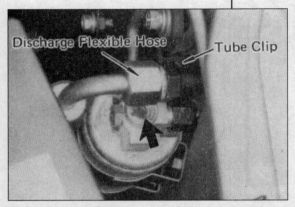

The sight glass (arrow) is a handy way to quickly check the condition of the refrigerant while the system is operating - sight glasses, if equipped, are usually on top of the receiver drier like this one, or, less frequently, in the liquid line between the condenser and the expansion valve

The sight glass (non-accumulator systems)

Many older and some newer non-accumulator systems are equipped with a built-in sight glass that allows you to quickly check the condition of the refrigerant while the system is in operation (**see illustration**). The sight glass is usually on the receiver-drier assembly; another, less common, location is the liquid line between the condenser and the expansion valve. For reasons that are explained later, most accumulator systems do not have a sight glass. On valves-in-receiver (VIR) units, the sight glass, if there is one, is in the VIR housing.

If the system in your vehicle is a non-accumulator type but doesn't have a sight glass, you can install an aftermarket in-line sight glass between the condenser and the thermostatic expansion valve. However, even though the sight glass affords a view of the refrigerant when the system is in operation, it's no substitute for a manifold test gauge set. Sight glass symptoms are not necessarily positive identification of a problem - they should be considered an adjunct to other system symptoms.

Using the sight glass

1   Start the engine, turn on the air conditioning system, put the controls at the maximum cooling and blower settings and allow it to run for 5 minutes to stabilize (this term is explained later in the chapter).

2   If the sight glass has a cap, remove it (make sure you replace it when you're done - the cap keeps the window clean).

3   Note the condition of the refrigerant in the sight glass. There are several conditions that you should watch for (**see illustration**):
   a) Clear sight glass - A clear sight glass can be good or bad. It indicates one of three possibilities:
      1) The system has the correct refrigerant charge.
      2) The system has no refrigerant in it. You will know if this is the case because there will be absolutely no cool air coming out of the heater/air conditioner vents.
      3) The system is overcharged (has too much refrigerant). This condition can only be verified with test gauges.

b) Occasional bubbles or foam in sight glass - An occasionally bubbly or foamy sight glass indicates the system is slightly low on refrigerant and air has probably entered the system. But if the bubbles are sporadic, or infrequent (usually during clutch cycling or system start-up), their presence may not indicate a problem.

c) Oil streaks in sight glass - Oil streaks indicate that the system's compressor oil is circulating through the system, which, in turn, may mean that the system refrigerant charge is extremely low.

d) Heavy stream of bubbles - A heavy stream of bubbles indicates a serious shortage of refrigerant in the system.

e) Dark or cloudy sight glass - A dark or cloudy sight glass indicates that the desiccant in the receiver-drier has deteriorated and is being circulated through the system. It also indicates that contaminants are present.

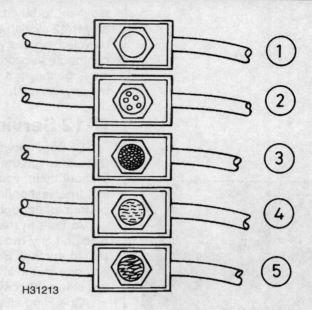

H31213

These are the five most common conditions indicated by the sight glass

1 Clear sight glass
2 Occasional bubbles or foam in sight glass
3 Heavy stream of bubbles
4 Oil streaks in sight glass
5 Dark of cloudy sight glass

As noted previously, accumulator systems do not have a sight glass. Why? Because, even with a full charge, bubbles are always present in the liquid line. In a non-accumulator system, the liquid and gaseous R-12 goes straight into the receiver-drier as it comes out of the condenser. The liquid settles to the bottom of the receiver-drier. Because the pick-up tube is located at the bottom of the receiver-drier, gaseous R-12 remains in the receiver-drier until it's converted into a liquid. Only liquid R-12 is released through the pickup tube. On conventional systems, therefore, all R-12 in the liquid line is in a liquid state and should have no bubbles.

Accumulator systems don't have a receiver-drier that separates the gas from the liquid as they come out of the condenser, so the liquid line always has some bubbles in it. Because this is the refrigerant's normal condition, a sight glass would be of little value.

Electronic sight glasses (discussed in Chapter 4), which were designed to sense bubbles in the lines of non-accumulator systems without sight glasses, are also of no value when servicing or diagnosing an accumulator system. **Warning:** *If refrigerant is added to an accumulator system until there are no more bubbles, the system will be overcharged and probably damaged, which could cause serious physical injury.*

Connecting the gauge set

In Chapter 4, we looked at the manifold test gauges, how to hook them up and how to read them. But there is one more topic that must be addressed before servicing the system - how to attach the service hoses to the valves.

Before getting started hooking up your gauges, keep in mind as you read through the following procedures that discharging either side of the system, accidentally or otherwise, is environmentally and fiscally irresponsible. R-12 is now a scare – and rapidly dwindling – substance whose price the rest of the decade will be determined by how much is available and how many people want to buy it. No more R-12 will be produced in the future – ever. The only R-12 available from now on must come from what can be recovered and recycled. So every time someone discharges R-12 into the atmosphere, they contribute to ozone depletion and shrink the available supply of remaining R-12 -- the longer it will last, the less it will cost. And the less harm it will do to the environment.

R-12 Service valves

System service valves are the "eyes' into an air conditioning system through which the manifold gauges are able to monitor system performance. Without them, you would be unable to do anything to the system. All checking, troubleshooting, discharging, evacuation and recharging procedures are performed through the service valves.

At first, system service valves never seem to be located at the same place on any two vehicles. Even the number of valves differs from one system to another. Some systems have only one service valve on the high side and one on the low side. Others use more than one valve on the high and/or low side so that system operation can be checked at different locations.

One thing all service valves have in common is a protective cap (see illustration) which keeps the core clean and prevents accidental discharge. The cap must be removed before the manifold gauges can be attached.

Two types of service valves are in common use on air conditioning systems today - the stem type and the Schrader type.

Stem type R-12 service valves

The stem type service valve features a unique three-connector design and an adjustable stem under a protective cap. When connecting a test gauge to this type of service valve or reading system pressures on the gauges after connection, you must manually position the valve stem. A special wrench should be used to protect it from damage. The stem type service valve has three operating positions (see illustration):

1) *Back-seated (open) position*
2) *Mid (test) position*
3) *Front-seated (closed) position*

Back-seated (open) position

The back-seated position of the stem type valve (stem turned out all the way) is the normal operating position. This position blocks the passageway

The protective cap on service valves performs two functions - it keeps the core clean so no contaminants get into the system when the service valve is open and it prevents accidental discharge of the system if the core fails

The three positions of the mechanical stem type valve:

A *Back-seated (stem turned all the way out) - normal operating position, valve blocks passage to service gauge port*

B *Mid-position (stem turned 1-1/2 to 2 turns in) - valve permits refrigerant to flow through system and allows it to flow through service port to the test gauges*

C *Front-seated (stem turned all the way in) - valve blocks refrigerant flow through the system*

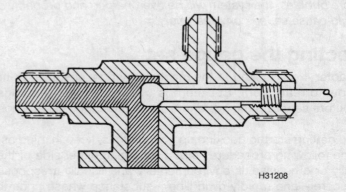

H31208

Stem-type service valve in back-seated position

to the service gauge port, preventing R-12 from flowing to the manifold test gauges, refrigerant can, vacuum pump, etc. It's the position the valve must be in when connecting or disconnecting the manifold gauge set or any other air conditioning service equipment.

Mid (test) position

After the service gauge set has been installed with the valve stem in the back-seated position, turn the valve stem 1-1/2 to 2 turns in. In this position, the valve stem still permits refrigerant to flow through the system but it also allows R-12 to flow through the service port and to the test gauges.

H31209

Stem-type service valve in mid (test) position

Front-seated (closed) position

With the service valve stem turned in as far as possible, the valve blocks refrigerant flow through the system. If the valve is installed on the compressor (it usually is), the flow of R-12 to or from the compressor is blocked. **Caution:** *If the air conditioning system is operated with the service valve(s) in the front-seated position, the compressor will be damaged.*

Schrader type R-12 valves

The Schrader type service valve is basically the same in design and operation as a tire valve. It had a spring-loaded mechanism that's normally (when no gauges are attached) in a closed position, preventing the escape of refrigerant from the system **(see illustration).** When a test gauge hose fitting (with

H31210

Stem-type service valve in front-seated (closed) position

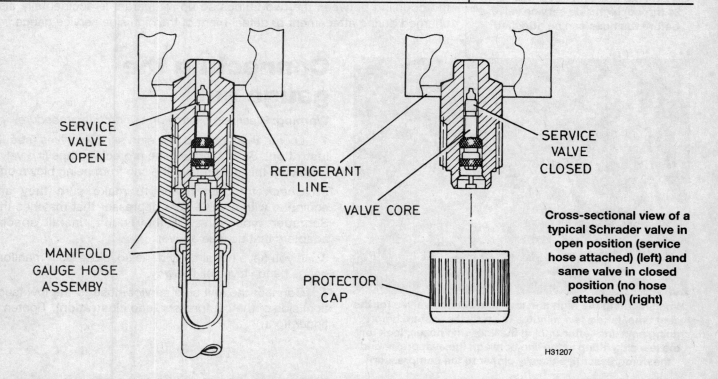

SERVICE VALVE OPEN

REFRIGERANT LINE

SERVICE VALVE CLOSED

VALVE CORE

MANIFOLD GAUGE HOSE ASSEMBY

PROTECTOR CAP

Cross-sectional view of a typical Schrader valve in open position (service hose attached) (left) and same valve in closed position (no hose attached) (right)

H31207

an integral valve core depressor) is connected to the Schrader valve, the stem is pushed to the open position and the pressurized refrigerant flows through the valve to the test gauge.

Schrader type valves have pretty much displaced stem type service valves on most air conditioning systems now in use. They are convenient, safe and environmentally superior to stem types. However, a few words to the wise are in order here: Always try to use a test hose with a built-in core depressor when working with Schrader type service valves. If a hose does not have a built-in depressor, attach an adapter to the hose that does. And NEVER attach hoses or adapters to a Schrader valve before the hose has been connected to the manifold gauge set. If you fail to remember this, it could result in a total loss of the R-12 in the system at best, and personal injury at worst. Finally, it should be noted that the Schrader valve, though basically similar in design and operation to a tire valve, cannot be replaced with a tire valve.

Special high-side R-12 service valves

Recently, many manufacturers have resorted to using different size fittings for high and low side service valves. Because of the high system pressures which occur in the discharge (high) side of the system, accidentally reversing the high and low side connections must be avoided at all costs.

In 1976, General Motors introduced a high side service valve with a different thread size (3/8-24 thread) than on the low side (7/16-20 thread). This simple measure prevents the novice and the experienced technician alike from unintentionally hooking up a can of refrigerant to the high side. Special adapters are needed to make the connection **(see illustration)**. The adapters can be purchased in straight fixed and flexible configurations and even in 45° and 90° angle models where necessary.

A special quick-disconnect fitting for the high side service valve is available for Ford systems. The fitting has a mechanism that immediately seals the coupling between the two fittings so no refrigerant is accidentally discharged during attachment or detachment of the high side service gauge.

A typical high side adapter fitting like this must be used with the General Motors post-1976 type (3/8-24 thread) high side service valve before the hose can be attached

Connecting the gauge set

Warning: *Wear eye protection during this procedure.*

1 Locate the high and low side service valves **(see illustration)**. Slowly remove the protective caps (if a valve is leaking, this will prevent the cap from being blown off).

2 Check the test hoses to make sure they are equipped with a valve core depressor that matches the Schrader type valve. If they don't, install special adapters that do (see above).

3 If you have not already done so, close both manifold gauge hand valves all the way.

4 Connect the low side service hose to the low (suction) side of the compressor **(see illustration)**. Tighten it finger tight.

When locating the high and low side service valves for the first time, take a few minutes to study the system before doing anything- after tracing the lines and hoses, look for the low side fitting in the line between the evaporator and the compressor (it's usually closer to the compressor)

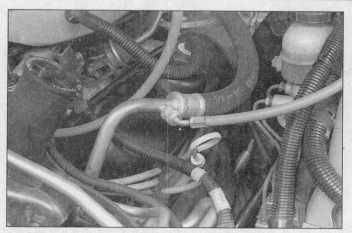

After removing the protective cap very slowly (in case there's a leak at the service valve), attach the low side hose fitting and route the hose out of the way of all moving and hot parts

The high side fitting is usually in the high side line between the condenser and the evaporator - if it's difficult to get at, like this one, you may need to use a 6-inch flexible extension adapter to hook up the high side hose

Note the angled metal line on this high side service hose - though not absolutely necessary, this design offers more flexibility when trying to attach it to hard to reach fittings

It's a good idea to protect the surrounding area of the engine compartment, and your eyes and skin, from refrigerant and oil with a shop rag when tightening or loosening a high side adapter fitting

Ditto for hooking up service hoses to service adapter fittings

Once the manifold gauge set is hooked up, make sure both hoses are routed away from all moving and hot components

5   Connect the high side service hose to the high (discharge) side of the compressor **(see illustrations)**. Again, tighten it finger tight. **Note:** *If the high side service hose connector doesn't fit on the high side Schrader valve, that's because it takes a special adapter.* Later model Ford and General Motors valves are smaller than earlier valves. The smaller size prevents accidental attachment of the low side service hose to the high side of the system.

6   Connect a separate service hose to the center fitting on the gauge set.

Stem type service valves

Warning: *Wear eye protection during this procedure.*

1   Locate the high and low side service valves. Slowly remove the protective caps (if the valve is leaking, this will prevent the cap from being blown off).

2   If you have not already done so, close both manifold gauge hand valves all the way.

3   Connect the low side service hose to the low (suction) side of the compressor. Tighten it finger tight.

4   Connect the high side service hose to the high (discharge) side of the compressor. Again, tighten it finger tight.

5   Connect a separate service hose to the center fitting on the gauge set.

R-134a service valves

The bad news is R-134a service valves are completely different from R-12 valves. The good news is they're all the same. Both the high and the low side valves on R-134a systems:

1   Have caps unique to the high and low side fittings, respectively.

2   Have no external threads on the valves (the internal threads are for the caps only).

3   Have external shapes unique to the high and low side fittings, respectively.

4   Have valves cores unique to R-134a fittings.

The R-134 valves are different so there is no chance of confusing the service valves on an R-134a system with any of various valves used on R-12 systems. The reason for this, of course, is that the EPA and the manufacturers don't want you to even THINK about trying to hook up a can or drum of R-12 or a set of R-12 manifold gauges to these new valves! And there's no way you can, because fitting adapters to hook up R-12 service hoses to R-134a valves will never be commercially available, so don't even try to find such fittings.

Stabilizing the system

Before actually beginning any tests, operate the system for a few minutes to stabilize the pressures and temperatures and ensure accurate gauge readings. To stabilize the system:

1   Always make sure the manifold gauge set, test hoses and other equip-

ment are kept away from moving engine parts and hot surfaces such as rocker arm covers, exhaust manifolds, etc.

2   Start the engine and, if necessary, adjust the engine speed to a fast idle (to speed up system stabilization).

3   Position the air conditioner controls at maximum cooling. Set the blower at the highest speed.

4   Open the doors and/or windows to quickly eliminate the heat from the passenger compartment.

5   Operate the system like this for at least 5 minutes (no more than 10 minutes should be necessary). The system is now stabilized and ready for testing.

Make sure the system is fully charged

Once the system is stabilized, it's ready for testing. There is, however, one more thing you must do before starting: Make sure the system is fully charged. How do you know whether the system is fully charged?

1   Using a thermometer, measure the "ambient' (outside) air temperature about 2 inches in front of the condenser. System pressures (particularly the high side) are directly affected by the ambient temperature. Jot down your reading and compare it to the ambient temperature column on the accompanying chart showing the relationship between pressure and temperature.

2   Insert a thermometer into the air conditioning outlet (see illustration) nearest the evaporator. Turn the blower switch to Low and note the indicated outlet air temperature. Again, jot down your reading and compare it to the evaporator temperature column on the accompanying chart.

3   Note the high and low side gauge readings and jot them down too. Then compare the preliminary readings to the columns for low and high side pressures, respectively, on the chart.

4   If the system is equipped with a sight glass (usually on the receiver drier), inspect the refrigerant flowing past the window. If there are some bubbles in the window, the system refrigerant level is low or there is a small leak in the system. If the sight glass is clear or oil-streaked, the system refrigerant is excessively low or there is a major leak. **Note:** *If the system hasn't been checked in the last year, the loss of some refrigerant is normal. Vibration loosens the fittings, the hoses are a little porous and even the design of the system itself allows some leakage.*

The best place to check the output of the evaporator is at the dash vent nearest the evaporator (usually one of the center vents)

A rule of thumb guide to the relationship between pressure and temperature

Low side Gauge (psi)	Evaporator temp. (degrees F.)
10	2
12	6
14	10
16	14
18	18
20	20
22	22
24	24
26	27
28	29

Low side Gauge (psi)	Evaporator temp. (degrees F.)
30	32
35	36
40	42
45	48
50	53
55	58
60	62
65	66
70	70

High side Gauge (psi)	Ambient temp. (degrees F.)
130 to 160	60
140 to 170	65
150 to 180	70
160 to 190	75
170 to 210	80
180 to 220	85
190 to 230	90
205 to 250	95
220 to 270	100
240 to 290	105
260 to 310	110
285 to 335	115
310 to 370	120

Low side pressure gauge reading		Evaporator temperature	
psi	kPa	°F	°C
15 to 40	103 to 276	35 to 60	2 to 16
40 to 50	276 to 345	50 to 65	10 to 18

High side readings

High side pressure gauge reading		Ambient temperature	
psi	kPa	°F	°C
115 to 200	793 to 1379	70 to 80	21 to 27
140 to 235	965 to 1620	80 to 90	27 to 32
165 to 270	1138 to 1861	90 to 100	32 to 38
210 to 310	1448 to 2137	100 to 110	38 to 44

Testing for proper refrigerant charge with an electronic sight glass

Remember, as noted in Chapter 4, that the use of this device on accumulator systems isn't really appropriate. Also, be sure to read the section entitled "Cooling the condenser while using the electronic sight glass."

1   Attach the manifold gauge set to the system as described earlier in this chapter.

2   Connect the C-clamps to the liquid line near the expansion valve or orifice tube **(see illustration)**.

   a)   The sensors must be on the condenser side of the expansion valve or orifice tube.

   b)   The clamps should be tight enough to keep from moving, but not so tight that they can cause damage to the tube.

   c)   The C-clamps should be about 1 to 3 inches apart (they must not touch each other).

3 Set the idle speed at 900 to 1000 rpm, turn on the air conditioning system and wait five minutes.

4 Spray the condenser with a continuous mist of water before checking or charging the system. A high volume shop fan can also be used to cool the condenser. See the comments below regarding condenser cooling.

5 What the instrument detects is the presence of bubbles in the liquid line:

a) If there are no bubbles, the tester will beep every two seconds. No bubbles means the line is completely full of gas, completely full of liquid or completely empty. The electronic sight glass cannot distinguish between a system that is completely full or empty, so it's essential that you connect manifold gauges to the system to verify the status of the refrigerant charge. And the gauges still require regular monitoring while the system is being charged. An electronic sight glass is not a substitute for test gauges.

b) The second type of signal is an erratic beep or ringing. If this signal is emitted, there are bubbles in the liquid line, which is an indication of a low refrigerant charge.

When hooking up an electronic sight glass, connect the C-clamps (arrows) to the liquid line near the expansion valve or orifice tube

a) *The sensors must be on the condenser side of the expansion valve or orifice tube*
b) *The clamps should be tight enough to keep from moving, but not so tight that they can cause damage to the tube*
c) *The C-clamps should be 1 to 3 inches apart (they must not touch each other)*

Cooling the condenser while using the electronic sight glass

During testing, the vehicle is stationary. An air conditioning system does not operate efficiently when the vehicle is stationary. In a moving vehicle, the motion of the air over the condenser cools and condenses the hot gas to form a high pressure liquid. In a stationary vehicle, this air movement is absent. This situation can cause a condition known as "flash gas' in the air conditioning system (especially on General Motors vehicles and others with an orifice tube system). The electronic sight glass senses this flash gas and emits an erratic beeping sound indicating the system is in need of charging even when the charge level is okay. To eliminate flash gas, spray the condenser with water or set up a large shop fan in front of the vehicle. This will eliminate flash gas and keep the condensing pressure at approximately 150 psi.

System performance test

Once the system charge has been brought up to the proper level, it's ready for a performance test.

1 Since the engine and air conditioning system will be running while the vehicle is stationary, place a large fan right in front of the condenser and radiator. Turn the fan motor speed selection knob, if equipped, to its highest setting.

2 Place the transmission selector lever in Neutral or Park and set the emergency brake. Block the wheels as well. Start the engine and set it at a fast idle.

3 Always note the low side gauge/evaporator temperature and high side gauge/ambient temperature readings first, as previously described, comparing the readings to the figures in the system pressure/temperature chart. If the initial readings seem to indicate an abnormality, you might want to compare the readings to the various combinations of low side/high side gauge readings in the next chapter.

4   After the system has been stabilized (normal temperatures and pressures obtained), its performance can be tested. With the engine running, the air conditioning controls in the maximum cooling position, the blower adjusted to the highest setting and the doors and windows of the vehicle closed, read both gauges. Jot down the readings and compare them to the figures in the accompanying chart showing normal system operating pressures. If they more or less match the rule of thumb figures, the system is operating satisfactorily. If they don't match, go to the next chapter and find the combination of low side and high side gauge readings that most closely approximates your readings.

5   The air blowing from the vents should be quite cold. If it isn't, go to the next chapter and study the possible causes of inadequate or nonexistent cooling.

6   If the system on the vehicle is a non-accumulator type and is equipped with a sight glass, the refrigerant should be generally clear of bubbles. Most systems usually show some bubbling during system cycling, so don't rely too heavily on sight glass readings to determine whether the system is fully charged.

Leak testing

Any time more than 1/2-pound of refrigerant is required to charge the system over a period of a year, a leak is indicated. Leakage - either through loose fittings, deteriorated hoses or seals or damaged metal lines - is the usual cause for low refrigerant charge. Most leaks are caused by normal engine vibration, which loosens threaded fittings and even causes metal lines to fatigue and crack over a period of time. Snugging all the fittings usually eliminates most leaks. Repair or replacement is necessary to cure leaks caused by metal fatigue and cracks. Looking for, locating and repairing subtle leaks can be time consuming. If any of the testing procedures outlined thus far indicate a leak, find and fix it. Fortunately, there are several good leak detectors available (discussed in Chapter 4) to make the job easier.

Finding leaks with a bubble detector

This is a cheap way to find a leak, and a good one, especially if you're unable to pinpoint the location of the leak using other methods.

1   Simply apply a commercial bubble detector solution, or even a soap and water solution, to the suspected leak with a small brush. Apply the solution to all fittings and connections where the leak might be.

2   Start the engine, turn on the air conditioning system and let the pressures stabilize.

3   The leaking refrigerant will cause the detector or soapy solution to form bubbles.

4   Tighten the loose fitting or repair the leaking components.

5   Wipe off the solution and repeat the above procedure to ensure that the leak is fixed.

Finding leaks with a halide (propane) torch (R-12 systems)

Warning: *The following method is not recommended unless there is no other leak detection device available. When a refrigerant leak is detected with a propane leak tester, the normally harmless refrigerant is exposed to the leak detector's propane flame, forming poisonous phosgene gas. Never inhale vapors produced by a propane leak tester - keep the work area well ventilated.*

To use a propane torch to find a leak:

1   Open the propane can valve and light the torch. Adjust the flame just high enough to heat the reaction plate in the chimney to a cherry red (about 1/2-inch above the reaction plate).

2   Lower the flame when the plate is red and adjust the top of the flame even with (or 1/4-inch above) the reaction plate - just high enough to maintain the cherry red color. **Caution:** *If the flame burns too high, the reaction plate will be destroyed after a few uses.*

3   Holding the propane torch so the flame is visible, but away from any hazardous materials, move the pick-up hose slowly around the components of the system. Keep the hose on the underside of the components - refrigerant is heavier than air and will fall as it seeps from a leak. Be sure to check all joints, connections, seals, vacuum hoses and controls.

4   The flame color is normally a pale blue. A change in color indicates a leak:

   a)   A pale yellow flame indicates a very small leak.
   b)   A yellowish-green flame indicates the presence of a small leak.
   c)   A purplish-blue flame indicates a major leak.

5   Once the point of the leak is detected, repair the system as necessary.

6   Don't stop searching after finding a leak. Be sure to check the entire system. There may be other leaks.

Finding leaks with an electronic leak tester:

1   Start the engine and turn on the air conditioning system.

2   Turn on the leak tester. Most electronic leak testers have a battery voltage indicator, usually a light emitting diode (LED). Make sure the LED is illuminated. If it isn't, replace the batteries before proceeding.

3   Search for leaks by slowly moving the sensing tip near all system components, controls, seals and fittings **(see illustration)**.

4   The instrument will emit an audible alarm when the sensing tip detects the presence of refrigerant gases. Most electronic detectors have a thumbwheel to adjust the sensitivity of the alarm.

5   To increase the detection sensitivity of the sensing tip itself, you'll have to reduce the air flow rate of the pumping tip:

   a)   Cover the exhaust vents at the back of the pumping tip housing by wrapping a piece of tape over them. Masking tape or cellophane tape works well.
   b)   Reopen one of the vent slots by punching or slicing through the tape over the slot with a razor blade or a fingernail. The reduced air rate makes it possible for the electronic leak tester to detect leaks smaller than 1/10 ounce per year!

When using an electronic leak detector, search for leaks by slowly moving the sensing tip near all system components, controls, seals and fittings - the instrument will emit an audible alarm when the sensing tip detects the presence of refrigerant gases

Finding leaks with a vacuum pump leakdown test

Sometimes leaks can be so small that they don't always show up when looking for them. And sometimes you're not really looking for a leak, because none is indicated. But whenever you discharge and evacuate the system (discussed later in this chapter), it's a good idea to perform a vacuum pump leakdown test anyway. Why? Because of the well known effects of the release of fluorocarbons into the ozone layer, most manufacturers are "downsizing' their air conditioning systems to prepare for the anticipated stricter Federal regulations and tighter supplies of R-12. A few years ago, 4-1/2 pounds of refrigerant in a system for a full-sized vehicle was pretty typical; that same system today may have only 2 pounds of R-12. And many smaller vehicles have systems with 1-1/2 to 2 pound capacities. When systems had large refrigerant capacities, and before we knew what fluorocarbons did to the environment, the leakage of 1/4 to 1/2-pound per year was no big deal. Now, however, the same size leak has a significant effect on system cooling ability and, more importantly, has a pronounced effect on the ozone layer. So it's imperative that small leaks be eliminated.

When a vacuum pump is connected to the system and running, it's an excellent first step in leak detection. **Note:** *The procedure for attaching and using a vacuum pump can be found later in this chapter (See "Evacuating the system').*

Obviously, if the vacuum pump is in good condition, but can't pump the system down to its normal vacuum, there is a massive leak somewhere (any of the methods discussed above will locate it). But let's say the pump does pull down to its normal vacuum. Does that mean there are no leaks? Not necessarily. Close the valves on the test gauge manifold (including the shutoff valve for the pump at the center service hose), turn off the pump and wait five minutes. If the vacuum reading drops more than two inches, there is a leak somewhere that must be corrected.

Removing contaminants

Contaminated refrigerant

Eventually, contaminants such as air, moisture and dirt find their way into the air conditioning system. Sometimes they work their way in through a loose fitting, a bad compressor seal, a porous hose or some other defective component. Other times they get in during some service procedure that involves opening the system. Regardless of how they get in, foreign substances must be eliminated because they don't condense like refrigerant, obstruct the movement of refrigerant through the system and form corrosive acids when they chemically react with refrigerant.

Replacing contaminated refrigerant involves two, sometimes three, procedures:

1   The system must be discharged.

2   It must then be evacuated or pumped down with a vacuum pump to remove all traces of air, moisture and contaminated refrigerant.

3   Sometimes, to remove foreign material from a system, it must also be flushed.

Discharging

When is discharging necessary?

Besides being the first step in the removal of contaminated refrigerant from the system, discharging is also necessary whenever the system must be opened for repairs or replacement of any part, with one notable exception. Compressors with stem-type service valves can be "isolated' and removed from the system without performing a complete discharge (see "Isolating the compressor" later in this chapter). Since discharging now requires an approved recycling system, take the vehicle to an approved air conditioning shop for discharging.

Flushing to remove contaminants

Flushing removes solid contaminants - excess oil, sludge, casting flash, metal flakes from a failed compressor, etc. - that could cause poor cooling or even component failure. Flushing is essential when replacing a broken compressor. If the system isn't flushed, small particles of metal from the old compressor will remain, circulating throughout the system until they find their way back to the new compressor and destroy it. Excess oil in the system can result in poor performance - flushing removes it. Flushing is also a good preventive maintenance procedure whenever a system is disassembled for servicing.

Note: *The flushing procedure described here is for the flushing kit depicted, or one similar in design. If the instructions contained in your kit differ significantly from the following procedure, do it their way.*

1   Discharge all refrigerant from the system as outlined earlier.

2   Disconnect the refrigerant lines. **Caution:** *Always remove the expansion valve and Pilot Operated Absolute/Suction Throttling Valve (POA/STV) or orifice tube assembly. The filter screens on the valves and orifices should be cleaned by hand with a Q-tip. It's not usually necessary to remove the condenser or evaporator from the vehicle for flushing.*

3   Attach one end of the flush hose to the flush gun and the other to the flushing cylinder. Attach a compressed air hose to the other end of the flushing cylinder (you'll need to install your own quick-disconnect fitting to hook up a shop air hose to the cylinder) **(see illustration).**

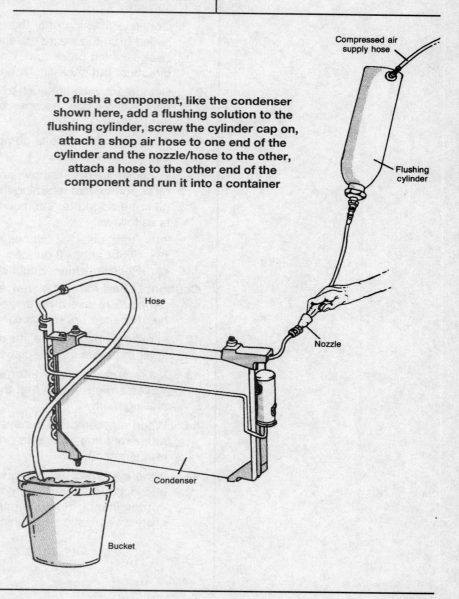

To flush a component, like the condenser shown here, add a flushing solution to the flushing cylinder, screw the cylinder cap on, attach a shop air hose to one end of the cylinder and the nozzle/hose to the other, attach a hose to the other end of the component and run it into a container

Compressed air supply hose

Flushing cylinder

Hose

Nozzle

Condenser

Bucket

4   You can flush any of the components in the system or the entire system. Don't attempt to flush the compressor itself. Flushing will remove the oil and may even damage the internal parts.

5   To flush the entire system, unscrew the cap from the flushing cylinder, pour about 20 ounces of flushing solvent (available at auto parts stores) into the cylinder and replace the cap.

6   Use proportionally smaller amounts of solvent for flushing single components.

7   Pressurize the flushing cylinder to 90 to 125 psi with a shop compressor. **Warning:** *Do not exceed 200 psi or serious injury could result if the flushing cylinder were to burst.*

8   When flushing an evaporator or condenser, fit one end of the waste discharge hose over the component's refrigerant inlet and route the other end into a waste container. Insert the flush gun into the refrigerant outlet and press the control button on the flush gun to release the flushing solvent.

Continue flushing until there is no evidence of oil or solids being dispelled from the waste hose with the flushing solvent. Note that this is a back-flushing procedure. Components can also be flushed in the other direction, but back-flushing is recommended.

9   Refrigerant lines are flushed in a similar manner, but the waste hose isn't needed since the open end of the line can be placed in the waste container.

10   After the procedure is complete, reassemble the system and replace any oil that was lost.

11   Because flushing removes oil, it's necessary to replenish the system's oil supply before returning the system to service. The correct amount of oil to be added for each component that has been flushed or replaced is as follows:

    a)   Condenser - 2 ounces
    b)   Evaporator - 2 ounces
    c)   Receiver-drier or suction-accumulator - 1 ounce

Caution: *Unless the unit is new and the desiccant is replaceable, do not attempt to re-use a receiver-drier or suction-accumulator once it has been opened up. Replace it with a new unit.*

12   In orifice tube systems, it's not a good idea to attempt to re-use the orifice tube assembly. Replace it with a new unit.

13   Make sure that any filter screens in expansion valves or POA/STV valves are clean and that the valves are in good condition before reinstalling them.

14   When reassembling the system components, replace all O-rings in the refrigerant line fittings to prevent leaks. Pre-lube the new O-rings with refrigerant oil.

15   If the system is not going to be reassembled right away, cap the inlet and outlet fittings on all components to prevent the incursion of new contaminants. Replacement components are usually equipped with protective plastic caps which can be used for this purpose.

Repairing the system

Once the system has been completely discharged, repairs can be performed. Some of the most common repairs include fixing leaks, repairing or replacing hoses or lines, replacing expansion valve screens, overhauling valves-in-receiver accumulators, replacing receiver-drier desiccant, replacing accumulators, replacing expansion tubes, replacing STV and EPR valves, replacing compressor reed valves and checking the oil level in the compressor.

All systems

Fixing leaks

Leaks are undoubtedly the most common problem associated with automotive air conditioning systems. Fortunately, they're also the easiest kind of problem to fix.

1   **Loose fittings or connections** - If a minor leak is traced to a connection, the fitting has probably loosened up from vibration. Try tightening it. After tightening a fitting or connection, always check it again for leakage to make sure the problem is solved.

2   **Deteriorated O-ring seals or gaskets** - If tightening a leaky connection doesn't stop the leak, the fitting O-ring seals or gaskets are probably deteriorated (though it's possible that the fitting itself is faulty or

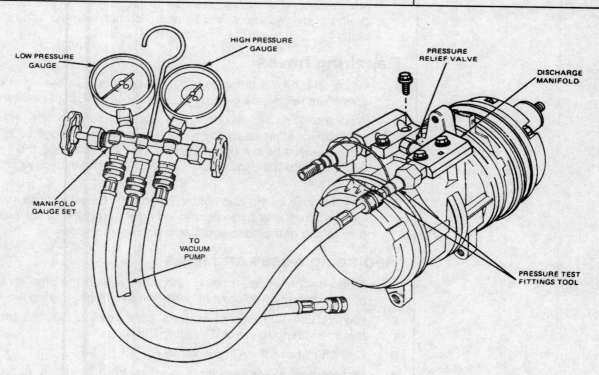

To leak test a compressor:

A   Remove the compressor and attach the high and low side hoses to the corresponding fittings on the compressor (some compressors may require an adapter plate to hook up the hoses to the compressor).

B   Attach the center gauge hose to a vacuum pump.

C   Open the low and high pressure manifold gauge valves, allowing vacuum to "pull down" the compressor.

D   Close the valves and check that the gauge needle remains steady and the vacuum does not leak out for at least 1/2 hour. Move the compressor shaft up and down to check the shaft seals.

damaged). Discharge the system and disconnect the fittings at the leaky connection. Be sure to clean the area around the fittings before disconnecting them to prevent dirt or grit from entering the system. Use two wrenches when loosening or tightening fittings to avoid kinking the metal refrigerant lines. If the fittings appear to be in good shape, you can probably get by with replacement of the O-ring seals or gaskets. Perform a leak test to check your work when the system is reassembled. If the connection still leaks, it's either faulty or damaged. Replace the hose, or hoses, of which it is a part.

3   **Faulty, porous or worn out hoses** - If the leak is due to a defective hose, or the fittings on either end of a hose, it must be replaced (see "Replacing hoses and lines' below).

4   **Suction Throttling Valve (STV) diaphragm leak** - If the leak is traced to the Suction Throttling Valve (STV), the problem is probably a torn diaphragm. Older STV units have an adjustable, replaceable diaphragm. Later Pilot Operated Absolute (POA) type STVs don't have a replaceable diaphragm. They must be replaced with a new unit (see "Replacing STV and EPR valves' later in this chapter).

5   **Compressor seal leak** - If the leak is at a compressor seal, the compressor must be rebuilt or replaced. Because of the large number of compressors in use on various systems and because of the large number of highly specialized, and different, tools necessary to rebuild each compressor, compressor overhaul is not covered in this book. We recommend that you exchange the old compressor for a new or rebuilt unit.

Repairing hoses

1   When attaching a fitting to a new hose, lubricate the hose and fitting with clean refrigerant oil. Do not use any other kind of lubricant.

2   Work the fitting into the hose end with a twisting motion. This helps to seat the locating beads or barbs in the hose. Fittings must be completely seated before use. If there's a locating bead on the fitting, push the fitting into the end of the hose until the bead is aligned with the end of the hose.

3   Install a hose clamp and tighten it securely. Some clamps have a locating tab which should be positioned against the end of the hose. Proper positioning of the hose and clamp ensures tightness.

Replacing hoses and lines

1   When disconnecting a fitting, thoroughly clean the area on both sides of the connection to prevent contaminants from entering the system.

2   Always use two wrenches (one as a back-up) when loosening a threaded fitting to prevent twisting the lines.

3   Cap off all hose ends immediately.

4   Manufacturers usually remove moisture from, then cap, all replacement hoses and lines. Do not remove the protective caps until the moment you install the part(s).

5   Replacement metal lines must be free of kinks. Inspect new lines when you buy them to ensure they are straight. Pack, stack or store them carefully to ensure that they aren't damaged between purchase and installation.

6 If the old lines are supported by brackets, make sure the new lines are attached to the same brackets. Failure to do so will most likely result in metal fatigue and cracks.

Expansion valve screen replacement

1 Discharge the system.

2 Detach the inlet line to the expansion valve from the condenser.

3 Remove the expansion valve from the evaporator.

4 The filter screen is located just inside the inlet passage. Remove and clean it thoroughly. If necessary, replace it.

5 No other service to the expansion valve is possible.

Defective fitting replacement

1 Cut off the defective fitting with a sharp knife by cutting through the hose behind the fitting clamp. Keep the hose end square. (Discard the defective fitting and hose remnant).

2 Inspect the shortened section of hose for adequate flexibility – it must not be so short that it will be stretched taut when the engine rolls and shakes during starting and at idle. Replace the old hose if necessary.

3 Slide the clamps onto the hose. Force the fitting into the hose with a rotating motion (you should be able to insert it rather easily by hand – don't use pliers, etc. or you could damage the fitting). Don't go past the shoulder on the fitting.

Defective hose replacement

1 Using a hacksaw, cut through the sleeve and the first wrap (layer) of bad hose.

2 Remove the sleeves and fittings from the hose. Discard the defective hose.

3 Cut the replacement hose to length with a sharp knife. Keep the hose ends square.

4 Assemble the original fittings to the hose with service band clamps.

5 Tighten the clamps securely.

Fitting O-rings

1 When disconnecting or connecting fittings between two metal tubes, be sure to use a backup wrench to prevent damage to the tubes.

2 After disconnecting the tubes, plug all openings immediately to prevent the entrance of dirt and moisture.

3 Discard all old O-rings.

4 Blow out all lines with refrigerant. Don't use compressed air.

5 When connecting the tubes, apply compressor oil to the portions shown.. Avoid applying oil to the threaded portions.

6 Make sure the O-ring is securely butted against the raised portion of the tube.

7 Insert the tube into the fitting until the O-ring is no longer visible.

8 Tighten the nut securely.

9 After connecting the line and recharging the system, be sure to conduct a leak test and make sure the connections aren't leaking.

R-134a hoses

The hoses used on R-134a systems look similar to those used in R-12 systems. Like R-12 hoses, they're made of reinforced rubber or thermoplastic. However, there is one major difference between the two: R-134a hoses are also lined with a nylon barrier that prevents HFC's from migrating through the hose wall. So don't try to use non-R-134a hoses for an R-134a system, or you'll lose refrigerant rapidly. If you're *converting* an R-12 system to R-134a, and if the old hoses are in good condition, you can use them with R-134a. But don't use *new* R-12 hoses that have never had R-12 run through them. "Used" R-12 hoses (those that have already been used in a R-12 system) have a protective layer formed by R-12 lubricant, which is absorbed into the inner hose wall to create a natural barrier to R-134a permeation. New R-12 hoses don't have this protective barrier, and will allow R-134a to leak out.

Expansion valve/Pilot Operated Absolute (POA) valve replacement

1 Thoroughly clean the exterior of the VIR unit.

2 Detach all connections and mounting hardware.

3 Remove the four inlet connector shell-to-valve housing screws. Remove the shell from the assembly.

4 Clean the upper part of the valve housing. Don't scratch the sealing surface.

5 Loosen one of the valve capsule retaining screws. Remove the other retaining screw completely. If there is any residual refrigerant pressure trapped in the VIR assembly, the screw will prevent the valves from popping out and causing injury.

6 Insert the correct end of the capsule removal tool into the tapered groove projection on the expansion valve. Press down on the tool to loosen the valve.

7 Turn the tool around and insert the other end into the baffle for the POA valve. Again, press down on the tool to free the valve. **Caution:** *Don't press down on the O-ring on top of the housing*.

8 Remove the other retaining screw and lift out both valves. Remove and discard the O-rings from the valves and valve cavities.

9 Coat the new O-rings with clean refrigerant oil. Install them.

10 Install the POA and expansion valves with thumb pressure. **Caution:** *Driving the valves into place with tools can damage them*.

11 Install the retaining screws and tighten them to 5 to 7 ft-lbs.

12 Install the inlet connector shell and the four shell-to-valve screws and tighten the screws securely.

Desiccant bag replacement

1 Always replace the desiccant bag after replacing the expansion valve, POA valve and/or O-rings.

2 To get at the desiccant bag, remove the screws which attach the bottom receiver shell to the VIR housing. If the shell is stuck, bump it with your hand to free it from the housing. **Caution:** *Do not pry the receiver shell free with a tool*.

3 Lower the shell carefully to clear the pick-up tube. Remove the old desiccant bag.

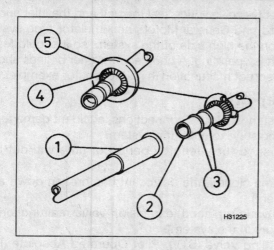

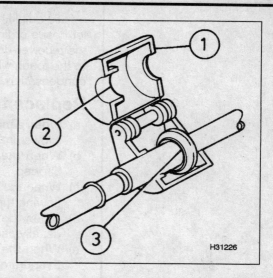

Spring-lock refrigerant line coupling components

1	Female fitting	4	Garter spring	
2	Male fitting	5	Cage	
3	O-rings			

Fit the tool (1) over the spring-lock coupling with the projecting boss (2) against the open garter spring (3)

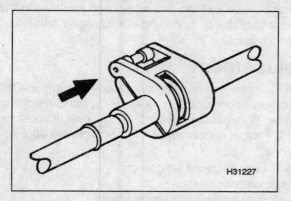

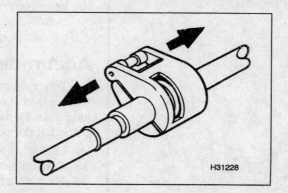

Push the tool so that the boss presses against the garter spring . . .

. . . and simultaneously pull the two pipes apart

4   If the receiver shell has an O-ring, remove and discard it. Drain, measure and discard any refrigerant oil present in the shell.

5   Remove the pick-up tube screen and clean the screen and the inside of the shell with solvent. Wipe it completely dry with a lint free cloth.

6   Replace the pick-up tube screen.

7   Install a new desiccant bag.

8   Replace the oil that was removed, measured and discarded with an equal amount of clean refrigerant oil, then add 1 additional ounce.

9   Place the shell back in position and attach it to the housing. Install the shell screws and tighten them to 5 to 7 foot pounds.

Receiver-drier or desiccant replacement

Unlike VIR and EEVIR type receivers, other receiver-drier units are usually sealed units and cannot be repaired. If the system becomes saturated with moisture (during, for example, a major leak), the receiver-drier must be replaced.

Heating and air conditioning

To quickly check a suspect receiver-drier, feel the unit and the inlet and outlet hoses or lines. Unlike Ford and General Motors accumulator type systems, the receiver-drier is located on the high side of the system, so it should feel hot to the touch when the system is operating. A cool receiver drier or lines showing condensation indicate some sort of malfunction (a restriction, for example).

Replace the receiver-drier:

a) When a major leak (broken hose, loose connections, accident damage, etc.) allows ambient air and moisture to enter the system.

b) When the system is opened for a lengthy period of time without being capped.

c) When the sight glass turns cloudy (the desiccant has broken down and is flowing through the system).

d) When the expansion valve is replaced (expansion valve malfunctions are usually caused by moisture in the system).

e) When the Suction Throttling Valve (STV), Pilot Operated Absolute (POA), Evaporator Pressure Regulator (EPR) or expansion valve is replaced (each of these components usually malfunctions when moisture enters the system).

f) When the normally warm or hot outlet lines from the receiver-drier are cool during system operation (excessive moisture build-up near the receiver-drier causes formation of condensation on the hoses, indicating a restriction).

g) When too much refrigerant oil (more than 5-ounces) accumulates in the receiver-drier (this indicates that the oil bleed hole is clogged and it usually causes poor system performance).

Accumulator replacement

The accumulator, which is connected to the evaporator inlet pipe on General Motors and Ford Motor Company accumulator type systems, performs the same functions as the receiver-drier. If the accumulator malfunctions, it must be replaced. It cannot be serviced. Typical accumulator malfunctions are caused by:

a) *Leaks.*

b) *A restricted orifice tube or compressor inlet screen.*

c) *An internally corroded evaporator.*

d) *Saturated desiccant (desiccant alone can't be replaced).*

The procedure for replacing the accumulator in specific vehicles is included in *Haynes Automotive Repair Manuals*. However, the following general procedure should enable you to replace the accumulator on a vehicle if you don't have the Haynes manual.

1 Detach the cable from the negative terminal of the battery.

2 Discharge the system (minimizing oil loss as much as possible) as outlined previously.

3 Disconnect the accumulator inlet and outlet lines and cap all openings to prevent contamination of the system by dirt or moisture. **Note:** *On some 1981 and later Ford Motor Company vehicles, the suction hose must be disconnected at the compressor because the line is not removable at the accumulator.*

4 If the accumulator has a pressure sensing switch, remove it and transfer it to the new accumulator.

5 Remove the accumulator mounting bracket screws and lift the accumulator from the engine compartment.

6 Pour 1-ounce of fresh, clean refrigerant oil into the new accumulator before installing it.

7 Installation is the reverse of removal.

Orifice tube (expansion tube) replacement

The accumulator type systems used in some Ford Motor Company and General Motors vehicles have a fixed orifice tube (expansion tube) instead of a standard expansion valve. The orifice tube is located in the line between the condenser and the evaporator (it's usually at the evaporator inlet; on some newer Ford vehicles, it's in the liquid line).

Because it's a relatively inexpensive part, the orifice tube assembly is normally replaced as a routine service procedure every time the system is opened for servicing. Orifice tube replacement is mandatory, however, when a clog causes a high side restriction or whenever a failed compressor is replaced. **Caution:** *NEVER clean and reinstall a used orifice tube - it could seriously damage the system*.

1   Discharge the system as previously outlined.

2   Disconnect the high side line from the evaporator. Remove and discard any O-rings, if equipped.

3   Pour a small amount of refrigerant oil into the inlet to lubricate the tube O-rings.

4   Insert the special tool **(see illustration)** into the tube. Turn the tool clockwise to engage the tangs on the tube. Turn the tool nut slowly to avoid breaking the orifice tube during removal. **Note:** *If the orifice tube breaks off during removal, you'll have to obtain a special broken orifice tube tool to extract the broken section. If the special tool fails to extract the tube, a special repair kit is available for some systems.*

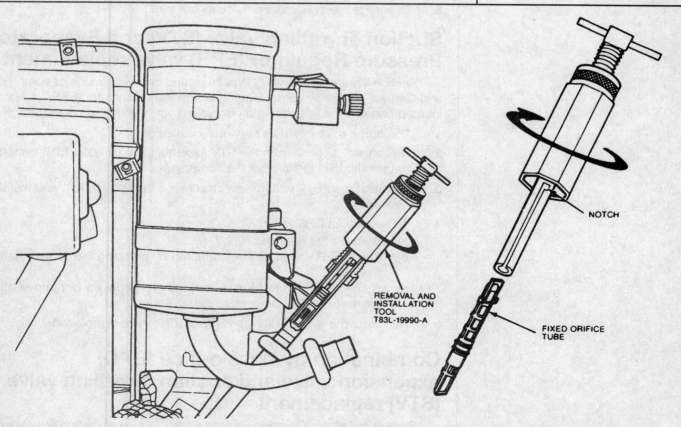

Insert the special tool into the tube, turn the tool clockwise to engage the tangs on the tube, then turn tool nut slowly to avoid breaking the orifice tube during removal

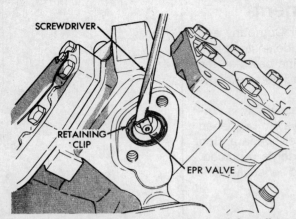

To replace the EPR valve, remove the retaining clip and pry out the valve (some valves can even be removed by simply grasping the center shaft of the valve and pulling it out - others may require a special extraction tool)

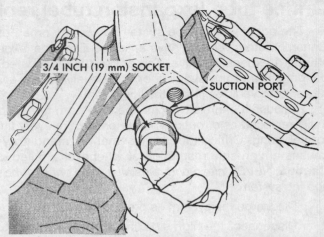

To install a new EPR valve, use a 3/4-inch or 19mm socket and carefully tap the valve into place

5   Lubricate the new O-ring(s) on the new orifice tube with clean refrigerant oil.

6   Insert the new orifice tube into the evaporator inlet pipe with the short end of the tube facing the evaporator. Push the tube in until it's seated.

7   Reconnect the high side line.

8   Recharge the system as previously outlined.

Suction Throttling Valve (STV) and Evaporator Pressure Regulator (EPR) valve replacement

Suction Throttling Valves (STVs) are found on the low side of some Ford and General Motors systems. Expansion Pressure Regulator (EPR) valves are located beneath the inlet fitting on Chrysler twin-cylinder compressors.

1   Discharge the system as previously outlined.

2   Disconnect all lines from the STV assembly. On Chrysler EPR systems, detach the inlet fitting from the compressor.

3   To replace an STV unit, simply unscrew it from the mount and install a new one.

4   To replace an EPR valve:
     a)   Remove the retaining clip.
     b)   Some EPR valves can be extracted by grasping the center shaft of the valve.
     c)   A special tool **(see illustration)** may be required to remove other valves from the compressor cavity.

5   Recharge the system after the STV or EPR valve is replaced.

Combination by-pass orifice (BPO) expansion valve and suction throttling valve (STV) replacement

Some Ford Motor Company systems feature a combination by-pass orifice (BPO) expansion valve and suction throttling valve (STV).

1   Discharge the system as previously outlined.

2   Disconnect the two refrigerant lines from the STV housing manifold tube assembly.

3   Remove the two mounting bolts and detach the BPO expansion valve and STV housing manifold and tube assembly from the evaporator manifold plate.

4   Remove the two socket head screws that attach the STV housing manifold to the expansion valve body.

5   Using a special wrench or a pair of curved jaw channel-lock pliers, grasp the STV body near the tapered end. Remove it by turning it counterclockwise.

6   Remove and discard the STV O-ring from the expansion valve body. Be sure to install a new one.

7   Installation is the reverse of removal.

Compressor reed valve replacement

If moisture has entered the system, reed valve corrosion is a common compressor problem. On the compressor models included below, reed valve replacement is a relatively straightforward procedure.

However, some common compressor units are not included here. On some Harrison (Frigidaire) compressors (the four-cylinder R-4, five-cylinder V5 and the six-cylinder A6 and DA-6), for instance, the reed valves cannot be replaced unless the compressor is overhauled. But because of the number of special tools required, and the difficulty of including accurate, up-to-date overhaul procedures for every compressor, the procedures for compressor overhaul are not included in this book. If reed valve replacement is indicated and your compressor is not included below, exchange it for a rebuilt unit.

Chrysler, Tecumseh and York two-cylinder and Sanden (Sankyo) five-cylinder units

1   Thoroughly clean the compressor.

2   Discharge the system.

3   Remove the head bolts and service valves (if equipped) from the compressor (note the location of any long head bolts - usually at the service valves).

4   Gently pry or tap under the tabs extending from the head plate to free it from the compressor body. Remove the head plate(s). Wrap the head(s) in a clean cloth while it's off.

5   Remove the reed valve assemblies.

6   Remove all old gasket material from the compressor body, the head and the service valve mount. Use extreme care to avoid scratching the mating surfaces.

7   Coat a new gasket with clean refrigerant oil and position it on the compressor body (use the alignment pins, if present).

8   Install the replacement reed valve assemblies. **Caution:** *Be sure the discharge valves are facing up (you can tell the two apart because the discharge valves are smaller than the suction valves)*.

9   Using the alignment pins (if present), install the head(s) on the compressor.

10   If the compressor is equipped with service valves, lubricate the new valve O-rings and install the service valves and O-rings.

11   Tighten the head bolts in a criss-cross pattern and work from the inside to the outside edge of the head(s). If service valves are installed on the compressor head, tighten those bolts first.

Chrysler C-171 and Ford FS-6 6-cylinder compressors

1   Discharge the system.

2   Remove the compressor from the vehicle.

3   Remove the clutch assembly (see clutch coil replacement later in this chapter).

4   Pour the refrigerant oil in the compressor into a calibrated container and note the amount.

5   Cap the openings and thoroughly clean the compressor.

6   Mount the compressor in a vise or special holding fixture.

7   Remove the bolts and the front and/or rear head assembly, dowel pins, gaskets, plate and reed assembly.

Installation

8   Clean all parts with solvent and blow them dry with clean compressed air.

9   Lubricate all parts with clean refrigerant oil.

10   Install the dowel alignment pins, the reed assembly, the plate, the gaskets and the head(s) in the opposite order in which they were removed.

11   Using new brass washers (if originally equipped), tighten the through bolts.

12   Add fresh refrigerant oil (see "Compressor oil check' later in this chapter).

13   Install the clutch assembly.

14   Install the compressor.

Nippondenso 10-cylinder compressor

1   Remove the magnetic clutch assembly.

2   Remove the service valve and drain the compressor oil.

3   Remove and discard the O-rings in the service valve.

4   Remove the shaft seal assembly.

5   Remove the through bolts. Discard the washers.

6   Remove the front housing by tapping on the protrusion with a hammer and punch. Be careful not to scratch the sealing surface of the rear housing.

7   Remove the front and rear O-rings from the cylinder block.

8   Clean and inspect the front and rear valve plates for scratched, bent or otherwise damaged parts. Replace any damaged parts.

9   Clean and inspect both cylinder heads and both valve plate assemblies for nicks or burrs on the sealing surfaces. Replace any damaged parts.

10   Make sure that all passages in the valve plate are unobstructed. If either the cylinder head or the valve plate is cracked, it must be replaced.

11 Install the two pins in the rear cylinder.

12 Lubricate the new rear cylinder O-ring with compressor oil and install it in the rear cylinder.

13 Install the rear suction valve over the pins on the rear cylinder (the front and rear suction valves are identical).

14 Install the rear valve plate together with the discharge valve over the pins on the rear cylinder (Note that the rear valve plate is marked with an "R').

15 Lubricate the gasket with compressor oil and install it on the valve plate.

16 Install the rear housing on the rear cylinder.

17 Install the two pins in the front cylinder.

18 Lubricate the new rear housing O-ring with compressor oil and install it in the rear housing.

19 Install the front suction valve over the pins on the front cylinder.

20 Install the front valve plate and the discharge valve over the pins on the front cylinder.

21 Lubricate the new gasket with compressor oil and install it on the valve plate.

22 Install the front housing on the front cylinder and tighten the six through bolts in two or three passes to 19 ft-lbs.

23 Check the compressor shaft rotating torque. It should be 16 in-lbs.

24 Install the shaft seal assembly.

25 Fill the compressor with Denso oil 6, Suniso No. 5GS or equivalent.

26 Install the service valve with the new O-ring and tighten it to 19 ft-lbs.

27 Install the magnetic clutch assembly.

Compressor oil check

The oil level on some older compressors can be checked and topped up with the compressor installed. Other units must be removed before oil can be measured or added. Unless the compressor can be isolated (in other words, is equipped with stem-type service valves), the system must be discharged first. Only those compressors which can be checked for oil level are included in this chapter. But first, here's a list of some DOs and DON'Ts pertinent to oil level checks and oil replacement:

a) **Always use new, moisture-free refrigerant oil**. This oil is highly refined and dehydrated. Its container must be kept tightly closed at all times unless you're using it. If the container is allowed to remain open even for a short time, moisture will be absorbed from the atmosphere and introduced into the system.

b) **Always run the engine and system for 10 minutes** to allow proper oil distribution through the system.

c) **If the oil level in the compressor is checked with a dipstick**, each ounce of new refrigerant oil added to the compressor will raise the dipstick reading approximately 1/4-inch.

d) **Always replace the oil plug sealing gasket or O-ring**.

e) **If you use "charging cans' to add oil to the system**, the procedure for adding oil is identical to that for adding refrigerant. The can capacity most commonly used for adding oil this way is 4 ounces. But bear in mind that only 2 ounces of each can is oil. The other 2 ounces is refrigerant.

Rule of thumb guide for adding oil to individual components

If no major oil loss has occurred, and if only a single component must be replaced, oil can be added to the system by putting it into a specific component. Use the amounts shown below:

Condenser - 1 ounce
Receiver-drier - 1 ounce
Desiccant bag in VIR - 1 ounce plus the amount drained from the receiver-drier
Evaporator - 3 ounces
Accumulator
   a)   Ford - 1 ounce plus the amount measured
   b)   General Motors
       1)   DA-6 - 3 ounces plus the amount measured
       2)   A-6, R-4 or V5 - 2 ounces plus the amount measured

It's important to note that, since oil distributes itself throughout the system during operation, it isn't absolutely necessary to add the oil to the component being replaced. With one notable exception, as long as the amount of oil lost during the replacement procedure is added somewhere, the system will be fine. The exception? The compressor. If the compressor is being replaced, always put the oil into the compressor and not somewhere else.

Chrysler, Tecumseh and York two-cylinder compressors

1   Obtain a dipstick or fabricate one.

2   Discharge the system (or isolate the compressor, if equipped with stem-type service valves).

3   Remove the oil filler plug. **Caution:** *Loosen the plug very slowly - there may be residual crankcase pressure.*

4   Clean the dipstick.

5   Insert the dipstick and check the oil level. **Note:** *You may have to rotate the dipstick to be sure it clears the crankshaft.*

6   Add oil, if necessary, to bring it to the specified level.

Harrison (Frigidaire) A-6 six-cylinder compressor

1   If you're replacing either the accumulator or the compressor, or find evidence of excessive oil loss, remove the accumulator and the compressor, then drain, measure and replace the oil.

   a)   If the amount of oil measured from the accumulator and compressor is 6 ounces or more, add the same amount of new oil plus 2 ounces to replace the amount captured in the desiccant of the old accumulator.

   b)   If the amount recovered is less than 6 ounces, add 6 ounces of new oil plus 2 ounces to replace the amount captured in the desiccant of the old accumulator.

Note: *Normally, a system will have 6 ounces of oil in the accumulator and/or compressor together. Neither unit will necessarily have 3 ounces or all 6 ounces, so both units must be measured.*

2   New compressors are normally supplied with fresh oil already inside them, but don't assume that it's the correct amount. If a new compres-

sor is being installed, drain and measure the oil inside it before installing it. Add only the specified amount to the compressor.

3   If the old compressor is inoperable, use the following rule of thumb measurements:

   a)   If the amount drained and measured is more than 1-1/2 ounces and the system shows no signs of major oil loss, add the same amount as drained to the new compressor or that amount plus an additional ounce for a new or rebuilt compressor.

   b)   If the amount of oil drained is less than 1-1/2 ounces, and the system appears to have lost oil, add 6 ounces to the new or rebuilt compressor, or add 7 ounces to the old compressor after it has been overhauled.

Note: *If the oil drained from the system contains metal chips or other foreign material, remove the receiver-drier, flush the system and install a new receiver drier or accumulator (and any other components that may have been damaged).*

Harrison (Frigidaire) R-4 four-cylinder compressor

The Harrison (Frigidaire) compressor is charged, when new, with 6 ounces of refrigeration oil. Because it doesn't have an oil sump, and retains very little oil, it doesn't normally have to be removed for oil level measurement. **Caution:** *Since this compressor has no sump, it must be well lubricated. If it runs dry, it will quickly self destruct.*

There are several conditions which warrant checking and adding oil to this compressor:

1   When replacing components (even if no oil leak is noted):

   a)   If only the compressor is being replaced - remove, drain, measure and add the correct amount of new oil.

   b)   If the evaporator is being replaced, add 3 ounces.

   c)   If the condenser is being replaced, add 1 ounce.

2   When there is a loss of refrigerant over a period of time, (and a component is being replaced to correct the leak), add refrigerant oil to the component in accordance with the amount previously specified in the "Rule-of-thumb guide for adding oil to individual components."

3   When there's evidence of a major oil leak - If the system loses excessive oil, remove the accumulator, then drain and measure the oil.

   a)   If more than 3 ounces is measured, put in the same amount of new oil as you drained, plus an extra 2 ounces of new oil to compensate for that lost by replacing the accumulator (held by the desiccant).

   b)   If less than 3 ounces is measured, add 3 ounces of new oil, plus an additional 2 ounces of new oil to compensate for that lost by replacing the accumulator (held by the desiccant).

Caution: *If oil drained from the accumulator (or any other component) contains metal chips or other foreign particles, repair or replace the defective component, flush the entire system and add 6 ounces of new refrigerant oil to the compressor suction port. And be sure to replace the accumulator - if the desiccant bag has trapped any of the particles, they will circulate in the restored system, causing further damage.*

4   When the system oil level is unknown or system performance and efficiency are marginal, drain and flush the system and add a new 6 ounce charge of refrigerant oil to the system.

Harrison (Delco Air) DA-6 six-cylinder compressor

Like the Harrison (Frigidaire) described above, the Delco Air compressor has no sump, so it doesn't have to be removed for oil measurement. Check or add oil under the following conditions:

1 **Components being replaced, but no evidence of excessive oil leakage**
   a) If the compressor is being replaced, remove it, then drain and measure the oil. Add the same amount of new oil plus an extra ounce.
   b) If the evaporator is being replaced, add 3 ounces of new oil.
   c) If the condenser is being replaced, add 1 ounce of new oil.
   d) If the accumulator is being replaced, remove, drain and measure the old oil. Replace it with the same amount of new oil, plus 3 ounces to compensate for the oil held by the desiccant. If no oil can be drained from the old accumulator, add 2 ounces of new oil.

2 **Evidence of excessive oil leakage**
   a) Remove the accumulator, drain the oil and measure (the DA-6 itself only holds a minimum amount of refrigeration oil because it has no sump).
   b) If the amount recovered is less than 3 ounces, add 3 ounces of new oil to the system.
   c) If the amount recovered is more than 3 ounces, add an amount of oil equal to that drained from the old accumulator.

Note: *If a new accumulator must be added to the DA-6 system, add an additional 3 ounces of oil to compensate for that retained by the original accumulator desiccant.*

Harrison V5 five-cylinder compressor

1 When the compressor is removed from the vehicle for service, drain the oil from the drain plug opening to insure an accurate measurement. Measure the oil, then discard it. Add an equal amount of new oil.

2 The V5 compressor has a unique lubrication system. The crankcase suction bleed is routed through the rotating swashplate to lubricate the swashplate bearing. The rotation of the swashplate separates the oil, removing some of it from the crankcase-suction bleed and rerouting it to the crankcase where it can lubricate the compressor mechanism.

3 Up to 4 ounces of oil can collect in the crankcase. But new or rebuilt compressors may be shipped from the factory with up to 8 ounces of oil in the crankcase. Drain the oil from the drain plug opening, measure it and put back in an amount equal to that drained and measured from the old compressor. **Note:** *If a new accumulator is being added to the system, put an additional 2 ounces of oil into the compressor to compensate for the oil retained by the desiccant in the old accumulator.*

Sanden (Sankyo) five-cylinder compressor

1 Start the engine and run the system for 5 minutes. Make sure the compressor cycles on during this time. Turn off the system and stop the engine.

2 Clean the dipstick and allow it to cool down.

3 Remove the compressor and place it on a workbench. Position the compressor with the oil fill plug at top dead center (TDC).

4 Thoroughly clean the oil fill plug and the area around it to prevent dirt from contaminating the compressor.

5 Slowly loosen the fill plug to allow any residual refrigerant pressure to escape.

6 The front plate hub has a lobe which is indexed with a notch at 180° from TDC of the cam rotor. Rotate the hub plate lobe until the index notch is 110° from bottom center **(see illustrations)**. Check this position by looking through the oil fill hole and noting that the ball end of the top piston rod lines up with the fill hole.

7 Looking at the front of the compressor, insert the dipstick diagonally from the upper left to the lower left until the dipstick stop contacts the filler hole surface. Remove the dipstick and note the oil level. It should be between the 4th and 6th increments on the dipstick (3 to 4 ounces). Add oil as necessary.

8 If system components are being replaced, add refrigerant oil in accordance with the amounts specified in the "Rule of thumb guide for adding oil to individual components."

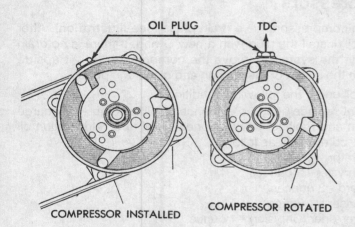

When you put the compressor on the workbench, make sure that the oil filler plug is at the top

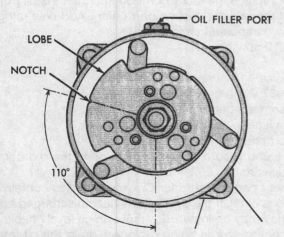

Rotate the hub plate lobe until the index notch is 110° from bottom dead center

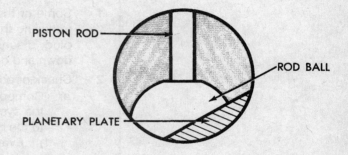

To verify that the hub plate lobe and index notch are aligned, look through the oil fill hole and verify that the ball end of the top piston rod lines up with the fill hole

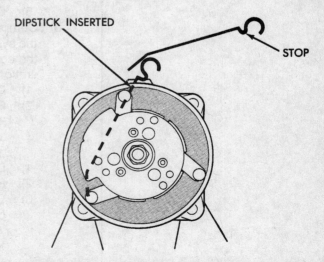

Insert the dipstick diagonally from the upper left to the lower left until the dipstick stop contacts the filler hole surface

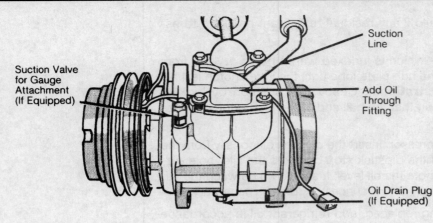

Suction Valve for Gauge Attachment (If Equipped)

Suction Line

Add Oil Through Fitting

Oil Drain Plug (If Equipped)

If the compressor on your vehicle has a drain plug, remove it and drain the oil, then reinstall the plug with a new O-ring - if it doesn't have a drain plug, you will have to remove the compressor, turn it upside down and drain the oil out of the suction and discharge ports

Chrysler C-171, Ford FS-6 and Nippondenso six-cylinder compressors

1 Some of these compressors have drain plugs **(see illustration)**. After removing the oil, install the plug with a new O-ring. If there is no drain plug, discharge the system, remove the compressor, turn it upside down and drain the oil out of the suction and discharge ports.

2 Check or add oil under the following conditions:

a) Component replacement, no evidence of oil leakage - Discharge the system and replace the component. Add new refrigeration oil to the new component as follows:

1) Evaporator
   (a) Chrysler - 2 ounces
   (b) Ford - 3 ounces
2) Condenser - 1 ounce
3) Receiver-drier (Chrysler) - 1 ounce
4) Accumulator (Ford) - amount drained from old accumulator plus 1 ounce
5) Compressor - see below

b) Component replacement, evidence of oil leakage - Slowly discharge the system, repair or replace the faulty component, drain the oil from the compressor and remove the suction port fitting. Add new refrigeration oil to the new component as follows:

1) Chrysler - 9 to 10 ounces
2) Ford
   (a) 1981 vehicles - 13 ounces
   (b) 1982 to 1987 vehicles - 10 ounces
   (c) Compressor replacement
1) Discharge the system.
2) Remove the compressor.
3) Drain, measure and record the amount of oil in the old compressor, then discard it.
   (a) Replacement compressors for Chrysler vehicles contain 9 to 10 ounces of oil. If the system has been discharged and flushed, they may be installed without an oil level check. If only the compressor is being replaced, drain the oil from the new compressor; even if more than 6 ounces are removed, pour no more than 6 ounces into the new compressor.

(b) Drain the oil from replacement compressors for 1981 Ford vehicles and add new oil in proportion to the amount removed from the old compressor. If less than 3 ounces were removed from the old compressor, add 6 ounces to the new compressor. If 3 to 6 ounces were removed, pour the same amount into the new compressor. If more than 6 ounces were drained, put no more than 6 ounces into the new compressor.

(c) Compressors for 1982 to 1987 Ford vehicles are charged with 10 ounces of oil. Drain 4 ounces from the new compressor before installing it.

Tecumseh HR980 4-cylinder compressor

This compressor must be charged with 8 ounces of refrigeration oil. But if a component is removed from the system, some oil will be lost. Add oil to the system as follows:

1 Compressor replacement - A new compressor is already charged with 8 ounces of refrigerant oil. Before installing the compressor, drain 4 ounces from the new compressor. This maintains the system total charge within the 8 ounce limit.

2 Component replacement
   a) Evaporator - 3 ounces
   b) Accumulator - Drain oil from the accumulator through the Schrader valve of the pressure sensing switch fitting. Measure the amount of oil removed and add that amount plus 1 ounce to the new accumulator.

York rotary vane compressor

1 Run the system for 10 minutes, then stop the engine.

2 Discharge the system (slowly, to prevent oil from escaping).

3 Remove the suction and discharge hoses.

4 Rotate the compressor shaft by hand in a counterclockwise direction for 10 revolutions.

5 If the compressor is on the vehicle, remove the drivebelt and tilt the compressor until the suction and discharge ports are level. Using a dipstick **(see illustration)**, measure the oil level.

6 If the compressor is removed from the vehicle, drain the oil from the sump and from the suction and discharge ports.
   a) If the oil measures less than 2 ounces, replace it with 2 ounces of fresh oil.
   b) If there are more than 2 ounces, replace the oil with an equal amount of fresh oil.

7 If any system components are being replaced, add refrigerant oil to them in accordance with the "Rule of thumb guide for adding oil to individual components."

8 If there is any evidence that a major leak has occurred, flush the system, then add oil in the following amounts:
   a) If the refrigerant charge capacity is under 2 pounds- 6 ounces.
   b) If the charge is up to 3 pounds - 7 ounces.
   c) If the charge is more than 3 pounds - 8 ounces.

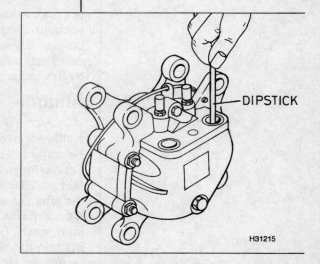

H31215

Using a dipstick to check the oil level on a York rotary vane compressor

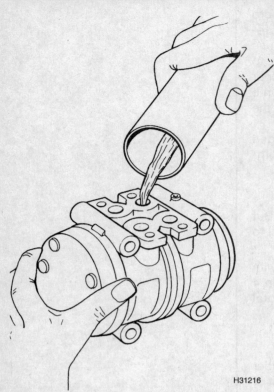

Refilling a Nippondenso 10-cylinder compressor with oil

9   Inspect the O-rings on the suction and discharge fittings and coat them with clean refrigerant oil before installing the lines.

Nippondenso 10-cylinder compressor

1   Discharge the system.

2   Remove the compressor.

3   Remove the service valve assembly.

4   Turn the compressor upside down and drain the oil.

5   Refill the compressor with 2.0 to 3.4 ounces of Denso oil 6, Suniso No. 5GS or an equivalent compressor oil **(see illustration)**.

Evacuating the system

Once the system has been opened up for repairs or component replacement, or has been found to be excessively low on refrigerant, it must be completely evacuated with a vacuum pump to remove all traces of moisture before a new refrigerant charge is added.

Any amount of moisture is very harmful to air conditioning systems. Moisture reacts with refrigerant to form hydrochloric acid (HCL), which damages the system's internal components. That's why every system is equipped with either a receiver-drier or an accumulator to trap and retain the moisture that invariably infiltrates the system. You will recall from Chapter 1 that air contains moisture. So even the smallest leak will allow air and moisture into the system.

Moisture can collect and freeze in the orifice of the expansion valve, restricting the flow of refrigerant. And it can do the same thing in a system equipped with a suction throttling valve (STV) or evaporator pressure regulator (EPR) valve. In fact, it can block the flow of refrigerant through any orifice in the system. Obviously, moisture must be prevented from entering the system. Once it gets in, the desiccant in the receiver-drier or accumulator is the system's only means of removing it.

Vacuum pumps

The basic tool for removing air and moisture from a system is the vacuum pump (see Chapter 4 for detailed descriptions of the various types of vacuum pumps). A vacuum pump simply lowers the pressure inside the system to a vacuum condition. When the system reaches a vacuum condition, the boiling point of any water in the system is also lowered, eventually to a point at which it can easily evaporate. This vaporized moisture is then sucked out of the system by the vacuum pump.

Altitude

Of course it's impossible to obtain a vacuum reading of 29.5 in-Hg at any altitude above sea level. For each 1000 feet of altitude, the vacuum gauge must be corrected by 1 in-Hg to compensate for the change in atmospheric pressure. For example, a gauge reading of 24.5 in-Hg will have the same results as 5000 feet ad 29.5 in-Hg has at sea level. (See Chapter 4 for detailed description of the effect of altitude on vacuum.)

Caution: *Don't attempt to use the air conditioning system compressor as a vacuum pump. Refrigerant oil circulates with the refrigerant, which has a high attraction for the oil. The system compressor depends on smooth, constant oil distribution for proper operation. The compressor must not be used for evacuation because the oil cannot be properly circulated while the system is being evacuated and a low level of refrigerant oil will cause internal damage.*

Evacuating a non-accumulator type system

Note: *The following procedure DOES NOT apply to accumulator type systems such as Ford Fixed Orifice Tube (FFOT) system or General Motors' Cycling Clutch Orifice Tube (CCOT) system. A special service procedure for these systems is discussed later in this chapter.*

1 The system must be fully discharges and the test gauges must still be attached.

2 Attach the center service hose of the manifold gauge set to the inlet fitting of the vacuum pump in accordance with the pump manufacturer's instructions (see Chapter 4 for more information regarding the pump) **(see illustration)**.

3 Open the discharge valve on the vacuum pump, or remove the dust cap (if equipped) from the discharge outlet.

4 Start the vacuum pump.

5 Open the low and high side manifold hand valves all the way. Observe the low side gauge and verify that the pump draws the system down to a vacuum.

6 After about 5 minutes, note the indicated high and low side gauge readings:

   a) The low side gauge should indicate a system vacuum of 20 in-Hg or less.

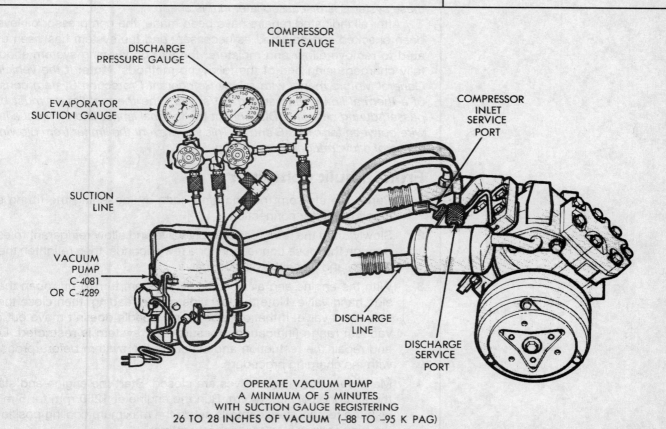

OPERATE VACUUM PUMP
A MINIMUM OF 5 MINUTES
WITH SUCTION GAUGE REGISTERING
26 TO 28 INCHES OF VACUUM (−88 TO −95 K PAG)

The correct setup for evacuating the typical non-accumulator system (Chrysler shown, others similar) - note that the center service hose of the manifold gauge set is attached to the inlet fitting of the vacuum pump

b) The high side gauge should read slightly below the zero mark on the gauge. If it doesn't, the gauge needle may be pegged against the stop. If the needle has no stop, there is a restriction in the system and evacuation cannot be continued until the restriction is located and removed.

7 After the system has been pulled down to its lowest vacuum point, close the high side valve on the manifold gauge set and turn off the vacuum pump, then note the reading on the low side gauge. Let the system stand for 5 minutes or longer and then recheck the reading on the low side gauge again.

a) If the system has lost vacuum, a leak exists. Charge the system, find the leak, repair as necessary and repeat the procedure.

b) If the reading is the same, there is no leak. Start the vacuum pump and open both hand valves. Operate the pump for 30 minutes. Then close both hand valves, turn off the vacuum pump and detach the service hose from the pump. Connect the service hose to a refrigerant supply and completely charge the system in accordance with the instructions below.

Charging (non-accumulator type systems)

Note: *The following procedure DOES NOT apply to accumulator type systems, such as Ford's Fixed Orifice Tube (FFOT) system or General Motors' Cycling Clutch Orifice Tube (CCOT) system. A special service procedure for these systems is discussed later in this chapter.*

After all indicated repairs have been made, the compressor oil level has been checked and adjusted as necessary and the system has been evacuated to remove all air and moisture, the air conditioning system should be fully charged using one of the following methods. **Note:** *If the vehicle is a General Motors model with a Low Refrigerant Protection System consisting of a thermal limiter and superheat switch, the thermal limiter must be bypassed during charging. Disconnect the thermal limiter and connect a jumper wire between terminals B and C. This will prevent the limiter from blowing because of a low refrigerant condition.*

From a bulk container

1 Purge the air from the charging hose by loosening the fitting at the manifold center connection.

2 Slowly open the refrigerant supply valve and allow refrigerant to escape through the loose connection for a few seconds, then retighten the connection and close the canister valve.

3 With the engine and air conditioning system turned off, open the high side hand valve. Note the low side gauge reading, then close the high side hand valve. If the low side gauge needle doesn't move out of the vacuum range (indicating pressure), the system is restricted. Locate and repair the restriction and evacuate the system before proceeding with the charging procedure.

4 Make sure both hand valves are closed. Start the engine and stabilize the air conditioning system. Run the engine at 1250 rpm for 5 minutes with the temperature controls set to the maximum cooling position and the blower switch on the highest setting.

5 Place the refrigerant canister on a scale, in an upright position and note its exact weight.

6   Open the valve on the bulk refrigerant container and the low side hand valve on the manifold and begin charging the system with refrigerant vapor. **Caution:** *Don't allow liquid refrigerant to enter the compressor (high) side of the system. Serious damage will result because liquid cannot be compressed.*

7   Monitor the weight change indicated on the scale. When the scale reading matches the specified amount, close the valves. **Note:** *If the capacity is not specified, add refrigerant until it just passes the sight glass, then put in an additional 4 ounces.*

8   Once the system is fully charged, close the low side hand valve and the valve on the bulk refrigerant container.

9   Detach the service hose between the bulk container and the manifold.

10 Run a performance test.

11 Remove the manifold gauge set and replace all protective caps.

Evacuating and charging accumulator systems

Note: *On the accumulator type systems used by Ford Motor Company and General Motors, evacuating and charging are combined into one service procedure. The procedures described here can be applied using either disposable cans or bulk (drum) containers.*

General Motors Cycling Clutch Orifice Tube (CCOT) system

1   If the system requires the addition of any refrigerant oil, add it now (see "Compressor oil check').

2   Place the container on a scale, weigh it and record the total weight before starting the charging procedure. Watch the scale during the charging procedure to determine when the proper amount has been dispensed into the system.

3   Connect the low side service hose to the accumulator service fitting, the center hose to the supply and the high side hose to the vacuum pump.

4   To start evacuation, slowly open the high side and low side manifold gauge hand valves and commence vacuum pump operation.
    a)   On all vehicles except 1981 and later models, evacuate the system for at least 15-minutes AFTER the low side gauge reads 28 to 29 in-Hg of vacuum or more at sea level.
    b)   On 1981 and later models, this extra 15-minutes isn't necessary.

Note: *For every 1000 feet above sea level, lower the vacuum requirement by an inch. Example: At 3000 feet, the necessary vacuum is 26.5 in-Hg (see Chapter 4).*

5   If the prescribed vacuum level cannot be reached - and maintained - close the vacuum control valve, shut off the pump and look for a leak at the hose fittings or the pump itself. When the system is completely evacuated, close the high side gauge hand valve and turn off the vacuum pump.

6   Watching the low side gauge, verify that the vacuum level holds steady for at least 5-minutes.
    a)   If it does, proceed with charging.

b) If it doesn't, add 1/2-pound of refrigerant (R134a systems only), leak test the system, repair the leaks(s) and repeat the evacuation procedure. **Note:** *R-12 systems should be brought to a qualified air conditioning repair shop.*

7 Warm up the engine to normal operating temperature. Set the air conditioning controls to the Off position. With the refrigerant supply inverted, open the can or drum valve and the low side hand valve.

8 After 1-pound of refrigerant has been dispensed, set the air conditioning controls at their normal positions and adjust the blower selector to the highest position. When the compressor engages, it acts as a suction pump, drawing in the rest of the charge. **Note:** *This procedure can be completed more quickly by placing a large volume fan in front of the condenser. Maintaining the condenser at a temperature lower than the refrigerant will enable the refrigerant to enter the system more rapidly.*

9 Turn off the valve on the refrigerant can or drum. Run the engine for another 30 seconds to clear the lines and manifold. Quickly remove the low side service hose from the accumulator fitting to prevent refrigerant loss while the engine is running. Replace the cap on the fitting.

10 Leak test the system while it's operating and verify that it works properly.

Ford Motor Company Ford Fixed Orifice Tube (FFOT) system

1 If refrigerant oil needs to be added, do so now (see "Compressor oil check').

2 Place the refrigerant drum on a scale, weigh it and record the total weight before charging begins. Watch the scale to determine when the system is fully charges.

3 Attach the manifold gauge set low side service hose to the accumulator low side service fitting. Attach the center hose to a vacuum pump. Using an adapter, connect the high side service hose to the high side service fitting on the compressor discharge line's condenser connection.

4 To begin evacuation, slowly open the high and low side **(see illustration)** manifold gauge set hand valves and start up the vacuum pump. Evacuate the system until the low side gauge reads at least 25 in-Hg and as close to 30 in-Hg as possible, then continue the evacuation an additional 15-minutes (if any components have been replaced, continue vacuum pump operation for an additional 20 to 30 minutes). **Note:** *For each 1000 feet above sea level, vacuum should be lowered by 1-inch. Example: At 4000 feet, it would have to be 25.5 in-Hg of vacuum. For other vacuum corrections, see Chapter 4.*

5 If the prescribed vacuum level cannot be reached and maintained, close the vacuum control valve, shut off the pump and look for a leak at the connections or at the pump.

6 When the system is fully evacuated, close the high side gauge valve and turn off the vacuum pump.

7 Watch the low side gauge to be sure the vacuum level holds for at least 5-minutes. If it does, proceed with charging. If it doesn't, add 1/2-pound of refrigerant and leak test the system (R134a-systems only). Repair the leak(s) and repeat the evacuation procedure. **Note:** *R-12 systems should be brought to a qualified air conditioning repair shop.*

8 With both manifold gauge set hand valves closed, detach the service hose from the vacuum pump and connect it to the refrigerant supply.

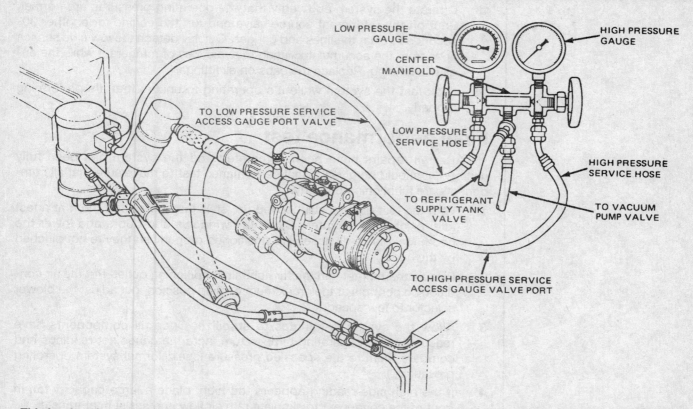

LOW PRESSURE GAUGE

HIGH PRESSURE GAUGE

CENTER MANIFOLD

LOW PRESSURE SERVICE HOSE

HIGH PRESSURE SERVICE HOSE

TO LOW PRESSURE SERVICE ACCESS GAUGE PORT VALVE

TO REFRIGERANT SUPPLY TANK VALVE

TO VACUUM PUMP VALVE

TO HIGH PRESSURE SERVICE ACCESS GAUGE VALVE PORT

This is what the gauges look like when you start the vacuum pump: both gauges read zero - and the low side gauge will continue to drop below zero into the vacuum range as the pump sucks the system dry - the reading you're looking for is at least 25 in-Hg and even 30, if you can get it

9   Loosen the center hose at the manifold gauge set and open the refrigerant drum or can tap. Allow a small amount of refrigerant to escape to purge the air and moisture from the center hose. Tighten the center hose connection at the manifold gauge set.

10   Disconnect the wiring harness snap-lock connector from the clutch cycling pressure switch. Attach a jumper wire across the 2 terminals of the connector. Open the manifold gauge set low side hand valve to allow refrigerant to enter the system. With the refrigerant supply inverted (to permit charging with liquid refrigerant), open the can or drum valve. **Warning:** *If the low side service port isn't on the accumulator, keep the refrigerant containers in an upright position, permitting charging with refrigerant vapor only.*

11   When no more refrigerant is being drawn into the system, start the engine. Move the air door lever to the vent-heat-A/C position and the blower switch to the High position. Depress the A/C On-Off pushbutton to draw the remaining refrigerant into the system.

12   Continue adding refrigerant until the specified amount is in the system. Then close the manifold gauge set low side hand valve and the refrigerant supply valve. Remove the jumper wire from the clutch cycling pressure switch connector and attach the connector to the switch. **Note:** *This charging procedure can be completed more rapidly by placing a large volume fan in front of the condenser. By keeping the condenser temperature below the temperature of the refrigerant supply, refrigerant will enter the system more rapidly.*

13 Operate the system and verify that the operating pressures are normal. Shut off the refrigerant source valve and run the engine for another 30-seconds to clear the lines and gauges. Quickly detach the low side service hose from the accumulator fitting to avoid loss of refrigerant while the engine is running. Replace the caps on all fittings.

14 Leak test the system while it's operating to ensure that it's performing properly.

Final performance test

After all repairs have been completed and the system has been fully charged, it should be given a final performance test to make sure that all components are functioning properly.

1 With the test gauges still hooked up, start the engine and run it at a fast idle for about 5-minutes. Close the windows and doors and lower the hood. Make sure all hoses are positioned properly so they're not pinched by the hood.

2 Place a thermometer in the far right air conditioning outlet. Put the air conditioning controls at their maximum cooling position, but adjust the blower selector to low speed.

3 Allow the system 5-minutes to stabilize. Once all components have reached normal operating temperature, note the gauge set readings and compare them to the specified pressure (see "Normal system operating pressures").

4 If the high side reading appears too high, place a large capacity fan in front of the condenser to simulate ram air flow and assist heat transfer.

5 The thermometer in the air conditioning outlet should read 35 to 45°F at approximately 75 to 80°F ambient temperature. Note that higher temperatures and high humidity will increase the outlet temperature.

6 If the system appears to be operating normally, stop the engine, disconnect the gauge set and replace the service fitting caps. If the system is not operating within specifications or displays other abnormal conditions, refer to the next chapter.

Converting from R-12 to R-134a
Why convert at all?

The obvious answer is: to protect the ozone layer in the upper atmosphere. Of course, it also adds resale value to your vehicle. Nevertheless, as long as your old R-12 system is still functioning correctly, there's no reason to change anything. But, if your system springs a major leak, or the compressor blows up, you may be *forced* to repair the system. At this point, you'll have to decide whether to stick with your vehicle's R-12 system or convert it to R-134a. As far as the price of the refrigerant itself, there is no question that you'll save money if you convert to R-134a. A pound of R-134a is significantly less expensive than a pound of R-12. However, the price of the refrigerant is not the only factor you'll have to consider. Converting from R-12 to R-134a can vary in price from well under a hundred to six or seven hundred dollars, depending on what components must be replaced, whether there's an aftermarket alternative to the factory retrofit kit and other factors. Deciding which way to go can be more complicated than the actual conversion procedure. And you're going to have to live with your choice as long as you own the vehicle, so we've included this section to help you decide what's best for you.

What about other refrigerants?

For now, automobile manufacturers have chosen R-134a as the long-term replacement for R-12 in automotive air conditioning systems, both in new vehicles and in retrofit applications. There are several other EPA-approved refrigerants available, but at the time this second edition was published in 2000, large-scale performance testing had not been performed on vehicles retrofitted with any refrigerants other than R-134a. If you decide to retrofit with some alternative refrigerant other than R-134a, not all of the following procedure will necessarily apply. Conversely, you may have to do some things to your system not covered here. Before you begin, make sure that you consult the refrigerant manufacturer to ensure that your vehicle's air conditioning system is suitable for conversion to that particular refrigerant. You may also want to review the EPA publications *Choosing and Using Alternative Refrigerants in Motor Vehicle Air Conditioning* and *Questions to Ask Before you Purchase an Alternative Refrigerant*. Both of these publications can be ordered by phone: EPA Ozone Protection Hotline Number: (800) 296-1996. They're also available online (http://www.epa.gov/ozone/title6/609/retrguid.html) In the future, the EPA may develop guidelines for retrofitting to refrigerants other than R-134a. At this time, however, R-134a is the only game in town.

Terminology

In the following section, we will discuss OEM vs. aftermarket options and then we'll describe the procedure for retrofitting a typical vehicle air conditioning system to R-134a. But before we begin, a brief note on terminology: When you start researching the conversion of your old R-12 system to R-134a, you will see or hear the terms "conversion" and "retrofit." Don't be confused by these two terms. In this book, they're interchangeable. They both refer to the procedure for converting an R-12 system to R-134a (or some other alternative refrigerant).

OEM retrofits

Vehicle manufacturers (also known as original equipment manufacturers, or OEMs) have developed detailed procedures and retrofit kits for most late-model R-12 equipped systems. Because late-model R-12 systems were purpose-built with the likelihood of eventual conversion in mind, they'll produce the best performance with R-134a when converted with an OEM kit. But though an OEM kit usually provides the best guarantee of retaining performance similar to the old R-12 system, it might well be an expensive solution. Some models can receive an OEM-warrantied retrofit for as little as $150, including labor, and even less, if you do the work yourself. But other OEM retrofits will run as high as $650 or more. If your vehicle is one of these expensive-to-convert models, you may want to explore the less-expensive solution of installing an aftermarket retrofit kit. If you're thinking about converting an older vehicle, you might find that - because OEM retrofit kits are mainly intended for late 1980s and early 1990s models - an aftermarket retrofit is your *only* option.

Aftermarket retrofits

Like OEM retrofit kits, aftermarket retrofits **(see illustration)** run the gamut from cheap to expensive. The "least-cost" retrofit is simple and doesn't require major component changes. Generally, the procedure consists of removing the old refrigerant, installing new fittings and an R-134a label,

A typical aftermarket R-134a retrofit kit

adding either a polyalkylene glycol (PAG) or polyol ester (POE or ester) lubricant and adding R-134a refrigerant. You will also have to replace the accumulator or receiver/drier too. For many vehicles, this simple, least-cost retrofit will provide performance that, although slightly diminished, is adequate for the climate and conditions under which the vehicle will be operated.

A least-cost retrofit, however, will not always provide a satisfactory solution for all vehicles. On such models, you might have to also replace the hoses or one of the more expensive components such as the compressor, condenser or evaporator. The cost of such a retrofit varies wildly but usually falls somewhere in between an expensive OEM retrofit and the least-cost aftermarket retrofit is a third option. Before going down this road, you will need to consult with an expert at your local automotive air conditioning shop or with a dealer service technician to learn as much as you can about the system in your vehicle.

Picking the right solution for you

When determining what kind of retrofit to do on your vehicle, discuss "the three C's" - cost, climate and components - with your local dealer or automotive air conditioning shop.

Cost: How much are you willing to spend? How much longer will you own the vehicle? Is the vehicle a refrigerant leaker or is this the first time in the life of the vehicle that the air conditioning system has been serviced?

Climate: Do you need adequate performance (you only take the car out on Sunday in St. Paul), or do you need polar-level performance (you use the car six days a week in San Antonio)? Even if you live in a hot and/or humid climate, are you so concerned about cost that you prefer the least-cost retrofit, even if that retrofit will not, in your technician's judgment, provide performance comparable to that of the old R-12 system?

Components: Are the components in the system in good shape? Are they compatible with R-134a or will they have to be replaced?

If the performance of an R-12 system is only marginal, retrofitting alone will not make it better. In fact, since all but a handful of late-model R-12 systems were *not* designed for use with R-134a, be ready for a slight drop in efficiency. In most parts of the country, this reduction won't be significant, and you may not even notice the difference.

In warmer climates, however, where an air conditioning system runs at full blast many months a year, a least-cost retrofit may not produce satisfactory performance. In that case, ask a professional technician to recommend what additional steps are most appropriate, a larger condenser, for example, or adding a fan or high-pressure cut-off switch. Also, on older models, it may be necessary to replace some components. R-134a operates at higher pressure than R-12, and this higher pressure puts more stress on the system, so older, worn components are more likely to fail. Look at it this way: Although these problems can drive up the price of a retrofit, they're still cost effective in comparison to replacing the entire air conditioning system!

Another problem with older vehicles is that some of the system components, even if they function satisfactorily with R-12, were not specifically designed to operate with R-134a, so they might wear out prematurely when subjected to the higher operating pressure of R-134a. Their service life could be shortened only slightly, or a great deal. Only large-scale durability testing on thousands of retrofitted vehicles will provide a better understanding of how retrofit affects the service life of each system component.

Keep in mind that there is no such thing as a "universal retrofit procedure," or a one-size-fits-all kit that will provide all the necessary parts to guarantee a successful retrofit for every make and model. Even within particular models, retrofit requirements may vary. A particular make, model and year vehicle driven for 90,000 miles in Houston may require a more extensive retrofit than the same make, model and year driven for 35,000 miles in Minneapolis.

EPA Requirements for Retrofit

The following modifications are the *minimum* steps required by EPA regulations before an alternative refrigerant is substituted as a replacement for R-12:

- Unique service fittings must be used in order to minimize the risk of cross-contamination of either the air-conditioning system or the service facility's recycling equipment.
- The new refrigerant must be identified by a uniquely colored label.
- All R-12 must be properly removed from the system before filling the system with an alternative refrigerant. Separate, dedicated EPA-approved equipment must be used to recover the R-12 from the system.
- In order to prevent the discharge of refrigerant into the atmosphere, a high-pressure compressor shutoff switch must be installed on any system equipped with a pressure relief device.
- In addition (even though this book is concerned only with R-134a), alternative refrigerant blends that contain HCFC-22 must be used with barrier hoses.

A few more words on non-R-134a refrigerants

A number of refrigerants other than R-134a have been listed by the EPA as "acceptable" under its Significant New Alternatives Policy (SNAP) program, or are under SNAP review. Keep in mind that the SNAP program evaluates substitutes *only for their effect on human health and the environment*, and *not* for performance or durability. None of these refrigerants have been endorsed by the OEMs, and none of them have undergone extensive testing in a wide range of vehicle models. In addition, most are currently not readily available in all areas of the country.

Although some manufacturers of alternative refrigerants may be marketing their products as "drop-ins," there is really no such thing as a drop-in product according to the minimum requirements of the EPA regulations described above. These regulations apply to *any* substitute for R-12, so there is no such thing as a refrigerant that can literally be dropped in on top of the existing R-12 in the system.

Some air conditioning service technicians seem to believe that R-134a is only a temporary replacement for R-12, to be used until a drop-in replacement that cools well and does not require a retrofit becomes available. If your neighborhood tech tells you such nonsense, don't believe him! Current research indicates that no such replacement refrigerant exists. The automotive industry conducted extensive research and testing on many potential substitutes for R-12 before selecting R-134a. The EPA is not aware of any plans by the automakers to use any refrigerant in new vehicles other than R-134a.

R-134a Refrigerant

Toxicity, flammability and corrosion

Based on current toxicity data, R-134a is regarded as one of the safest refrigerants ever introduced,. The chemical industry's Program for Alternative Fluorocarbon Toxicity Testing (PAFT) tested R-134a in a full battery of laboratory animal toxicity studies. The results indicate that R-134a does not pose a danger of cancer or birth defects. R-134a is even being used in metered-dose inhalers in Europe! But, when handling R-134a, as with any other chemical, be sure to work in a well-ventilated area. It is never a good idea to inhale any vapor to such an extent that it replaces the oxygen in your lungs.

OEM automotive engineers and chemical manufacturers have examined the flammability and corrosivity of each potential R-12 substitute. Like R-12, R-134a is not flammable at ambient temperatures and atmospheric pressures. However, R-134a service equipment and vehicle air conditioning systems should not be pressure tested or leak tested with compressed air. Some mixtures of air and R-134a are combustible at elevated pressures. These mixtures may be potentially dangerous, causing injury or property damage. If you're going to pressure test the system for leaks, use *nitrogen*, which is inert and won't produce an explosive or flammable mixture. Finally, regardless of what you may have heard about R-134a's corrosivity, it is *not* corrosive to steel, aluminum or copper.

How Much to Charge into the System

The amount of R-134a charged into the system is generally 80 to 90 percent of the amount of R-12 in the system. Refer to the refrigerant capacity specifications beginning on page 5-104.

Lubricants

PAGs vs. esters

The mineral oil used in an R-12 system cannot be sufficiently transported throughout the air conditioning system by R-134a. Automobile manufacturers tested both polyalkylene glycol (PAG) and polyol ester (POE or ester) for refrigerant/lubricant miscibility (how well it mixes with refrigerant in any proportion), lubricity (how slippery it is), chemical stability and materials compatibility. In the process of developing their recommendations, they also considered the additives and conditioners in the oils. Most - but not all -manufacturers chose to use PAG lubricants in new vehicles equipped with R-134a, and they also recommend PAG lubricants for retrofits. Some compressor manufacturers put PAG in new compressors, some use esters and some sell their compressors dry.

PAGs are "hygroscopic," which means that they will readily absorb moisture from the atmosphere when exposed. Many aftermarket air conditioning component suppliers choose to use ester lubricants because of their concern that the hygroscopic characteristics of PAGs may limit their lubricating ability and introduce corrosion into an air conditioning system. Esters are also hygroscopic (although less so than PAGs), so you must still be careful not to allow excess moisture into the system. **Warning:** *Use PVC-coated gloves (or, if that is impractical, barrier creams) and safety goggles when handling PAGs or esters. Prolonged skin contact and/or even brief eye contact can cause irritations such as stinging and burning sensations. Also, avoid breathing any vapors produced by these lubricants, and make sure to use them in well-ventilated areas. Finally, be sure to keep both PAGs and esters* *in tightly sealed containers, both so that humidity does not contaminate the oil, and so that vapors do not escape.*

Flushing

The amount of mineral oil that can safely be left in a system after retrofitting, without affecting performance, is still being debated, but appears to have been a subject of excessive concern. Back in the early 90s, when manufacturers began converting to R-134a, there was a widespread concern that *any* mineral oil left in the system might cause system failure. Eight years later, that fear has been proven unfounded. As long as *most* of the old mineral oil is removed, any residual R-12 oil remaining in the system seems to have no significant effect on system performance. (Nevertheless, removing the mineral oil may require draining some components on certain vehicles.) Unless the vehicle manufacturer - or the aftermarket kit instruction sheet - specifically recommends flushing the system during the retrofit procedure, you can assume that flushing is not necessary. (Readers who obtain the SAE's J1661 document will note that it recommends flushing before retrofit. However, you can disregard this information because the SAE no longer believes that flushing is critical to a successful retrofit.)

Hoses and O-Rings

When R-134a was first introduced, the OEMs recommended that all non-barrier/nitrile hoses be replaced during a retrofit. This was because early laboratory tests indicated that the small R-134a molecules leaked through the walls of non-barrier hoses more readily than the larger R-12 molecules did. In the lab, this resulted in unacceptably high leakage rates. More recent testing, however, has shown that the lubricant used in automotive air conditioning systems is absorbed into the hose to create a natural barrier to R-134a permeation. In most cases, the R-12 system hoses will perform well, provided they are in good condition. Of course, if you note that the old hoses are cracked or damaged, they should be replaced with barrier hoses.

Unless a fitting has been loosened during the retrofit, replacement should be unnecessary. However, most retrofit instructions specify that the O-rings be replaced and the new O-rings lubricated with mineral oil.

Compressors

The OEMs originally believed that a retrofit would require a new compressor. This belief helped create horror stories about the high expense of retrofitting. Now it is generally accepted that most compressors that are functioning well in R-12 systems will continue to operate effectively after the system has been retrofitted. When a compressor is first run with R-12, a thin film of metal chloride forms on bearing surfaces and acts as an excellent anti-wear agent. This film continues to protect even after a system has been converted to R-134a (which is one reason why a new R-12 compressor may fail prematurely if installed in an R-134a system without the benefit of a break-in period on R-12).

A few of the older compressor designs use seals that are not compatible with R-134a or the new lubricants. For example, any compressor that has seals made of Viton® should not be used with R-134a because the refrigerant will cause the seals to swell excessively. If you're not sure about the compressor in an older vehicle, check with the compressor manufacturer, a dealer service department or an automotive air conditioning shop. They can help you identify a compressor that's going to be incompatible with R-134a or the new lubricants.

Of course, any compressor that's leaking, making funny noises or worn out should be replaced during the retrofit procedure. If you're going to buy a new or rebuilt compressor, make sure that the replacement compressor is approved for R-134a by its supplier.

Desiccants, Accumulators, Receiver/Driers

R-12 systems use an XH-5 desiccant; R-134a systems use either XH-7 or XH-9 desiccant. Some manufacturers recommend routine replacement of the accumulator or receiver/drier to one containing XH-7 or XH-9 during the retrofit procedure. Other manufacturers recommend leaving it alone. They generally agree, however, that the accumulator or receiver/drier should be replaced if the system is opened up for major repair on a vehicle more than five years old, or on one with over 70,000 miles on the odometer. If your vehicle falls into that category, make sure that you use a new accumulator or receiver/drier that uses R-134a-compatible desiccant. In addition, systems with silica gel should also be switched to XH-7 or XH-9 desiccant.

Condensers and Pressure Cutout Switches

When retrofit kits were first developed several years ago, manufacturers thought that the condenser and perhaps even the evaporator would have to be replaced to maintain an acceptable level of cooling performance on a retro-fitted system. Now, it is generally accepted that if an R-12 system is operating within the manufacturer's specifications, there may be no need to replace either part.

However, R-134a operates at higher vapor pressures, which may result in reduced condenser capacity. When retrofitting, you should consider how the air flow and condenser design on the vehicle will affect the success of the retrofit. Based on recent real-world experience, the installation of a pusher-type engine/condenser cooling fan mounted in front of the condenser will improve the performance of an air conditioning system on a vehicle that has experienced of a loss of cooling capacity after a retrofit.

You should also be aware that bent, misshapen or incorrectly positioned airflow dams and directors can also affect performance. Some OEMs even include hood seal kits as part of the recommended retrofit procedure. In addition, systems that are not equipped with a high-pressure cutout switch should have one installed to prevent damage to air conditioning system parts and to prevent refrigerant emissions. The installation of a high-pressure cutout switch will shut off the compressor when high pressures occur, reducing the likelihood of venting the refrigerant and overheating the engine cooling system.

Refrigerant Controls

Refrigerant controls - whether orifice tubes or expansion valves that meter refrigerant flow, or pressure cycling switches or other pressure controls designed to protect against freezing - may have to be changed during the course of a retrofit.

Cautions

1   *Refrigerant is under pressure. Do NOT begin this procedure until you have obtained suitable protective eye wear.*

2   *Do not allow refrigerant and lubricant vapor or mist to contact any part of your body. Exposure can irritate your eyes, nose, throat and/or skin. Wear protective latex or rubber gloves when handling refrigerant oil.*

3   *Do NOT pressurize R-134a equipment or air conditioning systems with compressed air. Some mixtures of air and R-134a are combustible at higher pressure. If testing for leaks, use nitrogen instead.*

4   Always work in a well-ventilated area.

5   Always use U.L approved air conditioning service equipment.

6   Wipe off all spilled lubricant immediately. Some R-134a lubricants can damage painted surfaces and plastic parts.

A typical R-134a conversion

For the following procedure, we selected a 1986 Oldsmobile with a GM accumulator-type air conditioning system. Even though there's no such thing as a "typical" retrofit, the following conversion involves most of the issues with which you'll be confronted when converting your vehicle's air conditioning system.

Perform a visual inspection

1   Inspect the condition of the compressor drivebelt. If it's damaged or worn, replace it. Inspect the condition of the condenser fins. If they're bent or clogged up with bugs or dirt, clean and straighten them. Verify that the fan operates correctly. Check the engine coolant level.

2   Carefully inspect the condition of the refrigerant hoses. If they're in good condition, they should work fine with R-134a. But if there's any doubt about their condition, replace them. Make sure that the new hoses are approved for R-134a. Remember, new R-12 hoses which have never had any R-12 run through them will probably leak if installed in an R-134a system because they lack the protective barrier of the old mineral oil that coats the inside of used R-12 hoses.

Do a performance/leak check

3   Start the engine and let it warm up. Turn on the air conditioning system and let it get as cold as it can. Using a thermometer, measure the evaporator output temperature at the dash vent nearest the evaporator (usually one of the center vents) and jot down this figure (see page 89). You'll want to compare this value with the evaporator output temperature after the system has been converted to R-134a.

4   If you have a set of R-12 gauges, measure the high and low side pressures of the system. Again, jot down these numbers for future reference. If you don't have a set of gauges, ask the technician at your local air conditioning shop to make these measurements for you.

5   If you have a leak detector, check for leaks now. Mark any obvious leaks or suspicious areas and make a note to inspect and repair them once the system is opened up. If you don't have a leak detector, make sure that the air conditioning shop checks for leaks before recovering the R-12 in the system.

Flush the system, if necessary

6   If the compressor has failed, be sure to have the system thoroughly flushed by a professional air conditioning technician before proceeding. He will get most of the compressor material out of the system so that it doesn't harm the new compressor or clog up an expansion valve or some other component. On some expansion valve systems, he may even recommend installing an inline filter on the high side to catch any of the remaining bits and pieces (orifice valve systems aren't as susceptible to damage from tiny bits of compressor material in the refrigerant).

Recover all R-12 from the system

7   Unless you have your own EPA-approved recovery and recycling equipment, drive the vehicle to an automotive air conditioning shop and have the system discharged. Do NOT discharge R-12 into the atmosphere! R-12 destroys the protective layer of ozone in the upper atmosphere. Besides, it's worth money. Remember, they don't make R-12 anymore, so the R-12 in your system is going to be reused after it's been recovered and cleaned. So be SURE to ask for a credit for any R-12 that's recovered from your system. Most reputable shops will offer you a credit for the R-12 that's recovered from your system. The amount they'll offer is usually the current market value of R-12, minus their labor for recovering and recycling it. If a shop refuses to offer you a credit for the R-12 in your system, shop around and find one that does.

8   It is critical that all R-12 be completely removed before converting to R-134a, which is why this part of the conversion must be handled by an automotive air conditioning shop with specially designed EPA-approved recovery equipment. Failure to remove all R-12 will lead to high system pressures, poor air conditioning performance and system failure.

9   If you're curious about what's involved in recovering the R-12 from the system, the procedure is as follows. If the system is operational, the air conditioning technician will run the engine at a fast idle (about 1000 rpm) for ten minutes with the system blower on LOW and the maximum cold setting. This procedure will maximize the refrigerant oil left in the accumulator, or the receiver/drier, and the compressor before it's removed. He'll note the discharge/suction pressures and duct temperatures for future reference. It's not a bad idea to ask him specifically to measure the pressure and temperature because these figures will serve as a benchmark against which you can compare the performance of your system after it's been converted to R-134a. Then he'll check the system for refrigerant leaks using a leak detector. (If the system is already discharged, he'll pump it up with a static charge sufficient to produce at least 50 psi, which is adequate for leak detection purposes). Then he'll note any leaks detected so they can be repaired when the system is opened. The shop will then thoroughly recover all refrigerant from the system.

Remove the old oil from the compressor and install new compressor seals

10   Drive the vehicle home. Remove the compressor from the vehicle, then drain and carefully measure all residual refrigerant oil (see illustration). Jot down the amount of oil removed from the compressor. If the compressor has no drain plug, hold the compressor upside down (with the suction/discharge ports pointing down) and rotate the compressor shaft.

11   On GM vehicles, and on other vehicles (if included in the retrofit kit), remove the old compressor seals and install the new compressor seals (see illustrations). If the old compressor seals are left in the compressor on a GM vehicle, the system might begin to leak refrigerant. On Ford, Chrysler and import vehicles, the seals on most models are compatible with R-134a and shouldn't pose a problem. Of course, if the seals show any signs of damage or wear, now is the time to replace them. Make sure that you specify you want R-134a compatible seals.

Carefully pour the lubricant in the compressor into a graduated container so that you can determine how much oil was in there

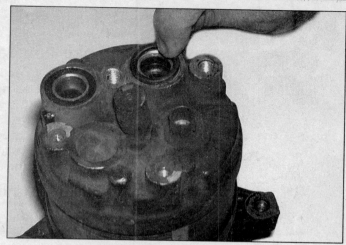

On GM vehicles, and on other vehicles (if included in the retrofit kit), remove the old compressor seals . . .

. . . and install the new compressor seals

Replace the accumulator or receiver/drier with an R-134a compatible unit

13 Remove the accumulator or receiver/drier. Drill a couple of holes in the bottom of the old unit, then drain the oil and carefully measure it **(see illustrations)**. Add this number to the amount already removed from the compressor. Look up the specified amount of refrigerant oil in the system. By now, you should have removed more than half of the old R-12 mineral oil in the system. (If not, you'll have to drain some of the other components.)

14 Make sure that the new accumulator or receiver/drier is R-134a compatible. The new unit should contain an R-134a compatible dessicant (XH-7 or XH-9). Most new accumulators and receiver/driers are compatible with R-12 and R-134a, so they can be installed in either type of system.

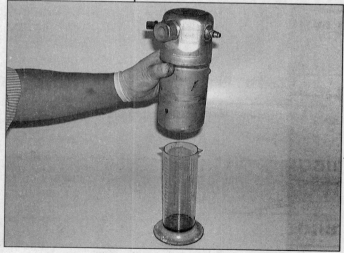

Drill a couple of holes in the bottom of the old accumulator or receiver/drier unit . . .

. . . then drain the oil into a graduate container and carefully measure it

Repair any damaged or worn components

16 Make any necessary repairs to the air conditioning system. If any hoses show signs of leakage, or have been damaged, replace them with R-134a compatible hoses. Ditto for any other damaged or worn components. Now is the time to do it, while you've got the system apart. If you need to replace a corroded or leaking condenser or evaporator, consider upgrading to a slightly larger capacity unit, if it will fit. Get advice on what works from a professional air conditioning technician and consult with your local automotive parts store.

Add R-134a compatible oil to the system

17 Referring to "Refrigerant oil capacity," determine the specified amount of oil in the system, then compare this figure to the amount of mineral oil already removed from the system when you drained the compressor and accumulator or receiver/drier. Verify that at least half of the old mineral oil has been removed from the system. If less than half of the original oil has been extracted, then you'll have to remove and drain some more system components (condenser, evaporator, hoses, etc.) until over half of the old oil has been removed. If you're unable to extract half of the old oil by draining components, flush out the components with an approved flushing solvent such as Dura 141 Flush solvent, or a suitable equivalent product. Or, have your local automotive air conditioning shop perform a closed-loop liquid flush.

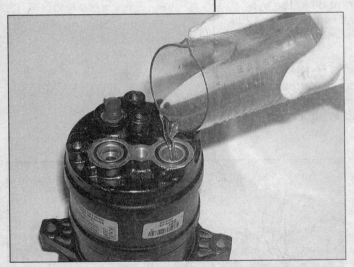

Add the new PAG or ester oil to the compressor

18 Add the new PAG or ester refrigerant oil to the system. Some technicians recommend putting half of the oil in the accumulator or receiver/drier and putting the other half in the compressor. Others put all of it in the compressor **(see illustration)**. **Warning:** *Do not allow PAG or ester lubricant vapor or mist to contact any part of your body. Exposure can irritate your eyes, nose, throat and/or skin. Wear protective latex or rubber gloves when handling PAG or ester lubricants.* **Caution:** *If you have any PAG or ester oil left over, make sure that the container is tightly sealed. PAG and ester oils are extremely hygroscopic.*

Install the compressor and accumulator or receiver/drier

19 Install the compressor. Make sure you don't spill any of the new oil inside the compressor.

20 Install the accumulator or receiver/drier. Again, make sure you don't spill any of the new oil inside the unit.

21 Install any other components that were removed for replacement, draining or flushing.

Replace the O-rings and reconnect all fittings

22 Your retrofit kit may or may not include a complete set of O-rings. Most GM kits include them (if your GM kit doesn't include new O-rings, go get a set of R-134a compatible O-rings for your system at an automotive parts

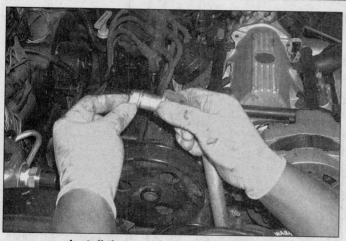

Install the new O-rings at all fittings

Remove the old R-12 service ports . . .

store). Most Ford, Chrysler and import kits don't include O-rings. Why? Because these manufacturers have for some time now used O-rings and compressor seals that are compatible with R-134a and with the new synthetic refrigerant lubricants. Yet we have heard first-hand accounts of converted systems on vehicles with supposedly compatible O-rings leaking because the O-rings weren't replaced. A month after a retrofit, the owner had to disassemble the system, replace all the O-rings (and the compressor seals), then evacuate and recharge the system. So our recommendation is to REPLACE all the O-rings. "Better safe than sorry," as the old saying goes. Besides, you already have the system apart anyway, so it's not that big a deal. If your retrofit kit doesn't include the O-rings and compressor seals, buy an O-ring kit from an automotive parts store. Make sure that the O-rings are R-134a and PAG or ester oil compatible.

23 Lubricate the new O-rings with PAG or ester oil. **Warning:** *Do not allow PAG or ester lubricant vapor or mist to contact any part of your body. Exposure can irritate your eyes, nose, throat and/or skin. Wear protective latex or rubber gloves when handling PAG or ester lubricants.*

24 Install the new O-rings at all fittings **(see illustration)**.

25 Tighten all fittings securely.

26 With the system now sealed up, manually turn the compressor clutch hub a dozen or more revolutions to circulate oil from the compressor. **Caution:** *Failure to circulate refrigerant oil throughout the compressor could result in damage to the compressor. Fluid is not compressible, so if all the lubricant is located in one chamber inside the compressor, it might create a hydrostatic lock, damaging the compressor internals.*

Install R-134a conversion ports

27 Remove the old R-12 service ports **(see illustrations)**, and install the R-134a conversion service ports, which should be included in your retrofit kit.

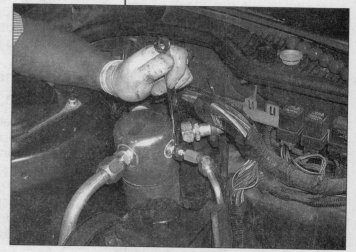

. . . and install the new R-134a ports

Some kits include special plastic bands that can be heat shrunk onto the new fittings to remind service people that the system has been retrofitted for R-134a

Install the refrigerant conversion label

Conversion ports are designed to disable the R-12 ports. Once they're installed, only R-134a compatible equipment can be used on the system. Some kits provide plastic tags that can be installed on the new fittings to indicate that only R-134a equipment can be used on the fittings **(see illustration)**.

28 Block off any service ports that are no longer utilized with permanent service caps, which should also be included in your kit, if this step applies to your system.

Install the R-134a label

29 Install the refrigerant conversion label **(see illustration)**, which should be included in your retrofit kit. This label alerts a future owner, or a technician who might service your vehicle (and you, if you forget!), that the system has been converted to R-134a. Conversion labels also provide specific information regarding the amount of R-134a in the system and the type and amount of refrigerant oil used. If there is a R-12 service label, either cover it up with the new R-134a label, or remove it or cross it out with a laundry marker to make sure that nobody is confused about the contents of your system.

Evacuate the system and recharge the system with R-134a

30 Drive the vehicle to an automotive air conditioning shop to have the system evacuated and recharged. The shop will evacuate the system **(see illustration)** for at least 30 minutes (at least 45 minutes for dual-evaporator systems) at 29 in-Hg of vacuum (minus 1.0 in-Hg for each 1000 feet above sea level) **(see illustration)**.

31 The shop will then recharge the system with R-134a. The amount they'll use varies from one model to another, but is approximately 80 to 85 percent of the originally specified R-12 charge.

Typical evacuation setup

Typical charging setup

32 Then the shop will leak test the system with an R-134a compatible leak detector to make sure that all fittings are tight enough and none of the new O-rings are leaking.

Perform a post-retrofit performance/leak check

33 Unless you have a set of R-134a gauges, have the shop performance check the system so you can compare the post-retrofit readings with the pressure and temperature readings taken before converting the system. Expect to see about a 5 to 20 percent increase in discharge pressures and vent outlet temperature during a hot idle.

34 If the vehicle tends to run a little hot, or is operated in extremely hot climates, the retrofitted system may not be able to maintain discharge pressures within reasonable limits, or may put out insufficient cooling air. On such vehicles, the easiest fix is to install either an extra pusher-type condenser fan, or even a higher-efficiency condenser.

Resources

The above summary should be all the information that most do-it-yourselfers will need to perform a successful and satisfactory conversion. However, we've included the following list of resources for those who want to know even more about retrofitting older systems.

1 Most refrigerant, lubricant and both OEM and aftermarket component manufacturers include documentation for their own guidelines and recommendations with their respective products. Some suppliers also provide information at their own websites. And some individuals - both professional technicians and do-it-yourselfers - have published their own experiences with retrofitting over the Net. Go to your search engine and type in: "R-134a air conditioning retrofit" or something similar. We found over a hundred websites devoted exclusively to retrofitting older systems.

2   The EPA is compiling a list of organizations that offer either classroom or home-study (videotape/workbook) retrofit training (these courses are intended for training professional technicians, but a knowledgeable enthusiast should be able to purchase such materials from the EPA). For EPA's current list, see "Resources for Retrofit Training" at http://www.epa.gov/ozone/title6/609/retrguid.html.

3   The Society of Automotive Engineers (SAE) provides guidelines for air conditioning system retrofits in publication J1661. This and other SAE air conditioning documents can be ordered from the SAE website at http://www.sae.org.

System Operating pressures (domestic vehicles)

Manufacturer Year Model (or type of system)	Low side gauge (evaporator suction)	High side gauge (discharge)

Note: *The following pressure specifications are for systems in good operating condition, at sea level and (unless otherwise noted) at an ambient air temperature of 80°F.*

American Motors Corporation (AMC)

1980 through 1988 (all models)	15 to 24	208 to 250

Buick

1980 and 1981	24 to 35	150 to 220
1982 through 1987		
FWD vehicles	22 to 29	165 to 205
RWD vehicles	24 to 30	130 to 190
1989 and 1990		
Automatic systems		
Reatta and Riviera	27	178
All other automatic systems	22 to 29	165 to 200
Manually operated systems		
CCOT systems	22 to 28	165 to 200
V5 systems	29 to 35	not available
1991		
Automatic systems		
Electra and LeSabre	22 to 29	165 to 200
Reatta and Riviera	27	178
Manual systems		
Century	37 to 47	150 to 335
LeSabre	22 to 40	135 to 300
Park Avenue	not available	not available
Regal	32 to 47	225 to 335
Roadmaster	29 to 36	190 to 265
Silhouette	not available	not available
Skylark	37 to 47	150 to 450
1992		
Automatic systems		
LeSabre, Park Avenue and Riviera	22 to 40	135 to 300
Roadmaster	not available	not available
Manual systems		
Century	37 to 47	150 to 335
LeSabre and Park Avenue	22 to 40	135 to 300
Regal	32 to 47	225 to 335
Roadmaster	29 to 36	190 to 265
Skylark	37 to 47	150 to 450
1993		
Automatic systems		
LeSabre, Park Avenue and Riviera	22 to 40	135 to 300
Roadmaster	29 to 42	150 to 330
Manual systems		
Century	43	320
LeSabre and Park Avenue	22 to 40	135 to 300
Regal	32 to 47	225 to 335
Roadmaster	29 to 36	190 to 265
Skylark	37 to 47	150 to 450

Manufacturer Year Model (or type of system)	Low side gauge (evaporator suction)	High side gauge (discharge)
1994		
Automatic systems		
LeSabre and Park Avenue	26 to 43	150 to 240
Roadmaster	36	315
Manual systems		
Century	26	200
LeSabre and Park Avenue	22 to 40	135 to 300
Regal	42	340
Roadmaster	36	315
Skylark	25 to 55	150 to 350
1995 and 1996		
Automatic systems		
LeSabre and Park Avenue	26 to 43	150 to 240
Regal	37	275
Riviera	25 to 30	140 to 190
Roadmaster	36	315
Manual systems		
Century	21 to 29	115 to 200
LeSabre and Park Avenue	35 to 43	190 to 240
Regal	42	340
Roadmaster	36	315
Skylark	25 to 55	150 to 350
Skylark	25 to 55	150 to 350
1997		
Automatic systems		
Century and Regal	42	340
LeSabre and Regency	29 to 37	185 to 245
Park Avenue	37 to 43	180 to 240
Riviera	25 to 36	140 to 205
Manual systems		
Century and Regal	42	340
LeSabre	29 to 37	185 to 245
Skylark	25 to 45	150 to 350
1998		
Automatic systems		
Century and Regal	42	340
LeSabre and Regency	29 to 37	185 to 245
Park Avenue	37 to 43	180 to 240
Riviera	25 to 36	140 to 205
Manual systems		
Century and Regal	42	340
LeSabre	29 to 37	185 to 245
Skylark	25 to 45	150 to 350
1999		
Automatic systems		
Century and Regal	42	340
LeSabre	29 to 37	185 to 245
Park Avenue	37 to 43	180 to 240
Riviera	25 to 36	140 to 205
Manual systems		
Century and Regal	42	340
LeSabre	29 to 37	185 to 245

Heating and air conditioning

Manufacturer Year Model (or type of system)	Low side gauge (evaporator suction)	High side gauge (discharge)
Cadillac		
1980 and 1981	24 to 35	150 to 220
1982 through 1989		
FWD vehicles	22 to 29	165 to 205
RWD vehicles	24 to 30	130 to 190
1990 and 1991	22 to 29	165 to 200
1992		
Brougham, Deville and Fleetwood	22 to 29	165 to 200
Eldorado and Seville	not available	not available
1993		
Brougham	32	235
DeVille and Fleetwood	22 to 29	165 to 200
Eldorado and Seville	not available	not available
1994		
DeVille, Eldorado and Seville	not available	not available
Fleetwood	33	300
1995		
Concours, DeVille, Eldorado and Seville	not available	not available
Fleetwood	36	315
1996		
Concours, DeVille, Eldorado and Seville	21 to 36	165 to 205
Fleetwood	36	315
1997		
Catera	28 to 30	145 to 261
Concours, DeVille, Eldorado and Seville	31 to 36	165 to 205
1998		
Catera	28 to 30	145 to 261
Concours, DeVille and Eldorado	31 to 36	165 to 205
Seville	34 to 40	
1999		
Catera	28 to 30	145 to 261
DeVille and Eldorado	31 to 36	165 to 205
Escalade	34	228
Seville	34 to 40	200 to 220
Chevrolet		
1980 and 1981	24 to 35	150 to 220
1982 through 1984		
FWD vehicles	22 to 29	165 to 205
RWD vehicles	24 to 30	130 to 190
1985 through 1988		
Spectrum and Sprint	21 to 28	206 to 213
All other models		
FWD vehicles	22 to 29	165 to 205
RWD vehicles	24 to 30	130 to 190
1989 and 1990		
Automatic systems		
Corvette	32	235
All other automatic systems	22 to 29	165 to 200
Manually operated systems		
CCOT systems	22 to 28	165 to 200
V5 systems	29 to 35	not available
1991		
Camaro	29 to 42	150 to 330
Caprice	29 to 36	190 to 265
Cavalier	37 to 47	150 to 325
Corvette		
Automatic system	32	235
Manual system	not available	not available
Lumina	32 to 47	225 to 335
All other models	not available	not available
1992		
Camaro	29 to 42	150 to 330
Caprice	29 to 36	190 to 265
Cavalier	37 to 47	150 to 325
Lumina	32 to 47	225 to 335
All other models	not available	not available
1993		
Blazer, Lumina and S-10 pick-up	32 to 47	225 to 335
Camaro	25 to 43	165 to 270
Caprice and Corvette	29 to 36	190 to 265
Cavalier	37 to 47	150 to 325
Corvette		
Automatic system	29 to 36	190 to 265
Manual system	not available	not available
Lumina APV	30 to 49	260 to 380
All other models	not available	not available
1994		
Astro van, full-size pick-up and Suburban	37	290
Beretta and Corsica	25 to 55	150 to 350
Blazer	32	225
Camaro	21 to 29	115 to 200
Caprice	36	315
Cavalier	27 to 65	150 to 325
Corvette		
Automatic system	22 to 29	165 to 200
Manual system	22 to 29	165 to 200
Full-size van	32	175
Lumina	42	340
Lumina APV	42	325
S-10 pick-up	21	259
1995		
Astro and full-size vans	37	290
Beretta and Corsica	25 to 45	150 to 330
Blazer and S-10 pick-up	26	299
Camaro	21 to 29	115 to 200
Caprice and Impala SS	36	315
Cavalier	27 to 65	150 to 325
Corvette		
Automatic system	22 to 29	165 to 200
Manual system	28	170
Full-size pick-up, Suburban and Tahoe	28	320
Lumina and Monte Carlo	42	340
Lumina APV		
3.1L engine	36	315
3.8L engine	42	325
1996		
Astro van	37	290
Beretta and Corsica	25 to 45	150 to 330
Blazer and S-10 pick-up	26	299
Camaro	21 to 29	115 to 200
Caprice, Impala SS and Lumina Van	36	315
Cavalier	27 to 65	150 to 325
Corvette		
Automatic system	25 to 28	211 to 238
Manual system	28	170
Full-size pick-up and van, Suburban and Tahoe	28	320
Lumina and Monte Carlo	42	340

Manufacturer Year Model (or type of system)	Low side gauge (evaporator suction)	High side gauge (discharge)
1997		
Astro van	37	290
Blazer and S-10 pick-up	26	299
Camaro		
3.8L engine	25 to 37	115 to 200
5.7L engine	21 to 29	115 to 200
Cavalier	32 to 65	150 to 324
Corvette		
Automatic system	30	not available
Manual system	not available	not available
Full-size pick-up, Suburban and Tahoe	28	320
Full-size van	39	251
Grand Prix, Lumina and Monte Carlo	42	340
Malibu	32 to 50	150 to 325
Venture van	32	286
1998		
Automatic systems		
Blazer	26	299
Corvette	30	210
Manual systems		
Astro van	37	290
Blazer and S-10 pick-up	26	299
Camaro		
3.8L engine	25 to 37	115 to 200
5.7L engine	21 to 29	115 to 200
Cavalier	32 to 65	150 to 324
Corvette	30	175
Full-size pick-up, Suburban and Tahoe	28	320
Full-size van	39	251
Lumina and Monte Carlo	42	340
Malibu	32 to 50	150 to 325
Metro	30 to 47	185 to 228
Prizm	34 to 40	270 to 305
Tracker	34 to 40	228 to 263
Venture van		
Without rear A/C	32	286
With rear A/C	42	325
1999		
Automatic systems		
Blazer and Envoy van	26	299
Corvette	30	155
Manual systems		
Astro van	37	290
Blazer and S-10 pick-up	32	228
Camaro		
3.8L engine	25 to 37	115 to 200
5.7L engine	21 to 29	115 to 200
Cavalier	32 to 65	150 to 324
Corvette	30	155
Full-size pick-up, Suburban and Tahoe	34	228
Full-size van	39	251
Lumina and Monte Carlo	42	340
Malibu	32 to 50	150 to 325
Metro	30 to 47	185 to 228
Prizm	34 to 40	270 to 305
Silverado full-size pick-up	44	204
Venture van		
Without rear A/C	32	286
With rear A/C	42	325

Manufacturer Year Model (or type of system)	Low side gauge (evaporator suction)	High side gauge (discharge)
Chrysler		
1980 (all models)	10 to 30	140 to 240
1981 through 1983		
FWD vehicles	20 to 30	140 to 240
RWD vehicles	20 to 30	115 to 240
1984 through 1987		
FWD vehicles	16 to 30	180 to 235
RWD vehicles	12 to 22	170 to 210
1990		
Automatic systems		
Fixed displacement compressor	16 to 30	180 to 235
Variable displacement compressor	16 to 38	180 to 235
Manual systems	20 to 35	140 to 240
1991		
Fifth Avenue and Imperial	20 to 30	140 to 240
Town and Country	10 to 35	140 to 210
All other models	20 to 35	140 to 240
1992		
Automatic systems		
Fifth Avenue and Imperial	20 to 30	140 to 240
Manual systems		
Fifth Avenue, LeBaron and New Yorker	20 to 35	180 to 240
Town and Country	10 to 35	140 to 210
1993		
Automatic systems		
Concorde	17 to 38	131 to 214
Fifth Avenue and Imperial	20 to 35	140 to 240
Manual systems		
Fifth Avenue, LeBaron and New Yorker	20 to 30	140 to 240
Concorde	17 to 38	131 to 214
Town and Country	10 to 35	140 to 210
1994		
Automatic systems		
Concorde, LHS and New Yorker	17 to 38	131 to 214
Manual systems		
LeBaron	16 to 38	180 to 235
Concorde, LHS and New Yorker	17 to 38	131 to 214
Town and Country	10 to 35	140 to 210
1995		
Automatic systems		
Concorde, LHS and New Yorker	17 to 38	131 to 214
Manual systems		
Sebring		
SOHC engine	27	129
DOHC engine	30 to 33	206 to 229
Cirrus	not available	not available
Concorde and New Yorker	17 to 38	131 to 214
Town and Country	10 to 35	140 to 210
1996		
Automatic systems		
Concorde, LHS and New Yorker	17 to 38	131 to 214
Manual systems		
Sebring		
SOHC	27	129
DOHC	30 to 33	206 to 229
Cirrus and Sebring Convertible	not available	not available
Concorde	17 to 38	131 to 214
Town and Country	10 to 37	112 to 210

Heating and air conditioning

Manufacturer Year Model (or type of system)	Low side gauge (evaporator suction)	High side gauge (discharge)
Chrysler		
1997		
Automatic systems (Concorde and LHS)	17 to 38	131 to 214
Manual systems		
Cirrus and Sebring convertible	17 to 38	131 to 214
Concorde	17 to 38	131 to 214
Sebring		
SOHC	27	129
DOHC	30 to 33	206 to 229
Town and Country	10 to 37	112 to 210
1998		
Automatic systems (Concorde)	20 to 30	210 to 250
Manual systems		
Sebring		
SOHC	27	129
DOHC	30 to 33	206 to 229
Cirrus and Sebring convertible	17 to 38	131 to 214
Concorde	20 to 30	210 to 250
Town and Country	10 to 37	112 to 210
1999		
Automatic systems		
Concorde, LHS and 300M	20 to 30	210 to 250
Manual systems		
Cirrus and Sebring Convertible	not available	not available
Concorde	20 to 30	210 to 250
Sebring Coupe		
SOHC	27	129
DOHC	30 to 33	206 to 229
Town and Country	10 to 37	112 to 210
Dodge		
1980		
Challenger, Colt and D-50 pick-up	15 to 30	210 to 230
All other models	10 to 30	140 to 240
1981 through 1983		
Challenger, Colt and Ram 50 pick-up	15 to 30	210 to 230
All other models		
FWD vehicles	20 to 30	140 to 240
RWD vehicles	20 to 30	15 to 240
1984 through 1986		
Colt, Colt Vista, Conquest and Ram 50 pick-up	15 to 30	170 to 200
All other models		
FWD vehicles	16 to 30	180 to 235
RWD vehicles	12 to 22	170 to 210
1987		
Colt, Colt Vista, Ram Raider and Ram 50 pick-up	19 to 25	172 to 252
Conquest	15 to 30	170 to 200
All other models		
FWD vehicles	16 to 30	180 to 235
RWD vehicles	12 to 22	170 to 210
1988		
Automatic system (Conquest)	15 to 30	170 to 200
Manual systems		
Colt, Colt Vista, Raider and Ram 50 pick-up	19 to 25	172 to 252
All other models		
FWD vehicles	16 to 30	180 to 235
RWD vehicles	12 to 22	170 to 210
1989		
Automatic system (Conquest TSi)	15 to 30	170 to 200
Manual systems		
Colt	30 to 33	299 to 384
Colt Vista and Colt wagon	20 to 26	130 to 220
Raider	19 to 32	102 to 142
Ram 50 pick-up	19 to 23	152 to 220
All other models		
FWD vehicles	16 to 30	180 to 235
RWD vehicles	12 to 22	170 to 210
1990		
Automatic systems		
Fixed displacement compressor	16 to 30	180 to 235
Variable displacement compressor	16 to 38	180 to 235
Manual systems		
Colt	19 to 25	172 to 252
Colt Vista, Colt wagon and Ram 50 pick-up	20 to 26	130 to 220
All other models	20 to 35	140 to 240
1991		
Automatic systems		
Monaco	22 to 45	125 to 225
Stealth	18 to 28	112 to 119
Manual systems		
Caravan	10 to 35	140 to 210
Colt	19 to 25	172 to 252
Colt Vista and Ram 50	20 to 26	130 to 220
Dakota	10 to 52	140 to 350
Ramcharger, full-size pick-up and full-size van	18 to 47	120 to 340
Stealth	19 to 28	111 to 118
All other models	20 to 35	140 to 240
1992		
Automatic systems		
Monaco	22 to 45	125 to 225
Stealth	18 to 28	112 to 119
Manual systems		
Caravan	10 to 35	140 to 210
Colt	19 to 25	172 to 252
Dakota	10 to 52	140 to 350
Daytona and Dynasty	20 to 35	180 to 240
Ram 50 pick-up	20 to 26	130 to 220
Ramcharger, full size pick-up and full-size van	18 to 47	120 to 340
Shadow and Spirit	20 to 35	180 to 240
Stealth	19 to 28	111 to 118
1993		
Automatic systems		
Intrepid	17 to 38	131 to 214
Stealth	19 to 28	111 to 118
Manual systems		
Caravan	10 to 35	140 to 210
Colt	20 to 30	105 to 148
Dakota	16 to 30	180 to 235
Daytona and Dynasty	20 to 30	140 to 240
Intrepid	17 to 38	131 to 214
Ram 50 pick-up	20 to 26	130 to 220
Ramcharger, full-size pick-up and full-size van	20 to 35	160 to 235
Shadow and Spirit	20 to 30	140 to 240
Stealth	19 to 28	111 to 118

Manufacturer Year Model (or type of system)	Low side gauge (evaporator suction)	High side gauge (discharge)
1994		
Automatic systems		
Intrepid	17 to 38	131 to 214
Stealth	19 to 28	111 to 118
Manual systems		
Caravan	10 to 35	140 to 210
Colt	20 to 30	104 to 148
Dakota	20 to 32	190 to 250
Full-size pick-up	32 to 40	190 to 220
Full-size van	20 to 35	160 to 235
Intrepid	17 to 38	131 to 214
Shadow and Spirit	16 to 38	180 to 235
Stealth	19 to 28	111 to 118
1995		
Automatic systems		
Intrepid	17 to 38	131 to 214
Manual systems		
Avenger		
SOHC engine	27	129
DOHC engine	30 to 33	206 to 229
Caravan	10 to 35	140 to 210
Dakota	20 to 32	190 to 250
Full-size pick-up	32 to 40	190 to 220
Full-size van	20 to 35	160 to 235
Stealth	19 to 28	111 to 118
Stratus	not available	not available
Intrepid	17 to 38	131 to 214
1996		
Automatic systems		
Intrepid	17 to 38	131 to 214
Manual systems		
Avenger		
SOHC	27	129
DOHC	30 to 33	206 to 229
Caravan	10 to 37	112 to 210
Dakota and full-size pick-up	32 to 40	190 to 220
Full-size van	20 to 35	160 to 235
Intrepid	17 to 38	131 to 214
Stratus	not available	not available
1997		
Automatic systems (Intrepid)	17 to 38	131 to 214
Manual systems		
Avenger		
SOHC	27	129
DOHC	30 to 33	206 to 229
Caravan	10 to 37	112 to 210
Dakota and Ram full-size pick-up	32 to 40	190 to 220
Intrepid	17 to 38	131 to 214
Ram full-size van	20 to 35	160 to 235
Stratus	17 to 38	131 to 214
1998		
Automatic systems (Intrepid)	20 to 30	210 to 250
Manual systems		
Avenger		
SOHC	27	129
DOHC	30 to 33	206 to 229
Caravan	10 to 37	112 to 210
Dakota, Durango and Ram full-size pick-up	32 to 40	190 to 220
Intrepid	20 to 30	210 to 250
Ram full-size van	20 to 35	160 to 235
Stratus	17 to 38	131 to 214

Manufacturer Year Model (or type of system)	Low side gauge (evaporator suction)	High side gauge (discharge)
1999		
Automatic systems		
Intrepid	20 to 30	210 to 250
Manual systems		
Avenger		
SOHC	27	129
DOHC	30 to 33	206 to 229
Caravan	10 to 37	112 to 210
Dakota, Durango and Ram full-size pick-up	32 to 40	190 to 220
Intrepid	20 to 30	210 to 250
Ram full-size van	20 to 35	160 to 235
Stratus	not available	not available

Eagle

1980 through 1987 (all models)	5 to 24	208 to 250
1988 and 1989		
Premier		
Accumulator type systems	24 to 50	160 to 250
Other models	22 to 45	125 to 225
Premier	24 to 50	160 to 250
Medallion and Summit	19 to 25	172 to 252
1990		
Premier	22 to 45	125 to 225
Summit	19 to 25	172 to 252
Talon	11 to 26	142 to 199
Vista	20 to 26	130 to 220
1991		
Premier	22 to 45	125 to 225
Summit	19 to 25	172 to 252
Talon	11 to 26	142 to 199
1992		
Premier	22 to 45	125 to 225
Summit	19 to 25	172 to 252
Summit wagon	30 to 33	299 to 384
Talon	11 to 26	142 to 199
1993		
Automatic systems		
Vision	17 to 38	131 to 214
Manual systems		
Summit	20 to 30	105 to 148
Summit wagon	30 to 33	299 to 384
Talon	30 to 33	299 to 384
Vision	17 to 38	131 to 214
1994		
Automatic systems		
Vision	17 to 38	131 to 214
Manual systems		
Summit	20 to 30	104 to 148
Summit wagon	27	164
Talon	30 to 33	199 to 384
Vision	17 to 38	131 to 214
1995 and 1996		
Summit	20 to 30	105 to 148
Summit wagon	27	164
Talon	20 to 31	107 to 160
Vision	17 to 38	131 to 214
1997		
Talon	20 to 31	107 to 160
Vision	17 to 38	131 to 214
1998 (Talon)	20 to 31	107 to 160

Heating and air conditioning

Manufacturer Year Model (or type of system)	Low side gauge (evaporator suction)	High side gauge (discharge)
Ford		
1980		
Systems with a suction throttling valve		
Granada with automatic		
temperature control	14 to 24	145 to 175
All other models	28 to 31	175 to 195
Accumulator type systems	24 to 52	160 to 200
1981		
Escort	20 to 45	130 to 230
All other models	24 to 52	160 to 250
1982 and 1983	24 to 52	160 to 250
1984 through 1986	24 to 50	160 to 250
1987 and 1988		
Festiva	More than 30	185 to 213
All other models	24 to 50	160 to 250
1989		
Aerostar, Crown Victoria		
and Taurus	25 to 50	160 to 250
Econoline full-size van	12 to 35	116 to 180
Festiva	30	185 to 213
All other models	9 to 45	130 to 230
1990		
Automatic systems	25 to 50	160 to 250
Manual systems		
Festiva	19 to 25	199 to 220
All other systems	25 to 52	160 to 250
1991		
Automatic systems		
Crown Victoria	25 to 50	160 to 250
All other automatic systems	25 to 45	130 to 230
Manual systems		
Aerostar	24 to 50	158 to 250
Bronco and F Series full-size		
pick-up	28 to 45	128 to 230
Capri	19 to 25	199 to 220
Crown Victoria	25 to 52	160 to 250
Econoline full-size van	12 to 35	115 to 180
Escort	21 to 23	171 to 223
Explorer and Ranger	22 to 50	160 to 250
Festiva	19 to 25	199 to 220
Mustang and Tempo	20 to 45	130 to 230
Probe	28 to 43	199 to 220
Taurus and Thunderbird	25 to 45	130 to 230
1992		
Automatic systems		
Crown Victoria	25 to 50	160 to 250
Taurus and Thunderbird	25 to 45	130 to 230
Manual systems		
Aerostar	24 to 50	158 to 250
Bronco and F Series		
full-size pick-up	28 to 45	128 to 230
Capri	19 to 25	199 to 220
Crown Victoria	25 to 52	160 to 250
Econoline full-size van	12 to 35	115 to 180
Escort	21 to 23	171 to 223
Explorer and Ranger	22 to 50	160 to 250
Festiva	19 to 25	199 to 220
Mustang	20 to 45	130 to 230
Probe	28 to 43	199 to 220
Taurus and Thunderbird	25 to 45	130 to 230
Tempo	20 to 45	130 to 230

Manufacturer Year Model (or type of system)	Low side gauge (evaporator suction)	High side gauge (discharge)
1993		
Automatic systems		
Crown Victoria	25 to 50	160 to 250
Taurus and Thunderbird	25 to 45	130 to 230
Manual systems		
Aerostar	20 to 50	160 to 250
Bronco and F Series full-size		
pick-up	28 to 45	128 to 230
Crown Victoria	25 to 52	160 to 250
Econoline full-size van	20 to 45	130 to 230
Escort	21 to 43	171 to 235
Explorer and Ranger	22 to 50	160 to 250
Festiva	19 to 25	199 to 220
Mustang and Tempo	20 to 45	130 to 230
Probe	24 to 46	154 to 209
Taurus and Thunderbird	25 to 45	130 to 230
1994		
Automatic systems		
Crown Victoria	22 to 47	160 to 245
Taurus	24 to 46	178 to 235
Thunderbird	25 to 45	130 to 230
Manual systems		
Aerostar	20 to 50	160 to 250
Aspire	20 to 41	185 to 263
Bronco and F Series		
full-size pick-up	28 to 45	128 to 230
Crown Victoria	22 to 47	160 to 245
Econoline full-size van	20 to 45	130 to 230
Escort	35 to 50	178 to 235
Explorer and Ranger	22 to 50	160 to 250
Mustang and Thunderbird	25 to 45	125 to 230
Probe		
R-12	24 to 46	154 to 209
R-134a	19 to 45	178 to 235
Taurus and Tempo	22 to 47	130 to 230
1995		
Automatic systems		
Crown Victoria	22 to 47	125 to 230
Explorer	20 to 50	160 to 250
Taurus	22 to 47	130 to 230
Thunderbird	25 to 45	130 to 230
Manual systems		
Aerostar	20 to 50	160 to 250
Aspire	19 to 41	202 to 263
Bronco and F Series		
full-size pick-up	28 to 45	128 to 230
Contour	22 to 47	125 to 225
Crown Victoria	22 to 47	160 to 245
Econoline full-size van	20 to 45	130 to 230
Escort	35 to 50	178 to 235
Explorer and Ranger	22 to 50	160 to 250
Mustang and Thunderbird	25 to 45	125 to 230
Probe	not available	not available
Taurus	22 to 47	130 to 230
Windstar	25 to 45	131 to 231
1996		
Automatic systems		
Crown Victoria and Thunderbird	25 to 45	125 to 230
Explorer	20 to 50	160 to 250
Taurus	22 to 45	125 to 230
Manual systems		
Aerostar	20 to 50	160 to 250
Aspire	19 to 41	202 to 263

Manufacturer Year Model (or type of system)	Low side gauge (evaporator suction)	High side gauge (discharge)
Bronco and F Series full-size pick-up	22 to 45	128 to 330
Contour	22 to 47	125 to 225
Crown Victoria	22 to 47	125 to 235
Econoline full-size van	20 to 45	130 to 230
Escort	20 to 45	125 to 235
Explorer and Ranger	22 to 50	160 to 250
Mustang and Thunderbird	25 to 45	125 to 230
Probe	not available	not available
Taurus	22 to 45	125 to 230
Windstar	22 to 47	250 to 420
1997		
Automatic systems		
Crown Victoria and Thunderbird	25 to 45	125 to 230
Explorer	20 to 50	160 to 250
Taurus	22 to 45	125 to 230
Manual systems		
Aerostar	22 to 47	160 to 250
Aspire	19 to 41	202 to 263
Contour	22 to 47	125 to 225
Crown Victoria	22 to 47	125 to 235
Econoline full-size van	20 to 45	130 to 230
Escort and Taurus	22 to 45	125 to 230
Expedition	not available	not available
Explorer and Ranger	22 to 50	160 to 250
F Series full-size pick-up		
F-250 Heavy Duty and F-350	24 to 47	128 to 230
All other models	22 to 45	128 to 230
Mustang and Thunderbird	25 to 45	125 to 230
Probe	23 to 46	220 to 445
Windstar	22 to 47	250 to 420
1998		
Automatic systems		
Crown Victoria	25 to 45	125 to 230
Explorer	22 to 50	160 to 250
Taurus	22 to 45	125 to 230
Manual systems		
Contour	22 to 47	125 to 225
Crown Victoria	22 to 47	125 to 235
Econoline full-size van	25 to 45	125 to 225
Escort and Escort Coupe	22 to 45	125 to 230
Expedition	25 to 45	125 to 230
Explorer	22 to 50	160 to 250
F Series full-size pick-up		
F-250 Heavy Duty and F-350	24 to 47	128 to 230
All other models	22 to 45	128 to 230
Mustang and Taurus	22 to 45	125 to 230
Ranger	22 to 50	160 to 250
Windstar	22 to 47	250 to 420
1999		
Automatic systems		
Crown Victoria	22 to 45	125 to 230
Expedition	25 to 45	125 to 230
Explorer	22 to 45	125 to 225
Taurus	22 to 45	125 to 230
Manual systems		
Crown Victoria	22 to 45	125 to 235
Contour and Mustang	25 to 45	125 to 230
Econoline full-size van	25 to 45	125 to 225
Escort	22 to 45	125 to 230
F Series full-size pick-up		
F-250 Super Duty and F-350	24 to 45	128 to 230
All other models	22 to 45	128 to 230

Manufacturer Year Model (or type of system)	Low side gauge (evaporator suction)	High side gauge (discharge)
Ranger	24 to 45	125 to 225
Taurus	22 to 45	125 to 230
Windstar	22 to 45	125 to 227

Geo

Manufacturer Year Model (or type of system)	Low side gauge (evaporator suction)	High side gauge (discharge)
1989 through 1992 (all models)	21 to 28	206 to 213
1993		
Metro, Tracker and Prizm	32 to 34	235 to 245
Storm	18 to 23	170 to 210
1994		
Metro	32 to 47	175 to 335
Prizm	30	384
Tracker	28	455
1995 and 1996 (all models)	34 to 40	270 to 305
1997		
Metro	30 to 47	185 to 228
Prizm	34 to 40	270 to 305
Tracker	34 to 40	228 to 263

GMC

Manufacturer Year Model (or type of system)	Low side gauge (evaporator suction)	High side gauge (discharge)
1980 and 1981	24 to 35	150 to 220
1982 through 1988	24 to 30	130 to 190
1989		
Manually operated systems		
CCOT systems	22 to 28	165 to 200
V5 systems	not available	not available
Automatic systems	not available	not available
1990 through 1993	not available	not available
Full-size and Safari vans	not available	not available
All other models	32 to 47	225 to 335
1994		
Full-size pick-up and Safari	37	290
Full-size van	32	175
Jimmy	32	225
Sonoma	21	259
1995		
Full-size and Safari vans	37	290
Full-size pick-up, Suburban and Yukon	28	320
Jimmy and Sonoma	26	299
1996		
Full-size pick-up, Suburban, Yukon and Savana full-size van	28	320
Jimmy and Sonoma	26	299
Safari	37	290
1997		
Full-size pick-up, Suburban and Yukon	28	320
Jimmy and Sonoma pick-up	26	299
Safari	37	290
Savana full-size van	39	251
1998		
Automatic systems (Jimmy)	26	299
Manual systems		
Full-size pick-up, Suburban and Yukon	28	320
Jimmy and Sonoma pick-up	26	299
Safari	37	290
Savana full-size van	39	251
1999		
Automatic systems (Jimmy)	26	299

Heating and air conditioning

Manufacturer Year Model (or type of system)	Low side gauge (evaporator suction)	High side gauge (discharge)
GMC (continued)		
1999		
Manual systems		
Full-size pick-up, Suburban and Yukon	34	228
Jimmy and Sonoma pick-up	32	228
Safari van	37	290
Savana full-size van	39	251
Sierra full-size pick-up	44	204
Jeep		
1980 through 1987 (all models)	15 to 24	208 to 250
1988 through 1991 (all models)	20 to 35	140 to 240
1992		
Cherokee, Comanche and Wrangler.	30 to 35	160 to 235
1993		
Cherokee and Wrangler	30 to 35	160 to 235
Grand Cherokee	30 to 40	170 to 260
1994 and 1995		
Cherokee and Wrangler	30 to 35	160 to 235
Grand Cherokee	32 to 41	200 to 260
1996		
Cherokee	20 to 35	160 to 235
Grand Cherokee	32 to 41	200 to 260
1997		
Cherokee and Grand Cherokee	32 to 41	200 to 260
Wrangler	20 to 35	160 to 235
1998 and 1999 (all models)	32 to 41	200 to 260
Lincoln		
1980		
Systems with a suction throttling valve		
Versailles with automatic temperature control	14 to 24	145 to 175
All other models	28 to 31	175 to 195
Accumulator type systems	24 to 52	160 to 200
1981 through 1983 (all models)	24 to 52	160 to 250
1984 through 1988		
Town Car	24 to 50	160 to 250
All other models	16 to 45	130 to 230
1989		
Town Car	25 to 50	160 to 250
All other models	9 to 45	130 to 230
1990		
Automatic systems	25 to 50	160 to 250
Manual systems	25 to 52	160 to 250
1991 and 1992		
Continental and Mark VII	25 to 45	130 to 230
Town Car	25 to 50	160 to 250
1993		
Continental	25 to 45	130 to 230
Mark VIII and Town Car	25 to 45	130 to 225
1994		
Continental	24 to 46	178 to 235
Mark VIII and Town Car	22 to 47	160 to 245
1995		
Continental	22 to 47	130 to 230
Mark VIII and Town Car	22 to 47	160 to 245
1996 and 1997		
Continental	22 to 47	130 to 230
Mark VIII and Town Car	25 to 45	125 to 230
1998		
Continental	22 to 47	130 to 230
Mark VIII, Navigator and Town Car	25 to 45	125 to 230
1999		
Continental	22 to 45	125 to 230
Navigator	25 to 45	125 to 230
Town Car	25 to 45	125 to 230
Mercury		
1980		
Systems with a suction throttling valve		
Monarch with automatic temperature control	14 to 24	145 to 175
All other models	28 to 31	175 to 195
Accumulator type systems	24 to 52	160 to 200
1981		
Lynx	20 to 45	130 to 230
All other models	24 to 52	160 to 250
1982 and 1983 (all models)	24 to 52	160 to 250
1984 through 1986 (all models)	24 to 50	160 to 250
1987 and 1988		
Tracer	More than 30	185 to 213
All other models	24 to 50	160 to 250
1989		
Grand Marquis and Sable	25 to 50	160 to 250
Tracer	30	185 to 213
All other models	9 to 45	130 to 230
1990		
Automatic systems	25 to 50	160 to 250
Manual systems	25 to 52	160 to 250
1991		
Automatic systems		
Grand Marquis	25 to 50	160 to 250
All other automatic systems	25 to 45	130 to 230
Manual systems		
Cougar and Sable	25 to 45	130 to 230
Grand Marquis	25 to 52	160 to 250
Tracer	21 to 23	171 to 223
Topaz	20 to 45	130 to 230
1992		
Automatic systems		
Cougar and Sable	25 to 45	130 to 230
Grand Marquis	25 to 50	160 to 250
Manual systems		
Cougar and Sable	25 to 45	130 to 230
Grand Marquis	25 to 52	160 to 250
Topaz	20 to 45	130 to 230
Tracer	21 to 23	171 to 223
1993		
Automatic systems		
Cougar and Sable	25 to 45	130 to 230
Grand Marquis	25 to 50	160 to 250
Manual systems		
Capri	19 to 25	199 to 220
Cougar, Sable and Topaz	25 to 45	130 to 230
Grand Marquis	25 to 52	160 to 250
Tracer	21 to 43	171 to 235
Villager	25 to 47	250 to 404
1994		
Automatic systems		
Cougar	24 to 45	130 to 230
Grand Marquis	22 to 47	160 to 245
Sable	24 to 46	178 to 235

Manufacturer Year Model (or type of system)	Low side gauge (evaporator suction)	High side gauge (discharge)
Manual systems		
Capri	not available	not available
Cougar	25 to 45	125 to 230
Grand Marquis	22 to 47	160 to 245
Sable and Topaz	22 to 47	130 to 230
Tracer	35 to 50	178 to 235
Villager	25 to 47	250 to 404
1995		
Automatic systems		
Cougar	25 to 45	130 to 230
Grand Marquis	22 to 47	125 to 230
Sable	22 to 47	130 to 230
Manual systems		
Mystique	22 to 47	125 to 225
Cougar	25 to 45	125 to 230
Grand Marquis	22 to 47	160 to 245
Sable	22 to 47	130 to 230
Tracer	35 to 50	178 to 235
Villager	25 to 47	250 to 404
1996		
Automatic systems		
Cougar and Grand Marquis	25 to 45	125 to 230
Sable	22 to 45	125 to 230
Villager	24 to 47	125 to 230
Manual systems		
Cougar	25 to 45	125 to 230
Grand Marquis	22 to 47	125 to 235
Mystique	22 to 47	125 to 225
Sable	22 to 45	125 to 230
Tracer	20 to 45	125 to 235
Villager	25 to 47	180 to 445
1997		
Automatic systems		
Cougar and Grand Marquis	25 to 45	125 to 230
Mountaineer	20 to 50	160 to 250
Sable	22 to 45	125 to 230
Villager	24 to 47	125 to 230
Manual systems		
Cougar	25 to 45	125 to 230
Grand Marquis	22 to 47	125 to 235
Mountaineer	22 to 50	160 to 250
Mystique	22 to 47	125 to 225
Sable and Tracer	22 to 45	125 to 230
Villager	25 to 47	180 to 445
1998		
Automatic systems		
Grand Marquis	25 to 45	125 to 230
Mountaineer	22 to 50	160 to 250
Sable	22 to 45	125 to 230
Villager	24 to 47	125 to 230
Manual systems		
Grand Marquis	22 to 47	125 to 235
Mountaineer	22 to 50	160 to 250
Mystique	22 to 47	125 to 225
Sable and Tracer	22 to 45	125 to 230
Villager	25 to 47	180 to 445
1999		
Automatic systems		
Grand Marquis	22 to 45	125 to 230
Mountaineer	22 to 45	125 to 225
Sable	22 to 45	125 to 230
Villager	24 to 47	125 to 230

Manufacturer Year Model (or type of system)	Low side gauge (evaporator suction)	High side gauge (discharge)
Manual systems		
Cougar and Mystique	25 to 45	125 to 230
Expedition	25 to 45	125 to 230
Explorer	22 to 45	125 to 225
Grand Marquis	22 to 45	125 to 235
Mountaineer	22 to 45	125 to 225
Sable	22 to 45	125 to 230
Tracer	22 to 45	125 to 230
Villager	25 to 47	125 to 230

Merkur

1985 and 1986 (XR4Ti)	20	160
1987 and 1988		
Scorpio	9 to 20	145 to 181
XR4Ti	27 to 41	334 to 435

Oldsmobile

1980 and 1981	4 to 35	150 to 220
1982 through 1988		
FWD vehicles	2 to 29	165 to 205
RWD vehicles	4 to 30	130 to 190
1989		
Manually operated systems		
CCOT systems	2 to 28	165 to 200
V5 systems	not available	not available
Automatic systems	not available	not available
1990		
Automatic systems		
Toronado	2	235
Cutlass Supreme	7	235
All other automatic systems	2 to 29	165 to 200
Manually operated systems		
CCOT systems	2 to 28	165 to 200
V5 systems	9 to 35	not available
1991		
Automatic systems		
Ninety Eight and Delta Eighty Eight	2 to 29	165 to 200
Cutlass Supreme	7	235
Toronado	2	235
Manual systems		
Eighty-Eight	2 to 40	135 to 300
Custom Cruiser	9 to 36	190 to 265
Calais	7 to 47	150 to 450
Cutlass Ciera and Cutlass Cruiser	7 to 47	150 to 335
Cutlass Supreme	2 to 47	225 to 335
Silhouette	not available	not available
Bravada	not available	not available
1992		
Automatic systems		
Custom Cruiser	not available	not available
Cutlass Supreme	2 to 47	225 to 335
Eighty-Eight	2 to 40	135 to 300
Ninety-Eight	2 to 28	135 to 170
Toronado and Trofeo	2 to 40	135 to 300
Manual systems		
Achieva	7 to 47	150 to 450
Custom Cruiser	9 to 36	190 to 265
Cutlass Ciera and Cutlass Cruiser	7 to 47	150 to 335
Cutlass Supreme	2 to 47	225 to 335

Heating and air conditioning

Manufacturer Year Model (or type of system)	Low side gauge (evaporator suction)	High side gauge (discharge)
Oldsmobile (continued)		
1992		
Eighty-Eight	2 to 40	135 to 300
Silhouette	not available	not available
1993		
Automatic systems		
Cutlass Supreme	2 to 47	225 to 335
Eighty-Eight	2 to 40	135 to 300
Ninety-Eight	2 to 28	135 to 170
Manual systems		
Achieva	7 to 47	150 to 450
Bravada	2 to 47	225 to 335
Cutlass Ciera and		
Cutlass Cruiser	3	320
Cutlass Supreme	2 to 47	225 to 335
Eighty-Eight	2 to 40	135 to 300
Silhouette	0 to 49	260 to 380
1994		
Automatic systems		
Cutlass Supreme	7	275
Eighty-Eight and Ninety-Eight	5 to 43	190 to 240
Manual systems		
Achieva	5 to 55	150 to 350
Bravada	32	225
Cutlass Ciera and		
Cutlass Cruiser	26	200
Cutlass Supreme	42	340
Eighty-Eight and Ninety-Eight	22 to 40	135 to 300
Silhouette	42	325
1995		
Automatic systems		
Aurora	25 to 30	140 to 190
Cutlass Supreme	37	275
Eighty-Eight and Ninety-Eight	35 to 43	190 to 240
Manual systems		
Achieva	25 to 55	150 to 350
Cutlass Ciera and		
Cutlass Cruiser	21 to 29	115 to 200
Cutlass Supreme	42	340
Eighty-Eight and Ninety-Eight	35 to 43	190 to 240
Silhouette		
3.1L engine	36	315
3.8L engine	42	325
1996		
Automatic systems		
Aurora	25 to 36	140 to 205
Cutlass Supreme	37	275
Eighty-Eight and Ninety-Eight	29 to 37	185 to 245
Manual systems		
Achieva	25 to 55	150 to 350
Bravada	26	299
Ciera	21 to 29	115 to 200
Cutlass Supreme	42	340
Eighty-Eight and Ninety-Eight	29 to 37	185 to 245
Silhouette	36	315
1997		
Automatic systems		
Aurora	25 to 36	140 to 205
Cutlass Supreme	42	340
LSS	29 to 37	185 to 245
Manual systems		
Achieva	25 to 45	150 to 350
Bravada	26	299
Cutlass	32 to 50	150 to 325
Cutlass Supreme	42	340
Eighty-Eight	29 to 37	185 to 245
Silhouette	32	286
1998		
Automatic systems		
Aurora	25 to 36	140 to 205
Bravada	26	299
LSS	29 to 37	185 to 245
Manual systems		
Achieva	25 to 45	150 to 350
Cutlass	32 to 50	150 to 325
Eighty-Eight	29 to 37	185 to 245
Silhouette		
Without rear A/C	32	286
With rear A/C	42	325
1999		
Automatic systems		
Aurora	25 to 36	140 to 205
Bravada	26	299
Intrigue	42	340
LSS	29 to 37	185 to 245
Manual systems		
Alero	25 to 45	150 to 350
Cutlass	32 to 50	150 to 325
Eighty-Eight	29 to 37	185 to 245
Intrigue	42	340
Silhouette		
Without rear A/C	32	286
With rear A/C	42	325
Plymouth		
1980		
Arrow, Arrow pick-up, Champ and Sapporo	15 to 30	210 to 230
All other models	10 to 30	140 to 240
1981 through 1982		
Arrow pick-up, Champ and Sapporo	15 to 30	210 to 230
All other models		
FWD vehicles	20 to 30	140 to 240
RWD vehicles	20 to 30	115 to 240
1983		
Colt, Colt pick-up and Sapporo	15 to 30	210 to 230
All other models		
FWD vehicles	20 to 30	140 to 240
RWD vehicles	20 to 30	115 to 240
1984 through 1987		
Colt, Colt Vista and Conquest	15 to 30	170 to 200
All other models		
FWD vehicles	16 to 30	180 to 235
RWD vehicles	16 to 22	170 to 210
1988		
Automatic system (Conquest)	15 to 30	170 to 200
Manual systems		
Colt and Colt Vista	19 to 25	172 to 252
All other models		
FWD vehicles	16 to 30	180 to 235
RWD vehicles	12 to 22	170 to 210
1989		
Colt	30 to 33	299 to 384
Colt Vista and Colt wagon	20 to 26	130 to 220

Manufacturer Year Model (or type of system)	Low side gauge (evaporator suction)	High side gauge (discharge)
All other models		
FWD vehicles	16 to 30	180 to 235
RWD vehicles	12 to 22	170 to 210
1990		
Automatic systems		
Fixed displacement compressor	16 to 30	180 to 235
Variable displacement compressor	16 to 38	180 to 235
Manual systems		
Colt	19 to 25	172 to 252
Colt Vista and Colt wagon	20 to 26	130 to 220
Laser	11 to 26	142 to 199
All other models	20 to 35	140 to 240
1991		
Colt Vista	20 to 26	130 to 220
Laser	11 to 26	142 to 199
Voyager	10 to 35	140 to 210
All other models	20 to 35	140 to 240
1992		
Acclaim	20 to 35	180 to 240
Colt Vista	30 to 33	299 to 384
Laser	11 to 26	142 to 199
Sundance	20 to 35	180 to 240
Voyager	10 to 35	140 to 210
1993		
Acclaim and Sundance	20 to 30	140 to 240
Colt	20 to 30	105 to 148
Colt Vista and Laser	30 to 33	299 to 384
Voyager	10 to 35	140 to 210
1994		
Acclaim and Sundance	16 to 38	180 to 235
Colt	20 to 30	105 to 148
Colt Vista	27	164
Laser	30 to 33	299 to 384
Voyager (front unit or rear auxiliary unit)	10 to 35	140 to 210
1995		
Neon	17 to 32	220 to 330
Voyager	10 to 35	140 to 210
1996		
Breeze	17 to 38	131 to 214
Neon	17 to 32	220 to 330
Voyager	10 to 37	112 to 210
1997		
Breeze	17 to 38	131 to 214
Neon	17 to 32	220 to 330
Voyager	10 to 37	112 to 210
1998		
Breeze	17 to 38	131 to 214
Neon	17 to 32	220 to 330
Voyager	10 to 37	112 to 210
1999		
Breeze	17 to 38	131 to 214
Neon	17 to 32	220 to 330
Voyager	10 to 37	112 to 210

Pontiac

Manufacturer Year Model (or type of system)	Low side gauge (evaporator suction)	High side gauge (discharge)
1980 and 1981	24 to 35	150 to 220
1982 through 1987		
FWD vehicles	22 to 29	165 to 205
RWD vehicles	24 to 30	130 to 190
1988		
LeMans	21 to 28	206 to 213
All other models		
FWD vehicles	22 to 29	165 to 205
RWD vehicles	24 to 30	130 to 190
1989		
LeMans	21 to 28	206 to 213
All other models		
CCOT systems	22 to 28	165 to 200
V5 systems	29 to 35	not available
1990		
Automatic systems	22 to 29	165 to 200
Manual systems		
LeMans	21 to 28	206 to 213
All other manually operated systems		
CCOT systems	22 to 28	165 to 200
V5 systems	29 to 35	not available
1991		
Automatic systems (Bonneville)	22 to 29	165 to 200
Manual systems		
6000	37 to 47	150 to 335
Bonneville	22 to 40	135 to 300
Firebird	29 to 42	150 to 330
Grand Am	37 to 47	150 to 450
Grand Prix	32 to 47	225 to 335
LeMans	21 to 28	206 to 213
Sunbird	37 to 47	150 to 325
Trans Sport	not available	not available
1992		
Automatic systems		
Bonneville	22 to 40	135 to 300
Manual systems		
Bonneville	22 to 40	135 to 300
Firebird	29 to 42	150 to 330
Grand Am	37 to 47	150 to 450
Grand Prix	32 to 47	225 to 335
LeMans	21 to 28	206 to 213
Sunbird	37 to 47	150 to 325
Trans Sport	not available	not available
1993		
Automatic systems		
Bonneville	22 to 40	135 to 300
Manual systems		
Bonneville	22 to 40	135 to 300
Firebird	25 to 43	165 to 270
Grand Am	37 to 47	150 to 450
Grand Prix	32 to 47	225 to 335
LeMans	32 to 34	235 to 245
Sunbird	37 to 47	150 to 325
Trans Sport	30 to 49	260 to 380
1994		
Automatic systems (Bonneville)	25 to 36	140 to 205
Manual systems		
Bonneville	22 to 40	135 to 300
Firebird	21 to 29	115 to 200
Grand Am	25 to 55	150 to 350
Grand Prix	42	340
Sunbird	27 to 65	150 to 325
Trans Sport	42	325
1995		
Automatic systems (Bonneville)	35 to 43	190 to 240
Manual systems		
Bonneville	35 to 43	190 to 240
Firebird	21 to 29	115 to 200
Grand Am	25 to 55	150 to 350

Heating and air conditioning

Manufacturer Year Model (or type of system)	Low side gauge (evaporator suction)	High side gauge (discharge)
Pontiac (continued)		
Manual systems (continued)		
Grand Prix	42	340
Sunfire	27 to 65	150 to 325
Trans Sport		
3.1L engine	36	315
3.8L engine	42	325
1996		
Bonneville	29 to 37	185 to 245
Firebird	21 to 29	115 to 200
Grand Am	25 to 55	150 to 350
Grand Prix	42	340
Sunfire	27 to 65	150 to 325
Trans Sport	36	315
1997		
Bonneville	29 to 37	185 to 245
Firebird		
3.8L engine	25 to 37	115 to 200
5.7L engine	21 to 29	115 to 200
Grand Am	25 to 45	150 to 350
Grand Prix	42	340
Sunfire	32 to 65	150 to 324
Trans Sport	32	286
1998		
Automatic systems		
Bonneville	29 to 37	185 to 245
Grand Prix	42	340
Manual systems		
Bonneville	29 to 37	185 to 245

Manufacturer Year Model (or type of system)	Low side gauge (evaporator suction)	High side gauge (discharge)
Firebird		
3.8L engine	25 to 37	115 to 200
5.7L engine	21 to 29	115 to 200
Grand Am	25 to 45	150 to 350
Grand Prix	42	340
Sunfire	32 to 65	150 to 324
Trans Sport		
Without rear A/C	32	286
With rear A/C	42	325
1999		
Automatic systems		
Bonneville	29 to 37	185 to 245
Grand Prix	42	340
Manual systems		
Bonneville	29 to 37	185 to 245
Firebird		
3.8L engine	25 to 37	115 to 200
5.7L engine	21 to 29	115 to 200
Grand Am	25 to 45	150 to 350
Grand Prix	42	340
Montana		
Without rear A/C	32	286
With rear A/C	42	325
Sunfire	32 to 65	150 to 324
Saturn		
1991 through 1994 (all models)	25 to 32	200 to 250
1995 through 1999 (all models)	24 to 28	180 to 215

System operating pressures (imported vehicles)

Manufacturer Year Model (or type of system)	Low side gauge (evaporator suction)	High side gauge (discharge)
Acura		
1986 (all models)	21 to 28	170 to 200
1987 through 1991		
Automatic system (Legend and Legend Coupe)	34	228
Manual systems (all models)	21 to 28	170 to 200
1992 and 1993 (all models)	21 to 28	170 to 200
1994		
Automatic system (Legend)	22 to 34	213 to 284
Manual systems		
Integra	11 to 28	210 to 280
Legend	22 to 34	213 to 284
Vigor	21 to 28	170 to 200
1995		
Automatic system		
Legend	22 to 34	213 to 284
2.5TL	14 to 28	210 to 280
Manual systems		
Integra	11 to 28	210 to 280
Legend	22 to 34	213 to 284
1996		
Automatic system		
2.5TL	14 to 28	210 to 280
3.2TL	20 to 36	215 to 310
3.5RL	14 to 26	205 to 245
Manual systems		
Integra	11 to 28	210 to 280
SLX	21 to 43	199 to 270

Manufacturer Year Model (or type of system)	Low side gauge (evaporator suction)	High side gauge (discharge)
1997		
Automatic systems		
2.2CL	22 to 29	250 to 300
3.0CL	19 to 26	260 to 305
2.5TL	14 to 28	210 to 280
3.2TL	20 to 36	215 to 310
3.5RL	14 to 26	205 to 245
Manual systems		
Integra	11 to 28	210 to 280
SLX	21 to 43	199 to 270
1998		
Automatic systems		
2.3CL	22 to 29	250 to 300
3.0CL	19 to 26	260 to 305
2.5TL	14 to 28	210 to 280
3.2TL	20 to 36	215 to 310
3.5RL	14 to 26	205 to 245
Manual systems		
Integra	11 to 28	210 to 280
SLX	21 to 43	199 to 270
1999		
Automatic systems		
2.3CL	22 to 29	250 to 300
3.0CL	19 to 26	260 to 305
3.2TL	20 to 36	215 to 310
3.5RL	14 to 26	205 to 245
Manual systems (Integra)	11 to 28	210 to 280

Manufacturer Year Model (or type of system)	Low side gauge (evaporator suction)	High side gauge (discharge)
Audi		
1980 through 1982		
4000	15 to 40	100 to 300
5000	28 to 32	not available
1983		
4000, Coupe and Quattro	15 to 40	100 to 300
5000	28 to 32	not available
1984		
Automatic system (5000)	19 to 25	240
Manual systems (4000, Coupe and Quattro)	15 to 40	100 to 300
1985 through 1987		
Automatic systems (5000 Series)	19 to 25	170
Manual systems (4000 Series and GT Coupe)	15 to 40	100 to 300
1988		
Automatic systems (5000 Series)	19 to 25	170
Manual systems (80 and 90)	19 to 46	154 to 255
1989 through 1991 (all models)	19 to 46	154 to 255
1992		
Automatic system (100 CS)	25 to 30	190 to 254
Manual systems		
80	19 to 46	154 to 255
100	25 to 30	190 to 254
1993		
Automatic systems (90 CS and 100 CS)	26 to 29	80
Manual systems (90 and 100)	26 to 29	290
1994		
Automatic systems (90 CS and 100 CS)	26 to 29	80
Manual systems (Cabriolet, 90 and 100)	32 to 36	279 to 350
1995 through 1997 (all models)	26 to 29	80 to 350
1998		
Automatic systems		
A4	26 to 29	80 to 350
A6	81	290
Manual systems (Cabrio)	26 to 29	80 to 350
1999		
A4	26 to 29	80 to 350
A6	81	290
BMW		
1980 through 1983 (all models)	24 to 34	284 to 394
1984		
633CSi	15 to 30	160 to 320
All other models	24 to 34	284 to 394
1985 and 1986		
635CSi	15 to 30	160 to 320
All other models	24 to 34	284 to 394
1987 and 1988		
Automatic systems (735i)	24 to 34	284 to 394
Manual systems (all models)	15 to 30	142 to 181
1989		
Automatic systems (525i, 535i and 735i)	24 to 34	284 to 394
Manual systems (all models)	15 to 30	142 to 181
1990		
Automatic systems 525i, 535i and 735i	24 to 34	284 to 394

Manufacturer Year Model (or type of system)	Low side gauge (evaporator suction)	High side gauge (discharge)
Manual systems		
325	15 to 30	185 to 205
1991 and 1992 (all models)	15 to 30	185 to 205
1993 through 1997 (all models)	36 to 42	164 to 215
1998 and 1999		
5-Series	not available	not available
All other models	36 to 42	164 to 215
Daihatsu		
1988 through 1992 (all models)	21 to 28	185 to 213
Fiat		
1980 through 1982 (all models)	7 to 42	142 to 284
Honda		
1980 through 1982		
Accord	30	200 to 220
Civic and Prelude	36	213
1983		
Accord and Civic	35	215
Prelude	37	320
1984 and 1985		
Accord, Civic and Civic CRX	35	215
Prelude	37	320
1986		
Accord	35	215
Civic and Civic CRX	36	320
Prelude	37	320
1987		
Accord	25 to 35	200
Civic and Civic CRX	36	320
Prelude	28	320
1988 through 1991		
Accord	25 to 35	200
Civic and Civic CRX	36	320
Prelude	33	340
1992		
Accord	25 to 35	200
Civic	36	320
Prelude	33	340
1993		
Accord	25 to 35	200
Civic and Civic Del Sol	36	320
Prelude	18 to 32	160 to 220
1994		
Accord	24 to 32	220 to 280
Civic and Civic Del Sol	22 to 36	220 to 295
Passport	23 to 31	313 to 370
Prelude	16 to 40	212 to 285
1995 and 1996		
Accord		
4-cylinder engine	24 to 32	220 to 280
V6 engine	17 to 32	210 to 260
Civic and Civic Del Sol	22 to 36	220 to 295
Odyssey		
Main unit	20 to 31	209 to 240
Main and auxiliary units		
With auxiliary unit on	28 to 43	220 to 280
With auxiliary unit off	20 to 31	209 to 240
Passport		
1995 models	19 to 28	213 to 242
1995-1/2 models	21 to 43	199 to 270
Prelude	16 to 40	212 to 285

Heating and air conditioning

Manufacturer Year Model (or type of system)	Low side gauge (evaporator suction)	High side gauge (discharge)
Honda (continued)		
1997		
Accord		
4-cylinder engine	24 to 32	220 to 280
V6 engine	17 to 32	210 to 260
Civic and Civic Del Sol	22 to 36	220 to 295
CR-V	20 to 35	200 to 280
Odyssey		
Main unit	20 to 31	209 to 240
Main and auxiliary units		
With auxiliary unit on	28 to 43	220 to 280
With auxiliary unit off	20 to 31	209 to 240
Passport	21 to 43	199 to 270
Prelude	16 to 40	212 to 285
1998		
Automatic system (Accord)		
Modine condenser	25 to 40	230 to 320
Showa condenser	21 to 35	210 to 350
Manual systems		
Accord		
Modine condenser	22 to 36	210 to 300
Showa condenser	18 to 31	200 to 275
Civic	23 to 36	240 to 300
CR-V	15 to 27	145 to 225
Odyssey		
Main unit	20 to 31	209 to 240
Main and auxiliary units		
With auxiliary unit on	28 to 43	220 to 280
With auxiliary unit off	20 to 31	209 to 240
Prelude	20 to 35	190 to 270
1999		
Automatic systems		
Accord		
Modine condenser	25 to 40	230 to 320
Showa condenser	21 to 35	210 to 350
Odyssey		
Without rear A/C	25 to 38	190 to 260
With rear A/C	34 to 48	220 to 300
Manual systems		
Accord		
Modine condenser	22 to 36	210 to 300
Showa condenser	18 to 31	200 to 275
Civic	23 to 36	240 to 300
CR-V	22 to 38	200 to 300
Odyssey		
Without rear A/C	25 to 38	190 to 260
With rear A/C	34 to 48	220 to 300
Prelude	20 to 35	190 to 270
Hyundai		
1986 and 1987 (all models)	14 to 28	298 to 384
1988 (all models)	28 to 30	299 to 384
1989 through 1993 (all models)	28 to 42	213 to 256
1994		
Elantra	28 to 32	199 to 228
Excel and Precis	23 to 45	125 to 225
Scoupe	28 to 42	213 to 256
Sonata	24 to 47	183 to 247
1995 and 1996		
Accent	23 to 45	199 to 228
Elantra	28 to 32	199 to 228
Scoupe	19 to 23	152 to 220
Sonata	24 to 47	183 to 247

Manufacturer Year Model (or type of system)	Low side gauge (evaporator suction)	High side gauge (discharge)
1997		
Automatic system (Sonata)	24 to 47	183 to 247
Manual systems		
Accent	23 to 45	199 to 228
Elantra and Tiburon	28 to 32	199 to 228
Sonata	24 to 47	183 to 247
1998		
Accent	23 to 45	199 to 228
Elantra and Tiburon	28 to 32	199 to 228
Sonata	not available	not available
1999		
Accent and Elantra	28 to 32	199 to 228
Sonata	not available	not available
Tiburon	28 to 32	199 to 228
Infiniti		
1990		
Automatic systems		
M30	18 to 24	193 to 239
Q45	27 to 33	142 to 173
Manual system (M30)	18 to 24	193 to 239
1991		
Automatic systems		
M30	18 to 24	193 to 239
Q45	27 to 33	142 to 173
Manual systems		
G20	14 to 26	162 to 210
M30	18 to 24	193 to 239
1992		
Automatic systems		
M30	18 to 24	193 to 239
Q45	27 to 33	142 to 173
Manual systems		
G20	14 to 26	162 to 210
M30	16 to 21	193 to 239
1993		
Automatic systems		
J30	23 to 28	182 to 223
Q45	27 to 33	142 to 173
Manual system (G20)	14 to 26	162 to 210
1994		
Automatic systems		
J30	23 to 28	182 to 223
Q45	28 to 32	192 to 232
Manual system (G20)	14 to 26	162 to 210
1995 and 1996		
Automatic systems		
I30	21 to 26	169 to 225
J30	24 to 31	182 to 223
Q45	28 to 32	192 to 232
Manual system (G20)	24 to 30	137 to 165
1997		
I30	21 to 26	169 to 225
J30	24 to 31	182 to 223
Q45	28 to 32	192 to 232
QX4	28 to 40	206 to 273
1998		
I30	21 to 26	169 to 225
Q45	28 to 32	192 to 232
QX4	28 to 40	206 to 273
1999		
G20		Refer to A/C specification label in engine compartment

Manufacturer Year Model (or type of system)	Low side gauge (evaporator suction)	High side gauge (discharge)
I30	21 to 26	169 to 225
Q45	36 to 47	178 to 240
QX4	28 to 40	206 to 273

Isuzu

1984 through 1989 (all models)	28 to 42	213 to 256
1990		
Impulse	28	213
All models except Impulse	30	228
1991 and 1992 (all models)	28	213
1993 (all models)	21 to 28	199 to 213
1994 (all models)	23 to 31	313 to 370
1995		
Pick-up	19 to 28	213 to 242
Rodeo		
1995 models	19 to 28	213 to 242
1995-1/2 models	21 to 43	199 to 270
Trooper	21 to 43	199 to 270
1996 and 1997		
Hombre	26	299
Rodeo and Trooper	21 to 43	199 to 270
1998		
Amigo, Rodeo and Trooper	21 to 43	199 to 270
Hombre	26	299
1999		
Amigo, Rodeo, Trooper and VehiCROSS	21 to 43	199 to 270
Oasis	not available (See A/C System Performance Test, PP. 30 and 31)	

Jaguar

1983 through 1987 (XJ6 and XJS)	34	228
1988 through 1992		
XJ6	30	205
XJS	34	228
1993		
XJ6	70	145 to 180
XJS	34	228
1994		
XJ6 and XJ12	70	145 to 180
XJS	29	3932
1995 and 1996		
XJ6, XJ12 and XJR	70	145 to 180
XJS	29	392
1997		
XJ6 and XJR	70	145 to 180
XK8	Refer to specification label in engine compartment	
1998		
XJ8 and XJR	70	145 to 180
XK8	Refer to specification label in engine compartment	
1999 (all models)	not available	not available

Kia

1994 through 1998 (all models)	21 to 43	171 to 235
1999		
Sephia	20 to 41	185 to 263
Sportage	25 to 32	384 to 526

Manufacturer Year Model (or type of system)	Low side gauge (evaporator suction)	High side gauge (discharge)

Land Rover

1997		
Defender 90	21 to 29	130 to 203
Discovery	27 to 37	256 to 341
Ranger Rover	20 to 25	140 to 190
1998		
Discovery	27 to 37	256 to 341
Ranger Rover	20 to 25	140 to 190
1999 (all models)	not available	not available

Lexus

1990 through 1992 (all models)	21 to 28	206 to 213
1993		
ES300, SC300 and SC400	21 to 28	206 to 213
GS300 and LS400	21 to 36	199 to 228
1994 through 1997 (all models)	21 to 36	199 to 228
1998		
LS400	21 to 36	199 to 213
All other models	21 to 36	199 to 228
1999		
LS400	21 to 36	199 to 213
RX300	21 to 36	199 to 214
All other models	21 to 36	199 to 228

Mazda

1986 through 1987 (all models)	14	225 to 275
1988 and 1989		
Automatic system (929)	28 to 43	210 to 260
Manual systems (all other models)	14	225 to 275
1990		
Automatic system (929)	28 to 43	210 to 260
Manual systems		
B2200 and B2600 pick-ups	14 to 24	149 to 185
Miata, MPV, Protégé and 323	21 to 43	171 to 235
MX-6 and 626	21 to 43	199 to 228
RX-7	14 to 24	149 to 192
1991		
Automatic system (929)	28 to 43	210 to 260
Manual systems		
B2200 and B2600 pick-ups	14 to 24	149 to 185
Miata, MPV, Protégé and 323	21 to 43	171 to 235
MX-6 and 626	28 to 43	199 to 228
Navajo	22 to 50	160 to 250
RX-7	14 to 24	149 to 192
1992		
Automatic system (929)	23 to 32	149 to 178
Manual systems		
B2200 and B2600 pick-ups	14 to 24	149 to 185
Miata, MPV, Protégé and 323	21 to 43	171 to 235
MX-3	21 to 43	185 to 214
MX-6 and 626	28 to 43	199 to 228
Navajo	18 to 45	130 to 230
1993		
Automatic system (929)	23 to 32	149 to 178
Manual systems		
B2200 and B2600 pick-ups	14 to 24	150 to 184
Miata, MPV, Protégé and 323	21 to 43	171 to 235
MX-3, MX-6 and 626	21 to 43	185 to 214
Navajo	18 to 45	130 to 230
RX-7	15 to 27	142 to 192

Heating and air conditioning

Mazda (continued)

1994

Model (or type of system)	Low side	High side
Automatic system (929)	17 to 25	160 to 200
Manual systems		
B2300, B3000 and B4000 pick-ups	22 to 52	160 to 250
Miata	22 to 35	200 to 227
MPV	17 to 28	171 to 227
MX-3	17 to 27	185 to 225
Protégé and 323	22 to 42	171 to 234
MX-6 and 626	21 to 26	185 to 213
Navajo	22 to 52	160 to 250
RX-7	22 to 35	199 to 288

1995 and 1996

Model	Low side	High side
Automatic systems		
929	16 to 24	157 to 199
Millenia	15 to 26	160 to 200
Manual systems		
B2300, B3000 and B4000 pick-ups	23 to 52	160 to 250
Miata	22 to 35	200 to 227
MPV	17 to 28	171 to 227
MX-3	17 to 27	185 to 225
Protégé	22 to 42	190 to 240
MX-6 and 626	21 to 26	185 to 213
RX-7	22 to 35	199 to 288

1997

Model	Low side	High side
Automatic system (Millenia)	15 to 26	160 to 200
Manual systems		
B2300, B3000 and B4000 pick-ups	23 to 52	160 to 250
Miata	22 to 35	200 to 227
MPV	17 to 28	171 to 227
MX-6 and 626	13 to 19	220 to 260
Protégé	22 to 42	190 to 240

1998

Model	Low side	High side
Automatic system (Millenia)	15 to 26	160 to 200
Manual systems		
626	14 to 28	185 to 230
B2500, B3000 and B4000 pick-ups	25 to 45	125 to 230
MPV	17 to 28	171 to 227
Protégé	22 to 42	190 to 240

1999

Model	Low side	High side
Automatic system (Millenia)	15 to 26	160 to 200
Manual systems		
626	14 to 28	185 to 230
B2500, B3000 and B4000 pick-ups	25 to 45	125 to 230
Miata	14 to 28	171 to 213
Protégé	22 to 42	190 to 240

Mercedes-Benz

1980

Model	Low side	High side
All models	22	205

1981

Model	Low side	High side
Automatic systems		
380SL and 380SLC	22	205
All other models (except 240D)	22	265
Manual system (240D)	28 to 30	265

1982

Model	Low side	High side
Automatic systems (all models except 240D)	22	265
Manual system (240D)	28 to 30	265

1983

Model	Low side	High side
Automatic systems (all models except 240D)	22	265
Manual system (240D)	15 to 30	160 to 320

1984 through 1986

Model	Low side	High side
190 Series	24 to 34	230 to 275
All other models	22	265

1987 through 1992 (all models) — 24 to 34 — 230 to 275

1993 and 1994

Model	Low side	High side
190E	24 to 34	230 to 275
All other models	not available	not available

1995 through 1999 (all models) — not available — not available

Mitsubishi

1983 through 1986 (all models) — 15 to 30 — 170 to 200

1987

Model	Low side	High side
Precis	28 to 42	213 to 256
Starion and Galant	15 to 30	170 to 200
All other models	19 to 25	172 to 252

1988

Model	Low side	High side
Automatic systems (Starion and Galant Sigma)	15 to 30	170 to 200
Manual systems		
Excel	28 to 30	299 to 384
All other models	19 to 25	172 to 252

1989

Model	Low side	High side
Automatic system (Starion ESI and Sigma)	15 to 30	170 to 200
Manual systems		
Mirage	30 to 33	299 to 384
Montero		
Without rear A/C	19 to 32	102 to 142
With rear A/C	16 to 30	142 to 199
Pick-up	19 to 23	152 to 220
Precis	28 to 42	213 to 256
Van	19 to 28	139 to 196
Wagon	31 to 41	145 to 202

1990

Model	Low side	High side
Automatic system (Sigma)	15 to 30	170 to 200
Manual systems		
Eclipse	11 to 26	142 to 199
Galant	18 to 23	152 to 220
Mirage	19 to 25	172 to 252
Montero		
Without rear A/C	18 to 32	102 to 142
With rear A/C	16 to 30	142 to 199
Pick-up	20 to 26	130 to 220
Van	19 to 28	139 to 196
Wagon	31 to 41	142 to 202

1991

Model	Low side	High side
3000GT		
Automatic system	18 to 28	112 to 119
Manual system	19 to 28	111 to 118
Eclipse	11 to 26	142 to 199
Galant	18 to 23	152 to 220
Mirage	19 to 25	172 to 252
Montero		
Without rear A/C	18 to 32	102 to 142
With rear A/C	16 to 30	142 to 199

Manufacturer Year Model (or type of system)	Low side gauge (evaporator suction)	High side gauge (discharge)
1992		
3000GT	19 to 28	111 to 118
Diamante	19 to 28	105 to 112
Eclipse	11 to 26	142 to 199
Expo and Montero	30 to 33	299 to 384
Galant	18 to 23	130 to 220
Mirage	19 to 25	172 to 252
Pick-up	20 to 26	130 to 220
1993		
Automatic systems		
Diamante		
Sedan	19 to 28	105 to 112
Wagon	21 to 28	206 to 213
3000GT	19 to 28	111 to 118
Manual systems		
3000GT	19 to 28	111 to 118
Eclipse	11 to 26	142 to 199
Expo	30 to 33	299 to 384
Galant	20 to 26	130 to 220
Mirage	20 to 30	105 to 148
Montero	17 to 33	149 to 185
Pick-up	20 to 26	130 to 220
1994		
Automatic systems		
3000GT	19 to 28	111 to 118
Diamante	19 to 28	105 to 112
Manual systems		
3000GT	19 to 28	111 to 118
Eclipse	11 to 26	142 to 199
Expo	27	164
Galant	6 to 20	111 to 139
Mirage	20 to 30	105 to 148
Montero	14 to 33	149 to 213
1995 and 1996		
Automatic systems		
3000GT	18 to 28	111 to 118
Diamante		
Sedan	19 to 28	105 to 112
Wagon	14 to 22	130 to 152
Manual systems		
3000GT	19 to 28	111 to 118
Eclipse	20 to 31	107 to 160
Galant	6 to 20	111 to 139
Expo	27	164
Montero	14 to 33	149 to 213
Pick-up	20 to 26	130 to 220
1997 and 1998		
Automatic systems		
3000GT	19 to 28	111 to 118
Diamante	19 to 28	105 to 113
Galant	6 to 20	111 to 139
Manual systems		
3000GT	19 to 28	111 to 118
Eclipse	20 to 32	107 to 160
Galant	6 to 20	111 to 139
Mirage	6 to 20	113 to 142
Montero	14 to 33	149 to 213
Montero Sport	20 to 23	130 to 220
1999		
Automatic systems		
3000GT	19 to 28	111 to 118
Diamante	19 to 28	105 to 113

Manufacturer Year Model (or type of system)	Low side gauge (evaporator suction)	High side gauge (discharge)
Manual systems		
3000GT	19 to 28	111 to 118
Eclipse	20 to 32	107 to 160
Galant	6 to 20	111 to 139
Mirage	6 to 20	111 to 139
Montero	14 to 33	149 to 213
Montero Sport	15 to 30	145 to 189

Datsun/Nissan

Manufacturer Year Model (or type of system)	Low side gauge (evaporator suction)	High side gauge (discharge)
1980 and 1981		
210, 510, 200SX and pick-up	16 to 24	148 to 205
310	26 to 34	155 to 190
810	16 to 22	143 to 175
280ZX	14 to 25	122 to 190
1982		
200SX	18 to 20	134 to 146
210 and pick-up	16 to 28	149 to 178
280ZX	13 to 22	121 to 148
310	26 to 34	154 to 188
Maxima	15 to 19	139 to 171
Sentra	17 to 23	175 to 189
Stanza	17 to 26	152 to 195
1983		
200SX	18 to 20	134 to 146
280ZX	13 to 22	121 to 148
Maxima	15 to 19	139 to 171
Pick-up	16 to 28	149 to 178
Pulsar and Sentra	18 to 30	162 to 196
Stanza	17 to 26	152 to 195
1984 and 1985		
200SX	6 to 17	109 to 154
300ZX	13 to 16	151 to 185
Maxima	15 to 19	139 to 171
Pick-up	11 to 28	141 to 171
Pulsar and Sentra	18 to 30	162 to 196
Stanza	17 to 26	152 to 195
1986		
200SX	6 to 17	109 to 154
300ZX	13 to 16	151 to 185
Maxima		
Automatic system	15 to 19	139 to 171
Manual system	7 to 17	142 to 192
Pick-up		
1986 model	11 to 28	141 to 171
1986-1/2 model		
SD engine	18 to 27	182 to 220
VG engine	17 to 26	176 to 210
Z engine	23 to 33	188 to 228
Pulsar NX and Sentra	18 to 30	162 to 196
Stanza	17 to 26	152 to 195
1987 and 1988		
200SX	14 to 27	138 to 185
300ZX		
Automatic system	13 to 16	151 to 185
Manual system	16 to 20	176 to 232
Maxima		
Automatic system	13 to 16	151 to 185
Manual system	14 to 27	176 to 232
Stanza	14 to 27	176 to 232
Pathfinder and pick-up	28 to 40	210 to 256
Pulsar NX and Sentra	27 to 38	186 to 220
Stanza Wagon	28 to 40	176 to 232
Van	28 to 40	191 to 220

Heating and air conditioning

Manufacturer Year Model (or type of system)	Low side gauge (evaporator suction)	High side gauge (discharge)

Datsun/Nissan (continued)

1989

240SX	24 to 31	203 to 247
300ZX		
Automatic system	13 to 16	151 to 185
Manual system	16 to 20	176 to 216
Maxima	18 to 28	162 to 232
Pathfinder and pick-up	23 to 31	205 to 247
Pulsar NX and Sentra	27 to 36	186 to 220
Stanza	14 to 26	179 to 232

1990

Automatic systems		
300ZX	12 to 21	128 to 186
Maxima	18 to 28	162 to 232
Manual systems		
Axxess	27 to 33	188 to 226
Maxima	12 to 21	128 to 186
Pathfinder and pick-up	20 to 28	162 to 196
Pulsar NX and Sentra	20 to 28	156 to 188
Stanza	25	185
240SX	18 to 25	173 to 213
300ZX	20 to 28	142 to 179

1991

Automatic systems		
300ZX	27 to 37	118 to 166
Maxima	16 to 27	155 to 213
Pathfinder	20 to 28	162 to 196
Manual systems		
Maxima	12 to 21	128 to 186
NX and Sentra	27 to 37	118 to 166
Pathfinder and pick-up	20 to 28	162 to 196
Stanza	25	185
240SX	18 to 25	173 to 213

1992

Automatic systems		
300ZX	27 to 37	118 to 166
Maxima	16 to 27	155 to 213
Pathfinder	17 to 26	176 to 210
Manual systems		
240SX	26 to 31	108 to 132
Maxima	12 to 21	128 to 186
NX and Sentra	27 to 37	118 to 166
Pathfinder and pick-up	17 to 26	176 to 210
Stanza	25	185

1993

Automatic systems		
300ZX	27 to 37	118 to 166
Altima	20 to 26	152 to 198
Maxima	16 to 27	155 to 213
Pathfinder	24 to 31	188 to 232
Manual systems		
240SX	26 to 31	108 to 132
300ZX	27 to 37	118 to 166
Altima	20 to 26	152 to 198
Maxima	16 to 27	151 to 213
NX and Sentra	27 to 37	118 to 166
Pathfinder and pick-up	24 to 31	188 to 232
Quest	22 to 46	119 to 220

1994

Automatic systems		
300ZX	27 to 33	162 to 199
Altima	20 to 26	152 to 198
Maxima	18 to 23	188 to 230
Pathfinder	24 to 31	188 to 232
Manual systems		
240SX	19 to 29	165 to 202
300ZX	27 to 33	162 to 199
Altima	20 to 26	152 to 198
Maxima	18 to 23	188 to 230
Pathfinder and pick-up	24 to 31	188 to 232
Quest	22 to 45	120 to 220
Sentra	24 to 40	129 to 182

1995

Automatic systems		
300ZX	27 to 33	162 to 199
Altima	20 to 26	152 to 198
Maxima	20 to 24	142 to 189
Pathfinder	24 to 31	188 to 232
Manual systems		
200SX and Sentra	17 to 33	179 to 232
240SX	21 to 33	134 to 162
300ZX	27 to 33	162 to 199
Altima	20 to 26	152 to 198
Maxima	20 to 24	142 to 189
Pathfinder	24 to 31	188 to 232
Pick-up	24 to 31	188 to 232
Quest	22 to 45	120 to 220

1996

Automatic systems		
300ZX	27 to 33	162 to 199
Altima	20 to 26	152 to 198
Maxima	20 to 24	142 to 189
Pathfinder	25 to 36	178 to 237
Manual systems		
200SX and Sentra	17 to 33	179 to 232
240SX	21 to 33	134 to 162
300ZX	27 to 33	162 to 199
Altima	20 to 26	152 to 198
Maxima	20 to 26	147 to 177
Pathfinder	25 to 36	178 to 237
Pick-up	24 to 31	188 to 232
Quest	22 to 45	120 to 220

1997

Automatic systems		
Altima	20 to 26	152 to 198
Maxima	20 to 24	142 to 189
Pathfinder	25 to 36	178 to 237
Quest	22 to 45	120 to 220
Manual systems		
200SX and Sentra	17 to 33	179 to 232
240SX	21 to 33	134 to 162
Altima	20 to 26	152 to 198
Maxima	20 to 26	147 to 177
Pathfinder	25 to 36	178 to 237
Pick-up	24 to 31	188 to 232
Quest	22 to 45	120 to 220

1998

Automatic systems		
Altima	20 to 26	152 to 198
Maxima	20 to 26	147 to 177
Pathfinder	25 to 36	178 to 237
Quest	22 to 45	120 to 220
Manual systems		
200SX and Sentra	17 to 33	179 to 232
240SX	21 to 33	134 to 162

Manufacturer Year Model (or type of system)	Low side gauge (evaporator suction)	High side gauge (discharge)
Altima	20 to 26	152 to 198
Frontier	24 to 31	186 to 228
Maxima	20 to 26	147 to 177
Pathfinder	25 to 36	178 to 237
Quest	22 to 45	120 to 220
1999		
Automatic systems		
Maxima	20 to 26	147 to 177
Pathfinder	25 to 36	178 to 237
Quest	25 to 36	120 to 220
Manual systems		
Altima	20 to 26	152 to 198
Frontier	24 to 31	186 to 228
Maxima	20 to 26	147 to 177
Pathfinder	25 to 36	178 to 237
Quest	22 to 45	120 to 220
Sentra	17 to 33	179 to 232

Peugeot

1986 through 1989 (505 Series)	not available	not available

Porsche

1989 through 1992 (911)	12 to 17	254 to 297
1993 through 1995 (911)	9 to 15	174 to 218
1997 through 1999		
911	9 to 15	174 to 218
Boxster	20 to 25	218 to 319

Saab

1989 through 1991		
Automatic system (9000)	37	172
Manual system (900)	21 to 28	149 to 220
1992		
Automatic system (9000)	40 to 46	391 to 441
Manual systems (900 and 9000)	21 to 28	149 to 220
1993		
Automatic system (9000)	15 to 44	174 to 239
Manual system (900)	21 to 28	149 to 220
1994 through 1998 (all models)	15 to 44	174 to 239
1999 (all models)	22 to 36	not available (varies in accordance with load)

Sterling

1988 (825)	34	228

Subaru

1983 (all models)	28	230
1984 through 1987 (all models)	28	256
1988 and 1989		
XT Coupe and XT6	30	228
All other models	28	256
1990		
Automatic system (Legacy)	25 to 35	200 to 227
Manual systems		
Legacy	28	256
Loyale	28	228
1991		
Automatic system (Legacy)	25 to 35	200 to 227

Manufacturer Year Model (or type of system)	Low side gauge (evaporator suction)	High side gauge (discharge)
Manual systems		
Legacy	28	256
Loyale	28	228
XT and XT6	30	228
1992		
Automatic system (SVX)	28	185 to 213
Manual systems		
Legacy	24 to 37	149 to 203
Loyale	28	228
1993 and 1994		
Automatic system (SVX)	28	185 to 213
Manual systems		
Impreza	26 to 31	356 to 412
Legacy	24 to 37	149 to 203
Loyale	28	228
1995 through 1997		
Automatic system (SVX)	28	185 to 213
Manual systems		
Impreza	23 to 31	356 to 412
Legacy	19 to 36	187 to 249
1998 and 1999		
Forester	23 to 31	413 to 441
Impreza	23 to 33	384 to 412
Legacy	19 to 36	187 to 249

Suzuki

1989 through 1993 (all models)	21 to 28	206 to 213
1994 (all models)		
R-12 systems	21 to 28	206 to 213
R-134a systems	21 to 28	256 to 213
1995 through 1997 (all models)	21 to 28	256 to 313
1998		
Esteem	37 to 51	239 to 296
Sidekick and X90		
SE Series	40 to 51	249 to 292
SZ Series	37 to 47	213 to 228
Swift	33 to 50	199 to 249
1999		
Esteem	37 to 51	239 to 296
Swift	33 to 50	199 to 249
Vitara and Grand Vitara	28 to 32	200 to 243

Toyota

1980 through 1982 (all models)	22 to 35	200 to 220
1983 and 1984		
Land Cruiser and pick-up	22 to 35	199 to 220
All other models	21 to 28	206 to 213
1985 (all models)	21 to 28	206 to 213
1986		
Automatic systems		
Celica, MR2 and van	21 to 28	199 to 220
Cressida and Supra	21 to 28	206 to 213
Manual systems (all models)	21 to 28	206 to 213
1987		
Automatic systems		
Celica	21 to 28	199 to 220
Cressida and Supra	21 to 28	206 to 213
Manual systems (all models)	21 to 28	206 to 213
1988 through 1990 (all models)	21 to 28	206 to 213
1991 and 1992		
Automatic systems (Celica, Cressida and Supra)	21 to 28	206 to 213
Manual systems (all models)	21 to 28	206 to 213

Heating and air conditioning

Manufacturer Year Model (or type of system)	Low side gauge (evaporator suction)	High side gauge (discharge)
Toyota (continued)		
1993		
Automatic systems		
Celica	21 to 28	206 to 213
Supra	28 to 36	199 to 228
Manual systems		
T100	21 to 36	199 to 228
All other models	21 to 28	206 to 213
1994		
Automatic system (Supra)	28 to 36	199 to 228
Manual systems		
Previa and T100	21 to 36	206 to 228
All other models	21 to 36	199 to 228
1995		
Automatic system		
Avalon	21 to 36	199 to 228
Supra	28 to 36	199 to 228
Manual systems		
Previa	21 to 36	203 to 228
Tacoma	22 to 37	205 to 235
All other models	21 to 36	199 to 228
1996 and 1997		
Automatic systems (Avalon and Supra)	21 to 36	199 to 228
Manual systems		
Previa	21 to 36	203 to 228
RAV4	22 to 37	206 to 235
Tacoma	22 to 37	205 to 235
All other models	21 to 36	199 to 228
1998		
Automatic systems (Avalon, Land Cruiser and Supra)	21 to 36	199 to 228
Manual systems		
RAV4	22 to 37	206 to 235
Sienna	21 to 36	205 to 235
Tacoma	22 to 37	205 to 235
All other models	21 to 36	199 to 228
1999		
Automatic systems		
4Runner, Avalon, Camry and Camry Solara	21 to 36	199 to 228
Land Cruiser	21 to 36	199 to 213
Manual systems		
4Runner	21 to 36	199 to 228
Avalon	21 to 36	199 to 228
Camry and Camry Solara	21 to 36	199 to 228
Celica	21 to 36	199 to 228
Corolla	21 to 36	199 to 213
RAV4	22 to 37	206 to 235
Sienna	21 to 36	205 to 235
Tacoma	22 to 37	205 to 235
Volkswagen		
1980 and 1981		
Dasher	15 to 30	175 to 250
All other models	15 to 30	150 to 270
1982		
Quantum	not available	not available
All other models	15 to 30	150 to 270
1983 and 1984		
Quantum	not available	not available
All other models	14 to 30	150 to 270
1985		
Quantum	not available	not available
All other models	26 to 40	150 to 210
1986 and 1987		
Quantum, Vanagon and Vanagon Synchro	not available	not available
All other models	26 to 40	150 to 210
1988		
Quantum	29	218
All other models	26 to 40	150 to 210
1989 through 1992 (all models)	26 to 40	150 to 210
1993		
Cabriolet and Fox	26 to 40	150 to 210
All other models	17 to 26	203
1994 through 1997 (all models)	17	203
1998		
Passat	22 to 36	232
All other models	17 to 26	203
1999		
New Beetle and Passat	22 to 36	232
Cabrio, Golf, GTI and Jetta	17	203
Volvo		
1980 and 1981 (all models)	31 to 38	180 to 230
1982 (all models)	18 to 22	140 to 190
1983 and 1984		
All models except diesel	20 to 37	115 to 170
Diesel	10 to 38	135 to 200
1985 through 1990 (all models)	20 to 37	115 to 170
1991 (all models)	31 to 38	185 to 227
1992 (all models)	20 to 37	114 to 170
1993		
Automatic systems (850 and 960)	not available	not available
Manual systems		
240	not available	not available
940	20 to 37	114 to 170
1994		
Automatic systems (850 and 960)	not available	not available
Manual system (940)	20 to 37	114 to 170
1995 and 1996		
Automatic systems		
850	25 to 33	406 to 450
960	not available	not available
Manual systems		
850	25 to 33	406 to 450
940	20 to 37	114 to 170
1997		
Automatic systems		
850	25 to 33	406 to 450
960	not available	not available
Manual systems		
850	25 to 33	406 to 450
1998		
C70, S70 and V70	25 to 33	406 to 450
S90 and V90	not available	not available
1999		
C70, S70 and V70	25 to 33	406 to 450
S80	not available	not available

System refrigerant oil capacity (domestic vehicles) (in ounces)

AMC

1980
All models
York 2-cylinder compressor...................... 7.00
Delco Air 4-cylinder compressor.................. 6.00

1981
All models
York 2-cylinder compressor...................... 700
Delco Air 4-cylinder compressor.................. 6.00
With Sankyo 5-cylinder compressor .... 7.00 to 8.00

1982 and 1983 (all models).................. 7.00 to 8.00
1984 and 1985 (all models).................. 4.00 to 6.00
1986 through 1988 (all models) .... 7.00 to 8.00

Buick

1980
Skyhawk.. 6.00
Skylark
Axial compressor 8.00
Radial compressor 5.00
All other models
Axial compressor 10.00
Radial compressor 6.00

1981 and 1982
Skyhawk (1982) 6.00
Skylark
Axial compressor 8.00
Radial compressor 5.00
All other models
Axial compressor 10.00
Radial compressor 6.00

1983
Century and Skylark
Axial compressor 8.00
Radial compressor 5.00
All other models 6.00

1984
Century, Skyhawk and Skylark
Axial compressor 8.00
Radial compressor 5.00
Electra, Estate Wagon,
Axial compressor 10.00
Radial compressor 6.00
All other models 6.00

1985
Century, Electra, Skyhawk and Skylark
Axial compressor 8.00
Radial compressor 5.00
Somerset Regal................................ 8.00
All other models 6.00

1986 and 1987
Century
Axial compressor 8.00
Radial compressor 5.00
Estate wagon and Regal 6.00
All other models 8.00

1988
Century
DA-V5 compressor........................... 6.00
HR-6 compressor............................ 8.00
Estate Wagon.................................. 6.00
All other models 8.00

1989 and 1990
Estate wagon.................................. 6.00
All other models 8.00

1991
Roadmaster.................................... 6.00
All other models 8.00

1992 and 1993
Century and Regal 9.00
Roadmaster.................................... 6.00
All other models 8.00

1994
Century....................................... 9.00
All other models 8.00

1995 and 1996
Century and Skylark 9.00
All other models 8.00

1997
Century, LeSabre and Regal 8.00
Park Avenue, Riviera and Skylark 9.00

1998 and 1999............................. 9.00

Cadillac

1980 through 1983 .... 6.00

1984 and 1985
Axial compressor.............................. 8.00
Radial compressor 5.00

1986
Brougham
Axial compressor 8.00
Radial compressor 5.00
All other models 8.00

1987 through 1992
Brougham...................................... 6.00
All other models 8.00

1993 through 1996
Fleetwood RWD 6.00
All other models 8.00

1997
Catera.. 9.00
All other models 8.00

1998.. 9.00

1999
Catera and Seville 9.00
DeVille, Eldorado and Escalade 8.00

Chevrolet

1980
Blazer K/V, C and K Series Pick-ups, El Camino,
G Series Van and Suburban
A-6 compressor 10.00
R-4 compressor 6.00

Heating and air conditioning

Chevrolet (continued)

1980 (continued)

Citation
- Axial compressor 8.00
- Radial compressor 5.00

Luv Pick-up 8.30

All other models
- Axial compressor 10.00
- Radial compressor 6.00

1981

Blazer K/V, C and K Series Pick-ups, El Camino,
G Series Van and Suburban
- A-6 compressor 10.00
- R-4 compressor 6.00

Citation
- Axial compressor 8.00
- Radial compressor 5.00

Luv Pick-up 5.00

All other models
- Axial compressor 10.00
- Radial compressor 6.00

1982

Blazer K/V, C and K Series Pick-ups, El Camino,
G Series Van and Suburban
- A-6 compressor 10.00
- R-4 compressor 6.00

Caprice, Impala, Malibu and Monte Carlo
- Axial compressor 10.00
- Radial compressor 6.00

Citation
- Axial compressor 8.00
- Radial compressor 5.00

All other models 6.00

1983

Blazer K/V, C and K Series Pick-ups, G Series Van
and Suburban
- A-6 compressor 10.00
- R-4 compressor 6.00

Celebrity and Citation
- Axial compressor 8.00
- Radial compressor 5.00

All other models 6.00

1984

Blazer K/V, C and K Series Pick-ups, G Series Van
and Suburban
- A-6 compressor 10.00
- R-4 compressor 6.00

Camaro, Cavalier, Celebrity and Citation
- Axial compressor 8.00
- Radial compressor 5.00

S/T Pickup
- DA-6 compressor 8.00
- R-4 compressor 6.00

All other models 6.00

1985

Astro
- Without rear A/C
  - 2.5L 8.00
  - 4.3L 6.00
- With rear A/C 9.00

Blazer K/V, C and K Series Pick-ups, G Series Van
and Suburban
- A-6 compressor 10.00
- R-4 compressor 6.00

Camaro, Cavalier, Celebrity and Citation
- Axial compressor 8.00
- Radial compressor 5.00

Nova .... 2.00 to 3.40

Spectrum 3.35

Sprint .... 2.00 to 3.50

S/T Pickup
- DA-6 compressor 8.00
- R-4 compressor 6.00

All other models 6.00

1986

Astro
- Without rear A/C
  - 2.5L 8.00
  - 4.3L 6.00
- With rear A/C 9.00

Blazer K/V, C and K Series Pick-ups and Suburban
- With gasoline engine 6.00
- With diesel engine 8.00

Camaro and Celebrity
- Axial compressor 8.00
- Radial compressor 5.00

Cavalier 8.00

G Series Van
- A-6 compressor 10.00
- R-4 compressor 6.00

Nova .... 2.00 to 3.40

Spectrum 3.35

Sprint .... 2.00 to 3.50

S/T Pickup
- DA-6 compressor 8.00
- R-4 compressor 6.00

All other models 6.00

1987

Astro
- Without rear A/C
  - 2.5L 8.00
  - 4.3L 6.00
- With rear A/C 9.00

Blazer K/V and Suburban
- With gasoline engine (except 7.4L) 6.00
- With diesel engine or 7.4L gasoline engine 8.00

Camaro and Celebrity
- Axial compressor 8.00
- Radial compressor 5.00

Cavalier 8.00

G Series Van
- A-6 compressor 10.00
- R-4 compressor 6.00

Nova .... 2.00 to 3.40

Spectrum 3.35

Sprint .... 2.00 to 3.50

S/T Pickup
- DA-6 compressor 8.00
- R-4 compressor 6.00

All other models 6.00

1988

Astro
- Without rear A/C
  - 2.5L 8.00
  - 4.3L 6.00
- With rear A/C 9.00

Blazer K/V
- R4 compressor 6.00
- HR6 compressor 8.00

C and K Series Pick-ups 6.00

Camaro and Celebrity
Axial compressor 8.00
Radial compressor 5.00
Cavalier and Corvette................................... 8.00
G Series Van
A-6 compressor 10.00
R-4 compressor 6.00
Nova .... 2.00 to 3.40
Spectrum.. 3.35
Sprint 2.96
S/T Pickup
DA-6 compressor 8.00
R-4 compressor 6.00
Suburban
R4 compressor 9.00
HR6 compressor 11.00
All other models 6.00

1989
Astro
Without rear A/C
2.5L 8.00
4.3L 6.00
With rear A/C 8.00
Blazer K/V
R4 compressor... 6.00
HR6 compressor 8.00
Blazer S/T
R4 compressor... 11.00
V-5 compressor... 8.00
C and K Series Pick-ups 6.00
Cavalier, Celebrity and Corvette 8.00
G Series Van
Without rear A/C
A-6 compressor 10.00
R-4 compressor 6.00
With rear A/C
A-6 compressor 13.00
R-4 compressor 9.00
S/T Pick-up
R-4 compressor 11.00
V-5 compressor... 8.00
All other models 6.00

1990 and 1991
Astro
Without rear A/C 8.00
With rear A/C 10.00
Blazer K/V
R4 compressor... 6.00
HR6 compressor 8.00
Blazer S/T
R4 compressor... 11.00
V-5 compressor... 8.00
C and K Series Pick-ups 6.00
Camaro, Caprice and Impala 6.00
G Series Van
Without rear A/C
A-6 compressor 10.00
R-4 compressor 6.00
With rear A/C
A-6 compressor 13.00
R-4 compressor 9.00
S/T Pick-up
R-4 compressor 11.00
V-5 compressor... 8.00
All other models 8.00

1992
3500HD.. 6.00
Astro
Without rear A/C 8.00
With rear A/C 10.00
Blazer K/V
R4 compressor.. 6.00
HR6 compressor 8.00
Blazer S/T
R4 compressor.. 11.00
V-5 compressor... 8.00
Camaro, Caprice and C and K Series Pick-ups........... 6.00
G Series van
Without rear A/C 8.00
With rear A/C 10.5
S/T Pick-up
R4 compressor.. 11.00
V5 compressor.. 8.00
Suburban.. 6.00
All other models 8.00

1993
3500HD.. 8.00
Astro
Without rear A/C 8.00
With rear A/C 10.50
Caprice 6.00
G Series and Lumina vans and Suburban
Without rear A/C 8.00
With rear A/C 11.00
Lumina.. 9.00
All other models 8.00

1994
3500HD.. 8.00
Astro, G Series and Lumina vans and Suburban
Without rear A/C 8.00
With rear A/C 11.00
Beretta and Corsica...................................... 9.00
R4 compressor 11.00
V5 compressor 8.00
S/T Pick-up
2.2L engine.. 9.00
4.3L engine.. 8.00
All other models... 8.00

1995 and 1996
3500HD.. 8.00
Astro, Express (1996), G Series and Lumina vans,
Suburban and Tahoe
Without rear A/C 8.00
With rear A/C 11.00
Beretta, Cavalier and Corsica........................... 9.00
S/T Pick-up
2.2L engine.. 9.00
4.3L engine.. 8.00
All other models... 8.00

1997
3500HD.. 8.00
Astro, Express and G Series vans, Suburban and Tahoe
Without rear A/C.. 8.00
With rear A/C 11.00
Cavalier, Corvette and Malibu 9.00
S/T Pick-up
2.2L engine.. 9.00
4.3L engine.. 8.00
Venture
Without rear A/C.. 8.00
With rear A/C .... Refer to label in engine compartment
All other models... 8.00

Heating and air conditioning

Chevrolet (continued)

1998
3500HD 8.00
Astro, Express and G Series vans, Suburban and Tahoe
  Without rear A/C 8.00
  With rear A/C 11.00
Metro 3.40
Prizm and C and K Series Pick-ups 8.00
S/T Pick-up
  2.2L engine 9.00
  4.3L engine 8.00
Tracker 3.04
Venture
  Without rear A/C 9.00
  With rear A/C .... Refer to label in engine compartment
All other models 9.00

1999
3500HD 8.00
Astro, Express and G Series vans, Suburban and Tahoe
  Without rear A/C 8.00
  With rear A/C 11.00
Malibu 9.50
Metro 3.40
Prizm and C and K Series Pick-ups 8.00
S/T Pick-up
  2.2L engine 9.00
  4.3L engine 8.00
Tracker .... not available
Venture
  Without rear A/C .... Refer to label in engine compartment
  With rear A/C .... Refer to label in engine compartment
All other models 9.00

Chrysler

1980 (all models)
RV-2 compressor .... 10.00 to 12.00
Sankyo compressor .... 7.00 to 8.00
C-171 compressor 9.00
1981 through 1984 .... 9.00 to 10.00
1985
Fifth Avenue .... 9.00 to 10.00
Laser 7.25
All other models .... 7.00 to 7.25
1986
Laser 7.25
All other models .... 7.00 to 7.25
1987
Conquest 5.70
Laser 7.25
All other models .... 7.00 to 7.25
1988
Conquest 5.70
Fifth Avenue 7.25
All other models .... 7.00 to 7.25
1989
Conquest 5.70
Fifth Avenue 7.25
All other models
  Fixed displacement compressor 7.25
  Variable displacement compressor 8.70
1990 through 1992
All models
  Fixed displacement compressor 7.25
  Variable displacement compressor 8.70

1993
Concorde 4.75
Town and Country
  Without rear A/C 4.73
  With rear A/C 7.40
All other models
  Fixed displacement compressor 7.25
  Variable displacement compressor 8.70
1994
Concorde 4.80
LeBaron 7.30
LHS and New Yorker 4.80
Town and Country
  Without rear A/C 4.73
  With rear A/C 7.40
1995
Cirrus 5.00
Concorde 4.80
LeBaron 7.30
LHS and New Yorker 4.80
Sebring Coupe
  SOHC .... 5.70 to 6.40
  DOHC .... 2.70 to 4.10
Town and Country
  Without rear A/C 4.73
  With rear A/C 7.40
1996
Cirrus 5.00
Sebring Coupe
  SOHC .... 5.70 to 6.40
  DOHC .... 2.70 to 4.10
All other models 7.00
Town and Country
  Without rear A/C 5.00
  With rear A/C 7.40
1997 through 1999
Sebring Coupe
  SOHC .... 5.70 to 6.40
  DOHC .... 2.70 to 4.10
Town and Country
  Without rear A/C 5.00
  With rear A/C 7.40
All other models 5.00

Dodge

1980
Challenger 8.00
Colt
  Hatchback .... not available
  Sedan 8.00
D50 and Ram 50 Pick-ups .... not available
All other models
  RV-2 compressor .... 10.00 to 12.00
  Sankyo compressor .... 7.00 to 8.00
  C-171 compressor .... 9.00 to 10.00
1981
Challenger and Colt .... Compressor oil level, 1.0 to 1.5 inches
D50 and Ram 50 Pick-ups .... not available
Diplomat, Mirada and St. Regis .... 9.00 to 10.00
All other models
  RV-2 compressor .... 10.00 to 12.00
  Sankyo compressor .... 7.00 to 8.00
  C-171 compressor .... 9.00 to 10.00
1982 and 1983
Challenger and Colt ...... Compressor oil level, 1.0 to 1.5 inches

D50 and Ram 50 Pick-ups .... not available
Full-size van and wagon .... 9.00 to 10.00
All other models .... 9.00 to 10.00

1984
Colt and Conquest .... Compressor oil level, 1.0 to 1.5 inches
D50 and Ram 50 Pick-ups .... not available
Full-size van and wagon .... 9.00 to 10.00
All other models .... 9.00 to 10.00

1985
Colt 3.80
Conquest .... not available
D50 and Ram 50 Pick-ups .... not available
Diplomat .... 9.00 to 10.00
All other models .... 7.00 to 7.25

1986
Colt 2.70
Conquest 5.70
D50 and Ram 50 Pick-ups 6.50
All other models .... 7.00 to 7.25

1987
Colt 2.70
D50 and Ram 50 Pick-ups 6.50
Ram Raider 3.70
All other models .... 7.00 to 7.25

1988
Colt 2.70
D50 and Ram 50 Pick-ups 2.70
Diplomat 7.25
Ram Raider 3.70
All other models .... 7.00 to 7.25

1989
Colt
    All Colt models except wagon 5.00
    Wagon 2.70
D50 and Ram 50 Pick-ups 2.70
Dakota, full-size Pick-up and Ramcharger .... 7.00 to 7.25
Diplomat 7.25
Ram Raider
    2.6L 3.70
    3.0L 2.70
All other models
    Fixed displacement compressor 7.25
    Variable displacement compressor 8.70

1990
Colt
    All Colt models except wagon 5.00
    Wagon 2.70
Dakota, full-size Pick-up and Ramcharger .... 7.00 to 7.25
D50 and Ram 50 Pick-ups .... 7.90 to 9.10
Monaco 8.10
All other models
    Fixed displacement compressor 7.25
    Variable displacement compressor 8.70

1991
Colt 5.00
D50 and Ram 50 Pick-ups .... 7.90 to 9.10
Dakota, full-size Pick-up and Ramcharger .... 7.00 to 7.25
Full-size van and wagon 7.25
Monaco 8.10
Stealth 5.40
All other models
    Fixed displacement compressor 7.25
    Variable displacement compressor 8.70

1992
Colt 5.00

Colt Vista 2.70
Dakota 7.25
Full-size Pick-up and Ramcharger .... 7.00 to 7.25
Full-size van and wagon 7.25
Monaco 8.10
Ram 50 Pick-up .... 7.90 to 9.10
Stealth 5.40
Viper .... not available
All other models
    Fixed displacement compressor 7.25
    Variable displacement compressor 8.70

1993
Caravan
    Without rear A/C 4.73
    With rear A/C 7.40
Colt 4.39
Colt Vista 2.70
Dakota 7.25
Full-size Pick-up and Ramcharger 4.60
Full-size van and wagon 7.25
Intrepid 4.80
Ram 50 Pick-up .... 7.90 to 9.10
Stealth 5.40
Viper .... not available
All other models
    Fixed displacement compressor 7.25
    Variable displacement compressor 8.70

1994
Caravan
    Without rear A/C 4.73
    With rear A/C 7.40
Colt 4.40
Colt Vista 2.70
Dakota and full-size Pick-up 7.75
Full-size van 4.73
Full-size wagon 7.25
Intrepid 4.80
Shadow and Spirit 7.25
Stealth 5.40
Viper 4.75

1995
Avenger
    SOHC .... 5.70 to 6.40
    DOHC .... 2.70 to 4.10
Caravan
    Without rear A/C 4.73
    With rear A/C 7.40
Dakota and full-size Pick-up 7.75
Full-size van 4.73
Full-size wagon 7.40
Intrepid 4.80
Neon 4.75
Spirit 7.25
Stealth 5.40
Stratus 5.00
Viper 4.75

1996
Avenger
    SOHC .... 5.70 to 6.40
    DOHC .... 2.70 to 4.10
Caravan
    Without rear A/C 5.00
    With rear A/C 7.40
Dakota and full-size Pick-up 7.75
Full-size van 5.25

Heating and air conditioning

Dodge (continued)

1996 (continued)
Full-size wagon 7.25
Intrepid 7.00
Neon.. 4.75
Stealth 5.40
Stratus 5.00
Viper 4.75

1997
Avenger
  SOHC .... 5.70 to 6.40
  DOHC .... 2.70 to 4.10
Caravan
  Without rear A/C 5.00
  With rear A/C 7.40
Dakota and full-size Pick-up 7.75
Full-size van and full-size wagon 7.25
Neon.. 6.75
Viper 4.75
All other models 5.00

1998
Avenger
  SOHC .... 5.70 to 6.40
  DOHC .... 2.70 to 4.10
Caravan
  Without rear A/C 5.00
  With rear A/C 7.40
Dakota and full-size Pick-up 8.10
Durango
  Without rear A/C 5.50
  With rear A/C 8.00
Full-size van 8.00
Full-size wagon 10.00
Neon.. 6.75
Viper 4.75
All other models 5.00

1999
Avenger.. 5.70 to 6.40
Caravan
  Without rear A/C 5.00
  With rear A/C 7.40
Dakota and full-size Pick-up 8.10
Durango
  Without rear A/C 5.50
  With rear A/C 8.00
Full-size van 8.00
Full-size wagon 10.00
Neon.. 4.75
Viper 4.75
All other models 5.00

Eagle

1988
Eagle 4X4... 7.0 to 8.0
Medallion........................... 4 to 6 dipstick increments
Premier 8.1

1989
Medallion........................... 4 to 6 dipstick increments
Premier 8.1
Summit 5.0

1990 and 1991
Premier 8.1
Summit 5.0
Talon 2.7

1992
Premier 8.1
Summit 5.0
Summit Wagon and Talon 2.7

1993
Summit 4.39
Summit Wagon and Talon 2.7
Vision 4.8

1994
Summit 4.4
Summit Wagon
  1.8L 4.1
  2.4L 2.7
Talon 2.7
Vision 4.8

1995 and 1996
Summit .... 4.4 to 5.1
Summit Wagon
  1.8L 4.1
  2.4L 2.7
Talon
  Without turbo........................... 2.7 to 4.1
  With turbo .... 5.7 to 6.4
Vision
  1995 .... 4.8
  1996 .... 7.0

1997 and 1998
Talon
  Without turbo........................... 2.7 to 4.1
  With turbo .... 5.7 to 6.4
Vision (1997) 5.0

Ford

1980
Econoline, F-Series Pick-ups and Super Duty Pick-ups
  Tecumseh compressor 11.00
  York compressor.................................... 10.00
Fiesta 9.00
Granada.. 10.50
LTD
  Motorcraft compressor 10.50
  Nippondenso compressor 13.00
All other models 10.00

1981
Econoline, F-Series Pick-ups and Super Duty Pick-ups
  Tecumseh compressor 11.00
  York compressor.................................... 10.00
Escort and LTD 13.00
All other models 10.00

1982
Econoline
  Tecumseh compressor 11.00
  York compressor.................................... 10.00
LTD.. 13
All other models 10.00

1983
Econoline... 10.00
Fairmont and LTD
  2.3L 8.00
  3.3L 10.00
Ranger
  Tecumseh HR-980 compressor 8.00
  All other compressors 10.00

Thunderbird
- 2.3L and 3.8L 8.00
- 5.0L 10.00
- All other models... 10.00

1984 and 1985

Bronco II
- Tecumseh HR-980 compressor 8.00
- All other compressors 10.00

Econoline 10.00

LTD and Thunderbird
- 2.3L and 3.8L 8.00
- 5.0L 10.00

Mustang
- 2.3L 8.00
- 3.8L and 5.0L 10.00

Ranger
- Tecumseh HR-980 compressor 8.00
- All other compressors 10.00

All other models.. 10.00

1986

Aerostar, Bronco and Econoline 10.00

Bronco II
- Tecumseh HR-980 compressor 8.00
- All other compressors 10.00

LTD
- 2.3L and 3.8L 8.00
- 5.0L 10.00

Mustang
- 2.3L 8.00
- 5.0L 10.00

Ranger
- Tecumseh HR-980 compressor 8.00
- All other compressors 10.00

Thunderbird
- 2.3L .... not available
- All other models 10.00

All other models.. 10.00

1987

Crown Victoria
- FS-6 compressor 10.00
- 6E171 compressor 13.00

Escort and EXP 7.00

Mustang
- 2.3L 8.00
- 5.0L 10.00

Ranger
- Tecumseh HR-980 compressor 8.00
- All other compressors 10.00

Taurus.. 10.00

Tempo 7.00

Thunderbird
- 2.3L .... not available
- All except 2.3L 10.00

All other models.. 10.00

1988

Crown Victoria
- FS-6 compressor 10.00
- 6E171 compressor 13.00

Escort, EXP and Tempo 8.00

Festiva 10.00

Mustang
- 2.3L 8.00
- 5.0L 10.00

Ranger
- Tecumseh HR-980 compressor 8.00
- All other compressors 10.00

Taurus
- 2.5L and 3.0L 10.00
- 3.0L SHO and 3.8L 8.00

Thunderbird
- 2.3L .... not available
- 3.8L 8.00
- 5.0L 10.00

All other models.. 10.00

1989

Aerostar
- Without rear A/C 7.00
- With rear A/C 10.00

Bronco and Thunderbird 7.00

Bronco II 10.00

Crown Victoria, Escort and Tempo 8.00

Econoline, F-Series Pick-ups and Super Duty Pick-ups
- Gasoline engine... 7.00
- Diesel engine.. 10.00

Festiva 10.00

Mustang
- 2.3L 8.00
- 5.0L 10.00

Probe 3.30

Probe
- 2.2L 3.30
- 3.0L 8.00

Ranger
- 2.3L 7.00
- 2.9L 10.00

Taurus
- 2.5L and 3.0L 10.00
- 3.0L SHO and 3.8L 8.00

1990

Aerostar
- Without rear A/C 7.00
- With rear A/C 10.00

Bronco and Thunderbird 7.00

Bronco II 10.00

Crown Victoria, Escort and Tempo 8.00

Econoline and Festiva 10.00

F-Series and Super Duty Pick-ups
- Gasoline engine... 7.00
- Diesel engine.. 10.00

Mustang
- 2.3L 8.00
- 5.0L 10.00

Probe
- 2.2L 3.30
- 3.0L 8.00

Ranger
- 2.3L 7.00
- 2.9L 10.00

Taurus
- 2.5L 10.00
- 3.0L 7.00
- 3.0L SHO and 3.8L 8.00

1991

Aerostar
- Without rear A/C 7.00
- With rear A/C 10.00

Bronco, Explorer and Thunderbird.......................... 7.00

Crown Victoria, Escort and Tempo 8.00

Econoline and Festiva 10.00

F-Series and Super Duty Pick-ups
- Gasoline engine... 7.00
- Diesel engine.. 10.00

Heating and air conditioning

Ford (continued)

1991 (continued)
- Mustang
  - 2.3L 8.00
  - 5.0L 10.00
- Probe
  - 2.2L 3.30
  - 3.0L 8.00
- Ranger
  - 2.3L 7.00
  - 2.9L 10.00
- Taurus
  - 2.5L 10.00
  - 3.0L and 3.8L 7.00
  - 3.0L SHO 8.00

1992
- Aerostar
  - Without rear A/C 7.00
  - With rear A/C 10.00
- Escort and ZX2 .... 8.00
- Econoline and Festiva 10.00
- F-150, F-250, F-350 and Super Duty Pick-ups
  - Gasoline engine 7.00
  - Diesel engine 10.00
- Mustang 8.00
- Probe 3.30
- Ranger
  - 2.3L, 3.0L and 4.0L 7.00
  - 2.9L 10.00
- Taurus
  - 3.0L and 3.8L 7.00
  - 3.0L SHO 8.00
- All other models 7.00

1993
- Aerostar
  - Without rear A/C 7.00
  - With rear A/C 10.00
- Crown Victoria
  - Without rear A/C 7.00
  - With rear A/C 10.00
- Econoline
  - Without rear A/C
    - FX-15 compressor 7.00
    - FS-6 compressor 10.00
  - With rear A/C 10.00
- Escort and ZX2
  - 1.8L with 10P13 compressor 7.75
  - 1.9L with FX-15 compressor 7.00
- F-150, F-250, F-350 and Super Duty Pick-ups 7.00*
- Festiva 10.00
- Mustang 8.00
- Probe 3.30
- Taurus
  - 3.0L and 3.8L
    - Without rear A/C 7.00
    - With rear A/C 10.00
  - 3.0L SHO and 3.2L SHO 8.00
- Thunderbird
  - Without rear A/C 7.00
  - With rear A/C 10.00
- All other models 7.00

1994
- Aerostar
  - Without rear A/C 7.00*
  - With rear A/C 10.00*

Bronco, Explorer, Mustang and Ranger 7.00*
- Econoline
  - Without rear A/C 7.00*
  - With rear A/C 10.00*
- F-150, F-250, F-350 and Super Duty Pick-ups 7.00*
- Probe 6.76
- Taurus
  - 10P15 compressor 8.00
  - All other compressors 7.00
- Thunderbird
  - 3.8L 7.00*
  - 5.0L 7.00
- All other models 7.00

1995
- Aerostar
  - Without rear A/C 7.00*
  - With rear A/C 10.00*
- Bronco, Explorer, Mustang and Ranger 7.00*
- Econoline
  - Without rear A/C 7.00*
  - With rear A/C 10.00*
- Escort and ZX2 .... 8.00
- F-150, F-250, F-350 and Super Duty Pick-ups 7.00*
- Probe 6.76
- Taurus
  - 10P15 compressor 8.00
  - All other compressors 7.00
- Thunderbird
  - 3.8L 7.00*
  - 5.0L 7.00
- Windstar
  - Without rear A/C 9.00*
  - With rear A/C 13.00*
- All other models 7.00

1996
- Aerostar
  - Without rear A/C 7.00*
  - With rear A/C 10.00*
- Bronco, Explorer and Mustang 11.00*
- Econoline
  - Without rear A/C 7.00
  - With rear A/C 10.00
- F-150, F-250, F-350 and Super Duty Pick-ups 11.00*
- Probe 6.76
- Ranger 7.00*
- Thunderbird
  - 3.8L 7.00*
  - 4.6L 7.00
- Windstar
  - Without rear A/C 9.00*
  - With rear A/C 13.00*
- All other models 7.00

1997
- Aerostar
  - Without rear A/C 9.00*
  - With rear A/C 13.00*
- Crown Victoria 7.50
- Econoline and Expedition
  - Without rear A/C 9.00
  - With rear A/C 13.00
- Escort and ZX2 .... 6.60
- Explorer, F-150 and F-250 LD 9.00
- F-250HD, F-350, Super Duty and Ranger Pick-ups 9.00*
- Mustang 8.60*
- Taurus 6.60

Thunderbird 7.00*
Windstar
    Without rear A/C 10.00
    With rear A/C 13.00
All other models 7.00
1998
Crown Victoria 7.50
Econoline and Expedition
    Without rear A/C 9.00
    With rear A/C 13.00
Explorer, F-150, F-250 and Ranger 9.00
Mustang 8.60
Taurus 6.60
Windstar
    Without rear A/C 10.00
    With rear A/C 14.00
All other models 7.00
1999
Crown Victoria 7.50
Econoline and Expedition
    Without rear A/C 9.00
    With rear A/C 13.00
F-150, F-250, F-Super Duty 250, 350 and
    Ranger Pick-ups 9.00
Windstar 14.00
All other models 7.00

On models with "Authorized Modification" decal (on radiator support near VECI label), add only the specified amount of refrigerant oil. On all models without this decal (except for the following exceptions), add the specified amount plus an additional 2.00 ounces. On 1993 through 1996 Bronco and F-Series Pick-ups without a decal, add the specified amount plus an additional 4.00 ounces. If there is no decal on 1994 and 1995 Econoline models with front and rear A/C, add the specified amount of oil plus an additional 3.00 ounces.

Geo

1989
Metro 2.70
Prizm 6.00
Spectrum 3.35
Tracker 2.70
1990 through 1991
Metro 2.70
Prizm 6.00
Storm 5.10
Tracker 2.70
1992 and 1993
Metro 2.70
Prizm 6.00
Storm 5.10
Tracker 4.90
1994
Metro 3.40
Prizm 5.10
Tracker 3.30
1995
Metro 3.50
Prizm 4.10
Tracker 3.30
1996 and 1997
Metro 3.40
Prizm 4.10
Tracker 3.30

GMC

1980 and 1981
All models
    A-6 compressor 10.00
    R-4 compressor 6.00
1982
S/T Pickup 6.00
All other models
    A-6 compressor 10.00
    R-4 compressor 6.00
1983
Caballero, S/T Pickup and Jimmy S/T 6.00
All other models
    A-6 compressor 10.00
    R-4 compressor 6.00
1984
Caballero and Jimmy S/T 6.00
S/T Pick-up
    DA-6 compressor 8.00
    R-4 compressor 6.00
All other models
    A-6 compressor 10.00
    R-4 compressor 6.00
1985
Caballero and Jimmy S/T 6.00
Safari
    Without rear A/C
        2.5L 8.00
        4.3L 6.00
    With rear A/C 9.00
S/T Pick-up
    DA-6 compressor 8.00
    R-4 compressor 6.00
All other models
    A-6 compressor 10.00
    R-4 compressor 6.00
1986
Caballero and Jimmy S/T 6.00
G Series Van
    A-6 compressor 10.00
    R-4 compressor 6.00
Safari
    Without rear A/C
        2.5L 8.00
        4.3L 6.00
S/T Pick-up
    DA-6 compressor 8.00
    R-4 compressor 6.00
    With rear A/C 9.00
All other models
    With gasoline engine 6.00
    With diesel engine 8.00
1987
Caballero and Jimmy S/T 6.00
G Series Van
    A-6 compressor 10.00
    R-4 compressor 6.00
Jimmy K/V and Suburban
    With gasoline engine (except 7.4L) 6.00
    With diesel engine or 7.4L gasoline engine............. 8.00
Safari
    Without rear A/C
        2.5L 8.00
        4.3L 6.00
    With rear A/C 9.00

Heating and air conditioning

GMC (continued)

1987 (continued)
S/T Pick-up
  DA-6 compressor 8.00
  R-4 compressor 6.00
All other models
  With gasoline engine 6.00
  With diesel engine 8.00
1988
Caballero and Jimmy S/T 6.00
G Series Van
  A-6 compressor 10.00
  R-4 compressor 6.00
Jimmy K/V and Suburban
  R4 compressor 6.00
  HR6 compressor 8.00
Safari
  Without rear A/C
    2.5L 8.00
    4.3L 6.00
  With rear A/C 9.00
S/T Pick-up
  DA-6 compressor 8.00
  R-4 compressor 6.00
All other models
  With gasoline engine 6.00
  With diesel engine 8.00
1989
Jimmy S/T
  R-4 compressor 11.00
  V-5 compressor 8.00
C and K Series Pick-ups 6.00
G Series Van
  Without rear A/C
    A-6 compressor 10.00
    R-4 compressor 6.00
  With rear A/C
    A-6 compressor 13.00
    R-4 compressor 9.00
Jimmy K/V and Suburban (without rear A/C)
  R4 compressor 6.00
  HR6 compressor 8.00
Suburban (with rear A/C)
  R4 compressor 9.00
  HR6 compressor 11.00
Safari
  Without rear A/C
    2.5L 8.00
    4.3L 6.00
  With rear A/C 8.00
S/T Pick-up
  R-4 compressor 11.00
  V-5 compressor 8.00
1990 and 1991
Jimmy S/T
  R-4 compressor 11.00
  V-5 compressor 8.00
C and K Series Pick-ups 6.00
G Series Van
  Without rear A/C
    A-6 compressor 10.00
    R-4 compressor 6.00
  With rear A/C
    A-6 compressor 13.00
    R-4 compressor 9.00

Jimmy K/V and Suburban (without rear A/C)
  R4 compressor 6.00
  HR6 compressor 8.00
Suburban (with rear A/C)
  R4 compressor 9.00
  HR6 compressor 11.00
Safari
  Without rear A/C 8.00
  With rear A/C 8.00
S/T Pick-up
  R-4 compressor 11.00
  V-5 compressor 8.00
1992
3500HD, C and K Series Pick-ups, Suburban 6.00
Denali and Yukon 9.00
Envoy, Jimmy S/T and Sonoma
  R4 compressor 11.00
  V5 compressor 8.00
G Series van
  Without rear A/C 8.00
  With rear A/C 10.50
Safari
  Without rear A/C 8.00
  With rear A/C 10.00
1993
3500HD, C and K Series Pick-ups 6.00
G Series van
  Without rear A/C 8.00
  With rear A/C 11.00
Safari
  Without rear A/C 8.00
  With rear A/C 10.50
Suburban
  Without rear A/C 8.00
  With rear A/C 11.00
All other models 8.00
1994 and 1995
G Series van, Safari and Suburban
  Without rear A/C 8.00
  With rear A/C 11.00
Sonoma
  2.2L engine 9.00
  4.3L engine 8.00
All other models 8.00
1996 and 1997
G Series van, Safari, Suburban and Savana
  Without rear A/C 8.00
  With rear A/C 11.00
Sonoma
  2.2L engine 9.00
  4.3L engine 8.00
All other models 8.00
1998 and 1999
Denali and Yukon
  Without rear A/C 8.00
  With rear A/C 11.00
Envoy and Jimmy S/T 9.00
G Series van, Safari, Suburban and Savana
  Without rear A/C 8.00
  With rear A/C 11.00
Sonoma
  2.2L engine 9.00
  4.3L engine 8.00
All other models 8.00

Jeep

1980 (all models)	7.00
1981 through 1983 (all models)	
Sankyo five-cylinder compressor	7.00 to 8.00
York two-cylinder compressor	7.00
1984 and 1985 (all models)	6.50
1986 through 1988	
Grand Wagoneer with V8 and J Series Pick-up with V8	7.00
All other models	6.50
1989	
Grand Wagoneer with V8	4.60
All other models	6.00
1990 and 1991 (all models)	4.60
1992 (all models)	4.60
1993	
Cherokee and Wrangler	4.60
Grand Cherokee and Grand Wagoneer	7.75
1994 and 1995	
Cherokee and Wrangler	4.60
Grand Cherokee	7.75
1996	
Cherokee	4.60
Grand Cherokee	7.75
1997	
Cherokee and Wrangler	8.10
Grand Cherokee	7.75
1998 and 1999	
Cherokee and Wrangler	8.10
Grand Cherokee	7.44

Lincoln

1980	
Continental and Mark VI	
Motorcraft compressor	10.50
Nippondenso compressor	13.00
Versailles	10.50
1981 and 1982	13.00
1983 through 1987	10.00
1988	
Continental	8.00
Mark VII and Town Car	10.00
1989 and 1990	8.00
1991 and 1992	
Continental and Town Car	7.00
Mark VII	8.00
1993	
Without rear A/C	7.00
With rear A/C	10.00
1994 through 1996	7.00
1997 through 1999	
Continental and Mark VIII	7.00
Navigator (1998 and 1999)	
Without rear A/C	9.00
With rear A/C	13.00
Town Car	7.50

Mercury

1980	
Marquis	
Motorcraft compressor	0.022 to 0.057 inch
Nippondenso compressor	0.021 to 0.036 inch
Monarch	10.50
All other models	10.00
1981	
Lynx 13.00	
All other models	10.00
1982	
Marquis	13.00
All other models	10.00
1983	
Cougar	
2.3L and 3.8L	8.00
5.0L	10.00
Marquis	
2.3L	8.00
3.3L and 3.8L	10.00
Zephyr	
2.3L	8.00
3.3L	10.00
All other models	10.00
1984 and 1985	
Capri	
2.3L	8.00
3.8L and 5.0L	10.00
Cougar and Marquis	
2.3L and 3.8L	8.0
5.0L	10.00
Marquis	
2.3L and 3.8L	8.00
5.0L	10.00
All other models	10.00
1986	
Capri	
2.3L	8.00
5.0L	10.00
Marquis	
2.3L and 3.8L	8.00
5.0L	10.00
All other models	10.00
1987	
Grand Marquis	
FS-6 compressor	10.00
6E171 compressor	13.00
Lynx	7.00
Topaz	7.00
All other models	10.00
1988	
Cougar	
3.8L	8.00
5.0L	10.00
Grand Marquis	
FS-6 compressor	10.00
6E171 compressor	13.00
Sable	
3.0L	10.00
3.8L	8.00
Topaz	8.00
Tracer	10.00
1989	
Cougar	7.00
Grand Marquis	8.00
Sable	
3.0L	10.00
3.8L	8.00
Topaz	8.00
Tracer	10.00
1990	
Cougar	7.00

Heating and air conditioning

Mercury (continued)

1990 (continued)
Grand Marquis 8.00
Sable
   3.0L 7.00
   3.8L 8.00
Topaz 8.00

1991
Capri 10.00
Cougar 7.00
Grand Marquis 8.00
Sable 7.00
Topaz 8.00

1992
Capri 10.00
Cougar 7.00
Grand Marquis 7.00
Sable 7.00
Topaz
   2.3L 7.00
   3.0L 8.00
Tracer 8.00

1993
Capri 10.00
Cougar, Grand Marquis and Sable
   Without rear A/C 7.00
   With rear A/C 10.00
Topaz
   2.3L 7.00
   3.0L 8.00
Tracer
   1.8L engine with 10P13 compressor 7.75
   1.9L engine with FX-15 compressor 7.00
Villager 7.00

1994
3.8L 7.00*
5.0L 7.00
Grand Marquis
   Without rear A/C 7.00
   With rear A/C 8.00
Sable
   3.0L
      Models with 10P15 compressor 8.00
      All other models 7.00
   3.8L 7.00*
Villager
   Without rear A/C 7.00
   With rear A/C 7.00*
All other models 7.00

1995
Cougar
   3.8L 7.00*
   5.0L 7.00
Sable
   Models with 10P15 compressor 8.00
   All other models 7.00
Tracer 8.00
Villager
   Without rear A/C 7.00
   With rear A/C 7.00*
All other models 7.00

1996
Cougar
   3.8L 7.00*
   4.6L 7.00

Villager
   Without rear A/C 7.00
   With rear A/C 7.00*
All other models 7.00

1997
Cougar
   3.8L 7.00*
   4.6L 7.00
Grand Marquis 7.50
Mountaineer 9.00*
Mystique 7.00
Sable and Tracer 6.60
Villager
   Without rear A/C 7.00
   With rear A/C 10.00

1998
Grand Marquis 7.50
Mountaineer 9.00
All other models 7.00
Villager
   Without rear A/C 7.00
   With rear A/C 10.00

1999
Grand Marquis 7.50
Mountaineer 7.00
Villager
   Without rear A/C 7.00
   With rear A/C 11.00
All other models 7.00

Merkur
1985 through 1989 .... 8.00

Oldsmobile

1980 and 1981
Omega
   Axial compressor 8.00
   Radial compressor 5.00
Starfire 6.00
All other models
   Axial compressor 10.00
   Radial compressor 6.00

1982
Omega
   Axial compressor 8.00
   Radial compressor 5.00
All other models 6.00

1983
Cutlass Ciera
   Axial compressor 8.00
   Radial compressor 5.00
Omega
   Axial compressor 8.00
   Radial compressor 5.00
All other models 6.00

1984
Cutlass Ciera and Cutlass Cruiser
   Axial compressor 8.00
   Radial compressor 5.00
Omega
   Axial compressor 8.00
   Radial compressor 5.00
Firenza 8.00
All other models 6.00

1985

Eighty Eight, Toronado and Trofeo 6.00
All other models
    Axial compressor 8.00
    Radial compressor 5.00

1986 and 1987

Cutlass Ciera and Cutlass Cruiser,
    Axial compressor 8.00
    Radial compressor 5.00
All other models 8.00

1988

Cutlass Ciera and Cutlass Cruiser,
    DA-V5 compressor 6.00
    HR-6 compressor 8.00
All other models 8.00

1989 through 1990 (all models) 8.00

1991

Bravada 6.00
All other models 8.00

1992

Bravada and Custom Cruiser 6.00
Cutlass Ciera, Cutlass Cruiser and Cutlass Supreme...... 9.00
Silhouette 8.00
All other models 8.00

1993

Cutlass Ciera, Cutlass Cruiser and Cutlass Supreme...... 9.00
Silhouette
    Without rear A/C 8.00
    With rear A/C 11.00
All other models 8.00

1994

Cutlass Ciera 9.00
Silhouette
    Without rear A/C 8.00
    With rear A/C 11.00
All other models 8.00

1995 and 1996

Achieva and Cutlass Ciera 9.00
Bravada 6.00
Silhouette
    Without rear A/C 8.00
    With rear A/C 11.00
All other models 8.00

1997

Achieva and Cutlass 9.00
Bravada 6.00
Silhouette
    Without rear A/C 8.00
    With rear A/C .... Refer to label in engine compartment
All other models 8.00

1998

Aurora and Bravada 8.00
Silhouette
    Without rear A/C 9.00
    With rear A/C .... Refer to label in engine compartment
All other models 9.00

1999

Alero .... not available
Aurora and Bravada 8.00
Cutlass 9.50
Silhouette
    Without rear A/C .... Refer to label in engine compartment
    With rear A/C .... Refer to label in engine compartment
All other models 9.00

Plymouth

1980

Arrow 8.00
Arrow Pick-up and Champ .... not available
Grand Fury, Horizon, TC3 and Volare
    RV2 compressor .... 10.00 to 12.00
    Sankyo compressor.. 7.00 to 8.00
    C-171 compressor 9.00
Sapporo.. 8.00
Trailduster and Voyager (RWD)
    RV-2 compressor .... 10.00 to 12.00
    C-171 compressor... 9.00 to 10.00

1981

Arrow Pick-up.. not available
Champ and Sapporo .... Compressor oil level, 1 to 1.5 inches
Grand Fury .... 9.00 to 10.00
Horizon, Reliant and TC3
    RV2 compressor... 10.00 to 12.00
    Sankyo compressor.. 7.00 to 8.00
    C-171 compressor 9.00
Trailduster and Voyager (RWD)
    RV-2 compressor .... 10.00 to 12.00
    C-171 compressor... 9.00 to 10.00

1982

Arrow Pick-up.. not available
Champ and Sapporo .... Compressor oil level, 1 to 1.5 inches
Scamp .... 9.00 to 10.00
All other models.. 9.00 to 10.00

1983

Arrow Pick-up.. not available
Colt and Sapporo .... Compressor oil level, 1 to 1.5 inches
Scamp .... 9.00 to 10.00
All other models.. 9.00 to 10.00

1984

Colt and Conquest .... Compressor oil level, 1 to 1.5 inches
Scamp .... 9.00 to 10.00
Voyager (FWD and AWD) without rear A/C .... 9.00 to 10.00
All other models.. 9.00 to 10.00

1985

Colt 3.8
Conquest
    All models except wagon... 2.25
    Wagon 2.00
Grand Fury... 9.00 to 10.00
Voyager (FWD and AWD) without rear A/C .... 7.00 to 7.25
All other models... 7.00 to 7.25

1986

Colt 2.7
Conquest 5.70
Voyager (FWD and AWD) without rear A/C .... 7.00 to 7.25
All other models... 7.00 to 7.25

1987

Colt 2.7
Voyager (FWD and AWD) without rear A/C .... 7.00 to 7.25
All other models... 7.00 to 7.25

1988

Colt 2.7
Grand Fury 7.25
Voyager (FWD and AWD) without rear A/C .... 7.00 to 7.25
All other models... 7.00 to 7.25

1989

Acclaim, Horizon, Reliant and Sundance
    Fixed displacement compressor................................. 7.25
    Variable displacement compressor............................. 8.70

Heating and air conditioning

Plymouth (continued)

1989 (continued)
Colt
- All models except wagon 5.00
- Wagon 2.70

Grand Fury 7.25

Voyager (FWD and AWD)
- Fixed displacement compressor 7.25
- Variable displacement compressor 8.70

1990
Acclaim, Horizon and Sundance
- Fixed displacement compressor 7.25
- Variable displacement compressor 8.70

Colt
- All models except wagon 5.00
- Wagon 2.70

Laser 2.70

Voyager (FWD and AWD)
- Fixed displacement compressor 7.25
- Variable displacement compressor 8.70

1991
Acclaim and Sundance
- Fixed displacement compressor 7.25
- Variable displacement compressor 8.70

Colt 5.00

Laser 2.70

Voyager (FWD and AWD)
- Fixed displacement compressor 7.25
- Variable displacement compressor 8.70

1992
Acclaim, Sundance and Voyager
- Fixed displacement compressor 7.25
- Variable displacement compressor 8.70

Colt 5.00

Colt Vista and Laser 2.70

1993
Acclaim and Sundance
- Fixed displacement compressor 7.25
- Variable displacement compressor 8.70

Colt 4.40

Colt Vista and Laser 2.70

Voyager
- Without rear A/C 4.73
- With rear A/C 7.40

1994
Acclaim and Sundance 7.30

Colt 4.40

Colt Vista and Laser 2.70

Voyager
- Without rear A/C 4.73
- With rear A/C 7.40

1995
Acclaim 7.30

Neon 4.75

Voyager
- Without rear A/C 4.73
- With rear A/C 7.40

1996
Breeze 5.00

Neon 4.75

Voyager
- Without rear A/C 5.00
- With rear A/C 7.40

1997 and 1998
Breeze 5.00

Neon 6.75

Prowler 5.08

Voyager
- Without rear A/C 5.00
- With rear A/C 7.40

1999
Breeze 5.00

Neon 4.75

Prowler 5.08

Voyager
- Without rear A/C 5.00
- With rear A/C 7.40

Pontiac

1980 and 1981
Phoenix
- Axial compressor 8.00
- Radial compressor 5.00

All other models
- Axial compressor 10.00
- Radial compressor 6.00

1982 and 1983
6000 (1983), Firebird and Phoenix
- Axial compressor 8.00
- Radial compressor 5.00

All other models 6.00

1984
Fiero 8.00

6000, Firebird, Phoenix and Sunbird
- Axial compressor 8.00
- Radial compressor 5.00

All other models 6.00

1985
Fiero and Grand Am 8.00

6000, Firebird, Phoenix and Sunbird
- Axial compressor 8.00
- Radial compressor 5.00

All other models 6.00

1986
Fiero, Grand Am and Sunbird 8.00

6000 and Firebird
- Axial compressor 8.00
- Radial compressor 5.00

All other models 6.00

1987
Bonneville, Fiero, Grand Am and Sunbird 8.00

6000 and Firebird
- Axial compressor 8.00
- Radial compressor 5.00

All other models 6.00

1988 and 1989
Firebird and Safari 6.00

All other models 8.00

1990 and 1991
Firebird 6.00

All other models 8.00

1992
Firebird 6.00

Grand Prix 9.00

All other models 8.00

1993
Grand Prix 9.00

Montana and Trans Sport
- Without rear A/C 8.00
- With rear A/C 11.00

All other models 8.00

1994

Sunbird	9.00
Montana and Trans Sport	
Without rear A/C	8.00
With rear A/C	11.00
All other models	8.00

1995 and 1996

Grand Am and Sunfire	9.00
Montana and Trans Sport	
Without rear A/C	8.00
With rear A/C	11.00
All other models	8.00

1997

Grand Am and Sunfire	9.00
Montana and Trans Sport	
Without rear A/C	8.00
With rear A/C	Refer to label in engine compartment
All other models	8.00

1998

Montana and Trans Sport	
Without rear A/C	8.00
With rear A/C	Refer to label in engine compartment
All other models	9.00

1999

Grand Am	8.00
Montana and Trans Sport	
Without rear A/C	Refer to label in engine compartment
With rear A/C	Refer to label in engine compartment
All other models	9.00

Saturn

1991 through 1996	6.75
1997	5.06
1998 and 1999	5.00

System refrigerant oil capacity (imported vehicles) (in ounces)

Acura

1987 through 1989

Integra	2.40 to 5.00*
Legend	2.70*

1990

Integra	2.00 to 3.4*
Legend	2.70*

1991

Integra	2.00 To 3.40*
Legend	3.70 to 4.70*

1992 and 1993

Integra	2.03 to 3.38
Legend	4.22
Vigor	4.73

1994 and 1995

Integra	4.70
Legend	5.00
Vigor (1994 only)	4.73

1996

Integra and 3.5RL	4.66
SLX	5.00
2.5TL	5.30
3.2TL	4.33

1997

Integra and 3.5RL	4.66
SLX	5.00
2.2CL and 3.0CL	5.33
2.5TL	5.30
3.2TL	4.33

1998

Integra and 3.5RL	4.66
SLX	5.00
2.3CL and 3.0CL	5.33
2.5TL	5.30
3.2TL	4.33

1999

Integra and 3.5RL	4.66
SLX	5.00
2.3CL, 3.0CL and 3.2TL	5.33

Audi

1977 Fox   10.00

1978 through 1981

Fox, 4000	10.00
5000	11.30

1982 through 1984

4000, Coupe and Quattro	10.00
5000	11.00

1985

GT Coupe, 4000S and 4000S Quattro	8.00
5000S, 5000S Turbo and 5000S Turbo Diesel	10.30

1986

GT Coupe, 4000S and 4000CS Quattro	8.00
5000S and 5000CS Quattro	10.30
5000CS Turbo	20.40

1987

Octagon head	8.00
Square head	6.00

1988 and 1989

80 and 90	2.70
100, 200 and 5000	3.80

1990 and 1991

80 and 90	2.70*
100 and 200	12.70*

1992

Coupe Quattro	not available
S4	10.10
100 and V8 Quattro	10.10
80	not available
90	not available

1993 on (all models)   8.50

Heating and air conditioning

BMW

1977 through 1982...	11.50
1983 and 1984	
320i, 318i and 325e...	11.50
All other models	5.70
1985 and 1986	5.70
1987 through 1989	5.70
1990 and 1991	10.00
1992	
318, 325, M3, 5 Series (including M5), 735 (with R-12) and 850	
Drum type compressor	10.13
Impeller cell type compressor	6.75
735 (with R-134a)	
Nippondenso compressor	
Without rear A/C	5.40
With rear A/C	6.08
Seiko Seiki compressor	6.08
1993	
318 and 325	
Nippondenso compressor	4.05
Seiko Seiki compressor	5.06
5 Series (including M5) and 850	
Nippondenso compressor	5.40
Seiko Seiki compressor	6.08
740 and 750	
Nippondenso compressor	
Without rear A/C	5.40
With rear A/C	6.08
Seiko Seiki compressor	6.08
1994 and 1995	
318, 325 and M3	
Nippondenso compressor	4.05
Seiko Seiki compressor	5.06
5 Series (including M5), 840 and 850	
Nippondenso compressor	5.40
Seiko Seiki compressor	6.08
740 and 750	
Nippondenso compressor	
Without rear A/C	5.40
With rear A/C	6.08
Seiko Seiki compressor	6.08
1996 through 1998	
318, 328, M3 and Z3,	
Nippondenso compressor	4.05
Seiko Seiki compressor	5.06
5 Series (including M5), 840 and 850	
Nippondenso compressor	5.40
Seiko Seiki compressor	6.08
740 and 750	
Nippondenso compressor	
Without rear A/C	5.40
With rear A/C	6.08
Seiko Seiki compressor	6.08

Daewoo

1999 (all models)	not available

Daihatsu

1989 (Charade)	not available
1990 and 1991	
Charade	not available
Rocky	not available

Datsun

1977	
6-cylinder compressor	9.10
2-cylinder compressor	9.00
1978	
F10, 510, 810 and pick-up	3.40
B210 and 280Z	9.10
200 SX	
6-cylinder compressor	9.10
2-cylinder compressor	8.00
1979	
510, 810 and pick-up	3.40
310 and 280ZX	5.10
210	8.10
200SX	
6-cylinder compressor	9.10
2-cylinder compressor	8.00
1980 and 1981	
210	8.10
280ZX	9.10
All other models	5.10
1982	
210	8.00
Diesel pick-up	6.00
All other models	5.00

Datsun/Nissan

1983	
Diesel pick-up	6.30
All other models	5.10

Fiat

1977 through 1982 (all models)	Checked with dipstick

Honda

1977 through 1981 Accord	7.90
1979 through 1982 Civic and Prelude	3.00
1982 Accord	8.00
1983 and 1984	
Accord and Prelude	7.90
Civic	2.00 to 3.00
1985 and 1986 (all models)	7.90
1987	
Accord	2.50
Civic	
Keihin compressor	2.00 to 3.00
Sanden compressor	6.00
Prelude	2.50
1988	
Accord	2.50
Civic	
Matsushita compressor	5.00
Sanden compressor	6.00
Prelude	5.00
1989	
Accord	2.50
Prelude	5.70
Civic and CRX	4.00
1990 and 1991	
Accord	3.00 to 4.00
Civic and CRX	4.00 to 4.40
Prelude	4.00

1992
Accord .... 3.00 to 4.10
Civic 4.06
Prelude 4.00
1993
Accord
Hadsys compressor .... 4.10 to 4.40
Nippondenso compressor .... 3.00 to 4.10
Civic (including Del Sol) 4.06
Prelude 4.30
1994
Accord 5.33
Civic (including Del Sol) and Prelude 4.00
Passport 5.00
1995
Accord
Four-cylinder 5.33
V6 .... 4.30
Civic (including Del Sol) and Prelude 4.00
Odyssey 5.33
Passport 5.00
1996 and 1997
Accord
Four-cylinder 5.33
V6 .... 4.30
Civic
All except Del Sol 4.33
Del Sol
Sanden compressor 4.33
Nippondenso compressor 4.00
CR-V (1997) 4.33
Odyssey 5.33
Passport 5.00
Prelude
1996 .... 4.30
1997 .... 4.33
1998 and 1999
Accord .... 5.33 to 5.92
Civic, CRV and Prelude 4.33
Odyssey
1998 .... 5.33
1999 .... 6.00
Passport 5.00

Hyundai

1986 .... 5.10
1987 through 1989 .... 5.00
1990 and 1991 .... 8.00
1992
Elantra 4.00
Excel and Scoupe 8.10
Sonata 7.80
1993
Elantra 4.05
Excel 8.10
Scoupe 2.70
Sonata .... 7.00 to 7.80
1994
Elantra and Scoupe .... 4.73 to 5.41
Excel .... 7.00 to 7.78
Sonata .... 7.00 to 7.80
1995
Accent, Elantra and Scoupe .... 4.73 to 5.41
Sonata .... 7.00 to 7.78

1996
Accent .... 4.73 to 5.41
Elantra .... 5.75 to 6.42
Sonata .... 7.00 to 7.78
1997
Accent, Elantra and Tiburon .... 5.75 to 6.42
Sonata .... 7.00 to 7.78
1998
Accent, Elantra and Tiburon .... 5.74 to 6.41
Sonata .... 7.09 to 7.76
1999
Accent, Elantra and Tiburon 6.08
Sonata 5.06

Infiniti

1990 and 1991
M30 and G20 .... 6.80
Q45 .... 8.00
1992
G20 and M30 .... 6.80
Q45 .... 8.00
1993
G20 .... 6.80
J30 .... 8.50
Q45 .... 9.70
1994 and 1995
G20 .... 6.80
J30 and Q45 .... 8.50
1996
G20 .... 6.80
I30 and J30 .... 8.50
Q45 .... 6.80
1997
I30 and J30 .... 8.50
Q45 and QX4 .... 6.80
1998 and 1999
G20 (1999 only), I30 and Q45 and QX4 .... 6.80

Isuzu

1984 (all models) 7.30
1985 and 1986 (all models) 5.00
1987 through 1989
I-Mark 3.50
Impulse, Pickup and Trooper II 5.00
1990
Amigo and Trooper II 5.00
Impulse 6.70
Pickup 6.00
1991
Amigo 6.00
Impulse and Stylus 6.70
Pickup
Kiki Diesel compressor 5.00
Harrison R4 compressor 6.00
1992
Amigo, Pick-up and Rodeo
R4 compressor 6.00
DKS-13 compressor 5.00
Impulse 5.07
Stylus 5.07
Trooper 5.00
1993
Amigo and Pick-up
R4 compressor 6.00
DKS-13 compressor 5.00

Heating and air conditioning

Isuzu (continued)
1993 (continued)
Impulse and Stylus.. 5.07
Rodeo and Trooper 5.00
1994 and 1995
All models 5.00
1996
Hombre 9.00
Oasis 5.33
Rodeo and Trooper 5.00
1997
Hombre
2.2L 9.00
4.3L 8.00
Oasis 5.33
Rodeo and Trooper 5.00
1998 and 1999
Amigo, Rodeo and Trooper...................................... 5.00
Hombre
2.2L 9.00
4.3L 8.00
Oasis 5.33

Jaguar
1980 through 1982
XJ6.. not available
XJ12 (1980) and XJS .... 10 to 11
1983 through 1987
XJ6.. 10 to 11
XJS 10.00
1988 and 1989
XJ6 .... 7.00
XJS
Delco compressor 7.00
Sanden compressor 4.6
1990 and 1991
XJ6 and XJS 7.00
1992
XJ6 and XJS 7.00
1993 and 1994
XJ6, XJR and XJS.. 4.06 to 5.07
XJ12 (1994) 4.50
1995 and 1996
XJ6 and XJ12 .... 7.50
XJR and XJS... 4.06 to 5.07
1997
XJ6 and XJ12 .... 7.50
XJR .... 4.06 to 5.07
XK8 .... 5.41 to 6.76
1998 and 1999
XJ8 and XK8 .... 5.41 to 6.76
XJR .... 4.06 to 5.07

Kia
1994 .... not available
1995 through 1997 .... not available
1998 and 1999
Sephia.. not available
Sportage... 6.075

Land Rover
1993 and 1994.. not available
1995
Defender .... not available

Land Rover (continued)
Discovery.. 6.3
Range Rover 5.06
1996 and 1997
Defender .... not available
Discovery.. 6.3
Range Rover and New Range Rover 5.06
1998
Discovery.. 6.3
Range Rover and New Range Rover 5.06
1999
Discovery.. 6.3
Range Rover... 6.08
New Range Rover 5.06

Lexus
1990 and 1991
ES250 and LS400...................................... 3.5 to 4.1
1992
ES300 .... 3.30
LS400, SC300 and SC400.......................... 3.50 to 4.10
1993
ES300 .... 3.30
GS300 and GS400 .... 9.80
LS400 .... 3.10 to 5.20
SC300 and SC400 .... 3.50 to 4.10
1994
GS300 and GS400 .... 4.10
LS400 .... 2.80 to 3.50
All other models 4.80
1995
GS300 and GS400 .... 4.10
All other models 4.80
1996 and 1997
ES300 and LS400... 4.80
All other models 4.10
1998 and 1999
ES300, SC300 and SC400 .... 4.10
LS400 .... 4.80
All other models .... not available

Mazda
1986
B2000 .... 5.90
626 .... 3.40
RX-7
Sanden compressor... 4.50
Nippondenso compressor .... 2.00 to 3.40
323 .... 2.00 to 3.40
1987 and 1988
B2200 .... 4.50
B2600 .... 4.00 to 5.90
RX-7
Nippondenso compressor .... 2.00 to 3.40
Sanden compressor .... 4.00 to 5.90
323... 2.00 to 3.40
626
1987 .... 3.40
1988 .... 2.10
929 .... 3.30
1989
B2200 .... 4.50
B2600i .... 4.00 to 5.90
MPV .... 2.60 to 3.30
MX6 and 626 .... 2.10*

RX-7
Nippondenso .... 2.10 to 3.40*
Sanden .... 4.00 to 5.90
323 .... 2.10 to 3.40*
929 .... 3.30*
1990
B2200 and B2600i 4.50
MPV .... 2.60 to 3.30
MX-6 and 626 .... 3.30 to 3.40
RX-7
Nippondenso .... 2.10 to 3.40*
Sanden 4.50
Protégé and 323 .... 3.80
929 .... 5.00
1991
B2200 and B2600i 8.20
Miata .... 2.70 to 3.30
MPV .... 4.90 to 6.10*
MX-6 and 626 .... 2.00 to 3.30*
RX7
Nippondenso .... 2.00 to 3.30*
Sanden 4.50*
Protégé and 323 .... 3.30 to 4.00*
Navajo 7.00
929 .... 2.00 to 3.30*
1992
B2200 and B2600 Pick-ups 4.60
Miata and MPV .... 2.70 to 3.40
MX-6 and 626 .... 3.40 to 3.70
Navajo 7.00
323 .... not available
1993
B2200 and B2600 Pick-ups 4.60
Miata and MPV .... 2.70 to 3.40
MX-3 .... 4.40
MX-6, 626 and RX-7 .... 3.40 to 3.70
Navajo 7.00
323 .... 3.90 to 4.60
929 .... 3.10
1994
B2300, B3000 and B4000 Pick-ups 7.00
Miata .... 4.40 to 5.07
MPV
Without rear A/C .... 5.55 to 5.70
With rear A/C .... 6.00 to 6.45
MX-3 .... 5.92 to 6.25
MX-6 and 626 .... 5.25
Navajo*
Without rear A/C 7.00
With rear A/C 10.00
Protégé .... 3.88 to 4.56
RX-7 .... 3.90 to 5.10
323 .... 3.90 to 4.60
929 .... 4.20 to 4.50
1995
B2300, B3000 and B4000 Pick-ups 7.00
Miata .... 4.40 to 5.07
Millenia 5.25
MPV
Without rear A/C .... 6.76 to 7.26
With rear A/C .... 8.16 to 8.66
MX-3 .... 5.92 to 6.25
MX-6 and 626 .... 5.92
Protégé 4.06
RX-7 .... 4.40 to 5.70
929 .... 4.20 to 4.50

1996
B2300, B3000 and B4000 Pick-ups 7.00
Miata .... 4.40 to 5.07
Millenia, MX-6 and 626 .... 5.92
MPV
Without rear A/C .... 6.76 to 7.26
With rear A/C .... 8.16 to 8.66
Protégé 4.06
1997
B2300, B3000 and B4000 Pick-ups 9.00
Miata .... 4.40 to 5.07
Millenia, MX-6 and 626 .... 5.92
MPV 6.76
Protégé 4.06
1998
B2500, B3000 and B4000 Pick-ups 9.00
Millenia 5.92
MPV 6.76
MX-6 and 626 .... 8.11
Protégé 4.06
1999
B2500, B3000 and B4000 Pick-ups 9.00
Miata 5.07
All other models .... not available

*If an "Authorized Modification" decal is located on the radiator support (next to the VECI label), add only the specified amount of refrigerant oil. If there is no modification decal, add specified amount plus another 2.00 ounces.

Mercedes-Benz

1977 through 1981 (manual system) .... 7.50 to 9.40
1977 (automatic system)
6.9L engine 10.10
All others 8.10
1978 through 1980 (automatic system)
280 Series, 300C and 300CD 8.10
300SD and 300 Series 5.80
450 Series and 6.9L engine 10.10
1981 (automatic system)
380 Series 10.10
All others .... 7.00 to 9.00
1982
Manual system (240D) .... 7.50 to 9.50
Automatic system
380 Series 10.00
All others .... 7.00 to 9.00
1983
240D .... 6.90 to 9.60
300 Series 5.80
380 Series 10.10
1984
190 Series .... 6.90 to 9.60
300 Series 5.80
380 and 500 Series 10.10
1985
190D 4.10
190E and 300 Series 5.80
380 and 500 Series 10.10
1986
190D 4.10
All others 5.80
1987 through 1989 (all models) 4.10
1990 and 1991
190E 5.00*
All others 4.00*

Heating and air conditioning

Mercedes-Benz (continued)

1992

300SD, 300SE, 400SE, 400SEL, 500SEC, 500SEL,
600SEC and 600SEL 5.41
All other models 4.06

1993

300SD, 300SE, 400SE, 400SEL, 500SEC, 500SEL,
600SEC and 600SEL 5.41
190E 4.06
C36, C43, C220, C230 and C280 .... 5.24
All other models 4.73

1994 through 1997

C36, C43, C220, C230 and C280 .... 5.24
E300, E320, E420, E430, E500, SL320, SL500
and SL600 .... 4.73
S320, S350, S420, S500 and S600 .... 5.41

1998 and 1999

C36, C43, C220, C230 and C280 .... 5.24
E300, E320, E420, E430, E500, SL320, SL500
and SL600 .... 4.73
S320, S350, S420, S500 and S600 .... 5.41
All other models .... not available

Mitsubishi

1984 .... 7.50

1985 and 1986

Cordia and Tredia 1.30*
Galant and Mirage 1.40*
Montero and Starion 3.70
Pick-up 6.80

1987

Cordia, Tredia, Galant and Mirage 1.30*
Montero and Starion 3.70
Pickup 4.00
Precis 5.10
Van/Wagon 5.00

1988 and 1989

Galant 2.70*
Montero 3.70
Precis 5.10
Van/Wagon 5.00
Other models 5.70

1990

Eclipse 2.60
Galant .... 5.00 to 5.70
Mirage and Wagon 5.00
Montero
2.6L 3.70
3.0L .... 2.10 to 3.30
Precis 8.10
Sigma and Van 2.70

1991

Eclipse and Montero 2.70*
Galant .... 5.00 to 5.70*
Mirage 5.00
Pickup .... 4.30 to 5.00
Precis 8.10
3000GT .... 4.60 to 6.00*

1992

3000GT .... 5.43 to 6.99
Diamante .... 5.41 to 6.09
Eclipse 2.70
Expo
1.8L .... 3.10 to 4.10
2.4L .... 2.00 to 3.40

Galant .... 5.07 to 5.75
Mirage 5.06
Montero 2.70
Precis 8.10
Pick-up .... 4.40 to 5.10

1993

3000GT .... 5.43 to 6.99
Diamante
Sedan .... 5.41 to 6.09
Wagon .... 4.73 to 5.41
Eclipse 2.70
Expo
1.8L .... 3.10 to 4.10
2.4L .... 2.00 to 3.40
Galant .... 5.07 to 5.75
Mirage .... 4.39 to 5.07
Montero 2.70
Precis 8.10
Pick-up .... 4.40 to 5.10

1994

3000GT .... 5.43 to 6.99
Diamante
Sedan .... 5.75 to 6.42
Wagon .... 4.73 to 5.41
Eclipse 2.70
Expo
1.8L .... 3.40 to 4.80
2.4L .... 2.00 to 3.40
Galant .... 5.07 to 5.75
Mirage .... 4.39 to 5.07
Montero 2.70
Pick-up .... 4.10 to 4.80

1995

3000GT .... 5.43 to 6.99
Diamante
Sedan .... 5.75 to 6.42
Wagon .... 4.73 to 5.41
Eclipse
Without turbo .... 2.70 to 4.10
With turbo .... 5.70 to 6.40
Expo
1.8L .... 3.40 to 4.80
2.4L .... 2.00 to 3.40
Galant .... 5.07 to 5.75
Mirage .... 4.39 to 5.07
Montero 2.70
Pick-up .... 4.10 to 4.80

1996

3000GT .... 5.43 to 6.99
Diamante .... 5.75 to 6.42
Eclipse
2.0L without turbo .... 2.70 to 4.10
2.0L with turbo and 2.4L .... 5.70 to 6.40
Galant .... 5.07 to 5.75
Mirage .... 4.39 to 5.07
Montero 2.70
Pick-up .... 4.10 to 4.80

1997

3000GT .... 5.43 to 6.99
Diamante .... 5.10 to 5.70
Eclipse
2.0L without turbo .... 2.70 to 4.10
2.0L with turbo and 2.4L .... 5.70 to 6.40
Galant 4.10
Mirage 4.10

Montero	4.10
Montero Sport	5.70

1998 and 1999

3000GT	4.73 to 6.08
Diamante	5.10 to 5.70
Eclipse	
2.0L without turbo	2.70 to 4.10
2.0L with turbo and 2.4L	5.70 to 6.40
Galant	4.10
Mirage	4.10
Montero	4.10
Montero Sport	5.70

Nissan/Datsun

1984

Diesel Pick-up	6.30
All others	5.10

Nissan

1985 and 1986

Maxima and 200SX	9.10
Pick-up (excluding 1986-1/2 Hardbody)	8.50
Pulsar, Sentra, Stanza and 300ZX	5.10

1987

Maxima, Stanza wagon, 200 SX and 300ZX	5.10
Pathfinder, Pickup, Pulsar NX, Sentra and Stanza	7.00
Van	8.50

1988

Pathfinder, Pickup, Pulsar NX, Sentra and Stanza	7.00
Van	8.10
All other models	5.10
1989 (all models)	7.00
1990 (all models)	6.80

1991

240SX	8.00
All other models	6.80

1992

240SX	8.00
All other models	6.80

1993 and 1994

240SX (1993 only)	8.00
Quest	
Without rear A/C	7.00
With rear A/C	10.00
All other models	6.80

1995 through 1997

240SX	8.50
Maxima	8.50
Quest	
Without rear A/C	7.00
With rear A/C	10.00
All other models	6.80

1998

240SX	8.50
Maxima	6.80
Quest	
Without rear A/C	7.00
With rear A/C	10.00
All other models	6.80

1999

Maxima	6.80
Quest	
Without rear A/C	7.00
With rear A/C	11.00
All other models	6.80

Porsche

1980 through 1983

911	10.00
911 Turbo	5.70
924	7.70
944 (1983) and 928	9.30

1984 and 1985

911	4.00
911 Turbo	5.70
924	7.70
928 and 944	9.30

1986 through 1988

911	4.00
911 Turbo	5.70
924	2.70
928	9.30
944	3.30

1989

911C	4.00
911C2 and 911C4	3.30
911 Turbo	5.70
928	9.30
944	2.60

1990 and 1991

911	3.30
928	9.30
944	2.60

1992

911	
R-12	3.37
R-134a	4.73
968	
R-12	2.60
R-134a	4.73

1993 through 1995

911	4.73
928	9.30
968	4.05

1996

911	4.73

1997 and 1998

911	4.73
Boxster	6.58

1999

All models	6.58

Saab

1980

99	not available
900	6.10

1981

900	5.90

1982 through 1985

900	
Sankyo compressor	5.75
Clarion compressor	4.05

1986 through 1991

900	
Sankyo compressor	5.75
Clarion compressor	4.05
9000	5.60

1992

900	5.75

9000
- Without rear A/C 5.60
- With rear A/C 6.75

1993 through 1996
- 900 (no 1993 model)... 6.76
- 9000 .... 6.76

1997 and 1998
- 900
  - Seiko Seiki compressor 6.76
  - Sanden compressor 5.07
- 9000 .... 6.76

1999
- 9-3 .... 5.07
- 9-5 .... 4.90

Subaru

1983 and 1984.. 4.10

1985 and 1986
- XT Coupe 2.10*
- All others 4.10

1987 through 1989 .... 4.10

1990 (legacy only)... 6.50

1991
- Legacy
  - Kiki Diesel compressor 2.40*
  - Calsonic compressor 3.20*
- Loyale, XT and XT6 .... 2.40*

1992 and 1993
- Impreza (1993)... 6.10
- Legacy
  - Calsonic compressor 8.00
  - Zexel compressor 5.10
- Loyale
  - Models built before March 5.06
  - Models built after March 4.72
- SVX... 5.06

1994 through 1996
- Impreza .... not available
- Legacy.. 5.30
- SVX... 5.06

1997
- Impreza... 4.90
- Legacy.. 5.30
- SVX 5.06

1998
- Forester 5.2
- Impreza... 4.90
- Legacy.. 5.30

1999
- Forester 5.2
- Impreza... 4.90
- Legacy .... not available

Suzuki

1989.. 2.70*
1990.. 5.00

1992 and 1993
- Sidekick 4.90
- Swift 4.90

1994
- Sidekick and Swift.. 3.30

1995
- Esteem 5.06
- Sidekick.. 3.30
- Swift 3.40

1996 through 1998
- Esteem.. 5.06
- Sidekick and X-90 .... 3.30
- Swift 3.40

1999
- Esteem.. 5.06
- Swift 3.40
- Grand Vitara .... not available

Toyota

1977 through 1979
- Celica 7.80
- Corolla .... Checked with dipstick
- Cressida 9.00
- Land Cruiser 10.00
- Pick-up
  - 1977 and 1978 .... 10.00
  - 1979 .... 7.60
- Corona
  - 1977 and 1978 .... 7.80
  - 1979 .... 7.60

1980 through 1982
- Celica, Corona and pick-up 7.50
- Corolla
  - 1980 .... 5.50
  - 1981 and 1982 .... 7.50
- Cressida
  - 1980 and 1981 .... 9.00
  - 1982 .... 8.00
- Tercel 5.00
- Land Cruiser 10.00
- Starlet 9.00
- Supra 6.00

1983 and 1984
- Corolla and pick-up .... 5.20 to 6.30
- Land Cruiser 10.00
- All others .... 2.00 to 3.40

1985 and 1986.. 3.40*

1987 through 1989
- Tercel 4.70
- Land Cruiser, Van, Cressida and Supra 2.70*
- All other models.. 3.40

1990 and 1991
- All models (except Supra and MR2)..................... 4.70
- Supra and MR2 .... 4.10

1992 .... not available

1993
- 4Runner and T-100 Pick-up................................. 4.80
- Camry.. 4.30
- MR2... 4.20
- Previa .... not available
- All other models.. 4.10

1994 and 1995
- Camry.. 4.90
- Previa .... not available
- T-100 Pick-up 4.80
- All other models.. 4.10

1996
- Camry.. 4.90
- Previa .... not available
- Supra and T-100 Pick-up...................................... 4.80
- All other models.. 4.10

1997
- 4Runner and Previa .... not available
- Supra, Tacoma and T-100 Pick-up 4.80
- All other models.. 4.10

1998 and 1999
4Runner, Land Cruiser and Tacoma Pick-up .... not available
RAV4
    Gasoline engine.. 4.10
    Electric motor .... not available
T-100 Pick-up (1998)... 4.80
All other models 4.10

Volkswagen

1977 and 1978
Dasher 10.00
All others
    R209 compressor.. 10.00
    SC209 compressor 8.00
    Sankyo compressor 6.00
1979 through 1981
R209 compressor.. 10.00
SC209 compressor 8.00
Sankyo compressor 6.00
1982 through 1984
Sankyo/Sanden SD-508 compressor 10.00
York SC-209 compressor 8.00
1985 and 1986
Cabriolet and Scirocco.. 6.00
All others (except Vanagon)...................................... 4.60
1987
Fox 1.40
Cabriolet, Scirocco and Vanagon 6.00
Quantum and all other models....................................... 4.60
1988 and 1989
Cabriolet and Scirocco.. 6.00
Fox 1.40*
Vanagon 5.00*
1990
Cabriolet... 4.80
Fox 1.40*
Corrado, Golf and Jetta.. 4.50
Vanagon 5.00*
1991
Cabriolet... 4.80
Corrado, Fox, Passat, Golf and Jetta.......................... 4.50
Vanagon 7.00
1992
Cabriolet... 4.75
Corrado 4.70
Fox 6.00
Golf, GTI and Jetta 4.60
Passat... 4.02
1993
Cabriolet... 4.75
Corrado
    R-12 system 4.70
    R-134a system 3.90
Eurovan
    Without rear A/C 4.60
    With rear A/C 8.10
Fox 6.00
Passat... 4.02
All other models 3.90
1994
Passat... 4.02
All other models 3.90

1995 through 1999
Eurovan
    Without rear A/C 4.60
    With rear A/C 8.10
New Beetle (1998 and 1999) 4.56
Passat... 4.02
All other models 3.90

Volvo

1977
240 .... 12.70
260 .... 12.50
1978 through 1981 .... 12.70
1982 .... 12.50
1983 through 1986
760 GLE
    Gas.. 5.10
    Diesel... 7.20
All others
    Gas.. 10.20
    Diesel... 4.60
1987 through 1989 (all models)........................... 6.80
1990
240 series 4.80
740, 760 and 940
    Delco compressor .... 4.30 to 6.80
    Sankyo compressor 4.50
    York compressor... 10.00
1991 (all models) 6.80
1992
240 .... 6.75
All other models
    Sanden SD 510 compressor 4.56
    Sanden SD 709 compressor 8.11
    Zexel compressor 6.76
1993 through 1995
240 (1993) 7.40
850 .... 6.80
940 and 960
    Sanden SD 510 compressor 4.56
    Sanden SD 709 compressor 8.11
    Seiko Seiki compressor 7.43
1996
850 .... 6.80
960
    Nippondenso compressor 6.09
    Seiko Seiki compressor 5.41
1997
850 .... 6.80
960
    Nippondenso compressor 6.09
    Seiko Seiki compressor 5.41
All other models 6.76
1998 and 1999
S90 and V90
    Sanden compressor.. 8.11
    Seiko-Seiki compressor 7.44
    Zexel compressor 6.76
All other models 6.76

System refrigerant capacity (domestic vehicles) (in pounds)

AMC

1980
Pacer 2.12
All other models 2.00
1981 through 1988 (all models) 2.00

Buick

1980
Century, Regal and Riviera.............................. 3.50
Electra, Estate Wagon and LeSabre 3.75
Skyhawk 2.50
Skylark 2.75
1981
Century, Electra, Estate Wagon and LeSabre.... 3.50
Regal and Riviera 3.25
Skylark 2.75
1982 through 1984
Century, Skyhawk and Skylark 2.75
Electra, Estate Wagon and LeSabre 3.50
Regal and Riviera 3.25
1985
Estate Wagon and LeSabre 3.50
Regal and Riviera 3.25
All other models 2.75
1986
Century and Riviera 2.75
Electra 2.87
Estate Wagon 3.50
LeSabre 2.40
Regal 3.25
Skyhawk
   Non-turbo models 2.25
   Turbo models 2.75
Skylark and Somerset 2.25
1987
Century and Riviera 2.75
Electra 2.87
Estate Wagon 3.50
LeSabre 2.40
Regal 3.25
Skyhawk
   Non-turbo models 2.25
   Turbo models 2.75
Skylark 2.25
1988
Century 2.75
Electra 2.40
Estate Wagon 3.50
LeSabre 2.40
Reatta and Riviera 2.38
Regal and Skylark 2.25
Skyhawk
   Non-turbo models 2.25
   Turbo models 2.75
1989
Century 2.75

Electra and LeSabre 2.40
Estate Wagon 3.50
Reatta and Riviera 2.38
Regal, Skylark and Skyhawk 2.25
1990
Century 2.75
Electra 2.40
Estate Wagon 3.50
LeSabre 2.40
Reatta and Riviera 2.38
Regal and Skylark 2.25
1991
Century 2.75
LeSabre 2.40
Park Avenue 2.42
Reatta 2.40
Regal
   Models with 3800 engine 2.75
   Models without 3800 engine 2.25
Riviera 2.37
Roadmaster 3.13
Skylark 2.25
1992
Century 2.38
LeSabre and Park Avenue 2.40
Regal
   Models with 3800 engine 2.75
   Models without 3800 engine 2.25
Riviera 2.38
Roadmaster 3.13
Skylark 2.65
1993
Century 2.38
LeSabre and Park Avenue 2.40
Regal
   Models with 3800 engine 2.75
   Models without 3800 engine 2.25
Riviera 2.38
Roadmaster 3.13
Skylark 2.63
1994
Century
   2.2L engine 1.75
   3.1L engine 2.00
LeSabre and Park Avenue 2.42
Regal 2.00
Roadmaster 1.75
Skylark 2.25
1995
Century
   2.2L engine 1.75
   3.1L engine 2.00
LeSabre and Park Avenue 2.42
Regal and Riviera 2.00
Roadmaster 1.75
Skylark 2.25

1996

Century	
2.2L engine	1.75
3.1L engine	2.00
Roadmaster	1.75
Skylark	2.25
All other models	2.00

1997 and 1998

Century and Regal	1.88
Skylark	2.25
All other models	2.00

1999

Century and Regal	1.88
All other models	2.00

Cadillac

1980 and 1981

Deville and Fleetwood	3.75
Eldorado and Seville	3.50

1982

Cimarron	2.75
All other models	3.25

1983 and 1984

Cimarron	2.75
All other models	3.50

1985

Brougham, Eldorado and Seville	3.50
Cimarron, Deville and Fleetwood	2.75

1986

Brougham	3.50
Cimarron	2.25
Deville and Fleetwood	2.87
Eldorado and Seville	2.75

1987 and 1988

Allante and Cimarron	2.25
Brougham	3.50
Deville and Fleetwood	2.87
Eldorado and Seville	2.75

1989

Allante	2.25
Brougham	3.50
All other models	2.40

1990

Allante	2.25
Brougham	3.50
Deville and Fleetwood	2.87
Eldorado and Seville	2.40

1991

Allante	2.25
Brougham	3.10
Deville and Fleetwood	2.42
Eldorado and Seville	2.37

1992

Allante	2.25
Brougham	3.10
Deville and Fleetwood (FWD)	2.42
Eldorado and Seville	2.38

1993

Allante	2.25
Deville	2.42
Eldorado and Seville	2.38
Fleetwood (RWD)	3.13

1994 through 1996

Fleetwood (RWD)	1.75
All other models	2.00

1997 and 1998

Catera	2.60
All other models	2.00

1999

Catera	2.56
Escalade	2.25

Chevrolet

1980

Camaro	3.25
Chevette	2.25
Citation	2.75
Corvette	3.00
G Series van	
Without rear A/C	3.00
With rear A/C	5.00
Luv Pick-up	1.88
Monza	2.81
Suburban	
Without rear A/C	3.75
With rear A/C	5.25
All other models	3.75

1981

Blazer K/V and C and K Series Pick-ups	3.75
Caprice and Impala	3.50
Chevette	2.25
Citation	2.75
Corvette	3.00
El Camino	3.25
G Series van	
Without rear A/C	3.00
With rear A/C	5.00
Luv Pick-up	1.88
Suburban	
Without rear A/C	3.75
With rear A/C	5.25
All other models	3.25

1982

Blazer K/V and C and K Series Pick-ups	3.75
Camaro and Corvette	3.00
Caprice and Impala	3.50
Chevette	2.25
El Camino	3.25
G Series van	
Without rear A/C	3.00
With rear A/C	5.00
Luv Pick-up	1.88
Malibu and Monte Carlo	3.25
S/T Pick-up	2.50
Suburban	
Without rear A/C	3.75
With rear A/C	5.25
All other models	2.75

1983

Blazer K/V and C and K Series Pick-ups	3.75
Blazer S/T	2.50
Camaro	3.00
Caprice and Impala	3.50
Chevette	2.25
El Camino	3.25
G Series van	
Without rear A/C	3.00
With rear A/C	5.00
Malibu and Monte Carlo	3.25
S/T Pick-up	2.50

Heating and air conditioning

Chevrolet (continued)

1983 (continued)
Suburban
- Without rear A/C 3.75
- With rear A/C 5.25

All other models 2.75

1984
Blazer K/V, C and K Series Pick-ups and Camaro 3.00
Blazer S/T 2.50
Caprice and Impala 3.50
Chevette 2.25
El Camino 3.25
G Series van
- Without rear A/C 3.00
- With rear A/C 4.50

Malibu and Monte Carlo 3.25
S/T Pick-up 2.50
Suburban
- Without rear A/C 3.00
- With rear A/C 5.33

All other models 2.75

1985
Astro
- Without rear A/C 2.00
- With rear A/C 3.00

Blazer K/V, C and K Series Pick-ups and Camaro 3.00
Blazer S/T 2.50
Caprice and Impala 3.50
Chevette 2.25
El Camino 3.25
G Series van
- Without rear A/C 3.00
- With rear A/C 4.50

Malibu and Monte Carlo 3.25
Nova 1.50
Spectrum and Sprint 1.54
S/T Pick-up 2.50
Suburban
- Without rear A/C 3.00
- With rear A/C 5.33

All other models 2.75

1986
Astro
- Without rear A/C 2.00
- With rear A/C 3.00

Blazer K/V, C and K Series Pick-ups and Camaro 3.00
Blazer S/T and S/T Pick-up 2.50
Caprice and Impala 3.50
Cavalier and Chevette 2.25
Celebrity and Corvette 2.75
El Camino, Malibu and Monte Carlo 3.25
G Series van
- Without rear A/C 3.00
- With rear A/C 4.50

Nova 1.50
Spectrum and Sprint 1.54
Suburban
- Without rear A/C 3.00
- With rear A/C 5.25

1987
Astro
- Without rear A/C 2.00
- With rear A/C 3.00

Beretta, Corsica, Celebrity and Corvette 2.75
Blazer K/V 3.50

Blazer S/T and S/T Pick-up 2.50
Camaro 3.00
Caprice and Impala 3.50
Cavalier and Chevette 2.25
El Camino, Malibu and Monte Carlo 3.25
G Series van
- Without rear A/C 3.50
- With rear A/C 4.50

Nova 1.50
Spectrum and Sprint 1.54
Suburban
- Without rear A/C 3.50
- With rear A/C 5.25

1988
Astro
- Without rear A/C 2.00
- With rear A/C 3.00

Blazer K/V, El Camino, Malibu and Monte Carlo 3.25
Blazer S/T, C and K Series Pick-ups and S/T Pick-up 2.50
Camaro 3.00
Caprice and Impala 3.50
Cavalier 2.25
G Series van
- Without rear A/C 3.50
- With rear A/C 4.50

Nova 1.50
Spectrum 1.76
Sprint 1.58
Suburban
- Without rear A/C 3.25
- With rear A/C 5.25

All other models 2.75

1989
Astro
- Without rear A/C 2.25
- With rear A/C 3.75

Blazer K/V 3.25
Blazer S/T, C and K Series Pick-ups and S/T Pick-up 2.50
Camaro and Cavalier 2.25
Caprice and Impala 3.50
G Series
- Models without rear A/C
  - Models with 7.4L engine 2.75
  - All other models 4.50
- Models with rear A/C 4.50

Suburban
- Without rear A/C 3.25
- With rear A/C 5.25

All other models 2.75

1990
Astro
- Without rear A/C 2.25
- With rear A/C 3.75

Beretta, Corsica, Celebrity and Lumina APV 2.75
Blazer K/V 3.25
Blazer S/T and S/T Pick-up 2.50
C and K Series Pick-ups 2.80
Caprice and Impala 3.50
G Series
- Models without rear A/C
  - Models with 7.4L engine 2.75
  - All other models 4.50

Suburban
- Without rear A/C 3.25
- With rear A/C 5.25

All other models 2.25

1991

Astro
- Without rear A/C 2.25
- With rear A/C 3.75

Blazer K/V 3.25

Blazer S/T and S/T Pick-up 2.50

C and K Series Pick-ups 2.80

Caprice and Impala 3.12

G Series
- Models without rear A/C
  - Models with 7.4L engine 2.75
  - All other models 4.50

Lumina APV 2.75

Suburban
- Without rear A/C 3.25
- With rear A/C 5.25

All other models 2.25

1992

3500HD, C and K Series Pick-ups and Suburban 2.80

Astro
- Without rear A/C 2.25
- With rear A/C 3.75

Beretta and Corsica 2.63

Blazer K/V 3.25

Blazer S/T and S/T Pick-up 2.50

Caprice 3.13

G Series van
- Without rear A/C 3.00
- With rear A/C 3.75

Lumina APV 2.75

All other models 2.25

1993

3500HD Pick-up 2.50

Astro
- Without rear A/C 2.25
- With rear A/C 3.75

Beretta and Corsica 2.63

Blazer K/V 3.00

Blazer S/T and S/T Pick-up 2.30

C and K Series Pick-ups
- Standard cab 2.50
- Crew Cab 3.00

Camaro 2.00

Caprice 3.13

G Series van
- Without rear A/C 3.00
- With rear A/C 4.25

Lumina APV
- Without rear A/C 2.62
- With rear A/C 3.50

Suburban
- Without rear A/C 3.00
- With rear A/C 4.25

All other models 2.25

1994

3500HD Pick-up
- Standard cab 2.00
- Crew cab 2.25

Astro
- Without rear A/C 2.00
- With rear A/C 3.00

Blazer K/V 2.25

Blazer S/T 2.50

C and K Series Pick-ups
- Standard cab 2.00
- Crew cab 2.25

Camaro, Corvette, Lumina and S/T Pick-up 2.00

Caprice and Impala SS 1.75

G Series van
- Without rear A/C 3.00
- With rear A/C 4.25

Lumina APV
- Without rear A/C 2.62
- With rear A/C 3.00

Suburban
- Without rear A/C 2.25
- With rear A/C 4.00

All other models 2.25

1995

Astro
- Without rear A/C 2.00
- With rear A/C 3.00

Beretta and Corsica 2.25

Blazer S/T and S/T Pick-up 2.00

C and K Series Pick-ups
- Standard cab 2.00
- Crew cab 2.25

Caprice and Impala SS 1.75

Cavalier 1.50

G Series van
- Without rear A/C 3.00
- With rear A/C 4.25

Lumina APV
- Without rear A/C 2.25
- With rear A/C 3.00

Suburban
- Without rear A/C 2.25
- With rear A/C 4.00

Tahoe 2.25

All other models 2.00

1996

Astro
- Without rear A/C 2.00
- With rear A/C 3.00

Beretta and Corsica 2.25

Blazer S/T and S/T Pick-up 2.00

C and K Series Pick-ups
- Standard cab 2.00
- Crew cab 2.25

Camaro
- 3.8L engine 1.75
- 5.7L engine 2.00

Caprice and Impala SS 1.75

Cavalier 1.50

Express van
- Without rear A/C 3.00
- With rear A/C 4.88

G Series van
- Without rear A/C 3.00
- With rear A/C 4.25

Lumina APV
- Without rear A/C 2.25
- With rear A/C 3.00

Suburban
- Without rear A/C 2.25
- With rear A/C 4.00

Tahoe 2.25

All other models 2.00

1997

Astro
- Without rear A/C 2.00
- With rear A/C 3.00

Heating and air conditioning

Chevrolet (continued)

1997 (continued)
- Blazer S/T and S/T Pick-up... 2.00
- C and K Series Pick-ups
  - Standard cab.. 2.00
  - Crew cab... 2.25
- Camaro
  - 3.8L engine... 1.63
  - 5.7L engine... 2.00
- Cavalier.. 1.50
- Corvette... 1.63
- Express van
  - Without rear A/C.. 3.00
  - With rear A/C.. 4.88
- G Series van
  - Without rear A/C.. 3.00
  - With rear A/C.. 4.25
- Lumina and Monte Carlo.. 1.88
- Malibu.. 1.75
- Suburban
  - Without rear A/C.. 2.25
  - With rear A/C.. 4.00
- Tahoe.. 2.25
- Venture
  - Without rear A/C.. 2.00
  - With rear A/C.. 2.90

1998
- Astro
  - Without rear A/C.. 2.00
  - With rear A/C.. 3.00
- Blazer S/T, S/T Pick-up, Lumina and Monte Carlo.......... 1.88
- C and K Series Pick-ups
  - Standard cab.. 2.00
  - Crew cab... 2.25
- Camaro and Cavalier... 1.50
- Corvette and Prizm... 1.63
- Express van
  - Without rear A/C.. 3.00
  - With rear A/C.. 4.88
- G Series van
  - Without rear A/C.. 3.00
  - With rear A/C.. 4.25
- Malibu.. 1.75
- Metro... 1.21 to 1.32
- Suburban
  - Without rear A/C.. 2.25
  - With rear A/C.. 4.00
- Tahoe
  - Without rear A/C.. 2.25
  - With rear A/C.. 4.00
- Tracker.. 1.33
- Venture
  - Without rear A/C.. 2.00
  - With rear A/C.. 2.90

1999
- Astro
  - Without rear A/C.. 2.00
  - With rear A/C.. 3.00
- Blazer S/T, S/T Pick-up, Lumina and Monte Carlo.......... 1.88
- C and K Series Pick-ups
  - Standard cab.. 2.00
  - Crew cab... 2.25
- Camaro and Cavalier... 1.50
- Corvette... 1.63

- Express van
  - Without rear A/C.. 3.00
  - With rear A/C.. 4.88
- G Series van
  - Without rear A/C.. 3.00
  - With rear A/C.. 4.25
- Malibu.. 1.75
- Metro... 1.10 to 1.32
- Prizm... 1.65
- Suburban
  - Without rear A/C.. 2.25
  - With rear A/C.. 4.00
- Tahoe
  - Without rear A/C.. 2.25
  - With rear A/C.. 4.00
- Tracker......................... Refer to label in engine compartment
- Venture
  - Without rear A/C.. 2.00
  - With rear A/C.. 2.90

Chrysler

1980
- Cordoba, LeBaron and Town and Country.................... 2.31
- Imperial, Newport and New Yorker (RWD).................... 2.87

1981 (all models).. 2.31

1982
- Cordoba and New Yorker (RWD)................................. 2.31
- LeBaron and Town and Country................................. 2.37

1983
- Cordoba and New Yorker (RWD)................................. 2.31
- All other models.. 2.37

1984 and 1985
- Fifth Avenue.. 2.31
- All other models.. 2.37

1986
- Fifth Avenue.. 2.62
- All other models.. 2.44

1987
- Conquest... 1.61
- Fifth Avenue.. 2.62
- All other models.. 2.37

1988 and 1989
- Conquest... 1.81
- Fifth Avenue.. 2.56
- All other models.. 2.37

1990 (all models).. 2.37

1991
- Imperial and New Yorker.. 2.12
- LeBaron... 2.00
- Town and Country
  - Without rear A/C.. 2.00
  - With rear A/C.. 2.70

1992
- Town and Country
  - Without rear A/C.. 2.10
  - With rear A/C.. 2.80
- All other models.. 2.00

1993
- Concorde... 1.75
- Town and Country
  - Without rear A/C.. 2.25
  - With rear A/C.. 3.13
- All other models.. 2.00

1994
- LeBaron... 1.63

Town and Country
    Without rear A/C 2.25
    With rear A/C 3.25
All other models 1.75
1995
    LeBaron 1.63
    Sebring Coupe .... 1.54 to 1.63
    Town and Country
        Without rear A/C 2.25
        With rear A/C 3.25
    All other models 1.75
1996
    Sebring Coupe .... 1.54 to 1.63
    Town and Country
        Without rear A/C 2.13
        With rear A/C 3.00
    All other models 1.75
1997
    Sebring Coupe .... 1.54 to 1.63
    Town and Country
        Without rear A/C 2.13
        With rear A/C 3.00
    All other models 1.75
1998
    Cirrus 1.63
    Concorde and Sebring Convertible 1.75
    Sebring Coupe .... 1.54 to 1.63
    Town and Country
        Without rear A/C 2.13
        With rear A/C 3.00
1999
    300M, Concorde and LHS 1.56
    Cirrus 1.25
    Sebring Convertible 1.75
    Sebring Coupe .... 1.54 to 1.63
    Town and Country
        Without rear A/C 2.13
        With rear A/C 2.88

Dodge
1980
    Aspen, Diplomat and Mirada 2.31
    B Series van/wagon
        Without rear A/C 3.38
        With rear A/C 4.00
    Challenger, Colt and D50 and Ram 50 Pick-ups 2.00
    D and W Series full-size Pick-ups and Ramcharger 2.63
    Omni and 024 .... 2.12
    St. Regis 2.87
1981
    Aries 2.37
    B Series van/wagon
        Without rear A/C 3.00
        With rear A/C 4.00
    Challenger, Colt and D50 and Ram 50 Pick-ups 2.00
    D and W Series full-size Pick-ups and Ramcharger 2.63
    Diplomat, Mirada and St. Regis 2.31
    Omni and 024 .... 2.12
1982
    400 and Aries 2.37
    B Series van/wagon
        Without rear A/C 3.00
        With rear A/C 4.00
    Challenger, Colt and D50 and Ram 50 Pick-ups 2.00
    D and W Series full-size Pick-ups and Ramcharger 2.63

Diplomat and Mirada 2.31
Omni and 024 .... 2.12
Rampage 2.13
1983
    B Series van/wagon
        Without rear A/C 3.00
        With rear A/C 4.00
    Challenger, Colt and D50 and Ram 50 Pick-ups 2.00
    D and W Series full-size Pick-ups and Ramcharger 2.63
    Diplomat and Mirada 2.31
    Omni 2.12
    Rampage 2.13
    All other models 2.37
1984
    B Series van/wagon
        Without rear A/C 3.00
        With rear A/C 4.00
    Caravan and Mini-Ram van 2.33
    Colt, Conquest and D50 and Ram 50 Pick-ups 2.00
    D and W Series full-size Pick-ups and Ramcharger 2.63
    Diplomat 2.31
    Omni 2.12
    Rampage 2.13
    All other models 2.37
1985
    B Series van/wagon
        Without rear A/C 3.00
        With rear A/C 4.00
    Caravan and Mini-Ram van 2.38
    Colt 1.61
    Conquest 1.54
    D50 and Ram 50 Pick-ups 2.00
    D and W Series full-size Pick-ups and Ramcharger 2.63
    Diplomat 2.31
    Omni 2.12
    All other models 2.37
1986
    B Series van/wagon
        Without rear A/C 3.00
        With rear A/C 4.00
    Caravan and Mini-Ram van 2.38
    Colt and Conquest 1.61
    D50 and Ram 50 Pick-ups 2.00
    D and W Series full-size Pick-ups and Ramcharger 2.63
    Diplomat 2.62
    All other models 2.44
1987
    B Series van/wagon
        Without rear A/C 3.06
        With rear A/C 4.06
    Caravan and Mini-Ram van 2.38
    Colt 1.61
    D50 and Ram 50 Pick-ups and Ram Raider 2.00
    D and W Series full-size Pick-ups and Ramcharger 2.63
    Dakota 2.75
    Diplomat 2.62
    All other models 2.37
1988
    B Series van/wagon
        Without rear A/C 3.06
        With rear A/C 4.06
    Caravan and Mini-Ram van 2.38
    Colt, D50 and Ram 50 Pick-ups and Ram Raider 2.00
    D and W Series full-size Pick-ups and Ramcharger 2.63
    Dakota 2.75

Heating and air conditioning

Dodge (continued)

1988 (continued)

Diplomat 2.56
All other models.. 2.37

1989

B Series van/wagon
   Without rear A/C...................................... 3.06
   With rear A/C 4.06
Caravan and Mini-Ram van
   Without rear A/C...................................... 2.38
   With rear A/C 2.70
Colt
   All models except wagon........................ 2.25
   Wagon 2.00
D50 and Ram 50 Pick-ups and Ram Raider 2.00
D and W Series full-size Pick-ups, Dakota
and Ramcharger.. 2.75
Diplomat 2.56
All other models.. 2.37

1990

B Series van/wagon
   Without rear A/C...................................... 2.80
   With rear A/C 4.10
Caravan and Mini-Ram van
   Without rear A/C...................................... 2.38
   With rear A/C 2.70
Colt
   All models except wagon........................ 2.25
   Wagon 2.00
D50 and Ram 50 Pick-ups 1.90
D and W Series full-size Pick-ups, Dakota
and Ramcharger.. 2.75
Monaco 2.25
All other models.. 2.37

1991

B Series van/wagon
   Without rear A/C...................................... 2.80
   With rear A/C 4.10
Caravan and Mini-Ram van
   Without rear A/C...................................... 2.38
   With rear A/C 2.70
Colt and Monaco... 2.25
D50 and Ram 50 Pick-ups 1.90
D and W Series full-size Pick-ups, Dakota
and Ramcharger.. 2.75
Dynasty.. 2.12
All other models.. 2.00

1992

Caravan
   Without rear A/C...................................... 2.10
   With rear A/C 2.80
Colt and Monaco... 2.25
Colt Vista 1.86
Dakota.. 2.50
Ram full-size Pick-up 2.75
Ram full-size van/wagon
   Without rear A/C...................................... 2.80
   With rear A/C 4.06
Stealth 2.12
Viper 1.88
All other models.. 2.00

1993

Caravan
   Without rear A/C...................................... 2.25
   With rear A/C 3.13

Colt .... 1.62 to 1.87
Colt Vista 1.86
Dakota.. 2.50
Intrepid 1.75
Ram full-size Pick-up 2.75
Ram full-size van/wagon
   Without rear A/C...................................... 2.80
   With rear A/C 4.06
Stealth 1.81
Viper 1.88
All other models.. 2.00

1994

Caravan
   Without rear A/C...................................... 2.25
   With rear A/C 3.25
Colt .... 1.62 to 1.87
Colt Vista 1.86
Dakota and Ram Pick-ups 2.00
Intrepid and Stealth... 1.75
Ram full-size van/wagon
   Without rear A/C...................................... 2.80
   With rear A/C 4.06
Shadow and Spirit... 1.63
Viper 1.88

1995

Avenger.. 1.54 to 1.63
Caravan
   Without rear A/C...................................... 2.25
   With rear A/C 3.25
Dakota and Ram Pick-ups 2.00
Neon 1.81
Ram full-size van/wagon
   Without rear A/C...................................... 2.25
   With rear A/C 3.13
Spirit 1.63
Viper 1.88
All other models.. 1.75

1996

Avenger.. 1.54 to 1.63
Caravan
   Without rear A/C...................................... 2.13
   With rear A/C 3.00
Dakota and Ram Pick-ups 2.00
Intrepid and Stratus.. 1.75
Neon 1.81
Ram full-size van/wagon
   Without rear A/C...................................... 2.50
   With rear A/C 3.75
Stealth and Viper 1.88

1997

Avenger.. 1.54 to 1.63
Caravan
   Without rear A/C...................................... 2.13
   With rear A/C 3.00
Dakota and Ram Pick-ups 2.00
Intrepid and Stratus.. 1.75
Neon 1.57
Ram full-size van/wagon
   Without rear A/C...................................... 2.50
   With rear A/C 3.75
Viper 1.88

1998

Avenger.. 1.54 to 1.63
Caravan
   Without rear A/C...................................... 2.13
   With rear A/C 3.00

Dakota and Ram Pick-ups	2.00K
Durango	
Without rear A/C	1.75
With rear A/C	1.88
Intrepid and Stratus	1.75
Neon	1.57
Ram full-size van/wagon	
Without rear A/C	2.12
With rear A/C	2.87
Viper	1.88
1999	
Avenger	1.54 to 1.63
Caravan	
Without rear A/C	2.13
With rear A/C	2.88
Dakota and Ram Pick-ups	2.00
Durango	
Without rear A/C	1.75
With rear A/C	1.88
Intrepid	1.56
Neon and Stratus	1.75
Ram full-size van/wagon	
Without rear A/C	2.12
With rear A/C	2.87
Viper	1.88

Eagle

1988	
Eagle 4X4	2.00
Medallion	1.80
Premier	2.25
1989	
Medallion	1.80
Premier and Summit	2.25
1990 and 1991	
Premier and Summit	2.25
Talon	2.06
1992	
Premier and Summit	2.25
Summit Wagon	1.86
Talon	2.06
1993	
Summit	1.87
Summit Wagon	1.86
Talon	2.06
Vision	1.75
1994	
Summit	1.87
Summit Wagon	1.68
Talon	2.06
Vision	1.75
1995 and 1996	
Summit	1.88
Summit Wagon	1.68
Talon	1.54 to 1.63
Vision	1.75
1997	
Talon	1.54 to 1.63
Vision	1.75
1998 (Talon)	1.54 to 1.63

Ford

1980	
Econoline	
Without rear A/C	3.50
With rear A/C	4.50

Fiesta	2.50
Granada	4.00
LTD	3.25
Pinto	2.25
All other models	3.50
1981	
Econoline	
Without rear A/C	3.50
With rear A/C	4.50
Escort	2.50
LTD	3.25
All other models	3.50
1982	
Econoline	
Without rear A/C	3.50
With rear A/C	4.50
Escort	2.56
EXP	2.31
F-Series and Super Duty Pick-ups and LTD	3.25
All other models	2.50
1983	
Crown Victoria	3.00
Econoline	
Without rear A/C	3.50
With rear A/C	4.50
Escort	2.56
EXP	2.31
F-Series and Super Duty Pick-ups	3.25
All other models	2.50
1984 and 1985	
Crown Victoria	3.25
Econoline	
Without rear A/C	3.50
With rear A/C	4.25
Escort and Tempo	2.56
EXP	2.31
F-Series and Super Duty Pick-ups	3.00
All other models	2.50
1986	
Aerostar	3.50
Bronco and F-Series and Super Duty Pick-ups	3.00
Crown Victoria	3.25
Econoline	
Without rear A/C	3.50
With rear A/C	4.25
Escort, EXP and Tempo	2.56
Taurus	2.75
All other models	2.50
1987	
Aerostar	3.50
Bronco II	2.50
Econoline	
Without rear A/C	3.50
With rear A/C	4.25
Escort, EXP and Tempo	2.56
Mustang and Thunderbird	2.50
Ranger	2.50
Taurus	2.75
All other models	3.25
1988	
Aerostar	3.50
Bronco	3.25
Crown Victoria	3.25
Econoline	
Without rear A/C	3.50
With rear A/C	4.25

Heating and air conditioning

Ford (continued)

1988 (continued)
Escort, EXP and Tempo 2.25
F-Series and Super Duty Pick-ups 3.25
Festiva 1.56
Taurus
    2.5L, 3.0L and 3.0L SHO engines 2.75
    3.8L engine 2.50
All other models 2.50

1989
Aerostar 3.50
Bronco and F-Series and Super Duty Pick-ups 3.25
Bronco II 2.50
Crown Victoria 3.00
Econoline
    Without rear A/C 3.50
    With rear A/C 4.25
Escort, Tempo and Ranger 2.25
Festiva 1.56
Taurus
    2.5L, 3.0L and 3.0L SHO engines 2.75
    3.8L engine 2.50
Mustang, Probe and Thunderbird 2.50

1990
Aerostar 3.50
Bronco 3.25
Bronco II and Ranger 2.00
Crown Victoria 3.00
Econoline
    Without rear A/C 3.50
    With rear A/C 4.25
Escort and Tempo 2.25
F-Series and Super Duty Pick-ups 3.25
Festiva 1.56
Taurus
    2.5L, 3.0L and 3.0L SHO engines 2.75
    3.8L engine 2.50
Mustang, Probe and Thunderbird 2.50

1991
Aerostar 3.50
Bronco and F-Series and Super Duty Pick-ups 2.75
Crown Victoria 3.00
Econoline
    Without rear A/C 3.50
    With rear A/C 4.25
Escort 2.12
Explorer 2.00
Festiva 1.56
Ranger 2.00
Tempo 2.25
All other models 2.50

1992
Aerostar 3.50
Bronco and F-Series and Super Duty Pick-ups 2.75
Crown Victoria and Tempo 2.25
Econoline
    Without rear A/C 3.44
    With rear A/C 4.44
Escort and ZX2 .... 2.12
Explorer and Ranger 2.00
Festiva 1.56
All other models 2.50

1993
Aerostar
    Without rear A/C 2.87
    With rear A/C 3.81

Bronco and F-Series and Super Duty Pick-ups 2.75
Crown Victoria 2.38
Econoline
    Without rear A/C 3.44
    With rear A/C 4.50
Escort and ZX2 .... 2.13
Explorer, Ranger and Taurus 2.00
Festiva 1.56
Mustang, Probe and Thunderbird 2.50
Tempo .... 2.19 to 2.31

1994
Aerostar
    Without rear A/C 3.75
    With rear A/C 4.50
Aspire 1.56
Crown Victoria and Probe 2.50
Econoline
    Without rear A/C 3.00
    With rear A/C 4.00
Escort and ZX2 .... 1.75
Explorer and Ranger 2.25
Mustang 2.13
Thunderbird 2.25
All other models 2.00

1995
Aerostar
    Without rear A/C 1.50
    With rear A/C 2.25
Aspire 1.56
Bronco and F-Series and Super Duty Pick-ups 2.06
Contour and Explorer 1.63
Crown Victoria and Mustang 2.13
Econoline
    Without rear A/C 2.75
    With rear A/C 4.00
Escort, ZX2 and Probe 1.75
Ranger 1.38
Taurus 2.00
Thunderbird 2.25
Windstar
    Without rear A/C 2.75
    With rear A/C 3.50

1996
Aerostar
    Without rear A/C 1.50
    With rear A/C 2.25
Aspire 1.56
Bronco and F-Series and Super Duty Pick-ups 2.37
Contour and Explorer 1.63
Crown Victoria, Mustang and Taurus 2.13
Econoline
    Without rear A/C 2.75
    With rear A/C 4.00
Escort, ZX2 and Probe 1.75
Ranger 1.38
Thunderbird 2.25
Windstar
    Without rear A/C 2.75
    With rear A/C 3.50

1997
Aerostar
    Without rear A/C 1.50
    With rear A/C 2.25
Aspire 1.56
Contour 1.63

Crown Victoria, Mustang and Taurus 2.13
Econoline
    Without rear A/C 3.25
    With rear A/C 4.00
Escort, ZX2 and Probe 1.75
Expedition and F-Series LD ....Refer to label in
    engine compartment
Explorer and Ranger 1.38
F-Series (except LD) and Super Duty Pick-ups 2.38
Thunderbird 2.25
Windstar
    Without rear A/C 2.75
    With rear A/C 3.50

1998
Contour and Expedition................................... Refer to label in
    engine compartment
Crown Victoria 2.38
Econoline
    Without rear A/C 2.75
    With rear A/C 4.00
Escort and ZX2 .... 1.75
Explorer and Ranger 1.88
F-Series LD 2.00
Mustang and Taurus 2.13
Windstar
    Without rear A/C 2.75
    With rear A/C 4.00

1999
Crown Victoria.. 2.38
Econoline
    Without rear A/C 2.75
    With rear A/C 4.00
Escort and ZX2 .... 1.69
Explorer and Ranger 1.88
F-Series and Super Duty Pick-ups........................ 2.00
Taurus 2.13
Windstar 3.50
All other models .... Refer to label in engine compartment

Geo

1989
Metro 1.10
Prizm 1.70
Spectrum 1.90
Tracker 1.32
1990 and 1991
Metro 1.10
Prizm 1.70
Storm .... 1.30 to 1.70
Tracker 1.32
1992
Metro 1.10
Prizm 1.70
Storm .... 1.20 to 1.40
Tracker 1.33
1993
Metro 1.10
Prizm 1.54
Storm 1.32
Tracker 1.33
1994
Metro 1.10
Prizm 1.52
Tracker 1.33

1995
Metro 1.47
Prizm .... 1.30 to 1.70
Tracker 1.33
1996 and 1997
Metro .... 1.21 to 1.32
Prizm .... 1.30 to 1.70
Tracker 1.33

GMC

1980
C and K Series Pick-ups, Caballero and Jimmy K/V 3.75
G Series van
    Without rear A/C 3.00
    With rear A/C 5.00
Suburban
    Without rear A/C 3.75
    With rear A/C 5.25
1981
C and K Series Pick-ups and Jimmy K/V 3.75
Caballero 3.25
G Series van
    Without rear A/C 3.00
    With rear A/C 5.00
Suburban
    Without rear A/C 3.75
    With rear A/C 5.25
1982 and 1983
C and K Series Pick-ups and Jimmy K/V 3.75
Caballero 3.25
G Series van
    Without rear A/C 3.00
    With rear A/C 5.00
Jimmy S/T and S/T Pick-up 2.50
Suburban
    Without rear A/C 3.75
    With rear A/C 5.25
1984
Caballero 3.25
C and K Series Pick-ups and Jimmy K/V 3.00
G Series van
    Without rear A/C 3.00
    With rear A/C 4.50
Jimmy S/T and S/T Pick-up 2.50
Suburban
    Without rear A/C 3.00
    With rear A/C 5.33
1985 and 1986
Caballero 3.25
C and K Series Pick-ups and Jimmy K/V.................... 3.00
G Series van
    Without rear A/C 3.00
    With rear A/C 4.50
Jimmy S/T and S/T Pick-up 2.50
Safari
    Without rear A/C 2.00
    With rear A/C 3.00
Suburban
    Without rear A/C 3.00
    With rear A/C.. 5.33
1987
Caballero 3.25
G Series van
    Without rear A/C 3.50
    With rear A/C.. 4.50

Heating and air conditioning

GMC (continued)

1987 (continued)
Jimmy K/V	3.50
Jimmy S/T and S/T Pick-up	2.50
Safari	
Without rear A/C	2.00
With rear A/C	3.00
Suburban	
Without rear A/C	3.50
With rear A/C	5.25

1988
Caballero	3.25
Jimmy K/V	3.25
C and K Series Pick-ups, Jimmy S/T and S/T Pick-up	2.50
G Series van	
Without rear A/C	3.50
With rear A/C	4.50
Safari	
Without rear A/C	2.00
With rear A/C	3.00
Suburban	
Without rear A/C	3.25
With rear A/C	5.25

1989 through 1991
Caballero	3.25
G Series van	
Without rear A/C	
7.4L engine	2.75
Other engines	4.50
With rear A/C	4.50
Jimmy K/V	3.25
C and K Series Pick-ups	2.80
Jimmy S/T and S/T Pick-up	2.50
Safari	
Without rear A/C	2.25
With rear A/C	3.75
Suburban	
Without rear A/C	3.25
With rear A/C	5.25

1992
Envoy, Jimmy S/T and Sonoma	2.50
G Series van	
Without rear A/C	3.00
With rear A/C	3.75
Safari	
Without rear A/C	3.00
With rear A/C	3.75
All other models	2.80

1993
3500HD	2.50
C and K Series Pick-ups	
Standard cab	2.50
Crew cab	3.00
Denali and Yukon	3.00
Envoy, Jimmy S/T and Sonoma	2.30
G Series van	
Without rear A/C	3.00
With rear A/C	4.25
Safari	
Without rear A/C	3.00
With rear A/C	3.75
Suburban	
Without rear A/C	3.00
With rear A/C	4.25

1994
3500HD, C and K Series Pick-ups	
Standard cab	2.00
Crew cab	2.25
Denali and Yukon	2.25
Envoy and Jimmy S/T	2.50
G Series van	
Without rear A/C	3.00
With rear A/C	4.25
Safari	
Without rear A/C	2.00
With rear A/C	3.00
Sonoma	2.00
Suburban	
Without rear A/C	2.25
With rear A/C	4.00

1995
3500HD, C and K Series Pick-ups	
Standard cab	2.00
Crew cab	2.25
Denali and Yukon	2.25
Envoy, Jimmy S/T and Sonoma	2.00
G Series van	
Without rear A/C	3.00
With rear A/C	4.25
Safari	
Without rear A/C	2.00
With rear A/C	3.00
Suburban	
Without rear A/C	2.25
With rear A/C	4.00

1996
3500HD, C and K Series Pick-ups	
Standard cab	2.00
Crew cab	2.25
Denali and Yukon	2.25
Envoy, Jimmy S/T and Sonoma	2.00
G Series van	
Without rear A/C	3.00
With rear A/C	4.25
Safari	
Without rear A/C	2.00
With rear A/C	3.00
Savana	
Without rear A/C	3.00
With rear A/C	4.88
Suburban	
Without rear A/C	2.25
With rear A/C	4.00

1997
3500HD, C and K Series Pick-ups	
Standard cab	2.00
Crew cab	2.25
Denali and Yukon	2.25
Envoy, Jimmy S/T and Sonoma	2.00
G Series van	
Without rear A/C	3.00
With rear A/C	4.88
Safari	
Without rear A/C	2.00
With rear A/C	3.00
Savana	
Without rear A/C	3.00
With rear A/C	4.88

Suburban
  Without rear A/C.. 2.25
  With rear A/C... 4.00
1998 and 1999
  C and K Series Pick-ups
    Standard cab... 2.00
    Crew cab... 2.25
  Denali and Yukon
    Without rear A/C... 2.25
    With rear A/C.. 4.00
  Envoy and Jimmy S/T 1.88
  G Series van
    Without rear A/C... 3.00
    With rear A/C.. 4.88
  Safari
    Without rear A/C... 2.00
    With rear A/C.. 3.00
  Savana
    Without rear A/C... 3.00
    With rear A/C.. 4.88
  Sonoma 1.88
  Suburban
    Without rear A/C... 2.25
    With rear A/C.. 4.00
  3500HD
    Standard cab... 2.00
    Crew cab... 2.25

Jeep

1980 through 1983
  CJ Series and Scrambler...................................... 2.50
  All other models... 2.25
1984 through 1988
  Grand Wagoneer and J Series Pick-up
    Six-cylinder engine.. 2.00
    V8 engine 2.25
  All other models... 2.00
1989 (all models)... 2.00
1990 and 1991
  Cherokee and Comanche 2.38
  Grand Wagoneer and Wrangler.................................. 2.00
1992
  Cherokee and Comanche 2.38
  Wrangler... 2.00
1993
  Cherokee... 2.38
  Grand Cherokee and Grand Wagoneer............................ 1.75
  Wrangler... 2.00
1994
  Cherokee... 2.38
  Grand Cherokee 1.75
  Wrangler... 2.00
1995
  Cherokee and Wrangler.. 2.00
  Grand Cherokee 1.75
1996
  Cherokee... 2.00
  Grand Cherokee 1.75
1997
  Cherokee... 1.25
  Grand Cherokee 1.75
  Wrangler... 1.25
1998 and 1999
  Cherokee... 1.25
  Grand Cherokee 1.63
  Wrangler... 1.25

Lincoln

1980
  Continental and Mark VI...................................... 4.25
  Versailles 4.00
1981 (all models) 3.00
1982 and 1983
  Continental 2.50
  Mark VI and Town Car 3.00
1984 through 1990
  Continental and Mark VII..................................... 2.50
  Town Car... 3.00
1991 and 1992 (all models) 2.50
1993
  Continental 2.50
  Mark VIII 2.13
  Town Car... 2.25
1994 (all models) 2.50
1995 through 1997 (all models)................................. 2.13
1998 and 1999
  Navigator .... Refer to label in engine compartment
  All other models 2.38

Mercury

1980
  Bobcat... 2.25
  Capri, Cougar and Zephyr..................................... 3.50
  Marquis 3.25
  Monarch 4.00
1981
  Capri, Cougar and Zephyr..................................... 3.50
  Lynx 2.50
  Marquis 3.25
1982
  Capri and Cougar... 2.50
  LN7.. 2.31
  Lynx... 2.56
  Marquis 3.25
  Zephyr... 3.50
1983
  Grand Marquis 3.00
  LN7.. 2.31
  Lynx... 2.56
  All other models 2.50
1984
  Grand Marquis 3.25
  Lynx and Topaz... 2.56
  All other models 2.50
1985
  Grand Marquis 3.25
  Lynx and Topaz... 2.56
  All other models 2.50
1986
  Grand Marquis 3.25
  Lynx and Topaz... 2.56
  Sable 2.75
  All other models 2.50
1987
  Cougar... 2.50
  Grand Marquis 3.25
  Lynx and Topaz... 2.56
  Sable 2.75
1988 and 1989
  Cougar... 2.50
  Grand Marquis 3.25

Heating and air conditioning

Mercury (continued)

1988 and 1989 (continued)

Sable
- 3.0L engine 2.75
- 3.8L engine 2.50

Topaz 2.25
Tracer 1.55

1990

Cougar 2.50
Grand Marquis 3.00

Sable
- 3.0L engine 2.75
- 3.8L engine 2.50

Topaz 2.25

1991

Cougar and Sable 2.50
Grand Marquis 3.00
Topaz 2.25
Tracer 2.12

1992

Capri 1.55
Cougar and Sable 2.50
Grand Marquis and Topaz 2.25
Tracer 2.12

1993

Capri 1.55
Cougar 2.50
Grand Marquis 2.40
Sable 2.00
Topaz .... 2.19 to 2.31
Tracer 2.13

Villager
- Without rear A/C 2.25
- With rear A/C 3.50

1994

Capri 1.25
Cougar 2.25
Grand Marquis 2.50
Sable and Topaz 2.00
Tracer 1.75

Villager
- Without rear A/C 2.00
- With rear A/C 3.25

1995

Cougar 2.25
Grand Marquis 2.13
Mystique 1.63
Sable 2.00
Tracer 1.75

Villager
- Without rear A/C 2.00
- With rear A/C 3.25

1996

Cougar 2.25
Grand Marquis 2.13
Mystique 1.63
Sable 2.13
Tracer 1.75

Villager
- Without rear A/C 2.00
- With rear A/C 3.25

1997

Cougar 2.25
Grand Marquis 2.13
Mountaineer 1.38

Mystique 1.63
Sable 2.13
Tracer 1.75

Villager
- Without rear A/C 2.00
- With rear A/C 3.25

1998

Grand Marquis 2.38
Mountaineer 1.88
Mystique .... Refer to label in engine compartment
Sable 2.13
Tracer 1.75

Villager
- Without rear A/C 2.00
- With rear A/C 3.25

1999

Cougar .... Refer to label in engine compartment
Grand Marquis 2.38
Mountaineer 1.88
Mystique .... Refer to label in engine compartment
Sable 2.13
Tracer 1.69

Villager
- Without rear A/C 2.00
- With rear A/C 3.50

Merkur

1985 through 1989 (all models) 2.50

Oldsmobile

1980

Omega 2.75

Starfire
- Axial compressor 3.00
- Radial compressor 2.50

Cutlass Cruiser 3.75
All other models 3.75

1981

Cutlass Cruiser 3.25
Omega 2.75
All other models 3.50

1982 and 1983

Ciera, Firenza and Omega 2.75
Cutlass Cruiser 3.25
All other models 3.50

1984

Ciera, Cutlass Cruiser, Firenza and Omega ... 2.75
All other models 3.50

1985

Eighty-Eight, Toronado and Trofeo 3.50
All other models 2.75

1986

Eighty-Eight
- 3.0L engine 2.40
- All other engines 2.88

Ninety-Eight 2.40
All other models 2.75

1987

Eighty-Eight and Ninety-Eight 2.40
All other models 2.75

1988

Ciera and Cutlass Cruiser 2.75
Cutlass Supreme 2.25
Eighty-Eight and Ninety-Eight 2.40
Toronado and Trofeo 2.38

1989

Ciera and Cutlass Cruiser	2.75
Cutlass Supreme	2.25
Eighty-Eight	2.88
Ninety-Eight	2.40
Toronado and Trofeo	2.38

1990

Ciera and Cutlass Cruiser	2.75
Cutlass Supreme	2.25
Eighty-Eight	2.88
Ninety-Eight	2.40
Silhouette	2.75
Toronado and Trofeo	2.38

1991

Bravada	2.50
Ciera and Cutlass Cruiser	2.75
Cutlass Supreme	2.25
Eighty-Eight and Ninety-Eight	2.42
Silhouette	2.75
Toronado and Trofeo	2.38

1992

Achieva	2.63
Bravada	2.50
Custom Cruiser	3.10
Cutlass Supreme	2.25
Eighty-Eight, LS, LSS and Ninety-Eight	2.42
Silhouette	2.75
All other models	2.38

1993

Achieva	2.63
Bravada	2.30
Cutlass Ciera and Cutlass Cruiser	2.38
Cutlass Supreme	2.25
Eighty-Eight, LS, LSS and Ninety-Eight	2.42
Silhouette	2.62

1994

Achieva	2.25
Bravada	2.00
Cutlass Ciera and Cutlass Cruiser	
2.2L engine	1.75
3.1L engine	2.00
Cutlass Supreme	2.00
Eighty-Eight, LS, LSS and Ninety-Eight	2.42
Silhouette	2.62

1995

Achieva and Aurora	2.25
Bravada	2.00
Cutlass Ciera and Cutlass Cruiser	
2.2L engine	1.75
3.1L engine	2.00
Cutlass Supreme	2.00
Eighty-Eight, LS, LSS and Ninety-Eight	2.42
Silhouette	2.25

1996

Achieva and Aurora	2.25
Bravada	2.00
Cutlass Ciera and Cutlass Cruiser	
2.2L engine	1.75
3.1L engine	2.00
Silhouette	2.25
All other models	2.00

1997

Achieva	2.25
Bravada	2.00
Cutlass	1.75

Cutlass Supreme	1.88
Silhouette	2.00
All other models	2.00

1998

Achieva	2.25
Bravada	1.88
Cutlass	1.75
Intrigue	1.88
All other models	2.00

1999

Alero and Cutlass	1.75
Bravada	1.88
Intrigue	1.88
All other models	2.00

Plymouth

1980

Grand Fury	2.87
Horizon and TC3	2.12
Trailduster	2.63
Volare	2.31
Voyager	
Without rear A/C	3.38
With rear A/C	4.00
All other models	2.00

1981

Arrow Pick-up, Champ and Sapporo	2.00
Grand Fury	2.31
Horizon and TC3	2.12
Reliant	2.37
Trailduster	2.63
Voyager	
Without rear A/C	3.00
With rear A/C	4.00

1982

Arrow Pick-up, Champ and Sapporo	2.00
Grand Fury	2.31
Horizon and TC3	2.12
Reliant	2.37
Scamp	2.13
Voyager	
Without rear A/C	3.00
With rear A/C	4.00

1983

Arrow Pick-up, Colt and Sapporo	2.00
Grand Fury	2.31
Horizon	2.12
Reliant and Turismo	2.37
Scamp	2.13
Voyager	
Without rear A/C	3.00
With rear A/C	4.00

1984

Colt and Conquest	2.00
Grand Fury	2.31
Horizon	2.12
Reliant and Turismo	2.37
Scamp	2.13
Voyager	2.33

1985

Caravelle, Reliant and Turismo	2.37
Colt	1.61
Conquest	1.54
Grand Fury	2.31
Horizon	2.12
Voyager	2.38

Heating and air conditioning

Plymouth (continued)

1986
- Colt and Conquest 1.61
- Grand Fury 2.62
- Voyager 2.38
- All other models 2.44

1987
- Colt 1.61
- Grand Fury 2.62
- Voyager 2.38
- All other models 2.37

1988
- Colt 2.00
- Grand Fury 2.56
- Voyager 2.38
- All other models 2.37

1989
- Colt
  - Wagon 2.00
  - All models except wagon 2.25
- Grand Fury 2.56
- Voyager
  - Without rear A/C 2.38
  - With rear A/C 2.70
- All other models 2.37

1990
- Colt
  - Wagon 2.00
  - All models except wagon 2.25
- Laser 2.06
- Voyager
  - Without rear A/C 2.00
  - With rear A/C 2.70
- All other models 2.37

1991
- Acclaim and Sundance 2.00
- Colt 2.25
- Laser 2.06
- Voyager
  - Without rear A/C 2.00
  - With rear A/C 2.70

1992
- Acclaim and Sundance 2.00
- Colt 2.25
- Colt Vista 1.86
- Laser 2.06
- Voyager
  - Without rear A/C 2.10
  - With rear A/C 2.80

1993
- Acclaim and Sundance 2.00
- Colt 1.87
- Colt Vista 1.86
- Laser 2.06
- Voyager
  - Without rear A/C 2.25
  - With rear A/C 3.13

1994
- Acclaim and Sundance 1.63
- Colt 1.87
- Colt Vista 1.86
- Laser 2.06
- Voyager
  - Without rear A/C 2.25
  - With rear A/C 3.25

1995
- Acclaim 1.63
- Neon 1.81
- Voyager
  - Without rear A/C 2.25
  - With rear A/C 3.25

1996
- Breeze 1.75
- Neon 1.81
- Voyager
  - Without rear A/C 2.13
  - With rear A/C 3.00

1997
- Breeze 1.75
- Neon 1.57
- Prowler 1.50
- Voyager
  - Without rear A/C 2.13
  - With rear A/C 3.00

1998
- Breeze 1.63
- Neon 1.57
- Prowler 1.50
- Voyager
  - Without rear A/C 2.13
  - With rear A/C 3.00

1999
- Breeze 1.25
- Neon 1.75
- Prowler 1.50
- Voyager
  - Without rear A/C 2.13
  - With rear A/C 2.88

Pontiac

1980
- 1000 .... 2.25
- Bonneville and Catalina 3.50
- Firebird 3.25
- Grand Am, Grand Prix and LeMans 3.75
- Phoenix 2.75

1981
- 1000 .... 2.25
- Bonneville and Catalina 3.50
- Firebird, Grand Prix and LeMans 3.25
- Phoenix 2.75

1982
- 1000 .... 2.25
- 2000, 6000 and Phoenix 2.75
- Bonneville and Grand Prix 3.25
- Firebird 3.00

1983
- 1000 .... 2.25
- 2000, 6000 and Phoenix 2.75
- Bonneville and Grand Prix 3.25
- Firebird 3.00
- Parisienne 3.50

1984
- 1000 .... 2.25
- 6000 .... 2.75
- Bonneville and Grand Prix 3.25
- Fiero 2.50
- Firebird 3.00
- Parisienne 3.50
- Phoenix and Sunbird 2.75

1985

1000	2.25
Bonneville and Grand Prix	3.25
Fiero	2.50
Firebird	3.00
Parisienne	3.50
All other models	2.75

1986

1000	2.25
6000	
STE	2.25
All models except STE	2.75
Bonneville and Grand Prix	3.25
Fiero	2.50
Firebird	3.00
Grand Am and Sunbird	2.25
Parisienne and Safari	3.50

1987

1000	2.25
6000	
STE	2.25
All models except STE	2.75
Bonneville	2.40
Fiero	2.50
Firebird	3.00
Grand Am and Sunbird	2.25
Grand Prix and Safari	3.50

1988

6000	
STE	2.25
All models except STE	2.75
Bonneville	2.40
Fiero	2.50
LeMans	2.20
Safari	3.50
All other models	2.25

1989

6000	
STE	2.25
All models except STE	2.75
Bonneville	2.40
LeMans	2.20
Safari	3.50
All other models	2.25

1990

6000	
STE	2.25
All models except STE	2.75
Bonneville	2.40
LeMans	2.20
Trans Sport	2.75
All other models	2.25

1991

6000	2.75
Bonneville	2.42
LeMans	2.20
Trans Sport	2.75
All other models	2.25

1992

Bonneville	2.42
Firebird, Grand Prix and Sunbird	2.25
Grand Am	2.65
LeMans	2.20
Montana and Trans Sport	2.75

1993

Bonneville	2.42
Firebird	2.00
Grand Am	2.63
Grand Prix and Sunbird	2.25
LeMans	2.20
Montana and Trans Sport	
Without rear A/C	2.62
With rear A/C	3.50

1994

Bonneville	2.42
Firebird and Grand Prix	2.00
Grand Am and Sunbird	2.25
Montana and Trans Sport	
Without rear A/C	2.62
With rear A/C	3.50

1995

Bonneville	2.42
Firebird and Grand Prix	2.00
Grand Am	2.25
Montana and Trans Sport	
Without rear A/C	2.25
With rear A/C	3.00
Sunfire	1.50

1996

Bonneville and Grand Prix	2.00
Firebird	
3.8L engine	1.75
5.7L engine	2.00
Grand Am	2.25
Montana and Trans Sport	
Without rear A/C	2.25
With rear A/C	3.00
Sunfire	1.50

1997

Bonneville	2.00
Firebird	
3.8L engine	1.63
5.7L engine	2.00
Grand Am	2.25
Grand Prix	1.88
Montana and Trans Sport	
Without rear A/C	2.00
With rear A/C	2.90
Sunfire	1.50

1998

Bonneville	2.00
Firebird	1.50
Grand Am	2.25
Grand Prix	1.88
Montana and Trans Sport	
Without rear A/C	2.00
With rear A/C	2.90
Sunfire	1.50

1999

Bonneville	2.00
Firebird	1.50
Grand Am	1.75
Grand Prix	1.88
Montana and Trans Sport	
Without rear A/C	2.00
With rear A/C	2.90
Sunfire	1.50

Saturn

1991 through 1993 (all models)	2.25
1994 through 1999 (all models)	1.50

Heating and air conditioning

System refrigerant capacity (imported vehicles) (in pounds)

Acura

1986 through 1990
Integra	1.87 to 2.09
Legend	1.88

1991
Integra	1.87 to 2.09
Legend	1.66
NSX	2.13

1992
Integra	2.00 to 2.10
Legend	1.50 to 1.70
NSX	2.00 to 2.10
Vigor	1.80 to 1.90

1993
Integra	2.00 to 2.10
Legend	1.40 to 1.50
NSX	1.80 to 1.90
Vigor	1.80 to 1.90

1994
Integra	1.40 to 1.50
Legend	1.50 to 1.70
NSX	1.80 to 1.90
Vigor	1.80 to 1.90

1995
Integra	1.40 to 1.50
Legend	1.50 to 1.70
NSX	1.80 to 1.90

1996
Integra	1.40 to 1.50
NSX	1.80 to 1.90
SLX	1.70
2.5TL, 3.2TL and 3.5RL	1.50 to 1.70

1997
Integra	1.40 to 1.50
NSX	1.80 to 1.90
SLX	1.70
2.2CL	1.30 to 1.40
3.0CL	1.40 to 1.60
2.5TL, 3.2TL and 3.5RL	1.50 to 1.70

1998
Integra	1.40 to 1.50
NSX	1.80 to 1.90
SLX	1.30
2.3CL	1.30 to 1.50
3.0CL	1.40 to 1.60
2.5TL, 3.2TL and 3.5RL	1.50 to 1.70

1999
Integra	1.40 to 1.50
NSX	1.80 to 1.90
SLX	1.30
2.3CL	1.30 to 1.50
3.0CL	1.40 to 1.60
3.2TL	1.30 to 1.40
3.5RL	1.50 to 1.70

Audi

1980 through 1983
4000, Coupe, Quattro T	2.13
5000	3.06

1984 and 1985
4000, Coupe, Quattro T	2.13
5000	2.38

1986 and 1987
4000, Coupe, Quattro T	2.37
5000	3.06

1988
80 and 90	2.31
5000	3.06

1989
80 and 90	2.31
100 and 200	2.38
V8 Quattro	2.42

1990 and 1991
80 and 90	2.31
100 and 200	2.38
Coupe Quattro	2.55
V8 Quattro	2.42

1992
80 and 90	2.31
100	2.38
Coupe Quattro	2.55
S4 and V8 Quattro	2.42

1993 and 1994
90	1.44
100 and S4	1.66
V8 Quattro	1.88

1995
90 and Cabriolet	1.44
A6 and S6	1.66
V8 Quattro	1.88

1996
A4 and Cabriolet	1.44
A6	1.33
V8 Quattro	1.88

1997
A4 and Cabriolet	1.44
A6 and A8	1.33

1998 and 1999
A4 and Cabriolet	1.44
A6	1.75
A8	1.33

BMW

1980 through 1985
3-Series	2.15
5-Series	
524TD, 535 and M5	2.15
528e and 533	2.81
6-Series	
Without rear A/C	2.43
With rear A/C	3.97
7-Series	2.81

1986 and 1987
3-Series	2.15
5-Series	
524TD, 535 and M5	2.15
528e and 533	2.81

6-Series
  Without rear A/C 2.43
  With rear A/C 3.97
7-Series 2.59
1988
  3-Series 2.15
  5-Series
    525i and 535I 4.24
    M5 .... 3.31
  6-Series
    Without rear A/C 2.43
    With rear A/C 3.97
  7-Series 4.24
  M3 .... 1.93
1989 through 1991
  3-Series 2.15
  5-Series
    525i and 535I 4.24
    M5 .... 3.31
  7-Series 4.24
  M3 .... 1.93
1992
  318, 325 and M3 .... 2.65
  5-Series (except M5) and 850 .... 4.24
  735
    Without rear A/C 4.24
    With rear A/C 4.57
  M5 .... 3.31
1993
  318 and 325
    Round tube condenser 2.20
    Flat tube condenser 1.82
  5-Series (including M5)
    Round tube condenser 3.42
    Flat tube condenser 3.20
  740 and 750
    Without rear A/C 3.42
    With rear A/C 3.75
  850 .... 3.42
1994
  318, 325 and M3
    Round tube condenser 2.20
    Flat tube condenser 1.82
  5-Series (including M5)
    Round tube condenser 3.42
    Flat tube condenser 3.20
  740 and 750
    Without rear A/C 3.42
    With rear A/C 3.75
  840 and 850 .... 3.42
1995
  318, 325 and M3
    Round tube condenser 2.20
    Flat tube condenser 1.82
  5-Series (including M5)
    Round tube condenser 3.42
    Flat tube condenser 3.20
  740 and 750 .... 2.65
  840 and 850 .... 3.42
1996 and 1997
  318, 328, M3 and Z3
    Round tube condenser 2.20
    Flat tube condenser 1.82
  740 and 750 .... 2.65
  840 and 850 .... 3.42

1998
  318, 328, M3 and Z3
    Round tube condenser 2.20
    Flat tube condenser 1.82
  5-Series 2.70
  740 and 750 .... 2.65
  840 .... 3.42

Daewoo
1999 (Lanos, Leganza and Nubira) .... not available

Daihatsu
1989 (Charade) 1.43
1990 through 1992
  Charade 1.43
  Rocky 1.65

Fiat
1980 and 1981
  Brava 2.75
  Strada .... not available

Honda
1980 (Civic and Prelude) 1.40
1981 and 1982
  Accord 1.66
  Civic and Prelude 1.40
1983
  Accord 1.66
  Civic 1.40
  Prelude 1.75
1984
  Accord 1.87
  Civic, CRX and Prelude 1.75
1985
  Accord .... 1.90 to 2.10
  Civic, CRX and Prelude .... 1.50 to 1.88
1986 and 1987
  Accord 1.88
  Civic and CRX 1.76
  Prelude 1.76
1988
  Accord 1.88
  Civic and CRX 1.98
  Prelude 1.76
1989
  Accord 1.88
  Civic and CRX 1.98
  Prelude 2.13
1990
  Accord .... 2.00 to 2.10
  Civic and CRX
    CRX and Civic (except Wagon) 1.98
    Wagon .... 1.88 to 2.10
  Prelude 2.00
1991
  Accord .... 2.00 to 2.10
  Civic and CRX .... 1.88 to 2.10
  Prelude 2.00
1992
  Accord .... 2.00 to 2.10
  Civic .... 1.88 to 2.10
  Prelude 1.65

Heating and air conditioning

Honda (continued)

1993
- Accord .... 1.76 to 1.87
- Civic 1.36
- Civic Del Sol 1.43
- Prelude 1.15

1994
- Accord and Prelude 1.15
- Civic and Civic Del Sol 1.21
- Passport 1.43

1995
- Accord
  - Four-cylinder engine 1.43
  - V6 engine 1.33
- Civic and Civic Del Sol 1.21
- Odyssey
  - Without rear A/C 1.43
  - With rear A/C 1.88
- Passport and Prelude 1.43

1996
- Accord
  - Four-cylinder engine 1.43
  - V6 engine 1.33
- Civic .... 1.32 to 1.43
- Civic Del Sol 1.88
- Odyssey
  - Without rear A/C 1.43
  - With rear A/C 1.88
- Passport and Prelude 1.43

1997
- Accord
  - Four-cylinder engine 1.43
  - V6 engine 1.33
- Civic .... 1.32 to 1.43
- Civic Del Sol 1.88
- CR-V 1.54
- Odyssey
  - Without rear A/C 1.43
  - With rear A/C 1.88
- Passport 1.43
- Prelude 1.66

1998
- Accord .... 1.31 to 1.44
- Civic .... 1.32 to 1.43
- CR-V 1.54
- Odyssey
  - Without rear A/C 1.43
  - With rear A/C 1.88
- Passport 1.43
- Prelude 1.66

1999
- Accord .... 1.31 to 1.44
- Civic .... 1.32 to 1.43
- CR-V 1.54
- Odyssey
  - Without rear A/C 1.38
  - With rear A/C 1.90
- Passport 1.43
- Prelude 1.66

Hyundai

1985 through 1989 (all models) .... 1.90 to 2.20

1990
- Excel .... 1.76 to 1.87
- Sonata .... 1.90 to 2.20

1991 (all models) .... 1.90 to 2.20

1992
- Elantra 2.10
- All other models .... 1.90 to 2.20

1993
- Elantra 2.10
- Excel .... 1.88 to 2.00
- Scoupe 1.90
- Sonata .... 1.90 to 2.20

1994
- Elantra 1.50
- Excel .... 1.50 to 1.54
- Scoupe .... 1.43 to 1.54
- Sonata .... 1.90 to 2.20

1995
- Accent .... 1.48 to 1.50
- Elantra 1.50
- Scoupe .... 1.43 to 1.54
- Sonata .... 1.65 to 1.76

1996
- Accent .... 1.48 to 1.50
- Elantra .... 1.50 to 1.61
- Sonata .... 1.56 to 1.67

1997
- Accent .... 1.48 to 1.50
- Elantra .... 1.50 to 1.61
- Sonata .... 1.56 to 1.67
- Tiburon .... 1.50 to 1.61

1998
- Accent .... 1.48 to 1.50
- Elantra and Tiburon .... 1.50 to 1.61
- Sonata 1.60

1999
- Accent .... 1.49 to 1.51
- Elantra and Tiburon .... 1.50 to 1.61
- Sonata 1.48

Infiniti

1990
- M30 .... 2.00 to 2.20
- Q45 .... 2.54 to 2.76

1991
- G20 .... 1.50 to 1.80
- M30 .... 2.00 to 2.20
- Q45 .... 2.54 to 2.76

1992
- G20 .... 1.50 to 1.80
- M30 .... 2.00 to 2.20
- Q45 .... 2.54 to 2.76

1993
- G20 .... 1.50 to 1.80
- J30 .... 1.60
- Q45 .... 2.40 to 2.60

1994 and 1995 (all models) .... 1.54 to 1.76

1996
- G20 and J30 .... 1.54 to 1.76
- I30 .... 1.32 to 1.54
- Q45 .... 1.70 to 1.82

1997
- I30 and QX4 .... 1.32 to 1.54
- J30 .... 1.54 to 1.76
- Q45 .... 1.49 to 1.60

1998
- I30 and QX4 .... 1.32 to 1.54
- Q45 .... 1.49 to 1.60

1999
    G20 .... 1.21 to 1.43
    I30 and QX4 .... 1.32 to 1.54
    Q45 .... 1.38 to 1.49

Isuzu

1981 and 1982 (I-Mark and Pick-up) 1.87
1983
    I-Mark and Pick-up 1.87
    Impulse 2.10
1984
    I-Mark and Pick-up 1.87
    Impulse 2.10
    Trooper 2.06
1985
    I-Mark and Pick-up 1.87
    Impulse 2.20
    Trooper 2.12
1986 through 1989
    I-Mark 1.77
    Impulse 2.20
    Pick-up 1.87
    Trooper 2.10
1990
    Amigo and Pick-up 1.87
    Impulse 2.20
    Trooper 2.10
1991
    Amigo and Pick-up 1.87
    Impulse and Rodeo 2.20
    Stylus 1.66
    Trooper 2.10
1992
    Amigo and Pick-up 1.87
    Impulse and Stylus 1.32
    Rodeo 2.20
    Trooper 1.87
1993
    Amigo, Pick-up and Rodeo 1.65
    Stylus 1.32
    Trooper 1.87
1994
    Amigo, Pick-up and Rodeo 1.43
    Trooper 1.65
1995
    Pick-up and Rodeo 1.43
    Trooper 1.65
1996
    Hombre 2.00
    Oasis
        Without rear A/C 1.43
        With rear A/C 1.88
    Rodeo 1.43
    Trooper 1.65
1997
    Hombre 2.00
    Oasis
        Without rear A/C 1.43
        With rear A/C 1.88
    Rodeo 1.43
    Trooper 1.65
1998 and 1999
    Amigo 1.32
    Hombre 1.88

Oasis
    Without rear A/C 1.43
    With rear A/C 1.88
Rodeo 1.43
Trooper 1.32

Jaguar

1980
    XJ6 and XJ12 .... 3.50
    XJS 2.50
1981 and 1982
    XJ6 .... 3.50
    XJS 2.50
1983 through 1987 (all models) 3.50
1988 and 1989
    XJ6 .... 2.50
    XJS
        Delco compressor 2.50
        Sanden compressor 3.50
1990 through 1992 (all models) 2.50
1993 (all models) 2.50
1994
    XJ6, XJR and XJS 2.50
    XJ12 .... 2.75
1995 and 1996
    XJ6 and XJ12 .... 2.40
    XJR and XJS 2.50
1997
    XJ6 and XJ12 .... 2.40
    XJR 2.50
    XK8 .... 1.43 to 1.65
1998 and 1999
    XJ8 .... 1.43 to 1.54
    XJR 2.50
    XK8 .... 1.43 to 1.65

Kia

1994 (all models) 1.54
1995 through 1997
    Sephia 1.54
    Sportage .... not available
1998
    Sephia .... 1.43 to 1.65
    Sportage .... not available

Land Rover

1993
    Defender 2.40
1994
    Defender 2.40
    Discovery
        Without rear A/C 1.98
        With rear A/C 2.50
1995
    Defender .... not available
    Discovery
        Without rear A/C 2.00
        With rear A/C 2.50
    Range Rover 1.98
1996
    Defender .... not available
    Discovery
        Without rear A/C 2.00
        With rear A/C 2.50

Heating and air conditioning

Land Rover (continued)

1996 (continued)
New Range Rover 2.76
Range Rover 1.98

1997
Defender .... not available
Discovery
    Without rear A/C 2.00
    With rear A/C 2.50
New Range Rover 2.76
Range Rover 2.75

1998
Discovery
    Without rear A/C 2.00
    With rear A/C 2.50
New Range Rover 2.76
Range Rover 2.75

1999
Discovery
    Without rear A/C 2.00
    With rear A/C 2.50
New Range Rover 2.76
Range Rover .... not available

Lexus

1990 and 1991
ES250 .... 1.30 to 1.70
LS400 .... 2.30

1992
ES300, SC300 and SC400 .... 1.90 to 2.20
LS400 .... 2.30

1993
ES300, SC300 and SC400 .... 2.09
GS300 and GS400 .... 1.87
LS400 .... 2.10

1994
ES300 .... 1.87
GS300 and GS400 .... 1.87
LS400 .... 2.10
SC300 and SC400 .... 1.87

1995
LS400 .... 1.86
All other models 1.87

1996 and 1997
LS400 .... 1.86
SC300 and SC400 .... 2.09
All other models 1.87

1998 and 1999
ES300 .... 1.76
GS300 and GS400 .... 1.32
LS400 .... 1.54
LX470 .... 2.31
SC300 and SC400 .... 2.09

Mazda

1985
GLC, MX6 and 626 .... 2.00
RX-7 .... 1.50 to 1.70

1986 and 1987
RX-7 .... 1.50 to 1.70
All other models 2.00

1988
RX-7 .... 1.50 to 1.70
929 .... 1.77
All other models 2.00

1989
323 .... 1.70 to 1.90
929 .... 2.30 to 2.50
B-Series Pick-ups .... 1.80 to 2.00
MPV
    Without rear A/C 2.70
    With rear A/C 3.10
MX6 and 626 .... 2.10 to 2.30
RX-7 .... 1.80

1990
B-Series Pick-ups 1.70
Miata 1.80
MPV
    Without rear A/C 2.70
    With rear A/C 3.10
MX6 and 626 .... 2.10 to 2.30
RX-7 .... 1.80
323 .... 1.70 to 1.90
929 .... 2.30 to 2.50

1991
323 .... 1.70 to 1.90
929 .... 2.30 to 2.50
B-Series Pick-ups 1.70
Miata 1.80
MPV
    Without rear A/C 2.70
    With rear A/C 3.10
MX6 and 626 .... 2.10 to 2.30
Navajo 1.75
RX-7 .... 1.80

1992
323 .... 1.70 to 1.90
B-Series Pick-ups 1.70
Miata 1.80
MPV
    Without rear A/C 2.70
    With rear A/C 3.10
MX6 and 626 .... 2.10 to 2.30
Navajo 1.75

1993
323 .... 1.70 to 1.90
929 .... 1.77
B-Series Pick-ups 1.76
Miata and MX-3 .... 1.77
MPV
    Without rear A/C 2.70
    With rear A/C 3.10
MX6 and 626 .... 2.10 to 2.30
Navajo 1.75
RX-7 .... 1.33

1994
323, 929 and Protégé 1.76
B-Series Pick-ups 1.37
Miata 1.33
MPV
    Without rear A/C 2.32
    With rear A/C 2.76
MX-3 .... 1.66
MX6 and 626 .... 1.54
Navajo 1.75
RX-7 .... 0.99 to 1.21

1995
929 .... 1.76
B-Series Pick-ups 1.37
Miata and Protégé 1.33

Millenia and MX-3	1.66
MPV	
Without rear A/C	1.98
With rear A/C	2.20
MX6 and 626	1.54
RX-7	0.99 to 1.21
1996	
B-Series Pick-ups	1.37
Miata and Protégé	1.33
Millenia	1.66
MPV	
Without rear A/C	1.98
With rear A/C	2.20
MX6 and 626	1.54
1997	
B-Series Pick-ups	1.38
Miata and Protégé	1.33
Millenia	1.66
MPV	2.21
MX6 and 626	1.54
1998	
B-Series Pick-ups	1.88
Millenia, MX6 and 626	1.66
MPV	2.21
Protégé	1.33
1999	
B-Series Pick-ups	1.88
Miata and Protégé	1.25
Millenia	1.76
MX6 and 626	1.69

Mercedes-Benz

1980	
450 Series	2.20
All other models	2.66
1981 through 1985 (all models)	2.66
1986	
300D, CD and TD	2.65
380SL	2.20
All other models	2.87
1987	
300D, CD and TD	2.65
190D and E and 300SDL	2.87
1988 and 1989	
420SEL, 300SE and SEL, 560SEC and SEL	2.90
All other models	2.20
1990	
190E 2.6L, 300CE, E and TE, 300SL, 500SL and 560SL	2.20
All other models	2.90
1991	
190E 2.6L, 300CE, E and TE, 300SL, 500SL and 560SL	2.20
All other models	2.90
1992	
400E and 500E	
Without rear A/C	2.43
With rear A/C	2.76
300D	2.90
300SD, 300SE, 400SE, 500SEC, 500SEL, 600SEC and 600SEL	
Without rear A/C	2.60
With rear A/C	3.00
All other models	2.20
1993	
190E	2.20

300SD, 300SE, 400SE, 500SEC, 500SEL, 600SEC and 600SEL	
Without rear A/C	2.60
With rear A/C	3.00
All other models	2.09
1994 through 1997	
S320, S3530, S420, S500 and S600	
Without rear A/C	2.60
With rear A/C	3.00
All other models	2.09
1998 and 1999	
C36, C43, C220, C230 and C280	2.09
E300, E320, E420, E430 and E500	2.09
S320, S3530, S420, S500 and S600	
Without rear A/C	2.60
With rear A/C	3.00
SL320, SL500 and SL600	2.09

Mitsubishi

1983 (all models)	2.20
1984	
Starion	1.56
All other models	2.20
Montero	2.20
Pick-up	2.20
1985	
Pick-up	1.30 to 1.80
All other models	1.63
1986	
Cordia and Tredia	2.01
Galant	1.62 to 2.00
Mirage, Montero and Starion	1.61
Pick-up	1.30 to 1.80
1987	
Cordia, Tredia and Galant	1.60 to 2.00
Mirage	1.62 to 2.00
Montero	1.30 to 2.00
Precis	1.90 to 2.20
Starion and Pick-up	1.61 to 2.00
1988	
Montero	1.98
Precis	1.90 to 2.20
Pick-up	1.61 to 2.00
Van/wagon	
Without rear A/C	2.00
With rear A/C	3.20
All other models	2.00
1989	
Galant	2.06
Mirage	2.25
Montero, Sigma and Pick-up	2.00
Precis	1.90 to 2.20
Starion	1.81
Van/wagon	
Without rear A/C	2.00
With rear A/C	3.20
1990	
Eclipse and Galant	2.06
Montero, Sigma and van/wagon	2.00
Precis	1.76 to 1.87
Pick-up	1.88
1991	
3000GT	2.12
Eclipse and Galant	2.06
Montero	2.00

Heating and air conditioning

Mitsubishi (continued)

1991 (continued)

Precis .... 1.87 to 1.92
Pick-up 1.88

1992

3000GT
    Through September 2.13
    October on 1.81
Diamante .... 2.14 to 2.36
Eclipse and Galant 2.06
Expo 1.87
Mirage 2.25
Montero 1.75
Precis .... 1.88 to 2.00
Pick-up 1.88

1993

3000GT 1.81
Diamante
    Sedan .... 2.14 to 2.36
    Wagon 1.75
Eclipse 2.06
Expo 1.87
Galant 2.06
Mirage .... 1.62 to 1.88
Montero 1.75
Precis .... 1.88 to 2.00
Pick-up 1.88

1994

3000GT, Diamante and Pick-up .... 1.63 to 1.75
Eclipse 2.06
Expo 1.68
Galant .... 1.44 to 1.52
Mirage .... 1.62 to 1.88
Montero .... 1.31 to 1.44

1995

3000GT, Diamante and Pick-up .... 1.63 to 1.75
Eclipse .... 1.54 to 1.63
Expo 1.68
Galant .... 1.44 to 1.52
Mirage .... 1.62 to 1.88
Montero .... 1.31 to 1.44

1996

3000GT, Diamante and Pick-up .... 1.63 to 1.75
Eclipse .... 1.54 to 1.63
Galant .... 1.44 to 1.52
Mirage .... 1.62 to 1.88
Montero .... 1.31 to 1.44

1997

3000GT .... 1.63 to 1.75
Diamante and Galant .... 1.44 to 1.52
Eclipse .... 1.54 to 1.63
Mirage .... 1.23 to 1.31
Montero .... 1.31 to 1.44
Montero Sport .... 1.44 to 1.50

1998

3000GT .... 1.63 to 1.75
Diamante and Galant .... 1.44 to 1.52
Eclipse .... 1.54 to 1.63
Mirage .... 1.23 to 1.31
Montero .... 1.31 to 1.44
Montero Sport .... 1.44 to 1.50

1999

3000GT .... 1.63 to 1.75
Diamante .... 1.31 to 1.41
Eclipse .... 1.54 to 1.63

Galant .... 1.48 to 1.56
Mirage .... 1.23 to 1.31
Montero .... 1.31 to 1.44
Montero Sport .... 1.44 to 1.50

Nissan/Datsun

1980

Pick-up 2.10
200SX, 280ZX and 810 .... 2.40
210 and 510 .... 2.20
280Z 2.00
310 .... 2.60

1981

Pick-up 2.00
200SX and 810 .... 2.40
210, 280ZX and 510 .... 2.20
310 .... 2.60

1982 and 1983

200SX and Maxima 2.40
All other models 2.20

1984

200SX, 300ZX and Maxima 2.40
All other models 2.20

1985 through 1987

Pulsar, Sentra and Stanza .... 1.80 to 2.20
All other models .... 2.00 to 2.40

1988

Pathfinder and Pick-up .... 1.80 to 2.00
Pulsar and Sentra .... 1.90 to 2.10
Van
    Without rear A/C .... 2.90 to 3.30
    With rear A/C .... 3.10 to 3.50
All other models .... 2.00 to 2.40

1989

240SX and Maxima .... 2.00 to 2.20
300ZX and Stanza .... 2.00 to 2.40
Pathfinder and Pick-up .... 1.80 to 2.00
Pulsar and Sentra .... 1.90 to 2.10
Van
    Without rear A/C .... 2.90 to 3.30
    With rear A/C .... 3.10 to 3.50

1990

240SX and Maxima .... 2.00 to 2.20
300ZX
    Non-turbo .... 1.87 to 2.09
    Turbo .... 1.65 to 1.87
Axxess .... 2.00 to 2.40
Pathfinder and Pick-up .... 1.80 to 2.00
Pulsar and Sentra .... 1.90 to 2.10
Stanza .... 1.80 to 2.20
Van
    Without rear A/C .... 2.90 to 3.30
    With rear A/C .... 3.10 to 3.50

1991

240SX, Pathfinder and Pick-up .... 1.80 to 2.00
300ZX and Stanza .... 1.65 to 1.87
Maxima .... 1.87 to 2.09
NX .... 1.43 to 1.65
Sentra .... 1.43 to 1.65

1992

300ZX and Stanza 1.87
240SX, Pathfinder and Pick-up 2.00
Maxima 2.09
NX and Sentra 1.65

1993

240SX 2.00
300ZX 1.87
Altima .... 1.54 to 1.76
Maxima .... 1.87 to 2.09
NX and Sentra 1.65
Pathfinder and Pick-up .... 1.65 to 1.87
Quest
   Without rear A/C 2.25
   With rear A/C 3.50

1994

Altima .... 1.54 to 1.76
Maxima .... 1.87 to 2.09
Pathfinder .... 1.65 to 1.87
Quest
   Without rear A/C 2.00
   With rear A/C 3.25
Sentra .... 1.32 to 1.54
Pick-up .... 1.65 to 1.87
300ZX .... 1.21 to 1.43

1995

200SX, 240SX and Sentra .... 1.32 to 1.54
300ZX .... 1.21 to 1.43
Altima .... 1.54 to 1.76
Maxima .... 1.71 to 1.82
Pathfinder and Pick-up .... 1.65 to 1.87
Quest
   Without rear A/C 2.00
   With rear A/C 3.25

1996

300ZX .... 1.21 to 1.43
Altima .... 1.54 to 1.76
Quest
   Without rear A/C 2.00
   With rear A/C 3.25
Pick-up .... 1.65 to 1.87
All other models .... 1.32 to 1.54

1997

Altima .... 1.54 to 1.76
Quest
   Without rear A/C 2.00
   With rear A/C 3.25
Pick-up .... 1.65 to 1.87
All other models .... 1.32 to 1.54

1998

Altima .... 1.54 to 1.76
Quest
   Without rear A/C 2.00
   With rear A/C 3.25
All other models .... 1.32 to 1.54

1999

Altima .... 1.54 to 1.76
Quest
   Without rear A/C 2.00
   With rear A/C 3.25
All other models .... 1.32 to 1.54

Peugeot

1980 and 1981

505
   Gasoline engine 2.20
   Diesel engine 2.00

1982 and 1983

505
   Gasoline engine 2.20
   Diesel engine 2.00
604 .... 2.00

1984 through 1987

505
   Gasoline engine 2.20
   Diesel engine 2.00

1988 (all models) 2.20

1989 through 1991

405 .... 3.30
505 .... 2.20

Porsche

1980

911 .... 2.42
911 Turbo 2.86
924 .... 1.87
928 .... 2.31

1981 and 1982

911 .... 2.75
911 Turbo 2.86
924 .... 1.87
928 .... 2.31

1983

911 .... 2.75
911 Turbo 2.86
924 .... 1.87
928 .... 2.31
944 .... 2.53

1984

911 .... 2.97
911 Turbo 2.86
924 .... 1.87
928
   Without rear A/C 2.31
   With rear A/C 2.64
944 .... 2.53

1985

911 .... 2.97
911 Turbo 2.86
924 .... 1.87
928
   Without rear A/C 2.31
   With rear A/C 2.64
944
   Through January 2.53
   February on 2.09

1986 and 1987

911 .... 2.97
911 Turbo 2.86
924 and 944 .... 2.09
928
   Without rear A/C 2.31
   With rear A/C 2.64

1988

911 .... 2.97
911 Turbo 2.86
924 and 944 .... 2.09
928
   Through June
      Without rear A/C 2.31
      With rear A/C 2.64
   July on 2.31

1989

911
   911C 2.97
   911 Carrera 2 and Carrera 4 .... 1.84
911 Turbo 2.86

Heating and air conditioning

Porsche (continued)

1989 (continued)
928	2.31
944	2.09

1990
911	1.84
928	2.31
944	2.09

1991
911 and 911 Turbo	1.84
928	2.31
944	2.09

1992
911	
With R-12	2.05
With R-134a retrofit	2.69
968	
With R-12	2.09
With R-134a retrofit	1.90

1993 through 1995
911	1.85
928	1.89
968	1.89

1996 (all models) ... 1.85

1997 and 1998
911	1.85
Boxster	1.87

1999
911	1.98
Boxster	1.87

Renault

1981 and 1982 (all models)	1.60

1983 through 1986
Alliance and Encore	1.80
18I, Fuego and Sportwagon	1.60

1987 (all models)	1.80

Saab

1980
99	1.87
900	2.60

1981 (all models)
Through chassis number AB1009099	2.20
Chassis number AB1009100 and above	2.50

1982 through 1985 (all models)
Sankyo compressor	2.20
Seiko Seiki compressor	2.10 to 2.20
Clarion compressor	2.30

1986 through 1991
900	
Sankyo compressor	2.20
Seiko Seiki compressor	2.10 to 2.20
Clarion compressor	2.30
9000	2.43

1992
900	2.20
9000	
Without rear A/C	2.43
With rear A/C	2.97

1993 (all models)	2.09

1994 through 1998
900	1.60
9000	2.09

1999
9-3	1.76
9-5	1.93

Sterling

1987 through 1991 (all models)	not available

Subaru

1982 (all models)	1.76 to 2.20
1983 and 1989 (all models)	1.63 to 1.74

1990 and 1991
Legacy	1.80 to 2.00
Loyale	1.74

1992
Legacy	2.00
Loyale	
Models built up to March	1.74
Models built from March on	1.87
SVX	1.43

1993
Impreza	1.65
Legacy	2.00
Loyale	1.87
SVX	1.43

1994 through 1996
Impreza	1.50
Legacy	1.65
SVX	1.43

1997
Impreza	1.30
Legacy	1.65
SVX	1.43

1998
Forester	1.30
Impreza	1.30
Legacy	1.65

1999
Forester	1.30
Impreza	1.30
Legacy	1.43

Suzuki

1989 through 1991
Sidekick	1.33
Swift	1.10

1992 through 1994
Sidekick	1.33
Swift	1.10

1995
Esteem	1.31
Sidekick	1.33
Swift	1.10

1996 through 1998
Esteem	1.31
Sidekick and X-90	1.33
Swift	1.10

1999
Esteem	1.31
Swift	1.10
Grand Vitara	1.33

Toyota

1980 through 1982 (all models)	1.66
1983 (all models)	1.70

1984
- Van 3.10
- All other models.. 1.70

1985
- 4Runner .... 1.30 to 1.80
- MR2 .... 1.70 to 1.90
- Pick-up.. 1.30 to 1.80
- Van
  - Without rear A/C .... 1.40 to 1.70
  - With rear A/C .... 3.00 to 3.20
  - All other models .... 1.40 to 1.70

1986
- 4Runner and Pick-up .... 1.30 to 1.80
- Celica and MR2 .... 1.70 to 1.90
- Supra
  - Early models .... 1.40 to 1.70
  - 1986-1/2 models .... 1.70 to 1.90
- Van
  - Without rear A/C .... 1.40 to 1.70
  - With rear A/C .... 3.00 to 3.20
  - All other models .... 1.40 to 1.70

1987
- 4Runner and Pick-up .... 1.30 to 1.80
- Celica and MR2 .... 1.70 to 1.90
- Supra .... 1.70 to 1.90
- Van
  - Without rear A/C .... 1.40 to 1.70
  - With rear A/C .... 3.00 to 3.20
  - All other models .... 1.40 to 1.70

1988
- Land Cruiser .... 1.80 to 2.00
- Van
  - Without rear A/C .... 1.40 to 1.70
  - With rear A/C .... 3.00 to 3.20
  - All other models .... 1.30 to 1.70

1989 and 1990
- Cressida .... 1.70 to 1.90
- Land Cruiser .... 1.80 to 2.00
- MR2.. 1.80
- Supra .... 1.40 to 1.70
- Van
  - Without rear A/C .... 1.40 to 1.70
  - With rear A/C .... 3.00 to 3.20
  - All other models .... 1.30 to 1.70

1991
- 4Runner, Pick-up and Supra .... 1.40 to 1.70
- Camry .... 1.30 to 1.70
- Celica and Corolla........................... 1.47 to 1.70
- Cressida .... 1.70 to 1.90
- Land Cruiser .... 1.87 to 2.10
- MR2 .... 1.76 to 1.91
- Previa
  - Without rear A/C .... 1.98 to 2.20
  - With rear A/C .... 2.54 to 2.76
- Tercel 1.65

1992
- Camry 2.20
- Celica 1.70
- Corolla... 1.70
- Cressida 1.90
- Land Cruiser 2.10
- MR2 .... 1.98
- Paseo 1.76
- Previa
  - Without rear A/C .... 1.98 to 2.20
  - With rear A/C .... 2.54 to 2.76

- Supra 1.70
- Tercel 1.76
- Pick-up... 1.70
- 4Runner 1.90

1993
- 4Runner 1.90
- Camry 2.09
- Celica 1.59
- Corolla, Paseo and Tercel 1.65
- Land Cruiser 1.98
- MR2 .... 1.87
- Previa
  - Without rear A/C 2.09
  - With rear A/C 2.65
- Pick-up... 1.80
- T-100 .... 1.43

1994
- 4Runner, Paseo and Supra 1.56
- Camry 1.88
- Celica and T-100 .... 1.43
- Corolla and Pick-up 1.65
- Land Cruiser 1.87
- MR2 .... 1.61
- Previa
  - Without rear A/C 1.98
  - With rear A/C 2.54
- Tercel 1.54

1995
- 4Runner, Paseo, Supra and T-100.... 1.56
- Avalon and Land Cruiser 1.87
- Camry 1.88
- Celica and Tercel............................. 1.43
- Corolla... 1.65
- MR2 .... 1.61
- Pick-up... 1.27
- Previa
  - Without rear A/C 1.98
  - With rear A/C 2.54
- Tacoma 1.32

1996
- 4Runner, Celica, Tercel and T-100 .... 1.43
- Avalon and Land Cruiser 1.87
- Camry 1.88
- Corolla... 1.54
- Paseo and Tacoma 1.32
- Previa
  - Without rear A/C 1.98
  - With rear A/C 2.54
- RAV4 and Supra 1.56

1997
- 4Runner, Celica, Tercel and T-100 .... 1.43
- Avalon and Land Cruiser 1.87
- Camry 1.76
- Corolla and RAV4 .... 1.54
- Paseo and Tacoma 1.32
- Previa
  - Without rear A/C 1.98
  - With rear A/C 2.54
- Supra 1.56

1998
- 4Runner, Celica and T-100 .... 1.43
- Avalon.. 1.87
- Camry 1.76
- Corolla... 1.54

Heating and air conditioning

Toyota (continued)

1998 (continued)
Land Cruiser
- Without rear A/C 1.76
- With rear A/C 2.40

RAV4
- Gasoline engine 1.54
- Electric motor 1.98

Sienna
- Without rear A/C 1.76
- With rear A/C
  - 4-door 2.76
  - 5-door 2.98

Supra 1.56
Tacoma 1.32
Tercel 0.99

1999
4Runner, Celica and Corolla 1.43
Avalon 1.87
Camry 1.76
Land Cruiser
- Without rear A/C 1.76
- With rear A/C 2.40

RAV4 .... 1.54
Sienna
- Without rear A/C 1.76
- With rear A/C
  - 4-door 2.76
  - 5-door 2.98

Tacoma 1.32
Tercel 0.99

Triumph
1980 and 1981 (all models) 2.50

Volkswagen

1980
Dasher 2.12
Jetta, Rabbit, Pick-up and Scirocco 2.06
Vanagon 2.62

1981
Dasher 2.12
Jetta, Rabbit and Pick-up 2.00
Scirocco 2.06
Vanagon 2.62

1982 through 1984
Jetta, Rabbit and Pick-up 2.00
Quantum 2.12
Scirocco 2.06
Vanagon 2.62

1985
Cabriolet, Golf, Jetta and Scirocco 2.50
Quantum 2.12
Vanagon 2.62

1986
Cabriolet, Golf, Jetta and Scirocco 2.50
Quantum 2.42
Vanagon 3.17

1987 and 1988
Cabriolet, Fox, Golf, Jetta and Scirocco 2.50
Quantum 2.42
Vanagon 3.17

1989
Cabriolet, Fox, Golf, Jetta and Scirocco 2.50
Vanagon 3.17

1990
Cabriolet, Fox, Golf and Jetta 2.50
Corrado 2.37
Passat 2.62
Vanagon 3.17

1991
Cabriolet, Fox, Golf and Jetta 2.50
Vanagon 3.17

1992
Cabriolet 2.06
Corrado 1.86
Fox 2.38
Golf, GTI and Jetta 2.42
Passat 2.52

1993
Cabriolet 2.06
Corrado 2.21
Eurovan
- Without rear A/C 2.08
- With rear A/C 2.95
Fox 2.38
Golf, GTI and Jetta 1.76
Passat 2.54

1994
Cabrio, Golf, GTI and Jetta 1.76
Corrado 2.21
Passat 2.54

1995 and 1996
Cabrio, Golf, GTI and Jetta 1.76
Eurovan
- Without rear A/C 2.08
- With rear A/C 2.95
Passat 2.08

1997
Cabrio, Golf, GTI and Jetta 1.76
Eurovan
- Without rear A/C 2.09
- With rear A/C 2.98
Passat 2.08

1998 and 1999
Cabrio 1.76
Eurovan
- Without rear A/C 2.09
- With rear A/C 2.98
Golf, GTI and Jetta 1.76
New Beetle 1.54
Passat 1.43

Volvo

1980 through 1982
240 Series 2.86
260 Series 3.30

1983 through 1987
240 Series 2.86
700 Series 2.60

1988
240 Series 2.86
700 Series
- 740 and 780 .... 2.60
- 760 .... 2.40

1989 and 1990
240 Series 2.86
700 Series 2.60

1991
240 Series 2.42

700 Series and 900 Series
    Four-cylinder engine 2.42
    Six-cylinder engine.. 2.75
1992
    240   .... 2.42
    740 and 940 .... 2.53
    760, 780 and 960 .... 2.43
1993
    240 and 850 .... 1.65
    940 .... 2.09
    960 .... 1.98
1994
    850 .... 1.65
    940 .... 2.09
    960 .... 1.98
1995
    850 .... 1.65

    940 .... 2.09
    960 .... 1.98
1996
    850 .... 1.65
    960 .... 1.98
1997
    850 .... 1.65
    960 .... 1.98
    C70, S70 and V70
        Cold weather models 1.82
        Warm weather models 1.65
1998 and 1999
    C70, S70 and V70
        Cold weather models 1.82
        Warm weather models 1.65
    S90 and V90... 1.98

Notes

Troubleshooting

Heaters

Little can go wrong with a heater. If the fan motor will run at all speeds, the electrical part of the system is okay. The three basic heater problems fall into the following general categories:

1 Not enough heat
2 Heat all the time
3 No heat

If there's not enough heat, the control valve or door is stuck in a partially open position or the coolant coming from the engine isn't hot enough. If the coolant isn't hot enough, the thermostat in the engine cooling system is stuck open, allowing coolant to pass through the engine so rapidly that it doesn't heat up quickly enough. If the vehicle is equipped with a temperature gauge instead of a warning light, watch to see if the engine temperature rises to the normal operating range after driving for a reasonable distance.

If there's heat all the time, the control valve or the door is stuck wide open. If there's no heat, coolant is probably not reaching the heater core. The likely cause is a collapsed or plugged hose or a frozen heater control valve. If the heater is the type that flows coolant all the time, the cause is a stuck door or a broken or kinked control cable.

The following troubleshooting guide lists some of the more specific heating system problems that may occur.

Heater system trouble diagnosis

Cause	Correction

Insufficient, erratic or no heat

Low engine coolant level

Coolant leaks	Fill to proper level. Pressure test for engine cooling system and heater system leaks. Service as required.
Engine overheating	Remove bugs, leaves, etc. from radiator and/or condenser fins. Check for: Sticking thermostat Incorrect ignition timing Water pump impeller damaged Clogged radiator or hoses Slipping drivebelt Cooling fan inoperative

Heating and air conditioning

Heater system trouble diagnosis (continued)

Cause	Correction

Low engine coolant level (continued)

Engine fails to warm up .... Check the thermostat and radiator cap. Replace if necessary.
Check the coolant level.

Plugged heater core .... Clean and back flush engine cooling system and heater core separately.
If foreign material still obstructs flow of coolant through core, replace it.

Damaged or deteriorated hoses .... Replace damaged hoses and back flush engine cooling system, then
heater core, until all deposits have been removed.

Blocked air inlet .... Check cowl air inlet for leaves, foreign material, etc. Remove as required.

Improperly adjusted control cables .... Readjust cables.

Airflow control doors sticking .... Check to see if cable operated doors respond properly to movements
or binding of control levers. If hesitation in movement is noted, determine cause and
service sticking or binding door as required.

Vehicle interior warms up too .... Incorrect operation of controls. Read the owner's manual to make sure
slowly you know how to operate the controls and vents properly.
Are you using the High blower speed?
Check the engine coolant level.
Check control cable and blower operation.

Insufficient heat to rear seat .... Check for an obstruction on the floor, such as wrinkled or torn sound
deadener or insulation material between the seat and the floor.
Are you using the blower to force air to the rear seat area?

Cold drafts on floor .... Locate and seal any air leaks.
Check the operation and adjustment of the vent cables.
Are you operating the heating system controls and vents properly?
Make sure the front floor mat is not blocking a vent.

Air valves do not operate .... See "Vacuum system does not operate air valves."
Check for proper installation and/or adjustment of air control cable.
Check for proper installation and/or adjustment of air/de-ice control cable.

No high heat output

Blower switch .... Check the fuse.
Check for power and continuity.

Heater control valve .... Check for sticking. If closed, repair or replace.

Vacuum line leak .... Check vacuum lines to and from electro/vacuum control solenoid for
heater doors.

Open circuit at electro/vacuum .... Check for voltage at High output solenoid.
solenoid Check for a good circuit to ground at solenoid.

Blower motor operates only on high speed setting

Blower motor resistor .... Check resistor for open circuit with a self-powered test light. Replace
if open.
Make sure wire harness connector makes good contact with resistor
spade terminals. Service as necessary.

Blower motor wire harness .... Check wire harness from resistor assembly to blower switch for a
short to ground. Service as necessary.

Cause	Correction

Blower motor inoperative

Cause	Correction
Blown fuse	Check fuse for continuity. Replace fuse as necessary.
Thermal limiter	Check thermal limiter for an open condition.
Open circuit	Check for voltage at the blower motor. Check for a good circuit to ground at blower motor.
Blower motor	Check blower motor operation by it directly to the battery with jumper wires.
Blower switch	Perform a continuity check on the blower switch.

No defrost

Cause	Correction
Air valve doesn't open	See "Vacuum system does not operate air valves." Adjust operating linkage. Check cable operation.
Air door doesn't open	Check for proper installation and/or adjustment of air or air/de-ice control cable.
Temperature control door doesn't open	Check and adjust temperature control cable if necessary.
Obstructions in defroster outlets at windshield	Remove obstructions. Look for and fix loose instrument panel pad cover at defroster outlets.
Dinged defroster outlets	Reshape outlet flange with pliers (outlet should have a uniform opening).
Blower motor not connected	Connect wire.
Inoperative blower motor	Check heater fuse and wiring. Replace motor, if necessary.
Inoperative blower motor	Check connectors, switch and switch wiring - replace switch as necessary.

Too warm in vehicle

Cause	Correction
Temperature door improperly adjusted	Check air diaphragm and vacuum supply hose.
Incorrect operation of controls	Are you operating the heater system controls properly?
Inoperative blower switch	Replace switch, if faulty.
Shorted or open resistor	Check the resistor block.

Vacuum system doesn't operate air doors (doesn't apply to all vehicles)

Cause	Correction
Little or no vacuum at door diaphragm	Check for vacuum leaks and disconnected hoses.
Leak in vacuum system	Check the vacuum hoses for leaks and obstructions. Check the heater control panel vacuum switch - replace if necessary.
Air door sticking	Check for binding and obstructions at the air door.
Air door doesn't operate	Check for a loose vacuum hose connection at the diaphragm.
Defroster door doesn't operate	Check for a loose vacuum hose connection at the diaphragm.

Heating and air conditioning

Heater system trouble diagnosis (continued)

Cause	Correction

Miscellaneous

Blown fuses................................. Locate and correct the short.

Front floor mat wet under....................... Improperly sealed windshield - reseal windshield or lead-in from antenna.
heater core
Leaking heater core - repair, if possible, or replace heater core.
Check for proper seal at dash.
Check for leak at connection on heater core (a hose leaking into the heater core is often misdiagnosed as a leaking core).

Heater "gurgle".......................... Check engine coolant level.

Objectionable engine or exhaust............ Check the seals between the engine compartment and the heater/air
fumes in vehicle
conditioning box.
Check for proper sealing between the air inlet duct assembly and the dash.
Locate and seal any other leaks.

Air conditioning systems

Before troubleshooting the system

None of the information included thus far is much use unless you know when to use it. Remember that the manifold gauge set is the most important diagnostic tool available. The key to quick and accurate troubleshooting of most internal system problems is correct interpretation of the test gauges.

If the system isn't producing enough cool air, inspect it for defects and correct as necessary (see "Preliminary system inspection" in Chapter 5).

General system troubleshooting guidelines

If cool air output is inadequate:

1 Make sure the outside air vents are closed.

2 Inspect the condenser coils and fins to make sure they're clear.

3 Check the compressor clutch for slippage.

4 Make sure there's sufficient refrigerant in the system.

5 Check the blower motor for proper operation.

6 Inspect the blower discharge passage for obstructions.

7 Check the system air intake filter for clogging.

8 Inspect the evaporator. Make sure it's not clogged. Flush it if necessary.

Note: *The remaining general checks for this condition require that the manifold test gauges be hooked up.*

9 If the high side gauge indicates normal pressure and the low side gauge indicates high pressure, the evaporator pressure regulator, hot gas bypass valve or suction throttling valve is defective or improperly adjusted.

10 If the discharge air temperature is higher than it should be but is accompanied by normal gauge pressures, or slightly increased high side pressure and low suction pressure, the screen in the expansion valve is clogged.

11 If the low side gauge indicates a high pressure and there's excessive sweating of the evaporator and suction line, the expansion valve thermal bulb has lost its charge.

12 If the high side gauge indicates a higher than normal pressure, the low side gauge indicates a lower than normal pressure and the receiver drier and liquid lines are cold to the touch (even frosting), the screen in the receiver-drier is clogged.

13 If the high pressure gauge indicates a higher than normal pressure, there may be excessive moisture in the system. If there are also bubbles in the sight glass, there's air in the system.

14 If the low pressure gauge indicates high pressure or the clutch cycles at too high a pressure, the thermostat is defective or incorrectly adjusted.

If the system provides intermittent cooling air:

1 Check the circuit breaker, blower switch and blower motor for a malfunction.

2 Inspect the compressor clutch coil and solenoid for an open or bad ground or for a loose connection in the compressor clutch coil or solenoid.

3 Make sure the compressor clutch isn't slipping.

4 Inspect the plenum door to make sure it's operating properly.

5 Inspect the dashboard control head vacuum lines. Make sure they're securely attached.

6 Inspect the evaporator to make sure it isn't clogged.

7 If the unit is icing up, it may be caused by excessive moisture in the system, incorrect super heat switch adjustment or low thermostat adjustment.

Note: *The last two general checks for this condition require that the manifold test gauges be hooked up.*

8 If the low side gauge indicates low or excessively high pressure and adjustments to the thermostat don't correct the condition, the thermostat is defective.

9 If the low side gauge indicates low pressure and the high side gauge also indicates low pressure, there's moisture in the system and it has probably clogged the hot gas bypass valve or suction throttle valve.

If the system provides no cooling air:

1 Inspect the compressor drivebelt. Make sure it's not loose or broken.

2 Check for a blown fuse.

3 Check the system wire harness for a blown fusible link (not used on all systems).

4 Inspect the wire harness for a broken or disconnected wire.

5 Inspect the wire harness for a broken or disconnected ground wire.

6 Inspect the clutch coil and solenoid. Make sure that neither is burned out or disconnected.

7 Make sure the electrical switch contacts in the thermostat are not burned excessively and that the sensing element is not defective.

8 Make sure the blower motor is not disconnected or burned out.

9 Check the ignition switch ground and relay. Make sure they're not burned out.

10   Make sure the compressor isn't partially or completely frozen.

11   Inspect the refrigerant lines for leaks.

12   Check the components for leaks.

13   Inspect the receiver-drier/accumulator or expansion valve/tube for clogged screens.

14   Inspect the compressor shaft seal for leaks.

15   If there's hot water in the heater and hot discharge air from the evaporator, the heater valve is inoperative.

Note: *The remaining general checks for this condition require that the manifold test gauges be hooked up.*

16   If there is only a slight variation in both gauge readings at any engine speed, the compressor reed valves are inoperative.

17   If the high side gauge indicates normal pressure but the low side gauge indicates high pressure, and the evaporator is flooding, the expansion valve is stuck open.

If the system is noisy:

1   Look for loose panels in the passenger compartment.

2   Inspect the compressor drivebelt. It may be loose or worn.

3   Check the compressor mounting bolts. They should be tight.

4   Listen carefully to the compressor. It may be worn out.

5   Listen to the idler pulley and bearing and the clutch. Either may be defective.

6   Inspect the wiring to the compressor clutch coil and solenoid for defects.

7   The winding in the compressor clutch coil or solenoid may be defective.

8   The compressor oil level may be low.

9   The blower motor fan bushing or the motor itself may be worn out.

10   If there is an excessive charge in the system, you'll hear a rumbling noise in the high pressure line, a thumping noise in the compressor, excessive pressure indicated on the high and low side gauges, bubbles or cloudiness in the sight glass or low pressure on the high side gauge.

11   If there's a low charge in the system, you'll hear hissing in the evaporator case at the expansion valve, bubbles or cloudiness in the sight glass or low head pressure indicated on the high side gauge.

12   If there's excessive moisture in the system, the expansion valve will be noisy and suction side pressure will be low.

13   If the high side service valve is closed, the compressor will make a knocking noise and the high pressure gauge will indicate above normal pressure.

Fault diagnosis flowcharts

If the air conditioning system doesn't seem to be working at all, it can be fairly straightforward to diagnose. Bear in mind that the problem may not be due to a malfunction in the air conditioning system. First, always check for obvious problems, such as a problem with the heater/air conditioning controls or the air distribution system under the dash. The following flow charts should help steer you along a logical path of diagnosis.

Chart 1: The system provides no cooling airflow
Heater/ventilation system component checks

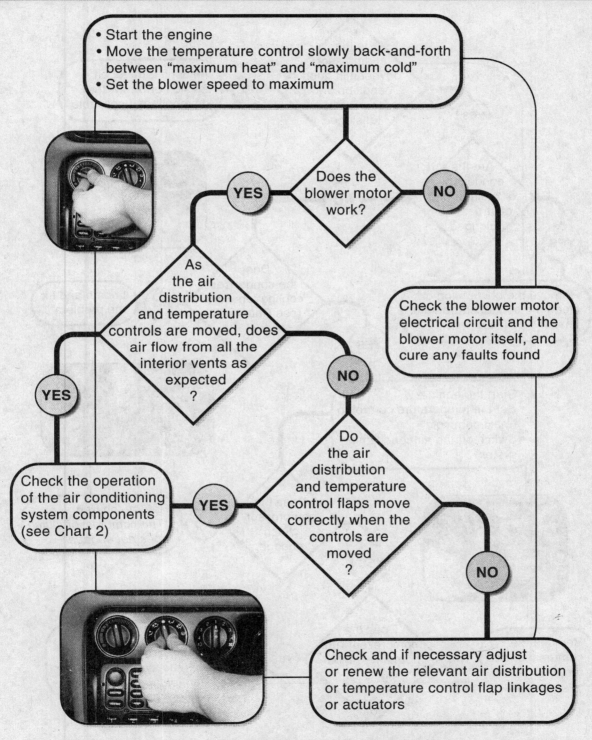

- Start the engine
- Move the temperature control slowly back-and-forth between "maximum heat" and "maximum cold"
- Set the blower speed to maximum

Does the blower motor work?

YES

NO

As the air distribution and temperature controls are moved, does air flow from all the interior vents as expected?

YES

NO

Check the blower motor electrical circuit and the blower motor itself, and cure any faults found

Check the operation of the air conditioning system components (see Chart 2)

Do the air distribution and temperature control flaps move correctly when the controls are moved?

YES

NO

Check and if necessary adjust or renew the relevant air distribution or temperature control flap linkages or actuators

Chart 1: The system provides no cooling airflow - Heater/ventilation system component checks

Heating and air conditioning

Chart 2: The system provides no cooling airflow
Air conditioning system component checks

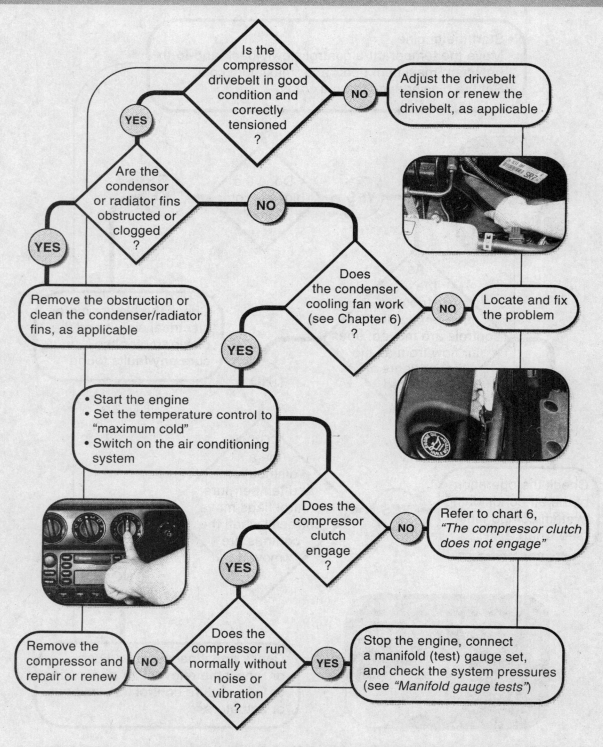

Is the compressor drivebelt in good condition and correctly tensioned?

NO → Adjust the drivebelt tension or renew the drivebelt, as applicable

YES ↓

Are the condensor or radiator fins obstructed or clogged?

YES → Remove the obstruction or clean the condenser/radiator fins, as applicable

NO →

Does the condenser cooling fan work (see Chapter 6)?

NO → Locate and fix the problem

YES ↓

- Start the engine
- Set the temperature control to "maximum cold"
- Switch on the air conditioning system

Does the compressor clutch engage?

NO → Refer to chart 6, "The compressor clutch does not engage"

YES ↓

Does the compressor run normally without noise or vibration?

NO → Remove the compressor and repair or renew

YES → Stop the engine, connect a manifold (test) gauge set, and check the system pressures (see "Manifold gauge tests")

Chart 2: The system provides no cooling airflow - Air conditioning system component checks

Chart 3: The cool air output is inadequate

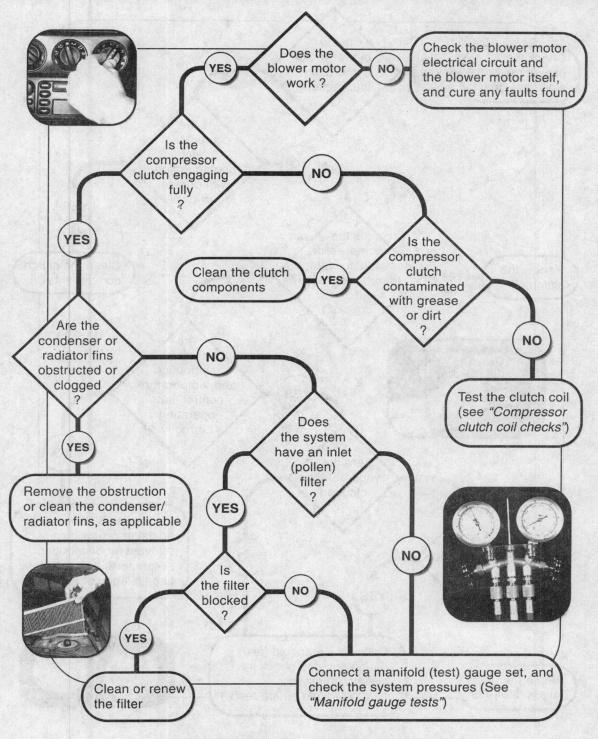

Does the blower motor work ?

YES

NO → Check the blower motor electrical circuit and the blower motor itself, and cure any faults found

Is the compressor clutch engaging fully ?

YES

NO → **Is the compressor clutch contaminated with grease or dirt ?**

YES → Clean the clutch components

NO → Test the clutch coil (see *"Compressor clutch coil checks"*)

Are the condenser or radiator fins obstructed or clogged ?

YES → Remove the obstruction or clean the condenser/radiator fins, as applicable

NO → **Does the system have an inlet (pollen) filter ?**

YES → **Is the filter blocked ?**

YES → Clean or renew the filter

NO → Connect a manifold (test) gauge set, and check the system pressures (See *"Manifold gauge tests"*)

NO → Connect a manifold (test) gauge set, and check the system pressures (See *"Manifold gauge tests"*)

Chart 3: The cool air output is inadequate

Heating and air conditioning

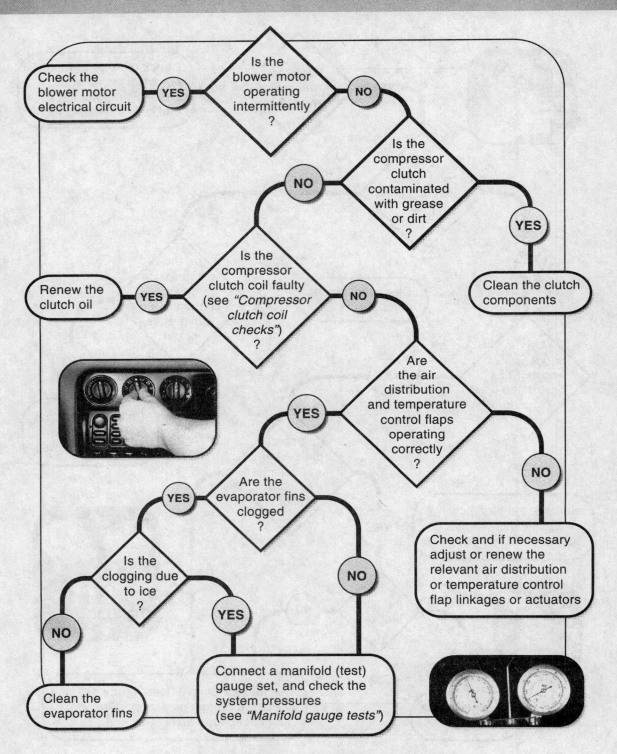

Chart 4: The system provides intermittent cooling airflow

Is the blower motor operating intermittently ?

YES → Check the blower motor electrical circuit

NO → Is the compressor clutch contaminated with grease or dirt ?

YES → Clean the clutch components

NO → Is the compressor clutch coil faulty (see *"Compressor clutch coil checks"*) ?

YES → Renew the clutch oil

NO → Are the air distribution and temperature control flaps operating correctly ?

NO → Check and if necessary adjust or renew the relevant air distribution or temperature control flap linkages or actuators

YES → Are the evaporator fins clogged ?

YES → Is the clogging due to ice ?

NO → Clean the evaporator fins

YES → Connect a manifold (test) gauge set, and check the system pressures (see *"Manifold gauge tests"*)

NO → Connect a manifold (test) gauge set, and check the system pressures (see *"Manifold gauge tests"*)

Chart 4: The system provides intermittent cooling airflow

Chart 5: The system is noisy in operation

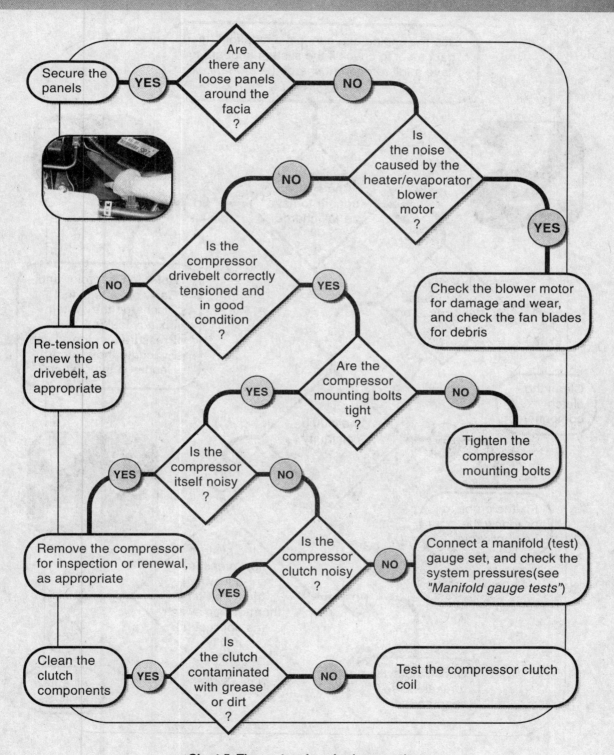

- Secure the panels — **YES** — Are there any loose panels around the facia ? — **NO** — Is the noise caused by the heater/evaporator blower motor ? — **YES** — Check the blower motor for damage and wear, and check the fan blades for debris
- **NO** — Is the compressor drivebelt correctly tensioned and in good condition ? — **NO** — Re-tension or renew the drivebelt, as appropriate
- **YES** — Are the compressor mounting bolts tight ? — **NO** — Tighten the compressor mounting bolts
- **YES** — Is the compressor itself noisy ? — **YES** — Remove the compressor for inspection or renewal, as appropriate
- **NO** — Is the compressor clutch noisy ? — **NO** — Connect a manifold (test) gauge set, and check the system pressures(see *"Manifold gauge tests"*)
- **YES** — Is the clutch contaminated with grease or dirt ? — **YES** — Clean the clutch components
- **NO** — Test the compressor clutch coil

Chart 5: The system is noisy in operation

Heating and air conditioning

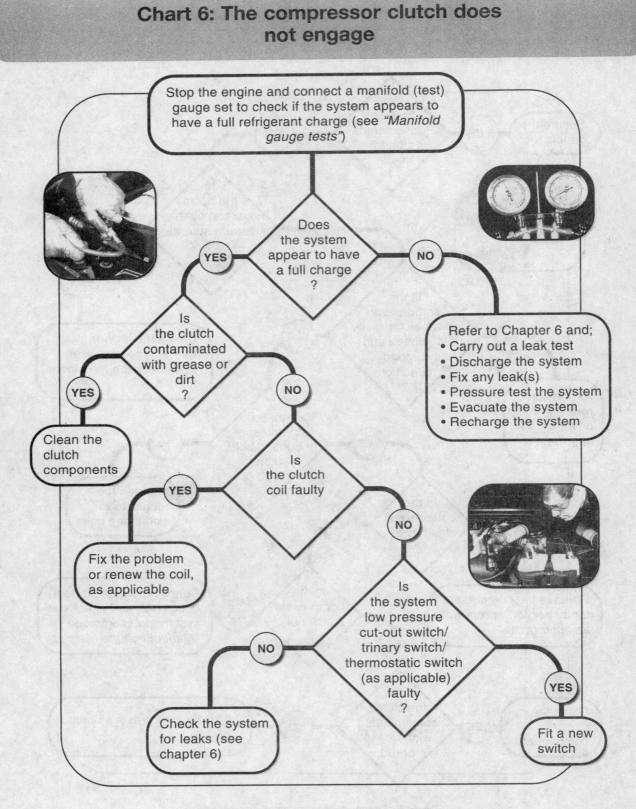

Stop the engine and connect a manifold (test) gauge set to check if the system appears to have a full refrigerant charge (see *"Manifold gauge tests"*)

Does the system appear to have a full charge ?

YES

NO

Is the clutch contaminated with grease or dirt ?

YES

NO

Refer to Chapter 6 and;
- Carry out a leak test
- Discharge the system
- Fix any leak(s)
- Pressure test the system
- Evacuate the system
- Recharge the system

Clean the clutch components

Is the clutch coil faulty

YES

NO

Fix the problem or renew the coil, as applicable

Is the system low pressure cut-out switch/ trinary switch/ thermostatic switch (as applicable) faulty ?

NO

YES

Check the system for leaks (see chapter 6)

Fit a new switch

Chart 6: The compressor clutch does not engage

Manifold gauge tests

The manifold gauge set is without question the most important tool used when troubleshooting a vehicle's air conditioning system. Manifold gauges allow you to measure the high side and low side pressures, which is vital information for determining whether the system is operating correctly, and for diagnosing problems. For a full description of the manifold gauge set, refer to Chapter 4.

Interpreting the readings shown on a manifold gauge set is the key to accurate fault diagnosis. Once the gauge has connected to the system, a large number of internal system problems can be diagnosed. The following pages provide typical examples of the readings likely to be obtained on manifold gauges due to a number of common problems that might need to be diagnosed.

Connect a manifold gauge set to the system as described in Chapter 5 (see "Connecting the gauge set"). **Note:** *The actual gauge readings shown in the following examples are typical, and varying equipment and ambient conditions may cause the actual values for the gauge readings to be different from those shown in the following pages. However, the relationship between the high and low side readings should be similar to the examples shown regardless of ambient conditions.*

Refer to the pressure/temperature relationship charts in Chapter 5 for general guidelines on how the system pressures will vary in accordance with the temperature.

Normal manifold gauge readings

If the system is operating normally, the high and low side pressures should always be the same when the system is switched off.

Typical pressures and temperatures for a system which is switched on and operating normally on a warm spring day would be:

Low side	35 psi (241 kPa)	39 degrees F. (4 degrees C.)
High side	180 psi (1241 kPa)	129 degrees F. (54 degrees C.)

The following gauge readings can be expected for a system that is operating normally, with no faults.

Air conditioning system switched off

70 LOW     *70 HIGH*

Gauge readings	Symptoms (when system is switched on)	Diagnosis
Low side pressure normal. High side pressure normal.	● Discharge air cold. ● Sight glass (where applicable) clear.	● System is functioning normally, and 'appears' to have a full refrigerant charge (not conclusive proof).

Heating and air conditioning

Air conditioning system switched on

35 LOW   180 HIGH

Gauge readings	Symptoms	Diagnosis
Low side pressure normal. High side pressure normal.	● Discharge air cold. ● Sight glass (where applicable) clear.	● System is functioning normally, and has a full refrigerant charge.

Abnormal manifold gauge readings

The following charts depict typical examples of gauge readings which may indicate a fault in the system. For each set of gauge readings, a list of possible additional symptoms and an interpretation of the readings are provided in order to help diagnose the cause of the problem.

Air conditioning system switched off

20 LOW   20 HIGH

Gauge readings	Symptoms	Diagnosis
Low side pressure low. High side pressure low.	● The compressor will not run.	● Low refrigerant charge.

Air conditioning system switched on

35 LOW   180 HIGH

Gauge readings	Symptoms	Diagnosis
Low side pressure normal. High side pressure normal.	● Sight glass (where applicable) clear, or a few bubbles. ● Cool air discharged for a few minutes, then discharge air temperature rises. ● Low side gauge does not fluctuate as compressor cycles on and off.	● Air and moisture in the system (moisture is freezing, causing minor restriction in system).

35 LOW

180 HIGH

Gauge readings	Symptoms	Diagnosis
Low side pressure normal-to-low, then moves into vacuum. High side pressure normal (may rise as low side moves into vacuum).	● Sight glass (where applicable) full of small bubbles. ● Cool air discharged for a few minutes, then discharge air temperature rises as low side moves into vacuum.	● Excessive air and moisture in the system (moisture is freezing and causing total blockage in system.

35 LOW

180 HIGH

Gauge readings	Symptoms	Diagnosis
Low side normal. High side normal.	● Compressor cycles on and off too quickly. ● Low side gauge does not indicate sufficient range.	● Faulty or incorrectly adjusted thermostatic switch, or pressure-sensitive (cycling) switch, as applicable (causing compressor to shut off too quickly).

35 LOW

180 HIGH

Gauge readings	Symptoms	Diagnosis
Low side low-to-normal, or normal-to-high. High side normal.	● Lack of cooling air, or fluctuating amount of cooling air. ● Compressor cycles at incorrect pressure or temperature.	● Faulty or incorrectly adjusted thermostatic switch, or faulty low pressure cut-out switch, as applicable (causing the compressor to operate for too long, resulting in freezing at the evaporator – the freezing restricts the airflow through the evaporator fins, and the refrigerant flow through the evaporator passages).

Heating and air conditioning

20 LOW  *150 HIGH*

Gauge readings	Symptoms	Diagnosis
Low side pressure low High side pressure low	● Discharge air only slightly cool ● Sight glass (where applicable) contains some bubbles	● Refrigerant charge slightly low.

5 LOW   *110 HIGH*

Gauge readings	Symptoms	Diagnosis
Low side pressure low High side pressure low	● Discharge air warm ● Compressor may stop	● Refrigerant charge very low (compressor may stop due to activation of low pressure cut-out switch).

10 LOW   *145 HIGH*

Gauge readings	Symptoms	Diagnosis
Low side pressure low. High side pressure low.	● Discharge air only slightly cool. ● Moisture or frost build-up on expansion valve.	● Expansion valve stuck closed (possibly due to blocked filter screen or faulty temperature sensing bulb), causing restriction of refrigerant flow.

10 LOW   *145 HIGH*

Gauge readings	Symptoms	Diagnosis
Low side pressure low. High side pressure low (may be normal-to-high if restriction is located immediately after the service valves).	● Discharge air only slightly cool. ● Moisture or frost on high side refrigerant lines.	● Restriction in high side of system (frost will build up immediately after the restriction).

-10 LOW   80 HIGH

Gauge readings	Symptoms	Diagnosis
Low side pressure zero-to-negative. High side pressure low.	• Discharge air only slightly cool. • Frost build-up on high side refrigerant lines (from filter/drier to evaporator).	• Refrigerant flow obstructed by dirt • Blocked filter/drier.

-10 LOW   80 HIGH

Gauge readings	Symptoms	Diagnosis
Low side pressure zero-to-negative. High side pressure low.	• Discharge air only slightly cool. • Frost build-up on high side refrigerant lines (before and after filter/drier).	• Refrigerant flow obstructed by dirt or moisture (ice). • Refrigerant flow obstructed by gas leakage from expansion valve temperature sensing bulb/capillary tube.

45 LOW   150 HIGH

Gauge readings	Symptoms	Diagnosis
Low side pressure high. High side pressure low	• Noisy compressor.	• Loose or worn compressor drivebelt. • Faulty compressor reed valve. • Compressor internal fault.

50 LOW   250 HIGH

Gauge readings	Symptoms	Diagnosis
Low side pressure high. High side pressure high.	• Discharge air warm. • High side refrigerant lines hot. • Possibly, bubbles in sight glass (where applicable).	• Restricted or blocked condenser fins. • Refrigerant overcharge. • Faulty condenser cooling fan. • Engine overheating. • Air in system. • Incorrect refrigerant in system.

50 LOW

250 HIGH

Gauge readings	Symptoms	Diagnosis
Low side pressure high. High side pressure high.	• Discharge air warm. • Moisture or frost on evaporator and/or low side refrigerant lines.	• Expansion valve stuck open allowing excessive amounts of refrigerant through evaporator.

Expansion valve system troubleshooting

1　Connect a manifold gauge set to the system and purge it (see Chapters 4 and 5).

2　The engine should be running at the normal fast idle speed.

3　Use a large fan to blow air through the condenser and radiator.

4　Run the air conditioning system for about 5 minutes to allow it to stabilize.

5　Conduct a system performance test (see Chapter 5).

6　Note the gauge readings and other symptoms indicated on the following pages. Since gauge readings can vary, and their interpretation is often based on personal opinion and previous experience, they should be considered only as a general guide.

7　Note any indicated symptoms as listed under "Symptoms" and perform additional tests if indicated. Perform the remedial procedures indicated under "Repair."

Interpreting the gauges when troubleshooting an expansion valve system

The high and low side system pressures on the following pages are typical pressure values you can expect to see on the gauges (assuming an ambient temperature of 85°F at sea level) when any of the following malfunctions occur.

An auxiliary low side gauge, and the typical pressure reading it would indicate for a given condition, are also included where appropriate. Of course, this assumes that you will use an auxiliary gauge on systems such as Chrysler's Evaporator Pressure Regulator (EPR) system and some Ford Suction Throttling Valve (STV) systems. If you're using a two-gauge set, disregard any information about the auxiliary gauge. **Note:** *The pressures shown in the following chart are intended as a general guide. They may or may not correlate exactly with the pressure values indicated on the gauges.*

PRESSURE/TEMPERATURE RELATIONSHIP

Low side gauge (psi)	Evap. temp (degrees F)	Low side gauge (psi)	Evap. temp (degrees F)	High side gauge (psi)	Ambient temp* (degrees F)
10	2	30	32	130 to 160	60
12	6	35	36	140 to 170	65
14	10	40	42	150 to 180	70
16	14	45	48	160 to 190	75
18	18	50	53	170 to 210	80
20	20	55	58	180 to 220	85
22	22	60	62	190 to 230	90
24	24	65	66	205 to 250	95
26	27	70	70	220 to 270	100
28	29			240 to 290	105
				260 to 310	110
				285 to 335	115
				310 to 370	120

Always try to measure ambient temperature two inches in front of the condenser.

Some air and moisture in the system

System pressure:

The low side gauge indicates normal pressure.
The high side gauge indicates normal pressure.
The auxiliary gauge indicates normal pressure.

Symptoms:

The sight glass is clear, or shows a few bubbles.
The discharge air slightly cool.
On a thermostatic switch system, the low side gauge doesn't fluctuate with the switch "on" and "off" cycles.

Diagnosis: There is some air and moisture in the system

Solution:

1   Leak test the system (check the compressor seal area very carefully).
2   Discharge the system.
3   Locate and repair any leaks found.

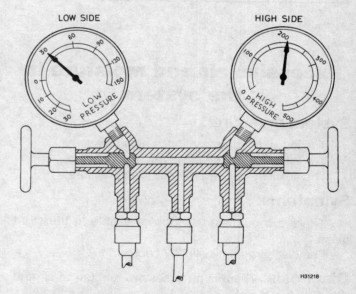

4   Replace the receiver-drier, accumulator or desiccant bag.
5   Evacuate the system for at least 30 minutes.
6   Charge the system.
7   Operate the system and check its performance.

Excessive moisture in the system

System pressure:

The low side gauge indicates normal pressure.
The high side gauge indicates normal pressure.
The auxiliary gauge indicates normal pressure.

Symptoms:

Tiny bubbles are visible in the sight glass.

The discharge air warms when the low side cycles into vacuum.

As moisture is released by the saturated desiccant, it becomes trapped -

and freezes - at the expansion valve, blocking the flow of refrigerant into the evaporator.

Diagnosis: There is excessive moisture in the system

Solution:

1   Discharge the system.

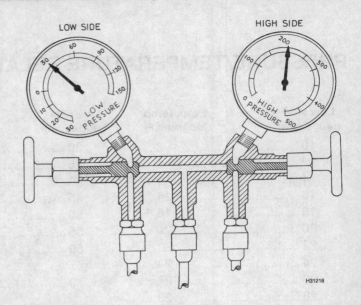

2   Replace the receiver-drier, accumulator or desiccant bag.

3   Evacuate the system with a vacuum pump.

4   Recharge the system.

5   Operate the system and check its performance.

Excessive air and moisture in the system

System pressure:

The low side gauge indicates high pressure.
The high side gauge indicates high pressure.
The auxiliary gauge indicates high pressure.

Symptoms:

There are occasional bubbles visible in the sight glass.

The discharge air is slightly cool.

Diagnosis: There is an excessive amount of air and moisture in the system

Solution:

1   Discharge the system.

2   Replace the receiver-drier, desiccant or accumulator.

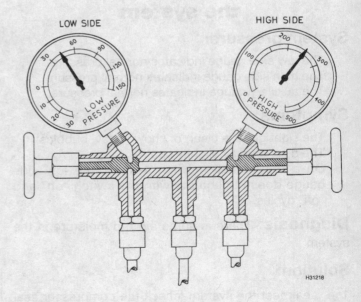

3   Evacuate the system.

4   Charge the system.

5   Operate the system and check its performance.

Defective thermostatic switch

System pressure:

The low side gauge indicates normal pressure.
The high side gauge indicates normal pressure.

Symptoms:

The compressor cycles on and off too quickly.
The low side gauge doesn't indicate sufficient range.

Diagnosis: The thermostatic switch is defective

Solution:

1   Remove and discard the old thermostatic switch.

2   Install a new switch. **Caution:** *Make sure the capillary tube is installed in the same position and to the same depth in the evaporator core as the old switch tube. Don't kink or bend the capillary tube sharply - it's gas-filled.*

3   Operate the system and check its performance.

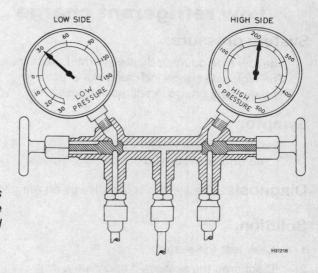

Misadjusted thermostatic switch or defective pressure sending switch

System pressure:

The low side gauge indicates low-to-normal pressure.
The high side gauge indicates normal pressure.

Symptoms:

The compressor cycles at the wrong temperature or pressure.

The evaporator freezes and restricts airflow if the switch allows the compressor to remain in operation too long.

Diagnosis: The thermostatic switch is misadjusted, or the pressure sensing switch (if equipped) is defective.

Solution:

Thermostatic switch

1   Remove whatever components necessary to gain access to the thermostatic adjustment screw.

2   Check for the presence of the adjusting screw or thermostatic switch (it's usually located under the cover on the end of the switch housing). **Note:** *If no adjusting screw is present, the switch is non-adjustable and must be replaced.*

3   Verify that the electrical wiring is routed so that a short circuit cannot occur.

4   Adjust the switch. **Note:** *The battery must be hooked up so the engine and air conditioning system can be operated during the adjustment.*

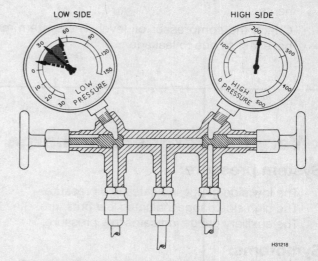

5   Operate the system and check its performance. Pressure sensing switch **Note:** *The pressure sensing switch, which is used on some late model Ford Motor Company and General Motors vehicles with accumulator type systems, performs the same function as the thermostatic switch. The switch is non-adjustable and is mounted on a Schrader valve fitting. No system discharge, therefore, is required.*

Solution:

Pressure sensing switch

1   Detach the electrical connector from the pressure sensing switch at the accumulator.

2   Remove the pressure sensing switch.

3   Install a new switch.

4   Operate the system and check its performance.

Heating and air conditioning

Low refrigerant charge

System pressure:

The low side gauge indicates normal pressure.
The high side gauge indicates low pressure.
The auxiliary gauge indicates low pressure.

Symptoms:

The discharge air is slightly cool.
Some bubbles are visible in the sight glass.

Diagnosis: The system is slightly low on refrigerant

Solution:

1   Leak test the system.
2   Discharge the system, if necessary.
3   Repair any leaks found, or replace leaking components.
4   Check the compressor oil level. The system may have lost oil due to leakage.

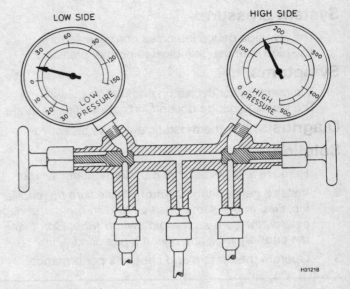

5   Evacuate the system.
6   Charge the system.
7   Operate the system and check its performance.

Very low refrigerant charge

System pressure:

The low side gauge indicates low pressure.
The high side gauge indicates low pressure.
The auxiliary gauge indicates low pressure.

Symptoms:

The discharge air is warm.
Clear, or oil, streaks are visible in the sight glass.
The compressor has ceased operation (will occur on a system equipped
with a refrigerant pressure sensing device).

Diagnosis: The system refrigerant level is very low.

Solution:

1   If compressor operation has ceased because of a pressure sensing device, bypass the device with a jumper wire until testing and repairs are completed.
2   Add a partial charge to the system (at least half of the system capacity).
3   Perform a leak test.

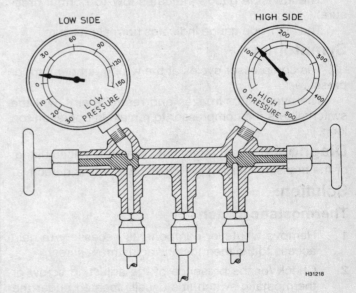

4   Discharge the system.
5   Check the compressor oil level. The system may have lost oil due to leakage.
6   Evacuate the system.
7   Charge the system.
8   Operate the system and check its performance.

Expansion valve stuck

System pressure:

The low side gauge indicates low pressure.
The high side gauge indicates low pressure.
The auxiliary gauge indicates low pressure.

Symptoms:

The discharge air is slightly cool.
The expansion valve is sweating or there is frost build-up.

Diagnosis: The expansion valve is stuck closed, the screen is plugged or the sensing bulb is malfunctioning.

Solution:

1   If the expansion valve inlet is cool to the touch:
   a)   Turn on the air conditioner and set it to its maximum cooling mode.
   b)   Spray liquid refrigerant onto the head of the valve or the capillary tube. Note the low side gauge reading. The low side gauge should drop into a vacuum. Note: This test may not be possible on some vehicles if the expansion valve or the capillary tube is not accessible.
   c)   If a low side vacuum reading is obtained, warm the expansion valve diaphragm chamber with your hand, then repeat the step above.
   d)   If the expansion valve test indicates that valve operation is satisfactory, clean the contact surface of the evaporator outlet pipe and the temperature sensing bulb. Make sure that the

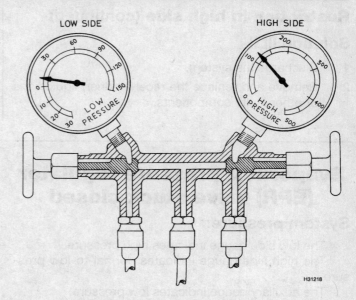

bulb is in snug contact with the pipe. Proceed to step 3.
   e)   If the expansion valve test indicates that the valve is defective, discharge the system, replace the valve and proceed to step 3.
2   If the expansion valve inlet shows sweating or frost:
   a)   Discharge the system.
   b)   Detach the inlet line from the expansion valve.
   c)   Clean and replace the screen and reconnect the inlet line.
   d)   Proceed to the next step.
3   Evacuate the system.
4   Charge the system.
5   Operate the system and check its performance.

Restriction in high side

System pressure:

The low side gauge indicates low pressure.
The high side gauge indicates low pressure (may be normal to high if a
restriction is located right after the service valve).
The auxiliary gauge indicates low pressure.

Symptoms:

The discharge air is slightly cool.
The high side lines are cool and show sweating or frost (which will appear immediately after the point at which the line is restricted).

Diagnosis: There is a restriction in the high side.

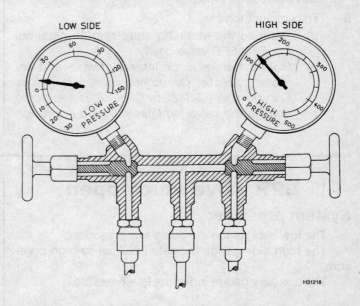

Heating and air conditioning

Restriction in high side (continued)

Solution:IILII

1 Discharge the system.
2 Remove and replace the receiver-drier, liquid lines or other faulty components.

3 Evacuate the system with a vacuum pump.
4 Charge the system.
5 Operate the system and check its performance.

Note: *The following two conditions apply only to Chrysler Corporation vehicles equipped with an Evaporator Pressure Regulator (EPR) valve.*

Evaporator pressure regulator (EPR) valve stuck closed

System pressure:

The low side gauge indicates high pressure.
The high side gauge indicates normal-to-low pressure.
The auxiliary gauge indicates low pressure.

Symptoms:

The evaporator outlet pipe is warm.
The discharge air is warm.
The difference in pressure between the low side gauge and the auxiliary
gauge is excessive (it shouldn't exceed 6 psi).

Diagnosis: The Evaporator Pressure Regulator (EPR) valve is stuck closed.

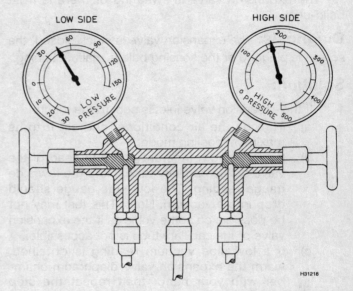

Solution:

1 Discharge the system.
2 To gain access to the valve, which is located in the suction passage, remove the fasteners from the suction line fitting on the rear of the compressor and detach the fitting.
3 To remove the valve:
   a) Remove the retaining snap-ring (if installed) from the EPR valve cavity.
   b) Rotate the valve counterclockwise and remove it. **Note:** *On earlier valves, a special Chrysler tool (C-3822 or C3822A) is needed to engage the valve; on later valves, a protrusion*

on the valve can be grasped with needle-nose pliers.

4 Lubricate the new O-ring with refrigerant oil and install it on the new valve.
5 Install the new valve (with the special tool, if necessary).
6 Clean the suction screen (if equipped).
7 Reposition the screen, spring and fitting. Tighten the fasteners to about 8 to 14 ft-lbs.
8 Evacuate the system.
9 Charge the system.
10 Operate the system and check its performance.

EPR valve stuck open

System pressure:

The low side gauge indicates low pressure.
The high side gauge indicates normal-to-high pressure.
The auxiliary gauge indicates low pressure.

Symptoms:

The evaporator outlet pipe is very cold.
The low side gauge indicates vacuum when the blower is disconnected.
The drop in pressure between the low side gauge and the auxiliary gauge is excessive (it should not exceed 6 psi).

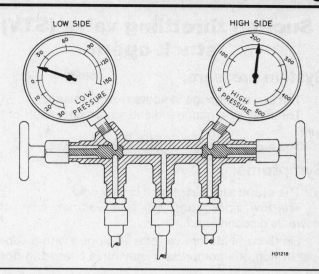

Diagnosis: The Evaporator Pressure Regulator (EPR) is stuck open.

Solution:

Same as solution for "EPR stuck closed".

STV/POA vale stuck closed

Note: *The following two conditions apply only to Ford and General Motors vehicles equipped with a Suction Throttling Valve (STV).*

System pressure:

The low side gauge indicates high pressure.
The high side gauge indicates normal-to-low pressure.
The auxiliary gauge indicates low pressure.

Symptoms:

The evaporator outlet pipe is warm.
The discharge air is warm.

Diagnosis: The STV/POA valve is stuck closed; there's a restriction in the low side of the system.

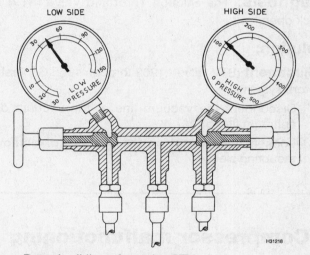

Solution:

Adjustment (Suction Throttling Valve [STV] - 1962 through 1965 General Motors systems)

1   Detach the vacuum line at the vacuum diaphragm fitting.
2   Loosen the locknut on the vacuum diaphragm mounting sleeve.
3   Rotate the vacuum diaphragm and sleeve counterclockwise (out of the valve body) to lower the pressure indicated on the low side gauge until it's within the normal range. **Caution:** *If the valve is rotated completely out of the body, immediate system discharge will occur.*
4   Tighten the locknut securely.
5   Reattach the vacuum line.

Replacement (Pilot Operated Absolute [POA] STV valve - 1965 and later models)

1   Discharge the system.

2   Detach all lines from the STV.
3   Remove the STV. **Note:** *If the STV is an integral component of a combination assembly (such as the Ford system, for example), it may be necessary to remove the combination assembly to gain access to the valve.*
4   Install a new STV. Make sure the replacement unit is the exact same model as the old unit.
5   Replace the receiver-drier, then evacuate the system.
6   If STV failure has caused the superheat switch to cut off compressor operation (on a General Motors system, for example), check the thermal limiter fuse (refer to the fuse guide in the owner's manual). Replace it if necessary.
7   Charge the system.
8   Operate the system and check its performance. If necessary, adjust the STV (older type only) to obtain the proper pressures.

Heating and air conditioning

Suction throttling valve (STV) stuck open

System pressure:

The low side gauge indicates low pressure.

The high side gauge indicates normal-to-high pressure.

The auxiliary gauge indicates low pressure.

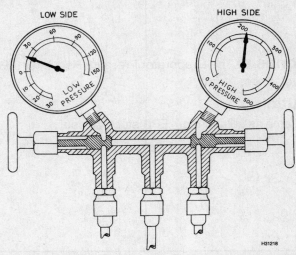

Symptoms:

The evaporator outlet pipe is very cold.

The low side gauge indicates vacuum when the blower is disconnected.

On General Motors vehicles equipped with a superheat switch, the compressor may have ceased to operate.

Diagnosis: The Suction Throttling Valve (STV) is stuck open.

Solution:

Adjustment (STV valve - 1962 through 1965 General Motors systems)

1 Disconnect the vacuum line at the vacuum diaphragm fitting.

2 Loosen the locknut on the vacuum diaphragm mounting sleeve.

3 Rotate the vacuum diaphragm and sleeve clockwise (into the body) to increase the pressure indicated on the low and auxiliary gauges. Continue turning until the indicated readings are normal.

4 If the valve cannot be adjusted to the correct setting, replace it (see "STV stuck closed" above).

Replacement (Pilot Operated Absolute [POA] type STV - 1965 and later models)

This design is not serviceable. If it's faulty, replace it (See "STV stuck closed" above).

Compressor malfunctioning

System pressure:

The low side gauge indicates high pressure.

The high side gauge indicates low pressure.

The auxiliary gauge indicates high pressure.

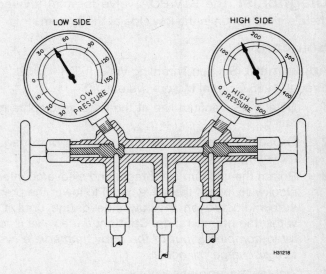

Symptoms:

The compressor is noisy (if the compressor is not noisy but the above gauge readings are indicated, the problem may be a loose or worn compressor drivebelt).

Diagnosis: The compressor is malfunctioning.

Solution:

1 Discharge the system (or isolate the compressor, if equipped with stem-type service valves).

2 Remove the compressor cylinder head and inspect it.

3 Replace the reed valve plate assembly if necessary.

4 Install the cylinder head. Use a new gasket.

5 Check the compressor oil level.

6 Replace the receiver-drier, desiccant or accumulator if:

a) The system has been previously opened.
b) The system has been operated two or more years with the present unit.
c) Compressor inspection reveals desiccant particles (very fine, brown or gold in color).

7 Evacuate the system (or the isolated, stem-type compressor).
8 Charge the system.
9 Operate the system and check its performance.

Condenser malfunction or overcharge

System pressure:

The low side gauge indicates high pressure.
The high side gauge indicates high pressure.
The auxiliary gauge indicates high pressure.

Symptoms:

The discharge air is warm.
The high side lines are very hot.
There are bubbles visible in the sight glass.

Diagnosis: The condenser is malfunctioning or the system is overcharged.

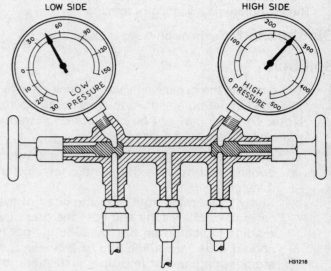

Solution:

1 Make sure the fan is working. Like the radiator, the condenser won't work well when the vehicle is at rest without the fan.

2 A slowly turning (clutch type) fan will also affect condenser performance. Inspect the fan drivebelt for loose adjustment and wear.

3 Inspect the front of the vehicle for a clogged bug shield or grille or any other obstruction that could prevent air from flowing through the condenser.

4 Check the clearance between the condenser and the radiator. Inspect the condenser mounting hardware, particularly any rubber bushings, for wear. Make sure all hardware is tight and in good condition.

5 After making the above inspections and necessary repairs, operate the system and check its performance.

6 If the indicated pressures are not lowered and/or the symptoms have not disappeared, inspect the system for an overcharge and correct as follows:

a) Discharge refrigerant until a stream of bubbles appears in the sight glass and the pressures indicated on both the high and low side gauges drop below normal.

b) Add refrigerant until the bubbles disappear and pressures return to normal, then add another 1/4 to 1/2 pound.

7 Operate the system and check its performance.

8 If the gauge readings are still too high:

a) Discharge the system.

b) Remove and inspect the condenser to ensure free passage of the refrigerant. Back flush it if necessary. Replace the condenser if flushing doesn't remove the obstruction(s).

9 Replace the receiver-drier, desiccant bag or accumulator.

10 Evacuate the system.

11 Charge the system.

12 Operate the system and check its performance.

Expansion valve stuck open

System pressure:

The low side gauge indicates high pressure.
The high side gauge indicates high pressure.
The auxiliary gauge indicates high pressure.

Symptoms:

The discharge air is warm.
The evaporator is sweating or frosting.

Diagnosis: The expansion valve is stuck open.

Solution:

1   To verify that the expansion valve is stuck open (or that the temperature sensing bulb is stuck open):
Note: *This test may not be possible on systems with an inaccessible sensing bulb.*

a) Set the air conditioner controls for maximum cooling and operate the system for several minutes.

b) Spray liquid refrigerant onto the head of the valve or capillary tube and note the pressure reading indicated on the low side gauge. It should drop into a vacuum. If it doesn't, a stuck open valve or improper installation of the bulb is indicated.

c) If a low side vacuum is indicated, warm the expansion valve diaphragm chamber with your hand, then repeat the test.

2   If the expansion valve test indicates that valve operation is satisfactory:

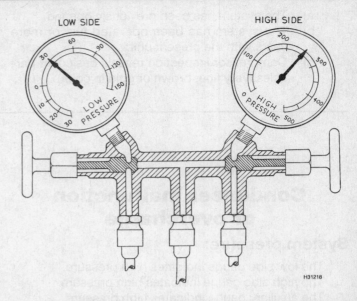

a) Clean the contact surface of the evaporator outlet pipe and the temperature sensing bulb, then clamp the bulb securely in contact with the pipe and recover with the proper insulation tape.

b) Operate the system and check its performance.

3   If the expansion valve test indicates that the valve is defective:

a) Discharge the system.

b) Replace the expansion valve. Make sure that all contacts are clean and secure.

c) Evacuate the system.

d) Recharge the system.

e) Operate the system and check its performance.

Ford fixed orifice tube (FFOT) system troubleshooting

The best way to troubleshoot an FFOT system is to analyze the clutch "cycle rate" and the refrigerant pressures, which vary between the lowest and highest points during the clutch cycle. (One complete cycle is equal to the time that the clutch is on plus the time that it's off.)

After noting and recording the system pressures and clutch cycle rate, simply compare your observations with the correct chart to determine whether the observed values correspond with the normal values.

To obtain accurate clutch cycle timing for the FFOT system, the following conditions must be met:

•   In-vehicle temperatures must be stabilized at 70 to 80°F.

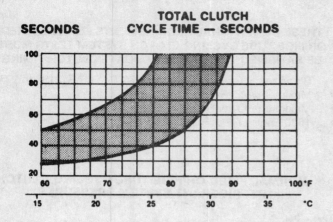

SECONDS

TOTAL CLUTCH CYCLE TIME — SECONDS

AMBIENT TEMPERATURES

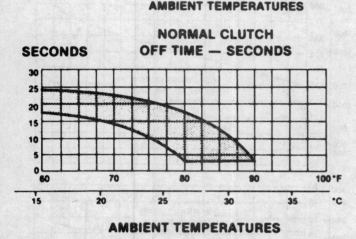

SECONDS

NORMAL CLUTCH OFF TIME — SECONDS

AMBIENT TEMPERATURES

THESE CONDITIONAL REQUIREMENTS FOR THE FIXED ORIFICE TUBE CYCLING CLUTCH SYSTEM TESTS MUST BE SATISFIED TO OBTAIN ACCURATE CLUTCH TIMING

- Stabilized in Car Temperature @ 70°F to 80°F (21°C to 27°C)
- Maximum A/C (Recirculating Air)
- Maximum Blower Speed
- 1500 Engine RPM For 10 Minutes

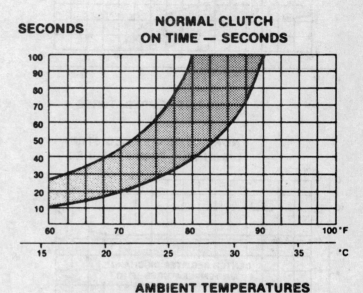

SECONDS

NORMAL CLUTCH ON TIME — SECONDS

AMBIENT TEMPERATURES

Refer to these charts to determine the normal clutch cycle rates and times for a Ford Fixed Orifice Tube (FFOT) system - Tempo/Topaz, Escort/Lynx shown - others similar

- The air conditioning system must be operating in the maximum cooling mode (recirculating the air).
- The blower speed must be at the highest setting.
- The engine must be running at 1500 rpm for 10 minutes.

The lowest pressure recorded on the low pressure gauge (observed when the clutch is disengaged) is the low pressure setting of the clutch cycling pressure switch. The high pressure setting for the switch is the pressure recorded when the clutch engages.

It should be noted that compressor clutch cycling doesn't normally occur in ambient temperatures above 100°F, and, in some cases, above 90°F, depending on local conditions and engine speed. In other words, the compressor just keeps running. Clutch cycling also doesn't usually occur when the engine is operating at curb idle speed.

Also, if the system contains no refrigerant or is extremely low on refrigerant, the clutch will neither engage nor operate. If the compressor cycles rapidly, it usually indicates the system is low on refrigerant.

Note: *Once a problem with the system has been corrected, repeat the following test procedure to make sure the problem has been eliminated.*

1   If insufficient cooling is noted and the vehicle's engine cooling system isn't equipped with an electric cooling fan system, proceed to step 2. If

Heating and air conditioning

NORMAL CLUTCH CYCLE RATE PER MINUTE

CYCLES/MINUTE

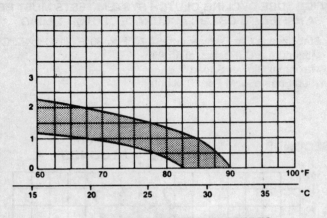

AMBIENT TEMPERATURES

NORMAL CENTER REGISTER DISCHARGE TEMPERATURES

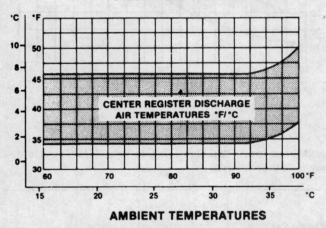

AMBIENT TEMPERATURES

THESE CONDITIONAL REQUIREMENTS FOR THE FIXED ORIFICE TUBE CYCLING CLUTCH SYSTEM TESTS MUST BE SATISFIED TO OBTAIN ACCURATE CLUTCH TIMING

- Stabilized in Car Temperature @ 70°F to 80°F (21°C to 27°C)
- Maximum A/C (Recirculating Air)
- Maximum Blower Speed
- 1500 Engine RPM For 10 Minutes

NORMAL FIXED ORIFICE TUBE CYCLING CLUTCH REFRIGERANT SYSTEM PRESSURES

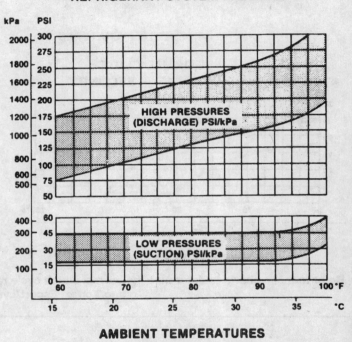

AMBIENT TEMPERATURES

Refer to these charts to determine normal Ford Fixed Orifice Tube (FFOT) cycling clutch refrigerant system pressure/temperature relationships - Tempo/Topaz, Escort/Lynx shown - others similar

---

the vehicle is equipped with an electric cooling fan system, verify that the compressor clutch engages.

   a)   If it doesn't, check the clutch electrical circuit.

   b)   If it does, verify that the cooling fan operates when the compressor clutch is engaged.

      1)   If the fan doesn't operate when the compressor clutch is engaged, check the cooling fan circuit.

      2)   If the fan does operate when the compressor clutch is engaged, proceed to the next step.

2   Inspect the compressor drivebelt. Make sure that it's not loose or deteriorated.

3   Inspect the compressor clutch wires and connectors. Make sure they're not frayed or otherwise damaged. Look at the electrical connectors.

Make sure they're not loose or unplugged. Be sure the resistor assembly is properly connected.

4   Check for blown fuses.

5   Make sure the blower operates properly.

6   Check all vacuum hoses and connections.

7   Make sure all vacuum motors and temperature doors move freely and open all the way.

8   Inspect all dashboard control head electrical and vacuum connections.

9   If cooling is still insufficient even after all the above items have been checked and, where necessary, repaired, the FFOT system must be examined more closely using the following pressure-cycle time charts.

10 Hook up a manifold gauge set, set the selector lever to the Maximum position, turn the blower switch to the highest setting and put the temperature lever at the coldest setting. Close all vehicle doors and windows.

11 Install a thermometer in the center vent (the one closest to the evaporator) and check the discharge temperature. Record the measurement. Also note and record the ambient (outside) temperature.

12 Run the engine for 10 to 15 minutes at approximately 1500 rpm with the compressor clutch engaged.

13 Measure the compressor clutch cycle time (on and off time) with a watch. Record the measurements and compare them to the accompanying charts.

   a)   If the compressor cycles very rapidly, proceed to step 14.
   b)   If the compressor cycles slowly, proceed to step 15.
   c)   If the compressor doesn't cycle at all (runs continuously), proceed to step 16.
   d)   If the compressor cycles normally, proceed to step 17.

14 If the compressor cycles very rapidly (1 second on, 1 second off), bypass the clutch cycling switch with a jumper wire. The compressor should operate continuously. Now feel the evaporator inlet and outlet tubes.

   a)   If they feel about the same temperature, replace the clutch cycling switch and retest the system.
   b)   If the evaporator inlet tube is warm, or if the outlet tube feels colder downstream from the orifice tube, leak-test the system, repair any leaks, evacuate, charge and retest the system. If no leaks are found, add about 1/4-pound of refrigerant to the system and feel the inlet and outlet tubes again.
   c)   If the evaporator inlet tube is colder, add 1/4-pound of refrigerant and feel the inlet and outlet tubes again. Continue to add refrigerant in 1/4-pound increments until both tubes feel about the same temperature (within a range of 28 to 40°F).
   d)   When the inlet tube feels about the same temperature as the outlet tube (about 28 to 40°F), add another 1/2 to 3/4 pounds of refrigerant and measure the discharge air temperature. It should be about 50°F.

15 If the compressor cycles slowly, feel the evaporator inlet and outlet tubes.

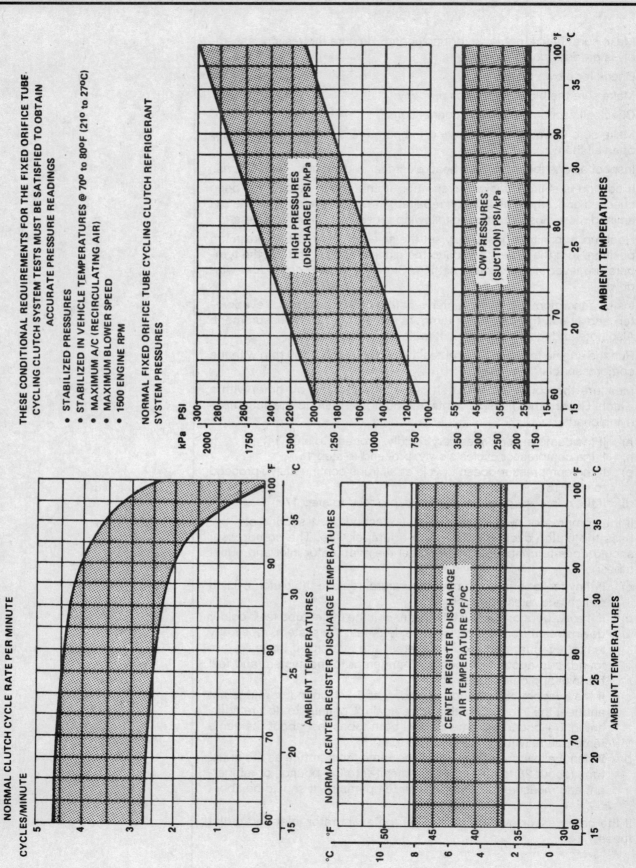

THESE CONDITIONAL REQUIREMENTS FOR THE FIXED ORIFICE TUBE CYCLING CLUTCH SYSTEM TESTS MUST BE SATISFIED TO OBTAIN ACCURATE PRESSURE READINGS

- STABILIZED PRESSURES
- STABILIZED IN VEHICLE TEMPERATURES @ 70° to 80°F (21° to 27°C)
- MAXIMUM A/C (RECIRCULATING AIR)
- MAXIMUM BLOWER SPEED
- 1500 ENGINE RPM

NORMAL FIXED ORIFICE TUBE CYCLING CLUTCH REFRIGERANT SYSTEM PRESSURES

HIGH PRESSURES (DISCHARGE) PSI/kPa

LOW PRESSURES (SUCTION) PSI/kPa

AMBIENT TEMPERATURES

NORMAL CLUTCH CYCLE RATE PER MINUTE

CYCLES/MINUTE

AMBIENT TEMPERATURES

NORMAL CENTER REGISTER DISCHARGE TEMPERATURES

CENTER REGISTER DISCHARGE AIR TEMPERATURE °F/°C

AMBIENT TEMPERATURES

Refer to these charts to determine the normal clutch cycle rates and times and pressure/temperature relationships for Ford Fixed Orifice Tube (FFOT) system on F-100 through F-350 trucks and Broncos

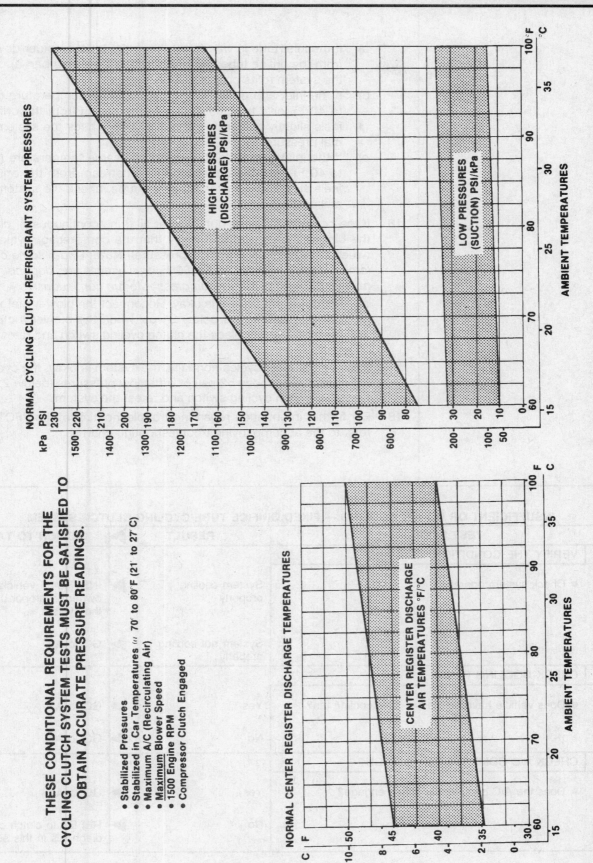

THESE CONDITIONAL REQUIREMENTS FOR THE CYCLING CLUTCH SYSTEM TESTS MUST BE SATISFIED TO OBTAIN ACCURATE PRESSURE READINGS.

- Stabilized Pressures
- Stabilized in Car Temperatures (70° to 80°F (21° to 27°C)
- Maximum A/C (Recirculating Air)
- Maximum Blower Speed
- <u>1500</u> Engine RPM
- Compressor Clutch Engaged

NORMAL CYCLING CLUTCH REFRIGERANT SYSTEM PRESSURES

HIGH PRESSURES (DISCHARGE) PSI/kPa

LOW PRESSURES (SUCTION) PSI/kPa

AMBIENT TEMPERATURES

NORMAL CENTER REGISTER DISCHARGE TEMPERATURES

CENTER REGISTER DISCHARGE AIR TEMPERATURES °F/°C

AMBIENT TEMPERATURES

Refer to these charts to determine the normal clutch cycle rates and times and pressure/temperature relationships for Ford Fixed Orifice Tube (FFOT) system on Econoline vans

a) If the inlet tube is warm or if the outlet tube is colder downstream from the orifice tube, perform step 14 (disregard part a), to restore the system to its proper charge level.

b) If the inlet and outlet tubes feel the same temperature (about 28 to 40°F), or if the outlet tube (downstream from the orifice tube) feels slightly colder than the inlet tube, check the system for normal pressure.

c) If the inlet and outlet tubes feel the same temperature (about 28 to 40°F), or if the outlet tube (downstream from the orifice tube) feels slightly colder than the inlet tube, check the system for normal pressure.

16 If the compressor does not cycle at all (runs continuously), disconnect the blower motor wire and verify that the compressor cycles off between 21 and 26 psi (low side pressure). **Note:** *Under some conditions (ambient temperatures above 80°F, or slightly lower, depending on humidity), it's normal for the compressor to run continuously.*

a) If it does, the system is okay. Reconnect the blower motor wire.

b) If the pressure falls below 21 psi when the blower motor wire is disconnected, replace the clutch cycling switch and retest the system.

17 If the compressor cycles normally, the system is okay. If it cycles on at high pressures (above 52 psi) or off at low pressures (below 21 psi), replace the clutch cycling switch and retest the system.

18 For further information regarding troubleshooting of the FFOT system, refer to the accompanying troubleshooting chart.

INSUFFICIENT OR NO A/C COOLING — FIXED ORIFICE TUBE CYCLING CLUTCH SYSTEM

TEST STEP		RESULT	▶	ACTION TO TAKE
A1	VERIFY THE CONDITION			
	• Check system operation.	System cooling properly	▶	INSTRUCT vehicle owner on proper use of the system.
		System not cooling properly	▶	GO to **A2**.
A2	CHECK COOLING FAN			
	• Does vehicle have an electro-drive cooling fan?	Yes	▶	GO to **A3**.
		No	▶	GO to **A5**.
A3	CHECK A/C COMPRESSOR CLUTCH			
	• Does the A/C compressor clutch engage?	Yes	▶	GO to **A4**.
		No	▶	REFER to clutch circuit diagnosis in this section.

INSUFFICIENT OR NO A/C COOLING — FIXED ORIFICE TUBE CYCLING CLUTCH SYSTEM — Continued

TEST STEP		RESULT ▶	ACTION TO TAKE
A4	CHECK OPERATION OF COOLING FAN		
	• Check to ensure electro-drive cooling fan runs when the A/C compressor clutch is engaged.	Yes ▶	GO to **A5**.
		No ▶	Check engine cooling fan circuit.
A5	COMPONENT CHECK		
	Under-hood check of the following:	OK but still not cooling ▶	GO to **A7**.
	• Loose, missing or damaged compressor drive belt.	Not OK ▶	REPAIR and GO to **A6**.
	• Loose or disconnected A/C clutch or clutch cycling pressure switch wires/connectors.		
	• Disconnected resistor assembly.		
	• Loose vacuum lines or misadjusted control cables.		
	Inside vehicle check for:		
	• Blown fuse/proper blower motor operation.		
	• Vacuum motors/temperature door movement — full travel.		
	• Control electrical and vacuum connections.		
A6	CHECK SYSTEM		
	• Check system operation.	(OK) ▶	Condition Corrected. GO to **A1**.
		(O̶K̶) ▶	GO to **A7**.
A7	CHECK COMPRESSOR CLUTCH		
	• Use refrigerant system pressure/clutch cycle rate and timing evaluation charts.	Compressor cycles very rapidly (1 second on) (1 second off) ▶	GO to **A8**.
	After preparing car as follows:		
	1. Hook up manifold gauge set.		
	2. Set function lever at max. A/C	Compressor runs continuously (normal operation in ambient temperature above 27°C (80°F) depending on humidity conditions) ▶	GO to **A9**.
	3. Set blower switch on high.		
	4. Set temperature lever full cold.		
	5. Close doors and windows.		
	6. Use a thermometer to check temperature at center discharge register, record outside temperature.	Compressor cycles slow ▶	GO to **A8**.
	7. Run engine at approximately 1500 RPM with compressor clutch engaged.		
	8. Stabilize with above conditions for 10-15 minutes.		
	• Check compressor clutch off/on time with watch. Refer to charts for normal clutch cycle timing rates.		

Heating and air conditioning

	TEST STEP	RESULT ▶	ACTION TO TAKE
A8	**CHECK CLUTCH CYCLING PRESSURE SWITCH**		
	• Bypass clutch cycling pressure switch with jumper wire. Compressor on continuously. • Hand feel evaporator inlet and outlet tubes.	▶ Outlet tube same temperature approximately −2°C - 4°C (28°F - 40°F) or slightly colder than inlet tube (after fixed orifice)	REPLACE clutch cycling pressure switch. Do not discharge system. Switch fitting has Schrader Valve. GO to **A9**.
		▶ Inlet tube warm or (after fixed orifice) colder than outlet tube	GO to **A10**.
A9	**CHECK SYSTEM PRESSURES**		
	• Compare readings with normal system pressure ranges.	▶ Clutch cycles within limits, system pressure within limits	System OK. GO to **A1**.
		▶ Compressor runs continuously (normal operation in ambient temperature above 27°C (80°F) depending on humidity conditions).	GO to **A11**.
		▶ Compressor cycles high or low ON above 359 kPa (52 psi) OFF below 144 kPa (21 psi).	REPLACE clutch cycling pressure switch. Do not discharge system. Switch fitting has Schrader valve. CHECK system. OK — GO to **A1**. NOT OK — GO to **A10**.
A10	**CHECK SYSTEM**		
	• Leak Check system.	▶ Leak found	REPAIR, discharge, evacuate and charge system. System OK, GO to **A1**.
		▶ No leak found	Low refrigerant charge or moisture in system. Discharge, evacuate and charge system. System OK.
A11	**CHECK CLUTCH CYCLING**		
	• Disconnect blower motor wire and check for clutch cycling off at 144 kPa (21 psi) (suction pressure).	▶ Clutch cycles OFF at 144-179 kPa (21-26 psi)	Connect blower motor wire. System OK, GO to **A1**.
		▶ Pressure falls below 144 kPa (21 psi)	REPLACE clutch cycling pressure switch. Do not discharge system. Switch fitting has Schrader valve. System OK, GO to **A1**.

General Motors cycling clutch orifice tube (CCOT) system troubleshooting

Preliminary inspection

Before attempting to troubleshoot the CCOT system, check the following components:

1   Inspect the compressor drivebelt. Make sure it's not loose, damaged or missing.

2   Inspect the air conditioning system wiring. Make sure that no wires are frayed or broken. Look for loose or unplugged electrical connectors. Check all fuses and make sure none of them are blown.

3   Verify that the temperature door strikes both stops when the lever is rapidly moved from hot to cold.

4   Verify that the engine cooling fan runs continuously in all air conditioning modes.

Preliminary test

5   After making the necessary repairs, turn on the engine and the air conditioning system and note whether the system is cooling effectively.

6   If the components listed in steps 1 through 4 are working properly but the system is still not cooling effectively, put the temperature lever at the maximum cold position, move the selector lever to normal mode, set the blower switch in the high position, open the doors and hood and warm up the engine at about 1500 rpm.

7   Watch the compressor clutch and see if it engages:
   a)   If the clutch doesn't engage, proceed to Step 10.
   b)   If the clutch "cycles" (alternately engages and disengages), feel the liquid line before the orifice tube.
      1)   If the tube feels warm, proceed to Step 8.
      2)   If the tube feels cold, inspect the high side tubes for a frost spot. Open the system and repair the restriction. Evacuate, charge and retest the system.

8   If the vehicle is equipped with a Harrison DA V5 compressor, proceed to "Troubleshooting systems with the Harrison DA V5 compressor."

9   If the vehicle is equipped with any compressor except the Harrison DA V5, feel the evaporator inlet and outlet pipes:
   a)   If the inlet is colder than the outlet, inspect the system for leaks and repair any found, evacuate and charge the system. If no leak is found, proceed to Step 15.
   b)   If the outlet pipe is colder, or the pipes are both the same temperature, proceed to Step 16.

Compressor clutch test

10   If the clutch did not operate, check the condition of the wire harness to the clutch and the adjustment of the throttle or vacuum cut-out switches. Connect a fused jumper wire between the positive battery terminal and the compressor clutch.
   a)   If the clutch doesn't operate, proceed to the next step.
   b)   If the clutch operates, proceed to Step 12.

11   Connect a ground wire from the clutch to the engine block. If the clutch still doesn't operate, remove and either repair or replace it.

12   If the clutch operates but cooling is inadequate, operate the clutch for a short time and check the low side pressure at the accumulator fitting.

a)   If the pressure is above 50 psi, proceed to the next step.

b)   If the pressure is below 50 psi, proceed to Step 14.

13   Connect a jumper wire across the pressure switch connector.

a)   If the compressor operates, the switch is faulty. Replace it and test the system.

b)   If the compressor doesn't operate with the jumper, look for an open or short circuit between the switch and the clutch.

14   Check the pressure on the high side.

a)   If the high side is above 50 psi, discharge the system and inspect the orifice tube and the high side for an obstruction.

b)   If the high side is below 50 psi, the charge is lost. Leak test the system, make the necessary repairs, then evacuate, charge and retest the system.

System charge test

Caution: *When conducting the system charge test, keep an eye on the gauges for any indication of overcharging (excessively high discharge pressures, for instance).*

15   If cooling is insufficient, add one pound of refrigerant, then check the clutch cycle rate.

a)   If the clutch cycles more than 8 times a minute, discharge the system and check for a plugged orifice tube.

b)   If the clutch cycles less than 8 times a minute, feel the accumulator inlet and outlet pipes.

1)   If the inlet pipe is warmer, or if both pipes are the same temperature as the inlet pipe, add another pound of refrigerant.

2)   If the inlet is colder than the outlet, add another pound of refrigerant. Feel the inlet and outlet pipes again.

(a)   If the outlet pipe is colder or the same temperature as the inlet pipe, add another pound of refrigerant.

(b)   If the inlet pipe is still colder than the outlet, discharge the system and check for a plugged orifice tube.

Pressure switch test

16   If the inlet and outlet pipe temperatures are okay but cooling is insufficient, verify (with a gauge set) that the clutch cycles on at 51 to 51 psi and off at 20 to 28 psi.

a)   If the clutch is cycling correctly, proceed to Step 17.

b)   If the clutch cycles at excessively high, or low, pressures, replace the pressure cycling switch.

c)   If the clutch runs continuously, unplug the evaporator blower motor connector. The clutch should now cycle off between 20 and 28 psi.

1)   If it doesn't (pressure falls below 20 psi), replace the pressure cycling switch.

2)   If the clutch does cycle off, proceed to Step 17.

Performance test

17   Slide the temperature lever to the coldest position, put the selector lever at the maximum mode, and turn the blower to the highest setting. Close the doors and windows, run the engine at 2000 rpm and place an auxiliary fan in front of the grille. Stick a thermometer in the dash vent

nearest the evaporator and check the temperature. It should be between 35 and 45°F (assuming an ambient temperature of about 85°F).

18   If the outlet temperature is too high, check compressor cycling time.

a)   If the clutch runs continuously, discharge the system and check for a missing orifice tube, plugged inlet screen or other restriction in the suction line.

b)   If none of these conditions are present, the system has been overcharged. Evacuate and recharge it.

c)   If the clutch cycles on and off, or remains off for a long time, discharge the system and check it for a plugged orifice tube. Replace the tube, then evacuate, charge and retest the system.

Troubleshooting systems with the Harrison V5 compressor

1   Complete the preliminary checks (Steps 1 through 7 in the previous section) first.

2   Connect a gauge set to the system, if you haven't already done so. Connect a fused jumper wire around the cooling fan switch. Put the selector lever in the normal mode and the blower switch in the highest position. With the engine idling at about 1000 rpm, measure the discharge air temperature at the center vent.

a)   If the temperature is no greater than 60°F, proceed to Step 4.

b)   If the temperature is greater than 60°F, check accumulator pressure.

1)   If the pressure is below 35 psi, proceed to Step 3.

2)   If the pressure is between 35 and 50 psi, proceed to Step 4.

3)   If the pressure is greater than 50 psi but less than 160 psi, proceed to Step 5.

4)   If the pressure is greater than 160 psi, proceed to Step 6.

3   If the accumulator pressure is below 35 psi, add one pound of refrigerant.

a)   If the pressure is now more than 35 psi, leak test the system.

b)   If the pressure is still low, discharge the system and inspect the orifice tube for restrictions or plugging. Replace the orifice tube, evacuate, charge and retest the system.

4   Move the selector lever to the Defrost mode. Disconnect the engine cooling fan. Allow the compressor to cycle on the high pressure cut-out switch.

a)   If the compressor makes a knocking noise as it engages, the system oil charge is high. Discharge the system, flush all components, charge the system and add fresh oil.

b)   If the compressor does not make a knocking noise during engagement, set the selector lever to Maximum cooling, adjust the blower to the low setting and allow the engine to idle for 5 minutes at 1000 rpm.

1)   If accumulator pressure is between 29 and 35 psi, the system is okay.

2)   If accumulator pressure is less than 28 psi, discharge the system and replace the compressor control valve. Evacuate, charge and retest the system.

3) If the pressure is more than 35 psi, discharge the system and replace the compressor control valve. Evacuate, charge and retest the system. If the accumulator pressure is still more than 35 psi, replace the compressor.

5   If the accumulator pressure was greater than 50 psi but less than 160 psi in Step 2, discharge the system and check for a missing orifice tube.

6   If the tube is still there, replace the compressor control valve. Evacuate, charge and retest the system. If the high pressure condition persists, replace the compressor.

7   If the accumulator pressure was greater than 160 psi in Step 2, the system is overcharged. Discharge, evacuate and retest the system.

NORMAL CCOT SYSTEM OPERATING PRESSURES

Model year	Low side psi	High side psi
1973 through 1978	20 to 28	185 to 235
1979 through 1981	24 to 35	150 to 220
1982 on		
Front wheel drive	22 to 29	165 to 205
Rear wheel drive	24 to 30	130 to 190

Glossary

Absolute humidity – The mass (actual amount) of water vapor present in a unit volume of moist air

Absolute pressure – Pressure measured from a starting point of 0 in a perfect vacuum. When measured by the absolute pressure scale, atmospheric pressure is 14.7 psi or 29.92 inches of mercury (in-Hg)

Absolute temperature scale – Also called the absolute scale temperature as measured on a scale in which the hypothetical lowest limit of physical temperatures is assigned the value zero. The Kelvin scale is an example of the absolute temperature scale

Absolute zero – The point at which there is a total absence of heat, approximately minus 459 or 460 degrees Fahrenheit

Accumulator – A refrigerant storage device used on General Motors and Ford systems that receives vapor and liquid refrigerant from the evaporator. The accumulator, which contains "desiccant," performs a function similar to that of a receiver-drier: it separates liquid from the vapor, retains the liquid and releases the vapor to the compressor. Always located on the low side of the system.

Air conditioner – A devise which controls the temperature, humidity and air movement, and sometimes the air purity, in an enclosed space

Air conditioning – A system or process for controlling the temperature, humidity, air movement and sometimes the purity of the air in an enclosed space

Air inlet valve – An adjustable door, often vacuum operated, in the plenum blower assembly that permits selection of outside or inside air for automotive heating and cooling systems

Air outlet valve – A vacuum operated door which directs air flow into the heater core or ducts, usually located in or near the plenum blower assembly

Ambient air temperature – The temperature of the surrounding air

Ambient sensor – A device which sample and detects changes in the temperature of the ambient (surrounding) air

Ambient switch – An outside air temperature sensing switch which prevents operation of the compressor and the recirculation air mode below an outside temperature of 40° F

Ambient temperature – See "ambient air temperature"

Amplifier – A device which increases the strength of an electrical or vacuum signal

Aspirator – The air intake of a sensor

Atmospheric pressure – The pressure exerted by the earth's atmosphere at any given point, and altitude, above or below sea level. The atmospheric pressure is calculated by multiplying the mass of the atmospheric column of the unit area above the given point and of the gravitational acceleration at the given point. It's also the common term used to denote a value of standard or normal atmospheric pressure equivalent to the pressure exerted by a column of mercury 29.92 in (760 m) high.

Auxiliary gauge – The gauge which indicates compressor inlet pressure on older Chrysler Corporation vehicles with an Evaporator Pressure Regulator (EPR) valve; also used to measure evaporator pressure on some Ford vehicles with a Suction Throttling Valve (STV)

Axial compressor – A compressor characterized by the unusual piston arrangement. The pistons are arranged horizontal around and parallel to the crankshaft axis or centerline.

Back seat – A term which means to route a service valve counterclockwise all the way down until the valve is "back-seated." When referring to a "stem type" ser-

Heating and air conditioning

vice valve, the term has a more specific meaning: in the back-seated position, the valve outlet to the system is open and the service port in the valve is closed (its normal operating position)

Bellows – A sealed, accordion-type chamber (gas filled or vacuum) which expands and contracts in accordance with temperature changes. Used as an air conditioning control device on many systems

Bi-metallic sensor – Also known as a bimetal sensor. Consists of a "thermocouple", an arm made of two dissimilar metals with different rates of thermal expansion, that flexes in accordance with temperature changes. Used as a temperature sensor

Blower fan – An electric motor-driven fan which forces air through the evaporator and duct assembly, then forces the cooled air out of the duct work and circulated it through the vehicle passenger compartment

Boiling point – The temperature at which a liquid converts to a vapor. In physics, this point is defined as the temperature at which the vapor pressure of a liquid is equal to the pressure of the atmosphere on the liquid, which is equal to 212° F (100° C) at sea level

Bowden cable – A cable or wire inside a metal or rubber housing used for remote control of a valve or other device

British Thermal Unit (TBU) – The amount of heat required to raise the temperature of one pound (.04 kg) of water one degree Fahrenheit. Commonly used as a measurement of heat quantity. 1 BTU = 778 pound feet or 252 calories

Bulk charging – Using large containers of R-12 to charge the system. Commonly employed with "charging stations" to perform complete system charges

Bulk refrigerant drum – Large (for example, 10 lbs., 25 lbs., 30 lbs.) container of refrigerant generally used in professional air conditioning service shops which employ charging stations to perform complete system charges

Capacity – A measure of theoretical maximum amount of refrigeration-produced output, measured in tons or BTUs per hour

Capillary tube – A tube, usually gas-filled, with a precisely calibrated length and inside diameter, used to connect the remote bulb or coil to the expansion valve or thermostat

Celsius – Also referred to as Celsius scale or Centigrade. Uses the freezing point of water as 0° and the boiling point of water at 100°. Celsius temperatures are computed from Kelvin values by subtracting 273.15 from the latter

Centigrade – See "celsius"

Change of state – Rearrangement of the molecular structure of matter as it changes between any two of the three physical states: solid, liquid or gas

Charge – A specific amount of refrigerant by volume or weight

Charging hose – A small diameter hose constructed to withstand high pressures. Connected between the air conditioning system and the manifold set

Charging station – A usually portable unit equipped with a manifold gauge set, charging cylinder, vacuum pump, refrigerant supply, auxiliary gauges, various valves and the plumbing necessary to hook everything together. Used for servicing air conditioning systems

Check valve – A one-way, in-live valve that permits flow of liquids or gases in one direction only. Used to control flow of vacuum, refrigerant, coolant, etc.

Clutch – An electrically operated coupling device that connects or disconnects the compressor pulley and compressor shaft

Clutch cycling switch – A device that turns the compressor on and off in response to changes in pressure or evaporator temperature

Clutch field – A clutch part, consisting of hundreds of windings of wire, that creates a magnetic field when current is applied, pulling in the armature to engage the clutch

Clutch pulley or rotor – The clutch part turned by the drivebelt. The pulley or rotor "free-wheels" until the clutch is engaged. On rotors which contain the field, the electrical connection is made through brushes similar to alternator and starter motor brushes.

Coefficient of expansion – The fractional change in length, area or volume per unit change in temperature of a solid, liquid or gas at a given constant pressure. For example, an aluminum bar stretches 13 millionths percent of its original length for each degree Fahrenheit rise in temperature. Also referred to as "expansivity"

Cold – The relative absence of heat

Compound gauge – Another name for the low side gauge, because it can indicate both pressure and vacuum

Compression – Reduction in volume and increase in pressure and temperature of a gas caused by squeezing it into a smaller space

Compressor – An air conditioning component which pumps, circulates and increases the pressure of refrigerant vapor

Compressor cut-off switch – A device used by some manufacturers to prevent compressor operation. Some typical examples: the Wide Open Throttle (WOT) cut-off switch, low pressure switch and high pressure switch

Compressor discharge switch – A devise that shuts off the compressor when refrigerant pressure is low. The switch is wired in series between the compressor clutch and the control panel switch

Compressor shaft seal – A seal, surrounding the compressor shaft, that permits the shaft to turn without the loss of refrigerant or oil

Condensation – The act or process of reducing a gas or vapor to a liquid or solid form

Condenser – The air conditioning system heat exchanger that turns refrigerant vapor into a liquid by removing heat from the vapor

Conduction - The transfer of heat between the closely packed molecules of a substance or between two substances that are touching, caused by a temperature differential between the two molecules or substances

Contaminants – Anything other than refrigerant or refrigerant oil in the system

Control head – The dashboard mounted assembly which houses the mode selector, the blower switch and the temperature control lever

Convection – The transfer of heat by the circulation of movement of heated, or cooled, parts of vapor or liquid

Corrosion – The eating or wearing away of a substance, such as metal, usually caused by chemical decomposition brought about by an acid

Cycling Clutch Orifice Tube (CCOT) system – The General Motors system that utilizes an accumulator (instead of a receiver-drier). The system uses a fixed orifice tube located at the evaporator outlet, instead of an expansion valve. A thermostatic switch or a pressure sensing switch cycles compressor operation off and on in accordance with system status

Cycling clutch system – Any system that controls compressor clutch operation as a means of temperature control

Dehumidify – To remove water vapor from the air

Density – The weight or mass per unit volume of a gas, liquid or solid

Desiccant – A drying agent (silica gel or similar substance) used in refrigeration systems to remove excess moisture from R-12 vapor

Diaphragm - A rubber-like piston or bellows assembly which divides the inner and outer chambers of back pressure regulated air conditioning devises

Dichlorodifluoromethane – The chemical substance (CCl_2F_2) used in earlier automotive air conditioning systems to absorb, carry and release heat. A member of the fluorocarbon family. Usually referred to as refrigerant, or R-12. See "fluorocarbon," "refrigerant –12."

Discharge – To bleed some or all of the refrigerant from a system by opening a valve or connection to permit refrigerant to escape slowly

Discharge air – Air conditioned air forced through the vents (ducts) into the passenger compartment

Discharge line – The line which connects the compressor outlet to the condenser inlet

Discharge pressure – The (high side) pressure of the refrigerant being discharged from the compressor

Discharge side - The part of the air conditioning system under high pressure, extending from the compressor outlet to the thermostatic expansion valve/tube inlet

Discharge valve – A device used to check high side pressures. Usually referred to as the high side service valve

Drier – A devise located in the liquid line, contains desiccant to absorb moisture from the system. Usually combined with the receiver

Drive pulley – The pulley attached to the nose of the engine crankshaft. Drives the compressor clutch pulley, usually with a V-type drivebelt

Drying pulley – See "desiccant"

Electro Vacuum Relay (EVR) – A combination solenoid vacuum valve and electrical relay which locks out blower operation and closed the fresh air door in cold weather, and switches the system to the recirculating air mode during maximum system use

Equalizer line – A line or connection used to operator certain control valves. Little or no refrigerant flows through the line

Evacuate – To pump the air, moisture and foreign material out of the system with a vacuum pump

Evaporation – A change of state, at the surface of liquid, from a liquid to a vapor. Evaporation can occur at various temperatures, depending on the liquid and the pressure

Evaporator – An air conditioning system component through which cool, liquid refrigerant is pumped at a reduced pressure. When heated by the warm passenger compartment air being forced through the evaporator, the refrigerant evaporates, drawing heat from the air as it passed over the cooling fins.

Evaporator Equalized Value in Receiver (EEVIR) – The EEVIR unit is similar in design to a valve-in-receiver type, except that it has an equalizer port on the expansion valve that allows for faster reaction time

Evaporator Pressure Regulator (EPR) valve – An evaporator temperature control device regulated by back pressure. Used on older Chrysler Corporation systems. Located in the compressor inlet. A system using this device is referred to as an EPR system.

Evaporator Temperature Regulator (ETR) valve – The ETR valve is a temperature-regulated evaporator temperature control device used on some early model Chrysler Corporation systems

Expansion tube – A device that converts high pressure liquid refrigerant into low pressure liquid refrigerant (thus lowering its boiling point) before it passes through the evaporator. The expansion valve replaces the thermostatic expansion valve. It's also referred to as a "fixed orifice tube."

Expansion valve – A device consisting of a metering valve and a temperature sensing capillary tube and bulb which meters refrigerant into the evaporator according to cooling requirements. Formally referred to as a "thermostatic expansion valve".

External equalizer – See "equalizer line"

Fahrenheit – A temperature scale which designates the freezing point of water as 32° and the boiling point of water as 212°

Fan clutch – A viscous (fluid) drive coupling device which permits variable engine fan speeds in relation to engine speeds

Feedback potentiometer – A variable resistance device which monitors the position of the shaft to which it is affixed and reports the position to the control head

Filter – A device used either with the drier or as a separate unit to remove foreign material (contaminants) from the refrigerant

Flooding – A term which refers to overcharging the system

Fluid – Any liquid or gas that is capable of flowing and that changes its shape at a steady rate when acted upon by a force tending to change its shape. A term used to refer to any substance having the above properties

Fluorocarbon – Any of a class of compounds produced by substituting fluorine for hydrogen in a hydrocarbon and characterized by great chemical stability. Fluorocarbons have numerous industrial application, but the chemical form dichlorodifluoromethane, known as R-12, is the form discussed in this book.

Flush – The removal of solid particles and sludge, such as metal flakes or casting flash, dirt or oil by running a pressurized cleaning solution through components and refrigerant lines

Foaming – The formation of bubbles in the oil and refrigerant caused by a rapid boiling out of the refrigerant dissolved in the oil when the pressure is suddenly reduced. If noted in the sight glass, this condition indicates a very low refrigerant level.

Ford Fixed Orifice Tube (FFOT) system – The FFOT system utilizes an accumulator instead of receiver-drier and an orifice tube instead of an expansion valve. The accumulator is located at the evaporator outlet. A pressure sensing switch cycles compressor operation.

Freeze-up – The failure of a unit to operate properly because of the formation of ice at the expansion valve orifice or on the evaporator coils or fins

Freezing point – The temperature at which a given liquid will turn to a solid. The freezing point varies with the pressure and the substance

Freon-12 – Another name for R-12, a type of refrigerant

Front-seat – A term used to denote the closed position of a stem type service valve to isolate the compressor. The system should never be operated with the valves in this position

Fuse – An electrical device used to protect a circuit against accidental overload

Gas – A vapor having no particles or droplets of liquid. In physics, a gas is a substance which possesses perfect molecular mobility and, unlike a liquid or a solid, the ability to expand indefinitely

Gauge manifold or gauge set – The one essential diagnostic tool required for every air conditioning service procedure. A typical gauge set includes high and low side gauges and valves for checking, measuring and controlling pressure and vacuum, and a third valve for controlling discharging, evacuation and charging procedures.

Head pressure – Refrigerant pressure in the lines and condenser between the discharge reed valve and the expansion valve orifice

Heat – The energy associated with the motion of atoms or molecules in solids, which can be transmitted through solid and fluid media by conduction, through fluid media by convection, and through empty space by radiation. All substances with temperatures above absolute zero contain heat.

Heat capacity – See "British Thermal Unit (BTU)"

Heater core – A finned unit through which coolant from the engine flows and over which air entering passenger compartment passes

Heat exchanger – A device which transfers the heat of one substance to another. The heater core, the condenser and the evaporator are heat exchangers.

Heat index – A number representing the effect of temperature and humidity on humans by combining the two variables into an "apparent " temperature. Introduced as a replacement for the temperature-humidity index. For example, a temperature of 90° and relative humidity of 65 percent combine to produce a heat index of 102.

Heat of condensation – The heat liberated by a unit mass of gas as its boiling point as it condenses to a liquid. Equal to the heat of vaporization.

Heat of vaporization – The heat absorbed per unit mass of a given material at its boiling point that completely converts the material to a gas at the same temperature. Equal to the heat of condensation.

Heat quantity – See "British Thermal Unit (BTU)"

Heat transmission – The flow of heat from one substance to another

Hg – The chemical symbol for Mercury. Used when referring to vacuum as inches of Mercury ("in-Hg").

High load condition – Denotes the condition that occurs when the air conditioning system must operate continuously at maximum capacity to supply enough cold air

High pressure line(s) – The line(s) carrying high pressure liquid and gas from the compressor outlet to the expansion valve inlet

"H" valve – The term used to denote a type of expansion valve used by Chrysler Corporation

High pressure relief valve – A safety valve located in the discharge line (six-cylinder compressors) or the compressor block (two-cylinder compressors)

High side – Another term for "discharge side." The part of the air conditioning system under high pressure, extending from the compressor outlet to the thermostatic expansion valve/tube inlet.

High side service valve – A device, located on the discharge or high side of the compressor, at which high side pressure can be checked and other service operations can be preformed

Hot gas – The state of refrigerant between the compressor and the condenser

Hot water vacuum valve – A vacuum actuated valve which controls the flow of coolant through the heater core

Humidity – The moisture or dampness in the air. Usually refers to an uncomfortably high level of humidity.

Icing switch – A device that cuts off the compressor when the evaporator temperature drops below a predetermined level

In-car sensor – A dual bimetal strip that samples passenger compartment air and controls a vacuum modulator

Inches of mercury – (in-Hg) A unit of measurement which designates the relative amount of vacuum present in a closed system

Incline compressor – Two-cylinder compressor with the pistons arranged side-by-side, like York or Tecumseh

Latent heat – The heat absorbed or radiated during a change of state at constant temperature and pressure. Called latent because it's "hidden," i.e. it cannot be felt or measured with a thermometer.

Latent heat of condensation – The amount of heat given of when a substance changes from a vapor to the liquid without changing temperature

Latent heat of evaporation – The amount of heat required to change a liquid into a vapor without raising the temperature of the vapor above that of the original liquid

Leak detector – Any device used to detect leaks in an air conditioning system (dye, solutions, electronic, propane, etc.)

Liquid line – The line between the drier outlet and the expansion valve. Sometimes, the line between the condenser outlet and the drier inlet is also referred to as a liquid line.

Low head pressure – Refers to a condition of lower-than-normal high side pressure caused by a system malfunction

Low pressure cut-out switch – A device that disengages the compressor clutch when the system pressure drops below a predetermined level

Low refrigerant protection system – A system which interrupts the electrical current to the compressor clutch in the event of refrigerant loss. A typical example is the General Motors superheat switch and thermal limiter.

Heating and air conditioning

Low side – Another term for "suction side." The low pressure part of the system between the expansion valve outlet and the compressor inlet.

Low side service valve – A device, located on the suction or low side of the compressor, at which low side pressure can be checked and other service operations can be performed

Low suction pressure – Refers to a condition of lower-than-normal high side pressure caused by a system malfunction

Magnetic clutch – A coupling device used to turn the compressor off and on electrically

Manifold - A device which controls refrigerant flow system test purposes by means of hand valves which can open or close various passageways connected together inside the manifold. Used in conjunction with manifold gauges and service hoses.

Manifold gauge set – A complete testing assembly consisting of a high side gauge, a low side gauge, an auxiliary gauge (optional), a test manifold and a set of service or charging hoses

Mercury – Sometimes referred to as "quicksilver." A heavy, silver-white, highly toxic metallic element, the only one that is liquid at room temperature. Used in thermometers and barometers. See "inches of mercury."

Mode door – A device which directs the flow of air through the heater/evaporator box

Muffler – A hollow, tubular device used in the discharge line of some systems to muffle the thumping sounds made by the compressor. Sometime used on the low side too.

Oil bleed line – An external oil line which circumvents the evaporator pressure regulator or bypass valve to ensure positive oil return to the compressor when rpms are high and the system is under a low charge or clogged

Oil bleed passage – An internal orifice which bypasses the evaporator pressure regulator, the bypass valve or the expansion valve to ensure positive oil return to the compressor

Operational test – A check of temperature and pressure conditions under controlled circumstances to determine whether the air conditioner is operating optimally

Overcharge – This term refers to the condition that occurs when too much refrigerant or oil is in the system

Performance test – "See "operational test"

Pilot Operated Absolute (POA) valve – The POA valve is suction throttling device used on some General Motors and Ford air conditioning systems. See "Suction Throttling Valve (STV)."

Plenum – One term for the air ducts, air valves and blower assembly inside the dash

Power servo – A vacuum-operated or electrically – powered device that actuates the duct doors and switches on systems equipped with automatic temperature control

Pressure – Force per unit area. As used in this book, the term refers to the refrigerant pressure, which is expressed in pounds per square inch (psi)

Pressure drop – The difference in pressure between two points in the system, usually caused by a restriction device

Pressure sending line – Also referred to as a capillary tube. Connects the remote bulb to the expansion valve.

Pressure sending switch – A device, used on some late model General Motors and Ford vehicles, which cycles compressor operation in accordance with pressure changes sensed at the accumulator

Programmer – The module that control blower speed, the air mix door, vacuum diaphragms and other devices in a system equipped with automatic temperature control

Propane – A flammable, heavier-than-air gas used in the Halide torch leak detector

psi – The abbreviation for pounds per square inch

psia – The abbreviation for pounds per square inch absolute

psig – The abbreviation for pounds per square inch gauge

Pump down – Another term for "evacuate"

Purging – Through evacuation of the air conditioning system

Radial compressor – A compressor with pistons radiating out from the centerline of the compressor. The Harrison (Frigidare) is a typical example.

Radiation – The process by which energy (such as heat) is emitted by one body, as particles or waves, transmitted through an intervening medium or space (like air), and absorbed by another body. Also refers to the energy transferred by this process

Ram air – A term referring to the air forced through the condenser coils by vehicle movement or fan action

Receiver drier – Also referred to as a receiver-dehydrator. A container for storing liquid refrigerant and a desiccant. Used in Chrysler Corporation and some import vehicles.

Reciprocating compressor – Any positive displacement compressor that has piston which travel back-and-forth in cylinders

Reed valves – Wafer-thin metal plates located in the valve plate of an automotive compressor which acts as suction and discharge valves. The suction valve is located on the underside of the valve plate; the discharge valve is situated on the top.

Refrigerant-12 – The chemical substance (CCl_2F_2) used in automotive air conditioning systems to absorb, carry and release heat. Usually referred to simply as R-12. A member of the fluorocarbon family. See "dichlorodifluoromethane," "fluorocarbon."

Refrigeration cycle – The complete circulation of refrigerant through an air conditioning system as it changes temperature and pressure, i.e. changes its state from vapor to liquid, then back to vapor

Refrigeration oil – A highly refined lubricating oil which is free from contaminants such as sulfur, moisture and tar

Relative humidity – The amount of water vapor in the air, expressed as a percentage of the maximum amount the air could hold at the given temperature. The ratio of the actual water vapor pressure to the saturation vapor pressure. Usually referred to as "humidity."

Remote bulb – A sensing device connected to the expansion valve by a capillary tube. The bulb senses the temperature of the evaporator outlet pipe and controls the expansion valve accordingly.

Resistor – An electronic device that reduces voltage to regulate an electric motor. In this book, the term refers to the blower motor resistor, which regulates fan speed.

Restrictor – A porous device located in vacuum lines to delay vacuum applied to diaphragms

Relay – An electrical switch that transmits impulses from one component to another

Rheostat – A variable resistor used to control blower speeds

Rotary compressor – A compressor which has rotating rotors, or vanes, that compress and pump refrigerant

Schrader valve – A spring-loaded valve, similar to a tire valve, located inside the service valve fitting to hold refrigerant in the system. Special adapters with built-in depressors must be used to attach service hoses to Schrader valves.

Service hose – Specially manufactured hose designed to withstand the operating pressures of air conditioning systems. Equipped with threaded fittings that can be attached to service valves, manifold gauge sets, vacuum pumps, refrigerant containers, etc.

Service port – A fitting, on stem-type service valves and some control devices, to which manifold gauge set service hoses can be connected

Service valve – Another name for either the high or low side service valves. See "high side service valve," "low side service valve."

Servo motor – A calibrated vacuum or electrical motor used to position valves or doors in an automotive air conditioning system

Shaft seal – See "compressor shaft seal"

Short cycling – A term referring to the condition in which the compressor in a cycling clutch system cycles too frequently

Sight glass – A glass window in the liquid line, the top of the receiver-drier, or a test manifold, for checking refrigerant flow

Silica gel – A highly absorbent drying agent, usually located in the accumulator or receiver-drier, used to remove moisture from refrigerant

Solenoid – An electro-magnetic relay

Specific heat – In physics, the number of calories to raise the temperature of 1 gram of a substance 1° C, or the number of BTUs per pound per degree F. In air conditioning, the quality of heat required to change the temperature of one pound of a substance by 1° F.

Suction line – The line between the evaporator outlet and the compressor inlet

Suction pressure – Compressor inlet pressure. Another name for "low side pressure"

Suction service valve – See "low side service valve"

Suction side – The low-pressure part of the air conditioning system between the orifice/expansion tube, or expansion vale outlet, and the compressor inlet

Suction Throttling Valve (STV) – A backpressure-regulated device, used on some Ford and General Motors systems, that controls refrigerant flow to prevent evaporator core freeze-up. See "Pilot Operated Absolute (POA) valve".

Superheat – Also known as superheated vapor. A gas or vapor that is not in contact with the generating liquid (steam not in contact with water, for example), that has been heated to such a degree that its temperature may

Heating and air conditioning

be lowered or its pressure increased without the conversion of any of the gas to liquid

Superheat switch – A device that is connected in series with a thermal limiter (fuse). Mounted on the rear of the compressor on General Motors systems equipped with low refrigerant protection.

Temperature – The measure of heat intensity or concentration, expressed in degrees. Measured by a thermometer. Temperature is not a measure of heat quantity.

Temperature dial – A calibrated control lever or wheel used to regulate automatic temperature control system modes

Temperature-humidity index – A number representing an estimate of the effect of temperature and moisture on humans, computed by multiplying the sum of dry-bulb and wet-bulb temperature readings by 0.4 and adding 15, with 65 assumed as the highest comfortable index.

Thermal – Of, pertaining to or caused by heat or temperature

Thermal limiter – A fuse like device that protects the low refrigerant protection system circuit on General Motors vehicles. Stops compressor operation when low pressure is sensed.

Thermistor – A temperature-sensitive, heat-activated resistor. Used in air conditioning system sensors.

Thermostatic expansion valve – A component which regulates the rate of refrigerant flow into the evaporator as determined by the outlet pipe temperatures sensed by the remote bulb.

Thermostatic switch – A temperature sensitive switch that prevents icing by cycling compressor operation control system temperature. Bellows and bimetallic switches are typical examples.

Throttling valve – See "Suction Throttling Valve (STV)" and "Evaporator Pressure Regulator (EPR) valve"

Transducer – Any device that converts an input signal into an output signal. Used to actuate electric or vacuum servo motors in an automatic temperature control system.

Undercharge – A term referring to a system low on refrigerant, resulting in improper cooling

Vacuum – A controlled, contained system, or condition, with lower-than-ambient-atmospheric pressure. Expressed in inches of mercury (in-Hg). A "perfect vacuum" is 29.92 in-Hg (a vacuum above a column of mercury will support the column to a height of 29.92 inches).

Vacuum motor – A vacuum-actuated device used to operate doors and valves

Vacuum power unit – A device for operating air conditioning doors and valves using vacuum as a source of power

Vacuum pump – A mechanical device used to evacuate an air conditioning system to rid it of moisture, air and contaminants

Valves-in-Receiver (VIR) unit – A component used on General Motors systems, in which the thermostatic expansion valve, POA suction throttling valve, the receiver-drier and, if equipped, the sight glass are all combined into one assembly

Vapor – The gaseous state of refrigerant

Vapor lines – Air conditioning system lines in which refrigerant is normally in a gaseous or vapor state

Variable displacement compressor – A compressor which can change it output in accordance with the conditions

Viscosity – The thickness of a liquid or its resistance to flow

Volatile liquid – A liquid that is easily evaporated

V-type compressor – A compressor with its pistons arranged in a vee-shaped configuration

Water valve – A shut-off valve, mechanically or vacuum operated, for stopping the flow of hot coolant to the heater

Index

A

Accumulator replacement, 5-28
Acknowledgements, 0-2
Aftermarket retrofits, 5-47
Air conditioning components, 2-3
    accumulator (orifice tube type systems), 2-10
    compressor, 2-4
    condenser, 2-9
    evaporator, 2-20
    receiver-drier, 2-10
Air conditioning system, 5-6
    control components, 2-21
    high-pressure fan switch, 2-27
    safety precautions, 5-6
Air power (venturi type) vacuum pumps, 4-8
Ambient temperature switch, 2-24
Anti-dieseling relay, 2-31
Attaching the manifold gauge set, 4-6

B

Basic air conditioning and heating system components, 2-1 through 2-32
    air conditioning components, 2-3
        accumulator (orifice tube type systems), 2-10
        compressor, 2-4
        condenser, 2-9
        receiver-drier, 2-10
    air conditioning system
        ambient temperature switch, 2-24
        compressor controls, 2-22
        compressor crankcase pressure control valve (variable displacement compressors), 2-26
        control components, 2-21
        high pressure cut-out switch, 2-23
        ON switch, 2-27
        pressure-sensitive (cycling) switch (orifice tube type systems), 2-24
        thermal fuse/superheat switch, 2-25
        thermostatic switch, 2-25
        trinary switch, 2-24
        using an expansion valve, 2-2
        using an orifice tube, 2-3
    anti-dieseling relay, 2-31
    basic types of air conditioning systems, 2-2
    closed throttle switch, 2-30
    compressor delay timer, 2-31
    condenser fan controls, 2-26
    constant run relay, 2-31
    controlling refrigerant flow to the evaporator, 2-11
    cooling system fan temperature switch, 2-27
    driveability controls, 2-30
    engine coolant high temperature switch, 2-31
    evaporator, 2-20
    evaporator controls, 2-27
    Evaporator Pressure Regulator (EPR) valve, 2-29
    Evaporator-Equalized Valves-In-Receiver (EEVIR), 2-29
    heating system components, 2-1
    high-pressure relief valve, 2-32
    low vacuum switch, 2-30
    orifice tubes, 2-19
    Pilot Operated Absolute Suction Throttling Valve (POA STV), 2-28
    power brake switch, 2-31
    power steering pressure switch, 2-30
    pressure-sensitive air conditioning system fan switch, 2-27
    R-134a system components, 2-32

Heating and air conditioning

Suction Throttling Valve (STV), 2-28
thermostatic expansion valve, 2-12
time delay relay, 2-30
Valves-In-Receiver (VIR), 2-29
wide-open throttle switch, 2-30
Basic theory of air conditioning system operation, 1-1 through 1-10
    air conditioners, 1-4
    convection, conduction and radiation, 1-3
    effect of pressure on boiling or condensation, 1-7
    heat, 1-2
    heat moves from warmer to cooler substances, 1-3
    heat transfer, 1-5
    latent heat of vaporization, 1-6
    pressure-temperature relationship of R-12, 1-9
    R-134a, 1-10
    Refrigerant-12, 1-8
    The comfort zone?, 1-1
    the heating system, 1-3
    What is automotive air conditioning?, 1-5
Bubble detector, 4-12

C

Closed throttle switch, 2-30
Combination by-pass orifice (BPO) expansion valve and suction throttling valve (STV) replacement, 5-30
Compressor
    controls, 2-22
    crankcase pressure control valve (variable displacement compressors), 2-26
    delay timer, 2-31
    oil check, 5-33
    reed valve replacement, 5-31
        Chrysler C-171 and Ford FS-6 6-cylinder compressors, 5-32
        Chrysler, Tecumseh and York two-cylinder and Sanden (Sankyo) five-cylinder units, 5-31
        Nippondenso 10-cylinder compressor, 5-32
Compressors, 5-51
Condenser fan controls, 2-26
Condensers and pressure cutout switches, 5-52
Constant run relay, 2-31
Contaminated refrigerant, 5-20
Cooling system fan temperature switch, 2-27
Correcting the gauge pressure reading for altitude, 4-4

D

Desiccant bag replacement, 5-26
Driveability controls, 2-30

E

Electronic sight glass (non-accumulator type systems), 4-14
Engine coolant high temperature switch, 2-31
EPA requirements for retrofit, 5-49
Evacuating and charging accumulator systems, 5-43
Evaporator controls, 2-27
Evaporator Pressure Regulator (EPR) valve, 2-29
Evaporator-Equalized Valves-In-Receiver (EEVIR), 2-29

F

Flushing to remove contaminants, 5-21

G

Glossary, GL-1 through GL-8

H

Halide (propane) torch leak detectors, 4-13
Halogen (electric) leak testers, 4-13
Heater and air conditioning ducts, 5-5
Heating and air conditioning system service and repair, 5-1 through 5-132
    a few more words on non-R-134a refrigerants, 5-49
    a typical R-134a conversion, 5-53
    accumulator replacement, 5-28
    aftermarket retrofits, 5-47
    air conditioning system, 5-6
    cautions, 5-52
    charging (non-accumulator type systems), 5-42
    combination by-pass orifice (BPO) expansion valve and suction throttling valve (STV) replacement, 5-30
    compressor oil check, 5-33
    compressor reed valve replacement
        Chrysler C-171 and Ford FS-6 6-cylinder compressors, 5-32
        Chrysler, Tecumseh and York two-cylinder and Sanden (Sankyo) five-cylinder units, 5-31
        Nippondenso 10-cylinder compressor, 5-32
    compressors, 5-51
    condensers and pressure cutout switches, 5-52
    connecting the gauge set, 5-9, 5-12
    contaminated refrigerant, 5-20
    converting from R-12 to R-134a, 5-46

cooling the condenser while using the electronic sight glass, 5-17
desiccant bag replacement, 5-26
desiccants, accumulators, receiver/driers, 5-52
discharging, 5-21
EPA Requirements for Retrofit, 5-49
evacuating a non-accumulator type system, 5-41
evacuating and charging accumulator systems, 5-43
    Ford Motor Company Ford Fixed Orifice Tube (FFOT) system, 5-44
    General Motors Cycling Clutch Orifice Tube (CCOT) system, 5-43
evacuating the system, 5-40
final performance test, 5-46
flushing the system, 5-2
flushing to remove contaminants, 5-21
heater and air conditioning ducts, 5-5
heating system, 5-1
hoses and O-rings, 5-51
inspecting the heating system, 5-1
leak testing, 5-18
lubricants, 5-50
make sure the system is fully charged, 5-15
OEM retrofits, 5-47
orifice tube (expansion tube) replacement, 5-29
picking the right solution for you, 5-48
preliminary system inspection, 5-7
R-12 service valves, 5-10
R-134a refrigerant, 5-50
R-134a service valves, 5-14
receiver-drier or desiccant replacement, 5-27
refrigerant controls, 5-52
removing contaminants, 5-20
repairing the system, 5-23
resources, 5-59
rule of thumb guide for adding oil to individual components, 5-34
safety precautions, 5-6
Schrader type R-12 valves, 5-11
special high-side R-12 service valves, 5-12
stabilizing the system, 5-14
stem type R-12 service valves, 5-10
stem type service valves, 5-14
Suction Throttling Valve (STV) and Evaporator Pressure Regulator (EPR) valve replacement, 5-30
system performance test, 5-17
terminology, 5-47
testing for proper refrigerant charge with an electronic sight glass, 5-16
the sight glass (non-accumulator systems), 5-8
Heating system, 5-1
    components, 2-1
    flushing, 5-2
High pressure cut-out switch, 2-23
High-pressure relief valve, 2-32

L

Leak testers, 4-12
    bubble detector, 4-12
    electronic sight glass (non-accumulator type systems), 4-14
    halide (propane) torch leak detectors, 4-13
    halogen (electric) leak testers, 4-13
Low vacuum switch, 2-30

M

Manifold gauge set (test gauges), 4-1
    auxiliary gauge, 4-2
    hoses, 4-3
    manifold hand valves, 4-2
    measuring pressure, 4-3
    pounds per square inch gauge (psig), 4-4
    the "high side" gauge, 4-2
    the "low side" gauge, 4-2
Manifold gauges for R-134a systems, 4-3

O

OEM retrofits, 5-47
Orifice tubes, 2-19

P

Pilot Operated Absolute Suction Throttling Valve (POA STV), 2-28
Power brake switch, 2-31
Power steering pressure switch, 2-30
Preface, 0-5
Pressure-sensitive (cycling) switch (orifice tube type systems), 2-24
Pressure specifications, 5-61 through 5-132

R

R-12 system charging tools and equipment, 4-10
R-134a system components, 2-32
R-134a systems, service requirements, 4-11
Refrigerant controls, 5-52
Repairing the system, 5-23
Rotary vane type vacuum pumps, 4-9

S

Service adapter for R-12 systems, 4-6
Service and diagnostic tools, 4-1 through 4-14
  attaching the manifold gauge set, 4-6
  correcting the gauge pressure reading for
    altitude, 4-4
  Don't mix refrigerants!, 4-12
  leak testers, 4-12
  manifold gauge set (test gauges), 4-1
    auxiliary gauge, 4-2
    hoses, 4-3
    manifold gauges for R-134a systems, 4-3
    manifold hand valves, 4-2
    measuring pressure, 4-3
    measuring vacuum, 4-5
    pounds per square inch gauge (psig), 4-4
    the "high side" gauge, 4-2
    the "low side" gauge, 4-2
  R-12 system charging tools and equipment, 4-10
  service adapter for R-12 systems, 4-6
  service fitting for R-134a systems, 4-7
  system evacuation tools, 4-8
  thermometers, 4-7
  What about R-134a systems?, 4-11
Service fitting for R-134a systems, 4-7
Sight glass (non-accumulator systems), 5-8
Suction Throttling Valve (STV), 2-28
Suction Throttling Valve (STV) and Evaporator
  Pressure Regulator (EPR) valve replacement, 5-30
System evacuation tools, 4-8
  air power (venturi type) vacuum pumps, 4-8
  rotary vane type vacuum pumps, 4-9
  vacuum pumps, 4-8

T

Testing for proper refrigerant charge with an
  electronic sight glass, 5-16

Thermal fuse/superheat switch, 2-25
Thermometers, 4-7
Thermostatic expansion valve, 2-12
Thermostatic switch, 2-25
Time delay relay, 2-30
Trinary switch, 2-24
Troubleshooting, 6-1 through 6-40
  air conditioning systems, 6-4
  expansion valve system troubleshooting, 6-18
  fault diagnosis flowcharts, 6-6
  Ford fixed orifice tube (FFOT) system
    troubleshooting, 6-28
  General Motors cycling clutch orifice tube (CCOT)
    system troubleshooting, 6-37
  heater system trouble diagnosis, 6-1
  heaters, 6-1
  manifold gauge tests, 6-13
  normal manifold gauge readings, 6-13
  pressure/temperature relationship, 6-19
  systems with the Harrison V5 compressor, 6-39
Typical automotive air conditioning systems,
  3-1 through 3-8
  automatic systems, 3-6
  high and low sides of the air conditioning
    system?, 3-1
  manually controlled systems, 3-2
  R-134a systems, 3-8

V

Vacuum pumps, 4-8
Vacuum, measuring, 4-5
Valves-In-Receiver (VIR), 2-29

W

What about R-134a systems?, 4-11
Wide-open throttle switch, 2-30

Haynes Automotive Manuals

NOTE: New manuals are added to this list on a periodic basis. If you do not see a listing for your vehicle, consult your local Haynes dealer for the latest product information.

ACURA
12020 Integra '86 thru '89 & Legend '86 thru '90
12021 Integra '90 thru '93 & Legend '91 thru '95

AMC
      Jeep CJ - see JEEP (50020)
14020 Mid-size models '70 thru '83
14025 (Renault) Alliance & Encore '83 thru '87

AUDI
15020 4000 all models '80 thru '87
15025 5000 all models '77 thru '83
15026 5000 all models '84 thru '88

AUSTIN-HEALEY
      Sprite - see MG Midget (66015)

BMW
*18020 3/5 Series not including diesel or
       all-wheel drive models '82 thru '92
18021 3-Series incl. Z3 models '92 thru '98
18025 320i all 4 cyl models '75 thru '83
18050 1500 thru 2002 except Turbo '59 thru '77

BUICK
*19010 Buick Century '97 thru '02
       Century (front-wheel drive) - see GM (38005)
*19020 Buick, Oldsmobile & Pontiac Full-size
       (Front-wheel drive) '85 thru '02
       Buick Electra, LeSabre and Park Avenue;
       Oldsmobile Delta 88 Royale, Ninety Eight
       and Regency; Pontiac Bonneville
19025 Buick Oldsmobile & Pontiac Full-size
      (Rear wheel drive)
      Buick Estate '70 thru '90, Electra'70 thru '84,
      LeSabre '70 thru '85, Limited '74 thru '79
      Oldsmobile Custom Cruiser '70 thru '90,
      Delta 88 '70 thru '85,Ninety-eight '70 thru '84
      Pontiac Bonneville '70 thru '81,
      Catalina '70 thru '81, Grandville '70 thru '75,
      Parisienne '83 thru '86
19030 Mid-size Regal & Century all rear-drive
      models with V6, V8 and Turbo '74 thru '87
      Regal - see GENERAL MOTORS (38010)
      Riviera - see GENERAL MOTORS (38030)
      Roadmaster - see CHEVROLET (24046)
      Skyhawk - see GENERAL MOTORS (38015)
      Skylark - see GM (38020, 38025)
      Somerset - see GENERAL MOTORS (38025)

CADILLAC
21030 Cadillac Rear Wheel Drive
      all gasoline models '70 thru '93
      Cimarron - see GENERAL MOTORS (38015)
      DeVille - see GM (38031 & 38032)
      Eldorado - see GM (38030 & 38031)
      Fleetwood - see GM (38031)
      Seville - see GM (38030, 38031 & 38032)

CHEVROLET
*24010 Astro & GMC Safari Mini-vans '85 thru '03
24015 Camaro V8 all models '70 thru '81
24016 Camaro all models '82 thru '92
24017 Camaro & Firebird '93 thru '02
      Cavalier - see GENERAL MOTORS (38016)
      Celebrity - see GENERAL MOTORS (38005)
24020 Chevelle, Malibu & El Camino '69 thru '87
24024 Chevette & Pontiac T1000 '76 thru '87
      Citation - see GENERAL MOTORS (38020)
24032 Corsica/Beretta all models '87 thru '96
24040 Corvette all V8 models '68 thru '82
24041 Corvette all models '84 thru '96
10305 Chevrolet Engine Overhaul Manual
24045 Full-size Sedans Caprice, Impala, Biscayne,
      Bel Air & Wagons '69 thru '90
24046 Impala SS & Caprice and
      Buick Roadmaster '91 thru '96
      Impala - see LUMINA (24048)
      Lumina '90 thru '94 - see GM (38010)
*24048 Lumina & Monte Carlo '95 thru '03
      Lumina APV - see GM (38035)
24050 Luv Pick-up all 2WD & 4WD '72 thru '82
      Malibu '97 thru '00 - see GM (38026)
24055 Monte Carlo all models '70 thru '88
      Monte Carlo '95 thru '01 - see LUMINA (24048)

24059 Nova all V8 models '69 thru '79
24060 Nova and Geo Prizm '85 thru '92
24064 Pick-ups '67 thru '87 - Chevrolet & GMC,
      all V8 & in-line 6 cyl, 2WD & 4WD '67 thru '87;
      Suburbans, Blazers & Jimmys '67 thru '91
24065 Pick-ups '88 thru '98 - Chevrolet & GMC,
      full-size pick-ups '88 thru '98,
      C/K Classic '99 & '00, Blazer &
      Jimmy '92 thru '94; Suburban '92 thru '99;
      Tahoe & Yukon '95 thru '99
*24066 Pick-ups '99 thru '03 - Chevrolet Silverado
      & GMC Sierra full-size pick-ups '99 thru '02,
      Suburban/Tahoe/Yukon/Yukon XL '00 thru '02
24070 S-10 & S-15 Pick-ups '82 thru '93,
      Blazer & Jimmy '83 thru '94,
*24071 S-10 & S-15 Pick-ups '94 thru '01, Blazer
      & Jimmy '95 thru '01, Hombre '96 thru '01
*24072 Chevrolet TrailBlazer & TrailBlazer EXT,
      GMC Envoy & Envoy XL, Oldsmobile
      Bravada '02 and '03
24075 Sprint '85 thru '88 & Geo Metro '89 thru '01
24080 Vans - Chevrolet & GMC '68 thru '96

CHRYSLER
25015 Chrysler Cirrus, Dodge Stratus,
      Plymouth Breeze '95 thru '00
10310 Chrysler Engine Overhaul Manual
25020 Full-size Front-Wheel Drive '88 thru '93
      K-Cars - see DODGE Aries (30008)
      Laser - see DODGE Daytona (30030)
25025 Chrysler LHS, Concorde, New Yorker,
      Dodge Intrepid, Eagle Vision, '93 thru '97
*25026 Chrysler LHS, Concorde, 300M,
      Dodge Intrepid, '98 thru '03
25030 Chrysler & Plymouth Mid-size
      front wheel drive '82 thru '95
      Rear-wheel Drive - see Dodge (30050)
*25035 PT Cruiser all models '01 thru '03
*25040 Chrysler Sebring, Dodge Avenger '95 thru '02

DATSUN
28005 200SX all models '80 thru '83
28007 B-210 all models '73 thru '78
28009 210 all models '79 thru '82
28012 240Z, 260Z & 280Z Coupe '70 thru '78
28014 280ZX Coupe & 2+2 '79 thru '83
      300ZX - see NISSAN (72010)
28016 310 all models '78 thru '82
28018 510 & PL521 Pick-up '68 thru '73
28020 510 all models '78 thru '81
28022 620 Series Pick-up all models '73 thru '79
      720 Series Pick-up - see NISSAN (72030)
28025 810/Maxima all gasoline models, '77 thru '84

DODGE
      400 & 600 - see CHRYSLER (25030)
30008 Aries & Plymouth Reliant '81 thru '89
30010 Caravan & Plymouth Voyager '84 thru '95
*30011 Caravan & Plymouth Voyager '96 thru '02
30012 Challenger/Plymouth Saporro '78 thru '83
30016 Colt & Plymouth Champ '78 thru '87
30020 Dakota Pick-ups all models '87 thru '96
*30021 Durango '98 & '99, Dakota '97 thru '99
30025 Dart, Demon, Plymouth Barracuda,
      Duster & Valiant 6 cyl models '67 thru '76
30030 Daytona & Chrysler Laser '84 thru '89
      Intrepid - see CHRYSLER (25025, 25026)
*30034 Neon all models '95 thru '99
30035 Omni & Plymouth Horizon '78 thru '90
30040 Pick-ups all full-size models '74 thru '93
*30041 Pick-ups all full-size models '94 thru '01
30045 Ram 50/D50 Pick-ups & Raider and
      Plymouth Arrow Pick-ups '79 thru '93
30050 Dodge/Plymouth/Chrysler RWD '71 thru '89
30055 Shadow & Plymouth Sundance '87 thru '94
30060 Spirit & Plymouth Acclaim '89 thru '95
*30065 Vans - Dodge & Plymouth '71 thru '03

EAGLE
      Talon - see MITSUBISHI (68030, 68031)
      Vision - see CHRYSLER (25025)

FIAT
34010 124 Sport Coupe & Spider '68 thru '78
34025 X1/9 all models '74 thru '80

FORD
10355 Ford Automatic Transmission Overhaul
36004 Aerostar Mini-vans all models '86 thru '97
36006 Contour & Mercury Mystique '95 thru '00
36008 Courier Pick-up all models '72 thru '82
*36012 Crown Victoria & Mercury Grand
       Marquis '88 thru '00
10320 Ford Engine Overhaul Manual
36016 Escort/Mercury Lynx all models '81 thru '90
36020 Escort/Mercury Tracer '91 thru '00
36022 Ford Escape & Mazda Tribute '01 thru '03
36024 Explorer & Mazda Navajo '91 thru '01
36025 Ford Explorer & Mercury Mountaineer
      '02 and '03
36028 Fairmont & Mercury Zephyr '78 thru '83
36030 Festiva & Aspire '88 thru '97
36032 Fiesta all models '77 thru '80
*36034 Focus all models '00 and '01
36036 Ford & Mercury Full-size '75 thru '87
36044 Ford & Mercury Mid-size '75 thru '86
36048 Mustang V8 all models '64-1/2 thru '73
36049 Mustang II 4 cyl, V6 & V8 models '74 thru '78
36050 Mustang & Mercury Capri all models
      Mustang, '79 thru '93; Capri, '79 thru '86
*36051 Mustang all models '94 thru '03
36054 Pick-ups & Bronco '73 thru '79
36058 Pick-ups & Bronco '80 thru '96
*36059 F-150 & Expedition '97 thru '02, F-250 '97
      thru '99 & Lincoln Navigator '98 thru '02
*36060 Super Duty Pick-ups, Excursion '97 thru '02
36062 Pinto & Mercury Bobcat '75 thru '80
36066 Probe all models '89 thru '92
36070 Ranger/Bronco II gasoline models '83 thru '92
*36071 Ranger '93 thru '00 &
      Mazda Pick-ups '94 thru '00
36074 Taurus & Mercury Sable '86 thru '95
*36075 Taurus & Mercury Sable '96 thru '01
36078 Tempo & Mercury Topaz '84 thru '94
36082 Thunderbird/Mercury Cougar '83 thru '88
36086 Thunderbird/Mercury Cougar '89 and '97
36090 Vans all V8 Econoline models '69 thru '91
*36094 Vans full size '92 thru '01
*36097 Windstar Mini-van '95 thru '03

GENERAL MOTORS
10360 GM Automatic Transmission Overhaul
38005 Buick Century, Chevrolet Celebrity,
      Oldsmobile Cutlass Ciera & Pontiac 6000
      all models '82 thru '96
*38010 Buick Regal, Chevrolet Lumina,
      Oldsmobile Cutlass Supreme &
      Pontiac Grand Prix (FWD) '88 thru '02
38015 Buick Skyhawk, Cadillac Cimarron,
      Chevrolet Cavalier, Oldsmobile Firenza &
      Pontiac J-2000 & Sunbird '82 thru '94
*38016 Chevrolet Cavalier &
      Pontiac Sunfire '95 thru '04
38020 Buick Skylark, Chevrolet Citation,
      Olds Omega, Pontiac Phoenix '80 thru '85
38025 Buick Skylark & Somerset,
      Oldsmobile Achieva & Calais and
      Pontiac Grand Am all models '85 thru '98
*38026 Chevrolet Malibu, Olds Alero & Cutlass,
      Pontiac Grand Am '97 thru '00
38030 Cadillac Eldorado '71 thru '85,
      Seville '80 thru '85, Oldsmobile
      Toronado '71 thru '85, Buick Riviera '79 thru '85
*38031 Cadillac Eldorado & Seville '86 thru '91,
      DeVille '86 thru '93, Fleetwood & Olds
      Toronado '86 thru '92, Buick Riviera '86 thru '93
38032 Cadillac DeVille '94 thru '02
      & Seville - '92 thru '02
38035 Chevrolet Lumina APV, Olds Silhouette
      & Pontiac Trans Sport all models '90 thru '96
*38036 Chevrolet Venture, Olds Silhouette,
      Pontiac Trans Sport & Montana '97 thru '01
      General Motors Full-size
      Rear-wheel Drive - see BUICK (19025)

GEO
      Metro - see CHEVROLET Sprint (24075)
      Prizm - '85 thru '92 see CHEVY (24060),
      '93 thru '02 see TOYOTA Corolla (92036)

(Continued on other side)

* Listings shown with an asterisk (*) indicate model coverage as of this printing. These titles will be periodically updated to include later model years - consult your Haynes dealer for more information.

Haynes North America, Inc., 861 Lawrence Drive, Newbury Park, CA 91320-1514 • (805) 498-6703

Haynes Automotive Manuals (continued)

NOTE: New manuals are added to this list on a periodic basis. If you do not see a listing for your vehicle, consult your local Haynes dealer for the latest product information.

40030 Storm all models '90 thru '93
Tracker - see SUZUKI Samurai (90010)

GMC
Vans & Pick-ups - see CHEVROLET

HONDA
42010 Accord CVCC all models '76 thru '83
42011 Accord all models '84 thru '89
42012 Accord all models '90 thru '93
42013 Accord all models '94 thru '97
*42014 Accord all models '98 thru '02
42020 Civic 1200 all models '73 thru '79
42021 Civic 1300 & 1500 CVCC '80 thru '83
42022 Civic 1500 CVCC all models '75 thru '79
42023 Civic all models '84 thru '91
42024 Civic & del Sol '92 thru '95
*42025 Civic '96 thru '00, CR-V '97 thru '00, Acura Integra '94 thru '00
42026 Civic '01 thru '04, CR-V '02 thru '04
42040 Prelude CVCC all models '79 thru '89

HYUNDAI
*43010 Elantra all models '96 thru '01
43015 Excel & Accent all models '86 thru '98

ISUZU
Hombre - see CHEVROLET S-10 (24071)
*47017 Rodeo '91 thru '02; Amigo '89 thru '94 and '98 thru '02; Honda Passport '95 thru '02
47020 Trooper & Pick-up '81 thru '93

JAGUAR
49010 XJ6 all 6 cyl models '68 thru '86
49011 XJ6 all models '88 thru '94
49015 XJ12 & XJS all 12 cyl models '72 thru '85

JEEP
50010 Cherokee, Comanche & Wagoneer Limited all models '84 thru '01
50020 CJ all models '49 thru '86
*50025 Grand Cherokee all models '93 thru '04
50029 Grand Wagoneer & Pick-up '72 thru '91 Grand Wagoneer '84 thru '91, Cherokee & Wagoneer '72 thru '83, Pick-up '72 thru '88
*50030 Wrangler all models '87 thru '00
50035 Liberty '02 thru '04

LEXUS
ES 300 - see TOYOTA Camry (92007)

LINCOLN
Navigator - see FORD Pick-up (36059)
*59010 Rear-Wheel Drive all models '70 thru '01

MAZDA
61010 GLC Hatchback (rear-wheel drive) '77 thru '83
61011 GLC (front-wheel drive) '81 thru '85
61015 323 & Protegé '90 thru '00
*61016 MX-5 Miata '90 thru '97
61020 MPV all models '89 thru '94
Navajo - see Ford Explorer (36024)
61030 Pick-ups '72 thru '93
Pick-ups '94 thru '00 - see Ford Ranger (36071)
61035 RX-7 all models '79 thru '85
61036 RX-7 all models '86 thru '91
61040 626 (rear-wheel drive) all models '79 thru '82
61041 626/MX-6 (front-wheel drive) '83 thru '91
61042 626 '93 thru '01, MX-6/Ford Probe '93 thru '97

MERCEDES-BENZ
63012 123 Series Diesel '76 thru '85
63015 190 Series four-cyl gas models, '84 thru '88
63020 230/250/280 6 cyl sohc models '68 thru '72
63025 280 123 Series gasoline models '77 thru '81
63030 350 & 450 all models '71 thru '80

MERCURY
64200 Villager & Nissan Quest '93 thru '01
All other titles, see FORD Listing.

MG
66010 MGB Roadster & GT Coupe '62 thru '80
66015 MG Midget, Austin Healey Sprite '58 thru '80

MITSUBISHI
68020 Cordia, Tredia, Galant, Precis & Mirage '83 thru '93
68030 Eclipse, Eagle Talon & Ply. Laser '90 thru '94
*68031 Eclipse '95 thru '01, Eagle Talon '95 thru '98
68035 Mitsubishi Galant '94 thru '03
68040 Pick-up '83 thru '96 & Montero '83 thru '93

NISSAN
72010 300ZX all models including Turbo '84 thru '89
72015 Altima all models '93 thru '04
72020 Maxima all models '85 thru '92
*72021 Maxima all models '93 thru '01
72030 Pick-ups '80 thru '97 Pathfinder '87 thru '95
*72031 Frontier Pick-up '98 thru '01, Xterra '00 & '01, Pathfinder '96 thru '01
72040 Pulsar all models '83 thru '86
Quest - see MERCURY Villager (64200)
72050 Sentra all models '82 thru '94
72051 Sentra & 200SX all models '95 thru '99
72060 Stanza all models '82 thru '90

OLDSMOBILE
73015 Cutlass V6 & V8 gas models '74 thru '88
For other OLDSMOBILE titles, see BUICK, CHEVROLET or GENERAL MOTORS listing.

PLYMOUTH
For PLYMOUTH titles, see DODGE listing.

PONTIAC
79008 Fiero all models '84 thru '88
79018 Firebird V8 models except Turbo '70 thru '81
79019 Firebird all models '82 thru '92
79040 Mid-size Rear-wheel Drive '70 thru '87
For other PONTIAC titles, see BUICK, CHEVROLET or GENERAL MOTORS listing.

PORSCHE
80020 911 except Turbo & Carrera 4 '65 thru '89
80025 914 all 4 cyl models '69 thru '76
80030 924 all models including Turbo '76 thru '82
80035 944 all models including Turbo '83 thru '89

RENAULT
Alliance & Encore - see AMC (14020)

SAAB
*84010 900 all models including Turbo '79 thru '88

SATURN
*87010 Saturn all models '91 thru '02
87020 Saturn all L-series models '00 thru '04

SUBARU
89002 1100, 1300, 1400 & 1600 '71 thru '79
89003 1600 & 1800 2WD & 4WD '80 thru '94

SUZUKI
90010 Samurai/Sidekick & Geo Tracker '86 thru '01

TOYOTA
92005 Camry all models '83 thru '91
92006 Camry all models '92 thru '96
*92007 Camry, Avalon, Solara, Lexus ES 300 '97 thru '01
92015 Celica Rear Wheel Drive '71 thru '85
92020 Celica Front Wheel Drive '86 thru '99
92025 Celica Supra all models '79 thru '92
92030 Corolla all models '75 thru '79
92032 Corolla all rear wheel drive models '80 thru '87
92035 Corolla all front wheel drive models '84 thru '92
92036 Corolla & Geo Prizm '93 thru '02
92040 Corolla Tercel all models '80 thru '82
92045 Corona all models '74 thru '82
92050 Cressida all models '78 thru '82
92055 Land Cruiser FJ40, 43, 45, 55 '68 thru '82
92056 Land Cruiser FJ60, 62, 80, FZJ80 '80 thru '96
92065 MR2 all models '85 thru '87
92070 Pick-up all models '69 thru '78
92075 Pick-up all models '79 thru '95
*92076 Tacoma '95 thru '00, 4Runner '96 thru '00, & T100 '93 thru '98
*92078 Tundra '00 thru '02 & Sequoia '01 thru '02
92080 Previa all models '91 thru '95

*92082 RAV4 all models '96 thru '02
92085 Tercel all models '87 thru '94

TRIUMPH
94007 Spitfire all models '62 thru '81
94010 TR7 all models '75 thru '81

VW
96008 Beetle & Karmann Ghia '54 thru '79
*96009 New Beetle '98 thru '00
96016 Rabbit, Jetta, Scirocco & Pick-up gas models '74 thru '91 & Convertible '80 thru '92
96017 Golf, GTI & Jetta '93 thru '98 & Cabrio '95 thru '98
*96018 Golf, GTI, Jetta & Cabrio '99 thru '02
96020 Rabbit, Jetta & Pick-up diesel '77 thru '84
96023 Passat '98 thru '01, Audi A4 '96 thru '01
96030 Transporter 1600 all models '68 thru '79
96035 Transporter 1700, 1800 & 2000 '72 thru '79
96040 Type 3 1500 & 1600 all models '63 thru '73
96045 Vanagon all air-cooled models '80 thru '83

VOLVO
97010 120, 130 Series & 1800 Sports '61 thru '73
97015 140 Series all models '66 thru '74
97020 240 Series all models '76 thru '93
97040 740 & 760 Series all models '82 thru '88
97050 850 Series all models '93 thru '97

TECHBOOK MANUALS
10205 Automotive Computer Codes
10210 Automotive Emissions Control Manual
10215 Fuel Injection Manual, 1978 thru 1985
10220 Fuel Injection Manual, 1986 thru 1999
10225 Holley Carburetor Manual
10230 Rochester Carburetor Manual
10240 Weber/Zenith/Stromberg/SU Carburetors
10305 Chevrolet Engine Overhaul Manual
10310 Chrysler Engine Overhaul Manual
10320 Ford Engine Overhaul Manual
10330 GM and Ford Diesel Engine Repair Manual
10340 Small Engine Repair Manual, 5 HP & Less
10341 Small Engine Repair Manual, 5.5 - 20 HP
10345 Suspension, Steering & Driveline Manual
10355 Ford Automatic Transmission Overhaul
10360 GM Automatic Transmission Overhaul
10405 Automotive Body Repair & Painting
10410 Automotive Brake Manual
10411 Automotive Anti-lock Brake (ABS) Systems
10415 Automotive Detailing Manual
10420 Automotive Eelectrical Manual
10425 Automotive Heating & Air Conditioning
10430 Automotive Reference Manual & Dictionary
10435 Automotive Tools Manual
10440 Used Car Buying Guide
10445 Welding Manual
10450 ATV Basics

SPANISH MANUALS
98903 Reparación de Carrocería & Pintura
98905 Códigos Automotrices de la Computadora
98910 Frenos Automotriz
98915 Inyección de Combustible 1986 al 1999
99040 Chevrolet & GMC Camionetas '67 al '87 Incluye Suburban, Blazer & Jimmy '67 al '91
99041 Chevrolet & GMC Camionetas '88 al '98 Incluye Suburban '92 al '98, Blazer & Jimmy '92 al '94, Tahoe y Yukon '95 al '98
99042 Chevrolet & GMC Camionetas Cerradas '68 al '95
99055 Dodge Caravan & Plymouth Voyager '84 al '95
99075 Ford Camionetas y Bronco '80 al '94
99077 Ford Camionetas Cerradas '69 al '91
99088 Ford Modelos de Tamaño Mediano '75 al '86
99091 Ford Taurus & Mercury Sable '86 al '95
99095 GM Modelos de Tamaño Grande '70 al '90
99100 GM Modelos de Tamaño Mediano '70 al '88
99110 Nissan Camioneta '80 al '96, Pathfinder '87 al '95
99118 Nissan Sentra '82 al '94
99125 Toyota Camionetas y 4Runner '79 al '95

Over 100 Haynes motorcycle manuals also available

2-05

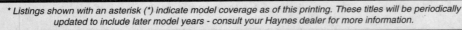